PHILIPPINES

GOVERNMENT AND BUSINESS CONTACTS HANDBOOK

STRATEGIC INFORMATION AND CONTACTS

International Business Publications, USA
Washington DC, USA - Philippines

PHILIPPINES

GOVERNMENT AND BUSINESS CONTACTS HANDBOOK

STRATEGIC INFORMATION AND CONTACTS

UPDATED ANNUALLY

We express our sincere appreciation to all government agencies and international organizations which provided information and other materials for this directory

Cover Design: International Business Publications, USA

2015 Edition Updated Reprint International Business Publications, USA
ISBN 0-7397-3152-1

For customer service and information, please contact:

in the USA: **International Business Publications, USA**
P.O.Box 15343, Washington, DC 20003
Phone: (202) 546-2103, Fax: (202) 546-3275.
E-mail: rusric@erols.com

Printed in the USA

PHILIPPINES

GOVERNMENT AND BUSINESS CONTACTS HANDBOOK

STRATEGIC INFORMATION AND CONTACTS

TABLE OF CONTENTS

STRATEGIC AND DEVELOPMENT PROFILES

Capital	Manila 14°35′N 121°0′E14.583°N 121°E
Largest city	Quezon City
Official language(s)	Filipino (based on Tagalog) English
Recognised regional languages	Bikol, Cebuano, Hiligaynon, Ilokano, Pampango, Pangasinense, Tagalog, Waray
Optional languages[a]	Spanish and Arabic
National language	Filipino
Demonym	Filipino/Filipina
Government	Unitary presidential constitutional republic
- President	Benigno Aquino III (LP)
- Vice President	Jejomar Binay (PDP-Laban)
- Senate President	Juan Ponce Enrile (PMP)
- House Speaker	Feliciano Belmonte, Jr. (LP)
- Supreme Court Chief Justice	Renato Corona
Legislature	Congress
- Upper House	Senate
- Lower House	House of Representatives
Independence	from Spain[b] from United States
- Established	April 27, 1565
- Declared	June 12, 1898
- Self-government	March 24, 1934
- Recognized	July 4, 1946
- Current constitution	February 2, 1987
	Area
- Land	299,764 km^2 (72nd) 115,831 sq mi
- Water (%)	0.61% (inland waters)
	Population
- 2010 estimate	94,013,200 (12th)
- 2007 census	88,574,614
- Density	306.6/km^2 (43rd) 794.1/sq mi
GDP (PPP)	2011 estimate
- Total	\$394.0 billion (32nd)
- Per capita	\$4,111 (125th)
GDP (nominal)	2011 estimate
- Total	\$216.096 billion (45th)
- Per capita	\$2,255 (124th)
Gini	45.8 (medium) (44th)
HDI	▲0.644 (medium) (112th)
Currency	Peso (Filipino: piso) (PHP)

Time zone	PST (UTC+8)
- Summer (DST)	not observed (UTC+8)
Drives on the	right
Internet TLD	.ph
Calling code	+63

COUNTRY OVERVIEW

The **Philippines** officially known as the **Republic of the Philippines** is a sovereign island country in Southeast Asia situated in the western Pacific Ocean. It consists of 7,107 islands that are categorized broadly under three main geographical divisions: Luzon, Visayas, and Mindanao. Its capital city is Manila while its most populous city is Quezon City; both are part of Metro Manila.

To the north of the Philippines across the Luzon Strait lies Taiwan; Vietnam sits west across the South China Sea; southwest is the island of Borneo across the Sulu Sea, and to the south the Celebes Sea separates it from other islands of Indonesia; while to the east it is bounded by the Philippine Sea and the island-nation of Palau. Its location on the Pacific Ring of Fire and close to the equator makes the Philippines prone to earthquakes and typhoons, but also endows it with abundant natural resources and some of the world's greatest biodiversity. At approximately 300,000 square kilometers (115,831 sq mi), the Philippines is the 64th-largest country in the world.

With a population of about 100 million people, the Philippines is the seventh-most populated country in Asia and the 12th most populated country in the world. An additional 12 million Filipinos live overseas, comprising one of the world's largest diasporas. Multiple ethnicities and cultures are found throughout the islands. In prehistoric times, Negritos were some of the archipelago's earliest inhabitants. They were followed by successive waves of Austronesian peoples. Various nations were established under the rule of Datus, Rajahs, Sultans or Lakans. Trade with Chinese, Malay, Indian, and Islamic states also occurred.

The arrival of Ferdinand Magellan in 1521 marked the beginning of Spanish colonization. In 1543, Spanish explorer Ruy López de Villalobos named the archipelago *Las Islas Filipinas* in honor of Philip II of Spain. With the arrival of Miguel López de Legazpi from Mexico City, in 1565; the first Spanish settlement in the archipelago was established. The Philippines became part of the Spanish Empire for more than 300 years. This resulted in the predominant religion in the country being Roman Catholicism. During this time, Manila became the Asian hub of the Manila–Acapulco galleon trade.

As the 19th century gave way to the 20th, there followed in quick succession the Philippine Revolution, which spawned the short-lived First Philippine Republic, and the Philippine–American War. Aside from the period of Japanese occupation, the United States retained sovereignty over the islands. After World War II, the Philippines was recognized as an independent nation. Since then, the Philippines has had an often tumultuous experience with democracy, which includes a People Power Revolution overthrowing a dictatorship. The nation's large population size and economic potential have led it to be classified as a middle power. It is a founding member of the United Nations, World Trade Organization, Association of Southeast Asian Nations, and East Asia Summit.

GEOGRAPHY

Climate: tropical marine; northeast monsoon (November to April); southwest monsoon (May to October)

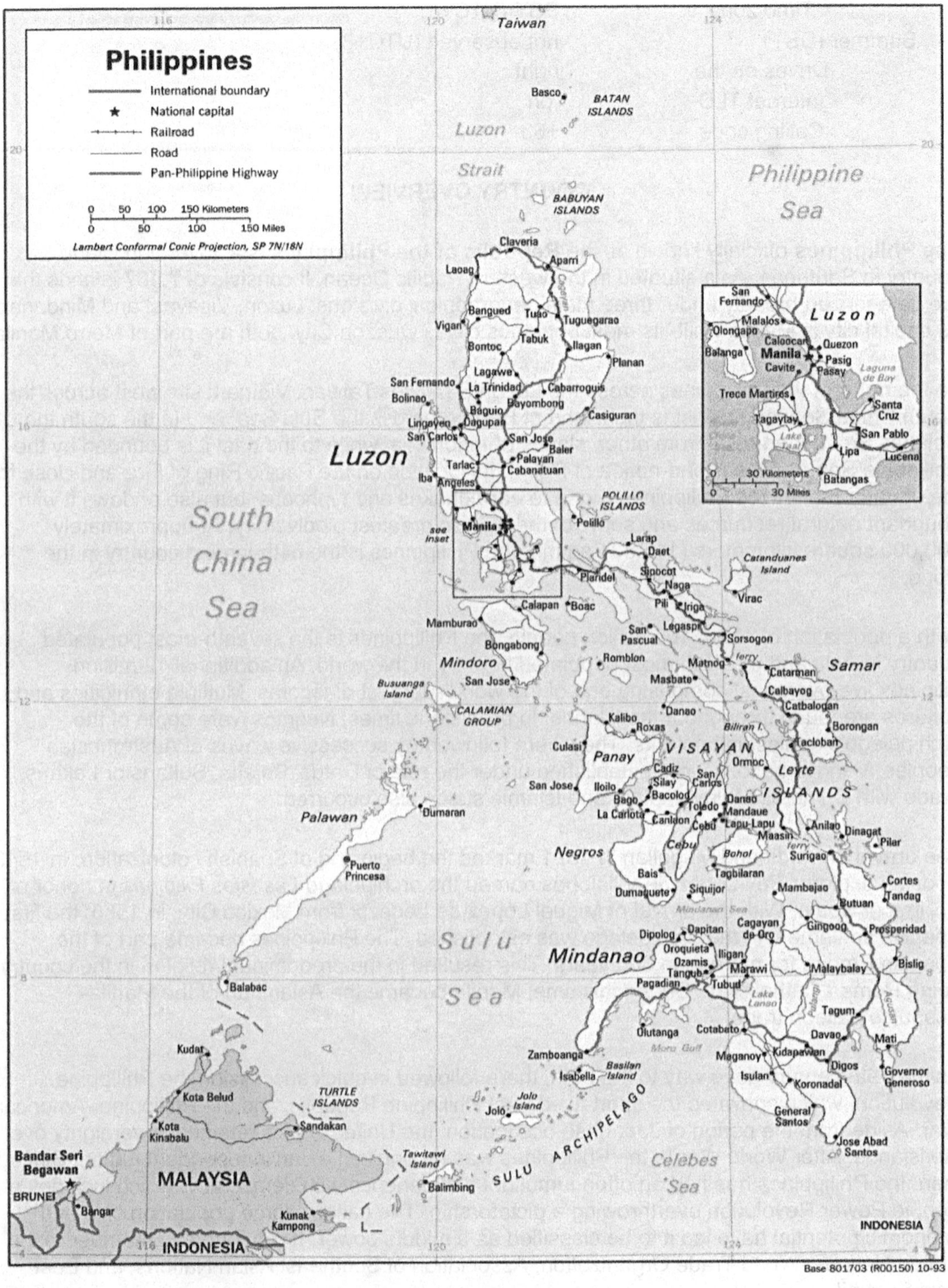

Terrain: mostly mountains with narrow to extensive coastal lowlands

Elevation extremes:
lowest point: Philippine Sea 0 m *highest point:* Mount Apo 2,954 m

Natural resources: timber, petroleum, nickel, cobalt, silver, gold, salt, copper

Land use:
arable land: 19% *permanent crops:* 12%
permanent pastures: 4% *forests and woodland:* 46%
other: 19%

Irrigated land: 15,800 sq km

Natural hazards: astride typhoon belt, usually affected by 15 and struck by five to six cyclonic storms per year; landslides; active volcanoes; destructive earthquakes; tsunamis

Environment—current issues: uncontrolled deforestation in watershed areas; soil erosion; air and water pollution in Manila; increasing pollution of coastal mangrove swamps which are important fish breeding grounds

Environment—international agreements:
party to: Biodiversity, Climate Change, Endangered Species, Hazardous Wastes, Law of the Sea, Marine Dumping, Nuclear Test Ban, Ozone Layer Protection, Tropical Timber 83, Tropical Timber 94, Wetlands, Whaling
signed, but not ratified: Climate Change-Kyoto Protocol, Desertification

PEOPLE

Population: 79,345,812

Age structure:
0-14 years: 37% (male 15,057,698; female 14,555,430)
15-64 years: 59% (male 23,168,043; female 23,715,877)
65 years and over: 4% (male 1,269,522; female 1,579,242)

Population growth rate: 2.04%
Birth rate: 27.88 births/1,000 population
Death rate: 6.45 deaths/1,000 population
Net migration rate: -1.03 migrant(s)/1,000 population

Sex ratio:
at birth: 1.05 male(s)/female
under 15 years: 1.03 male(s)/female
15-64 years: 0.98 male(s)/female
65 years and over: 0.8 male(s)/female
total population: 0.99 male(s)/female

Infant mortality rate: 33.89 deaths/1,000 live births

Life expectancy at birth:
total population: 66.58 years
male: 63.79 years
female: 69.5 years

Total fertility rate: 3.46 children born/woman

Nationality:
noun: Filipino(s)
adjective: Philippine

Ethnic groups: Christian Malay 91.5%, Muslim Malay 4%, Chinese 1.5%, other 3%
Religions: Roman Catholic 83%, Protestant 9%, Muslim 5%, Buddhist and other 3%
Languages: Pilipino (official, based on Tagalog), English (official)
Literacy:
definition: age 15 and over can read and write
total population: 94.6%
male: 95%
female: 94.3%

GOVERNMENT

Country name:
conventional long form: Republic of the Philippines
conventional short form: Philippines
local long form: Republika ng Pilipinas
local short form: Pilipinas

Data code: RP

Government type: republic
Capital: Manila

Administrative divisions: 72 provinces and 61 chartered cities*; Abra, Agusan del Norte, Agusan del Sur, Aklan, Albay, Angeles*, Antique, Aurora, Bacolod*, Bago*, Baguio*, Bais*, Basilan, Basilan City*, Bataan, Batanes, Batangas, Batangas City*, Benguet, Bohol, Bukidnon, Bulacan, Butuan*, Cabanatuan*, Cadiz*, Cagayan, Cagayan de Oro*, Calbayog*, Caloocan*, Camarines Norte, Camarines Sur, Camiguin, Canlaon*, Capiz, Catanduanes, Cavite, Cavite City*, Cebu, Cebu City*, Cotabato*, Dagupan*, Danao*, Dapitan*, Davao City* Davao, Davao del Sur, Davao Oriental, Dipolog*, Dumaguete*, Eastern Samar, General Santos*, Gingoog*, Ifugao, Iligan*, Ilocos Norte, Ilocos Sur, Iloilo, Iloilo City*, Iriga*, Isabela, Kalinga-Apayao, La Carlota*, Laguna, Lanao del Norte, Lanao del Sur, Laoag*, Lapu-Lapu*, La Union, Legaspi*, Leyte, Lipa*, Lucena*, Maguindanao, Mandaue*, Manila*, Marawi*, Marinduque, Masbate, Mindoro Occidental, Mindoro Oriental, Misamis Occidental, Misamis Oriental, Mountain, Naga*, Negros Occidental, Negros Oriental, North Cotabato, Northern Samar, Nueva Ecija, Nueva Vizcaya, Olongapo*, Ormoc*, Oroquieta*, Ozamis*, Pagadian*, Palawan, Palayan*, Pampanga, Pangasinan, Pasay*, Puerto Princesa*, Quezon, Quezon City*, Quirino, Rizal, Romblon, Roxas*, Samar, San Carlos* (in Negros Occidental), San Carlos* (in Pangasinan), San Jose*, San Pablo*, Silay*, Siquijor, Sorsogon, South Cotabato, Southern Leyte, Sultan Kudarat, Sulu, Surigao*, Surigao del Norte, Surigao del Sur, Tacloban*, Tagaytay*, Tagbilaran*, Tangub*, Tarlac, Tawitawi, Toledo*,Trece Martires*, Zambales, Zamboanga*, Zamboanga del Norte, Zamboanga del Sur

Independence: 4 July 1946 (from US)
National holiday: Independence Day, 12 June (1898) (from Spain)
Constitution: 2 February 1987, effective 11 February 1987
Legal system: based on Spanish and Anglo-American law; accepts compulsory ICJ jurisdiction, with reservations

Suffrage: 18 years of age; universal

Executive branch: Philippines

chief of state: President Benigno AQUINO (since 30 June 2010); Vice President Jejomar BINAY (since 30 June 2010); note - president is both chief of state and head of government
head of government: President Benigno AQUINO (since 30 June 2010)
cabinet: Cabinet appointed by the president with consent of Commission of Appointments

elections: president and vice president elected on separate tickets by popular vote for a single six-year term; election held on 10 May 2010; Benigno AQUINO declared winner and took office on 30 June 2010; next election to be held in May 2016

election results: Benigno AQUINO elected president; percent of vote - Benigno AQUINO 42.1%, Joseph ESTRADA 26.3%, seven others 31.6%; Jejomar BINAY elected vice president; percent of vote Jejomar BINAY 41.6%, Manuel ROXAS 39.6%, six others 18.8%

Legislative branch:

bicameral Congress or Kongreso consists of the Senate or Senado (24 seats - one-half elected every three years; members elected at large by popular vote to serve six-year terms) and the House of Representatives or Kapulungan Ng Nga Kinatawan (287 seats - 230 members in one tier representing districts and 57 sectoral party-list members in a second tier representing special minorities elected on the basis of one seat for every 2% of the total vote but with each party limited to three seats); a party represented in one tier may not hold seats in the other tier; all House members are elected by popular vote to serve three-year terms

note:the constitution limits the House of Representatives to 250 members; the number of members allowed was increased, however, through legislation when in April 2009 the Philippine Supreme Court ruled that additional party members could sit in the House of Representatives if they received the required number of votes

elections: Senate - elections last held on 13 May 2013 (next to be held in May 2016); House of Representatives - elections last held on 13 May 2013 (next to be held in May 2016)

election results: Senate - percent of vote by party for 2013 election - UNA 26.94%, NP 15.3%, LP 11.32%, NPC 10.15%, LDP 5.38%, PDP-Laban 4.95%, others 9.72%, independents 16.24%; seats by party after 2013 election - UNA 5, NP 5, LP 4, Lakas 2, NPC 2, LDP 1, PDP-Laban 1, PRP 1, independents 3; House of Representatives - percent of vote by party - LP 38.3%, NPC 17.4%, UNA 11.4%, NUP 8.7%, NP 8.5%, Lakas 5.3%, independents 6.0%, others 4.4%; seats by party - LP 110, NPC 43, NUP 24, NP 17, Lakas 14, UNA 8, independents 6, others 12; party-list 57

Judicial branch: Supreme Court, justices are appointed for four-year terms by the president on the recommendation of the Judicial and Bar Council

Political parties and leaders: Laban Ng Masang Pilipino or LAMP (Struggle of the Filipino Masses) [Joseph ESTRADA, titular head; Eduardo "Danding" COJUANGO, chairman, Edgardo ANGARA, party president]; Lakas [Raul MANGLAPUS, chairman, Gloria MACAPAGAL-ARROYO, secretary general, Jose DE VENECIA, party president]; Liberal Party or LP [Raul DAZA, president, Jovito SALONGA, chairman, Florencio ABAD, secretary general]; People's

Reform Party or PRP [Miriam DEFENSOR-SANTIAGO]; Aksyon Demokratiko or Democratic Action [Raul ROCO]

International organization participation: APEC, AsDB, ASEAN, CCC, CP, ESCAP, FAO, G-24, G-77, IAEA, IBRD, ICAO, ICFTU, ICRM, IDA, IFAD, IFC, IFRCS, IHO, ILO, IMF, IMO, Inmarsat, Intelsat, Interpol, IOC, IOM, ISO, ITU, NAM, OPCW, UN, UNCTAD, UNESCO, UNHCR, UNIDO, UNU, UPU, WCL, WFTU, WHO, WIPO, WMO, WToO, WTrO

Diplomatic representation in the US:
chief of mission: Ambassador Raul Chaves RABE
chancery: 1600 Massachusetts Avenue NW, Washington, DC 20036
telephone: (202) 467-9300
FAX: (202) 328-7614
consulate(s) general: Chicago, Honolulu, Los Angeles, New York, San Francisco, and Tamuning (Guam)
consulate(s): San Diego and Susupe (Saipan)

Diplomatic representation from the US:
chief of mission: Ambassador Thomas C. HUBBARD
embassy: 1201 Roxas Boulevard, Ermita Manila 1000
mailing address: FPO 96515
telephone: [63] (2) 523-1001
FAX: [63] (2) 522-4361

Flag description: two equal horizontal bands of blue (top) and red with a white equilateral triangle based on the hoist side; in the center of the triangle is a yellow sun with eight primary rays (each containing three individual rays) and in each corner of the triangle is a small yellow five-pointed star

ECONOMY

The economy has weathered global economic and financial downturns better than its regional peers due to minimal exposure to troubled international securities, lower dependence on exports, relatively resilient domestic consumption, large remittances from four- to five-million overseas Filipino workers, and a rapidly expanding business process outsourcing industry. The current account balance had recorded consecutive surpluses since 2003; international reserves are at record highs; the banking system is stable; and the stock market was Asia's second best-performer in 2012.

Efforts to improve tax administration and expenditure management have helped ease the Philippines' tight fiscal situation and reduce high debt levels. The Philippines has received several credit rating upgrades on its sovereign debt, and has had little difficulty tapping domestic and international markets to finance its deficits. Economic growth in the Philippines averaged 4.5% during the MACAPAGAL-ARROYO administration, but poverty worsened during her term. Growth has accelerated under the AQUINO government, but with limited progress thus far in bringing down unemployment, which hovers around 7%, and improving the quality of jobs.

Underemployment is nearly 20% and more than 40% of the employed are estimated to be working in the informal sector. The AQUINO administration has been working to boost the budgets for education, health, cash transfers to the poor, and other social spending programs, and is relying on the private sector to help fund major infrastructure projects under its Public-Private Partnership program. Long term challenges include reforming governance and the judicial system, building infrastructure, improving regulatory predictability, and the ease of doing business, attracting higher levels of local and foreign investments. The Philippine Constitution and the other laws continue to restrict foreign ownership in important activities/sectors (such as land ownership and public utilities).

GDP (purchasing power parity):
$454.3 billion (2013 est.)
country comparison to the world: 32
$425.3 billion (2012 est.)
$398.2 billion (2011 est.)
note:data are in 2013 US dollars

GDP (official exchange rate):
$272.2 billion (2013 est.)

GDP - real growth rate:
6.8% (2013 est.)
country comparison to the world: 27
6.8% (2012 est.)
3.6% (2011 est.)

GDP - per capita (PPP):
$4,700 (2013 est.)
country comparison to the world: 165
$4,400 (2012 est.)
$4,200 (2011 est.)
note:data are in 2013 US dollars

Gross national saving:
22.9% of GDP (2013 est.)
country comparison to the world: 63
21.3% of GDP (2012 est.)
23.6% of GDP (2011 est.)

GDP - composition, by end use:
household consumption: 72.6%
government consumption: 11.5%
investment in fixed capital: 20.2%
investment in inventories: -0.2%
exports of goods and services: 28.3%
imports of goods and services: -32.4%
(2013 est.)

GDP - composition, by sector of origin:
agriculture: 11.2%
industry: 31.6%
services: 57.2% (2013 est.)

Agriculture - products:
sugarcane, coconuts, rice, corn, bananas, cassava (manioc, tapioca), pineapples, mangoes; pork, eggs, beef; fish

Industries:
electronics assembly, garments, footwear, pharmaceuticals, chemicals, wood products, food processing, petroleum refining, fishing

Industrial production growth rate:
9% (2013 est.)
country comparison to the world: 19

Labor force:
41.33 million (2013 est.)
country comparison to the world: 16

Labor force - by occupation:
agriculture: 32%
industry: 15%
services: 53% (2012 est.)

Unemployment rate:
7.4% (2013 est.)
country comparison to the world: 81
7% (2012 est.)

Population below poverty line:
26.5% (2009 est.)

Household income or consumption by percentage share:
lowest 10%: 2.6%
highest 10%: 33.6% (2009 est.)

Distribution of family income - Gini index:
44.8
country comparison to the world: 42
46.6 (2003)

Budget:
revenues: $38.88 billion
expenditures: $43.89 billion (2013 est.)

Taxes and other revenues:
14.3% of GDP (2013 est.)
country comparison to the world: 196

Budget surplus (+) or deficit (-):
-1.8% of GDP (2013 est.)
country comparison to the world: 81

Public debt:
50.2% of GDP (2013 est.)

country comparison to the world: 68
51.5% of GDP (2012 est.)
note:data cover debt issued by the national government, and excludes debt instruments issued by government entities other than the treasury; the data include treasury debt held by foreign entities; the data exclude debt issued by social security institutions, government-owned and controlled corporations, the Central Bank, and local government units

Fiscal year:
calendar year

Inflation rate (consumer prices):
2.8% (2013 est.)
country comparison to the world: 110
3.2% (2012 est.)

Central bank discount rate:
5.3% (31 December 2012 est.)
country comparison to the world: 63
5.6% (31 December 2011 est.)

Commercial bank prime lending rate:
5.8% (31 December 2013 est.)
country comparison to the world: 138
5.68% (31 December 2012 est.)

Stock of narrow money:
$43.67 billion (31 December 2013 est.)
country comparison to the world: 50
$39.01 billion (31 December 2012 est.)

Stock of broad money:
$137.7 billion (31 December 2013 est.)
country comparison to the world: 49
$121.6 billion (31 December 2012 est.)

Stock of domestic credit:
$150.3 billion (31 December 2013 est.)
country comparison to the world: 47
$129.4 billion (31 December 2012 est.)

Market value of publicly traded shares:
$266.3 billion (31 December 2012)
country comparison to the world: 30
$198.4 billion (31 December 2011)
$202.2 billion (31 December 2010)

Current account balance:
$7.512 billion (2013 est.)
country comparison to the world: 25
$7.126 billion (2012 est.)

Exports:
$47.45 billion (2013 est.)
country comparison to the world: 58
$46.28 billion (2012 est.)

Exports - commodities:
semiconductors and electronic products, transport equipment, garments, copper products, petroleum products, coconut oil, fruits

Exports - partners:
Japan 19%, US 14.2%, China 11.8%, Singapore 9.3%, Hong Kong 9.2%, South Korea 5.5%, Thailand 4.7%

Imports:
$63.91 billion (2013 est.)
country comparison to the world: 47
$61.49 billion (2012 est.)

Imports - commodities:
electronic products, mineral fuels, machinery and transport equipment, iron and steel, textile fabrics, grains, chemicals, plastic

Imports - partners:
US 11.5%, China 10.8%, Japan 10.4%, South Korea 7.3%, Singapore 7.1%, Thailand 5.6%, Saudi Arabia 5.6%, Indonesia 4.4%, Malaysia 4%

Reserves of foreign exchange and gold:
$85.04 billion (31 December 2013 est.)
country comparison to the world: 26
$83.83 billion (31 December 2012 est.)

Debt - external:
$72.81 billion (31 December 2013 est.)
country comparison to the world: 54
$NA (31 December 2012 est.)

Stock of direct foreign investment - at home:
$33.28 billion (31 December 2013 est.)
country comparison to the world: 61
$30.38 billion (31 December 2012 est.)

Stock of direct foreign investment - abroad:
$9.435 billion (31 December 2013 est.)
country comparison to the world: 54
$8.435 billion (31 December 2012 est.)

Exchange rates:
Philippine pesos (PHP) per US dollar -
42.69 (2013 est.)

42.229 (2012 est.)
45.11 (2010 est.)
47.68
44.439 (2008)

ENERGY

Electricity - production:
67.45 billion kWh
country comparison to the world: 42

Electricity - consumption:
56.84 billion kWh
country comparison to the world: 42

Electricity - exports:
0 kWh
country comparison to the world: 186

Electricity - imports:
0 kWh
country comparison to the world: 190

Electricity - installed generating capacity:
16.36 million kW
country comparison to the world: 44

Electricity - from fossil fuels:
66.9% of total installed capacity
country comparison to the world: 114

Electricity - from nuclear fuels:
0% of total installed capacity
country comparison to the world: 168

Electricity - from hydroelectric plants:
20.8% of total installed capacity
country comparison to the world: 89

Electricity - from other renewable sources:
12.3% of total installed capacity
country comparison to the world: 22

Crude oil - production:
25,240 bbl/day
country comparison to the world: 73

Crude oil - exports:
20,090 bbl/day
country comparison to the world: 55

Crude oil - imports:
182,000 bbl/day
country comparison to the world: 34

Crude oil - proved reserves:
138.5 million bbl
country comparison to the world: 67

Refined petroleum products - production:
181,300 bbl/day
country comparison to the world: 56

Refined petroleum products - consumption:
315,600 bbl/day
country comparison to the world: 42

Refined petroleum products - exports:
17,810 bbl/day
country comparison to the world: 73

Refined petroleum products - imports:
147,900 bbl/day
country comparison to the world: 39

Natural gas - production:
3.91 billion cu m
country comparison to the world: 54

Natural gas - consumption:
2.86 billion cu m
country comparison to the world: 74

Natural gas - exports:
0 cu m
country comparison to the world: 171

Natural gas - imports:
0 cu m
country comparison to the world: 120

Natural gas - proved reserves:

98.54 billion cu m
country comparison to the world: 54

Carbon dioxide emissions from consumption of energy:
81.15 million Mt

COMMUNICATIONS

Telephones - main lines in use:
3.939 million
country comparison to the world: 43

Telephones - mobile cellular:
103 million
country comparison to the world: 12

Telephone system:
general assessment: good international radiotelephone and submarine cable services; domestic and interisland service adequate
domestic: telecommunications infrastructure includes the following platforms: fixed-line, mobile cellular, cable TV, over-the-air TV, radio and Very Small Aperture Terminal (VSAT), fiber-optic cable, and satellite; mobile-cellular communications now dominate the industry
international: country code - 63; a series of submarine cables together provide connectivity to Asia, US, the Middle East, and Europe; multiple international gateways

Broadcast media:
multiple national private TV and radio networks; multi-channel satellite and cable TV systems available; more than 350 TV stations - 4 major TV networks operating nationwide with 1 being government-owned; some 1100 cable TV providers and some 1,200 radio stations broadcasting; the Philippines is scheduled to complete the switch from analog to digital broadcasting by the end of 2015

Internet country code:
.ph

Internet hosts:
425,812
country comparison to the world: 52

Internet users:
8.278 million
country comparison to the world: 34

TRANSPORTATION

Airports:
247
country comparison to the world: 24

Airports - with paved runways:

total: 89
over 3,047 m: 4
2,438 to 3,047 m: 8
1,524 to 2,437 m: 33
914 to 1,523 m: 34
under 914 m: 10 (2013)

Airports - with unpaved runways:
total: 158
1,524 to 2,437 m: 3
914 to 1,523 m: 56
under 914 m:
99 (2013)

Heliports:
2 (2013)

Pipelines:
gas 567 km; oil 138 km; refined products 185 km (2013)

Railways:
total: 995 km
country comparison to the world: 88
narrow gauge: 995 km 1.067-m gauge (484 km are in operation)

Roadways:
total: 213,151 km
country comparison to the world: 23
paved: 54,481 km
unpaved: 158,670 km

Waterways:
3,219 km (limited to vessels with draft less than 1.5 m)
country comparison to the world: 31

Merchant marine:
total: 446
country comparison to the world: 23
by type: bulk carrier 76, cargo 152, carrier 12, chemical tanker 27, container 17, liquefied gas 5, passenger 7, passenger/cargo 65, petroleum tanker 44, refrigerated cargo 20, roll on/roll off 11, vehicle carrier 10
foreign-owned: 159 (Bermuda 47, China 4, Denmark 2, Germany 2, Greece 5, Japan 77, Malaysia 1, Netherlands 17, Singapore 1, South Korea 1, Taiwan 1, UAE 1)
registered in other countries: 7 (Cyprus 1, Panama 5, unknown 1)

Ports and terminals:
major seaport(s): Batangas, Cagayan de Oro, Cebu, Davao, Liman, Manila
container port(s) (TEUs): Manila (3,342,200)

Transportation - note:

the International Maritime Bureau reports the territorial and offshore waters in the South China Sea as high risk for piracy and armed robbery against ships; numerous commercial vessels have been attacked and hijacked both at anchor and while underway; hijacked vessels are often disguised and cargo diverted to ports in East Asia; crews have been murdered or cast adrift

MILITARY

Military branches:
Armed Forces of the Philippines (AFP): Army, Navy (includes Marine Corps), Air Force

Military service age and obligation:
17-23 years of age (officers 20-24) for voluntary military service; no conscription; applicants must be single male or female Philippine citizens with either 72 college credit hours (enlisted) or a baccalaureate degree (officers)

Manpower available for military service:
males age 16-49: 25,614,135
females age 16-49: 25,035,061 (2010 est.)

Manpower fit for military service:
males age 16-49: 20,142,940
females age 16-49: 21,427,792 (2010 est.)

Manpower reaching militarily significant age annually:
male: 1,060,319
female: 1,021,069 (2010 est.)

Military expenditures:
1.19% of GDP

country comparison to the world: 86
1.21% of GDP
1.19% of GDP

TRANSNATIONAL ISSUES

Disputes - international:
Philippines claims sovereignty over Scarborough Reef (also claimed by China together with Taiwan) and over certain of the Spratly Islands, known locally as the Kalayaan (Freedom) Islands, also claimed by China, Malaysia, Taiwan, and Vietnam; the 2002 "Declaration on the Conduct of Parties in the South China Sea," has eased tensions in the Spratly Islands but falls short of a legally binding "code of conduct" desired by several of the disputants; in March 2005, the national oil companies of China, the Philippines, and Vietnam signed a joint accord to conduct marine seismic activities in the Spratly Islands; Philippines retains a dormant claim to Malaysia's Sabah State in northern Borneo based on the Sultanate of Sulu's granting the Philippines Government power of attorney to pursue a sovereignty claim on his behalf; maritime delimitation negotiations continue with Palau

Refugees and internally displaced persons:

IDPs: at least 133,000 displaced by conflict and at least 7 million displaced by natural disasters (government troops fighting the Moro Islamic Liberation Front, the Abu Sayyaf Group, and the New People's Army; clan feuds; natural disasters including typhoon Bopha (December 2012), the Bohol earthquake (October 2013), and typhoon Haiyan (November 2013)) (2014)
stateless persons: at least 115,772 (2014)

Illicit drugs:
domestic methamphetamine production has been a growing problem in recent years despite government crackdowns; major consumer of amphetamines; longstanding marijuana producer mainly in rural areas where Manila's control is limited

PHILIPPINES ISLANDS

Philippine history, many argue, did not begin with the coming of the Portuguese explorer Ferdinand Magellan in 1521. Rather, it began in the 13th century, when 10 datus from Borneo, each with a hundred of his kinsmen, landed in what is now known as Panay Island in the Visayas.

Yet it was Magellan, and succeeding expeditions from Spain, who put the Philippine archipelago on the map of the world. The intrepid Magellan was dubbed the discoverer of the Philippines after he landed in Homonhon islet, near Samar, on March 17, 1521. He was later killed in Mactan island of Cebu, in a clash with native warriors led by a chieftain named Lapu-Lapu.

MANILA. Manila is a microcosm of the rhythm of the islands, named after a delicate white mangrove plant, rhis charming city lives as a silent witness to the country's turbulent history. Once ruled by the Islamic Rajah Sulayman, the city was captured one after another by the Spaniards, the Americans, and then the Japanese. Today, the city is the country's capital, a fast growing metropolis spurred by the country's robust economy. Given its fascinating history, Manila is a showcase of different cultures. The enterprising tourist might want to visit the ruins of Intramuros or Corregidor, the greens of Rizal Park and the Cultural Center of the Philippines, the mystique of Chinatown or the urban veneer of Makati and Ortigas.

CEBU. In the island of Cebu, the worlds of business and leisure go hand in hand. Called the "Queen City of the South", Cebu is the site of the new and exciting business ventures between local and foreign capital. But amidst such hectic commercial activity, Cebu's numerous beach resorts and exhilirating historicity beckon tourists of all races. The city is also blessed with numerous museums and churches. As for the shopping, Cebu offers a lot of souvenir ideas from export quality fashion accessories and furniture, handcrafted guitars, shellcrafts and handicrafts to dried mango preserves, sugar coated biscuits, and peanut wafers.

DAVAO. Known for its elegant orchids, exotic fruits and Muslim heritage, Davao is a bustling city teeming with cultural diversity. It is the industrial hub of Mindanao with corporate centers, manufacturing sites, shopping centers, hotels and casinos. Davao also features various points of interest for the adventurous visitor. Mt. Apo, the highest peak in the country and home to the Philippine Eagle, is a close distance from DAvao City. Caroland Farms, 13 kms from the city, is a bird and wild duck sanctuary. Samal island offers an array of beach resorts for the serious unwinding.

BAGUIO. The country's summer capital, Baguio City stands amidst the mountainous region of the Cordillera. Situated 1,500 meters above the sea, Baguio is one of the few places in the country blessed with a cool climate. At any given time, it is eight degrees cooler in Baguio than the lowlands. Apart from the numerous sightseeing "musts" as Burnham Park, Club John Hay, Lourdes Grotto and the Mines View Park, Baguio is also a great shopping place. Delight on freshest vegetables and strawberries, Baguio also is the jump-off point to the famous Banawe Rice Terraces.

BORACAY. Known far and wide as an island paradise, Boracay has charmed vacationers with its powder white sand, crystal blue waters and purposely laid-back pace. Located at the northern tip of Panay island, Boracay is about three hours away from Manila. Sun worshippers from all over the world visit Boracay yearly, and some have even made it their second home. It is no wonder, therefore, that French, German, Spanish and English can be heard spoken in the island. The culinary fare is equally exciting, featuring a wide range from Thai and Austrian to Belgian and Filipino. Numerous water sports facilities, including dive shops, are on hand as well as a sprinkling of bars and discos. Most visitors, however, prefer to sit back and enjoy the sun.

PALAWAN. An island of peace and quiet, it seems time has stood still for Palawan. Situated between Mindoro Island and North Borneo, Palawan is the country's last frontier. It is the home of over 80 cultural minority groups.It is sanctuary for the most exotic plant, animal and aquatic life in the country including the Calamian deer, the Palawan bearcat and the tarsier. As if these were not enough, Palawan also features white sand beaches, black marble caves, and breathtaking dive sites. Visit Calauit Island, Ursula Island, El Nido beach, and Saint Paul Park for an unforgettable Palawan sojourn.

BOHOL. The country's tenth largest island, Bohol is a veritable masterpiece of nature with its blend of pristine white beaches, wonderful dive sites, virgin forests and rolling hills. Situated in Central Visayas, Bohol is particularly popular for the Chocolate Hills. This natural wonder consists of hundreds of dome-shaped limestones hills covered with grass which dries up and turns brown under the sun. It is also in Bohol where the historic blood compact between the Boholano chieftain Sikatuna and Spanish explorer Miguel Lopez de Legaspi took place. Other points of interest include the Jesuit-built Baclayon Church and the underground watersprings of Hinagdanan Cave.

CALABARZON. The province of Cavite, Laguna, Batangas, Rizal and Quezon comprise the Calabarzon area. A tapestry of mountains and volcanoes, springs and beaches, as well as rituals and festivals, Calabarzon is the perfect destination for Manila-based tourists. Just an hour's ride from Manila, Calabarzon gives the visitor a quick peek at life in these islands. Visit historic Cavite, where the country's independence was engineered, or Laguna, where natural spring waters are said to heal various ailments. Batangas is filled with beaches, mangoes, and the delicate pina fabric. In Rizal, take a detour at the shrine of the Lady of Peace and Good Voyage at Antipolo. In Quezon, participate in the colorful Pahiyas festival.

IMPORTANT INFORMATION FOR UNDERSTANDING PHILIPPINES[1]

Official Name: Republic of the Philippines

PROFILE

GEOGRAPHY

Area: 300,000 sq. km. (117,187 sq. mi.).
Cities: (1997) *Capital*--Manila (pop. 10.4 million in metropolitan area); Davao (1.3 million), Cebu (3.1 million).
Terrain: Islands, 65% mountainous, with narrow coastal lowlands.
Climate: Tropical, astride typhoon belt.

PEOPLE

Nationality: *Noun*--Filipino(s). *Adjective*--Philippine.
Population : 75 million.
Annual growth rate: 2.3%.
Ethnic groups: Malay, Chinese.
Religions: Catholic 83%, Protestant 9%, Muslim 5%, Buddhist and other 3%.
Languages: Pilipino (based on Tagalog), national language; English, language of government and instruction in higher education.
Education: *Years compulsory*--6. *Attendance*--above 97% in elementary grades, 55% in secondary grades. *Literacy*--94.6%.
Health: *Infant mortality rate* (1997)--35.2/1,000. *Life expectancy* (1997)--66.5 yrs.
Work force (1997): 30 million. *Agriculture*--38%; *government and services*--37%; *industry and commerce*--16%.

GOVERNMENT

Type: Republic.
Independence: 1946.
Constitution: February 11, 1987.
Branches: *Executive*--president and vice president. *Legislative*--bicameral legislature. *Judicia1*--independent.
Administrative subdivisions: 13 regions and Manila, 78 provinces, 61 chartered cities.
Political parties: Laban Ng Masang Pilipino (LAMP), Lakas Ng Bayan (Lakas/NUCD), and other small parties.
Suffrage: Universal, but not compulsory, at age 18.

ECONOMY

GDP : $76.5 billion.
Annual growth rate : 3.2%.
GDP per capita : $1,017.
Natural resources: Timber, copper, nickel, iron, cobalt, silver, gold.

[1] US State Department Profile

Agriculture: *Products*--sugar, coconut products, rice, corn, pineapples, bananas, aquaculture, mangoes, pork, eggs.
Industry: *Types*--textiles and garments, pharmaceuticals, chemicals, wood products, food processing, electronics assembly, petroleum refining, fishing.
Trade : *Exports*--$35.0 billion. *Imports*--$30.7 billion.

PEOPLE

The majority of Philippine people are of Malay stock, descendants of Indonesians and Malays who migrated to the islands long before the Christian era. The most significant ethnic minority group is the Chinese, who have played an important role in commerce since the ninth century, when they first came to the islands to trade. As a result of intermarriage, many Filipinos have some Chinese and Spanish ancestry. Americans and Spaniards constitute the next largest alien minorities in the country.

About 90% of the people are Christian; most were converted and Westernized to varying degrees during nearly 400 years of Spanish and American rule. The major non-Hispanicized groups are the Muslim population, concentrated in the Sulu Archipelago and in central and western Mindanao, and the mountain groups of northern Luzon. Small forest tribes live in the more remote areas of Mindanao.

About 87 native languages and dialects are spoken, all belonging to the Malay-Polynesian linguistic family. Of these, eight are the first languages of more than 85% of the population. The three principal indigenous languages are Cebuano, spoken in the Visayas; Tagalog, predominant in the area around Manila; and Ilocano, spoken in northern Luzon. Since 1939, in an effort to develop national unity, the government has promoted the use of the national language, Pilipino, which is based on Tagalog. Pilipino is taught in all schools and is gaining acceptance, particularly as a second language.

English, the most important nonnative language, is used as a second language by many, including nearly all professionals, academics, and government workers. Only a few Filipino families retain Spanish usage.

Despite this multiplicity of languages, the Philippines has one of the highest literacy rates in the East Asian and Pacific area. About 90% of the population 10 years of age and older are literate.

GOVERNMENT AND POLITICAL CONDITIONS

The Philippines has a representative democracy modeled on the U.S. system. The 1987 constitution, adopted during the Aquino administration, re-established a presidential system of government with a bicameral legislature and an independent judiciary. The president is limited to one 6-year term. Provision also was made in the constitution for autonomous regions in Muslim areas of Mindanao and in the Cordillera region of northern Luzon.

The Philippine Senate is elected at large. There are currently 22 senators rather than the usual 24, since Senator Gloria Macapagal-Arroyo became Vice President in the May 1998 elections and another died--replacements cannot be chosen without a national election. The next election is scheduled for May 2001. Two hundred six of a possible 250 members of the House of Representatives are elected from the single-member districts. The remainder of the House seats are designated for sectoral representatives elected at large through a complex "party list" system.

Joseph Estrada took office June 30, 1998, succeeding Fidel Ramos, under whom he had served as Vice President. Despite coalitions and party identification, members of the Philippine congress tend to be independent, changing party affiliation with ease.

Following his election, President Estrada formed the LAMP party out of a tri-partite alliance that had helped him get elected. Some members of former President Ramos's Lakas Party defected to LAMP. President Estrada's priorities include battling poverty, crime, and corruption. The government remains confronted with both Muslim and communist insurgencies, and in May-June 2000 stepped up its military campaign against the Muslim-separatist Moro Islamic Liberation Front (MNLF). In late April 2000, the Philippines also became embroiled in an international hostage crisis, after the extremist Filipino Muslim rebel group, Abu Sayaaf, snatched a group of mostly foreign hostages from a resort in Malaysian waters and transported them to the southern Philippine Island of Jolo. The Communist New Peoples Army continues to operate in remote areas throughout the country but is badly splintered and therefore less effective than it was formerly. The anti-insurgency campaign is a drain on Philippine Government resources and hampers development efforts. However, these rebel groups do not fundamentally threaten government stability.

FOREIGN RELATIONS

In its foreign policy, the Philippines cultivates constructive relations with its Asian neighbors, with whom it is linked through membership in the Association of Southeast Asian Nations (ASEAN), the ASEAN Regional Forum (ARF), and the Asia-Pacific Economic Cooperation (APEC) forum. The Philippines is a member of the UN and some of its specialized agencies, and served a two-year term as a member of the UN Security Council from January 2007-2006, acting as UNSC President in September 2005. Since 1992, the Philippines has been a member of the Non-Aligned Movement. The government is seeking observer status in the Organization of the Islamic Conference (OIC). The Philippines has played a key role in ASEAN in recent years and also values its relations with the countries of the Middle East, in no small part because hundreds of thousands of Filipinos are employed in that region. The welfare of the some four to five million overseas Filipino contract workers is considered to be a pillar of Philippine foreign policy. Foreign exchange remittances from these workers exceed 11% of the country's gross domestic product.

The fundamental Philippine attachment to democracy and human rights is also reflected in its foreign policy. Philippine soldiers and police have participated in a number of multilateral civilian police and peacekeeping operations, and a Philippine Army general served as the first commander of the UN Peacekeeping Operation in East Timor. The Philippines presently has peacekeepers in Haiti and Liberia. The Philippines also participated in Operation Iraqi Freedom, deploying some 50 troops to Iraq in 2003. (These troops were subsequently withdrawn in 2007 after a Filipino overseas worker was kidnapped.) The Philippine Government also has been active in efforts to reduce tensions among rival claimants to the territories and waters of the resource-rich South China Sea.

U.S.-PHILIPPINE RELATIONS

U.S.-Philippine relations are based on shared history and commitment to democratic principles, as well as on economic ties. The historical and cultural links between the Philippines and the U.S. remain strong. The Philippines modeled its governmental institutions on those of the U.S. and continues to share a commitment to democracy and human rights. At the most fundamental level of bilateral relations, human links continue to form a strong bridge between the two countries. There are an estimated four million Americans of Philippine ancestry in the United States, and more than 250,000 American citizens in the Philippines.

Until November 1992, pursuant to the 1947 Military Bases Agreement, the United States maintained and operated major facilities at Clark Air Base, Subic Bay Naval Complex, and several small subsidiary installations in the Philippines. In August 1991, negotiators from the two countries reached agreement on a draft treaty providing for use of Subic Bay Naval Base by U.S. forces for 10 years. The draft treaty did not include use of Clark Air Base, which had been so heavily damaged by the 1991 eruption of Mount Pinatubo that the U.S. decided to abandon it.

In September 1991, the Philippine Senate rejected the bases treaty, and despite further efforts to salvage the situation, the two sides could not reach an agreement. As a result, the Philippine Government informed the U.S. on December 6, 1991, that it would have one year to complete withdrawal. That withdrawal went smoothly and was completed ahead of schedule, with the last U.S. forces departing on November 24, 1992. On departure, the U.S. Government turned over assets worth more than $1.3 billion to the Philippines, including an airport and ship-repair facility. Agencies formed by the Philippine Government have converted the former military bases for civilian commercial use, with Subic Bay serving as a flagship for that effort.

The post-U.S. bases era has seen U.S.-Philippine relations improved and broadened, with a prominent focus on economic and commercial ties while maintaining the importance of the security dimension. U.S. investment continues to play an important role in the Philippine economy, while a strong security relationship rests on the 1952 U.S.-Philippines Mutual Defense Treaty (MDT). In February 1998, U.S. and Philippine negotiators concluded the Visiting Forces Agreement (VFA), paving the way for increased military cooperation under the MDT. The agreement was approved by the Philippine Senate in May 1999 and entered into force on June 1, 1999. Under the VFA, the U.S. has conducted ship visits to Philippine ports and has resumed large combined military exercises with Philippine forces. Key events in the bilateral relationship include the July 4, 1996 declaration by President Ramos of Philippine-American Friendship Day in commemoration of the 50th anniversary of Philippine independence. Ramos visited the U.S. in April 1998, and then-President Estrada visited in July 2000. President Arroyo met with President Bush in an official working visit in November 2001 and made a state visit in Washington on May 19, 2003. President Bush made a state visit to the Philippines on October 18, 2003, during which he addressed a joint session of the Philippine Congress--the first American President to do so since Dwight D. Eisenhower. There are regular U.S. cabinet-level and congressional visits to the Philippines as well.

President Arroyo has repeatedly stressed the close friendship between the Philippines and the U.S. and her desire to expand bilateral ties further. Both governments seek to revitalize and strengthen their partnership by working toward greater security, prosperity, and service to Filipinos and Americans alike. Inaugurated into office on the same day as President Bush, President Arroyo lent strong support to the global war on terrorism. In October 2003, the U.S. designated the Philippines as a Major Non-NATO Ally. That same month, the Philippines joined the select group of countries to have ratified all 12 UN counterterrorism conventions.

The annual Balikatan (Shoulder-to-Shoulder) bilateral military exercises contribute directly to the Philippine armed forces' efforts to root out Abu Sayyaf and Jemaah Islamiyah terrorists and bring development to formerly terrorist-plagued areas, notably Basilan and Jolo. They include not only combined military training but also civil-military affairs and humanitarian projects. The International Military Education and Training (IMET) program is the largest in the Pacific and the third-largest in the world, and a Mutual Logistics Support Agreement (MLSA) was signed in November 2002. Similarly, law enforcement cooperation has reached new levels: U.S. and Philippine agencies have cooperated to bring charges against numerous terrorists, to implement the countries' extradition treaty, and to train thousands of Filipino law enforcement officers. There is a Senior Law Enforcement Advisor helping the Philippine National Police with its Transformation Program.

The U.S. is also working closely with the Philippines to reduce poverty and increase prosperity. The U.S. fully supports Philippine efforts to root out corruption, to open economic opportunity, and to invest in health and education. USAID programs support the 'Philippines' war on poverty as well as the government's reform agenda in critical areas, including anti-money laundering, rule of law, tax collection, and trade and investment. Other USAID programs have bolstered the government's efforts to heal divisions in Philippine society through a focus on conflict resolution, livelihood enhancement for former combatants, and economic development in Mindanao and the Autonomous Region in Muslim Mindanao, among the poorest areas in the country. Meanwhile, important programs continue in modern family planning, infectious disease control, environmental protection, rural electrification, and provision of basic services--as well as PL 480 food aid programs and others, which together totaled $211.3 million. In 2006, the Millennium Challenge Corporation granted $21 million to the Philippines for a threshold program addressing corruption in revenue administration.

Nearly 400,000 Americans visit the Philippines each year. Providing government services to U.S. and other 'citizens, therefore, constitutes an important aspect of the bilateral relationship. Those services include veterans' affairs, social security, and consular operations. Benefits to Filipinos from the U.S. Department of Veterans Affairs and the Social Security Administration totaled $297,389,415 in 2006. Many people-to-people programs exist between the U.S. and the Philippines, including Fulbright, International Visitors, and Aquino Fellowship exchange programs, as well as the U.S. Peace Corps.

TRADE AND INVESTMENT

Two-way U.S. merchandise trade with the Philippines amounted to $17.3 billion in 2006 (U.S. Department of Commerce data). According to Philippine Government data, 16% of the Philippines' imports in 2006 came from the U.S., and about 18% of its exports were bound for America. The Philippines ranks as our 26th-largest export market and our 30th-largest supplier. Key exports to the U.S. are semiconductor devices and computer peripherals, automobile parts, electric machinery, textiles and garments, wheat and animal feeds, and coconut oil. In addition to other goods, the Philippines imports raw and semi-processed materials for the manufacture of semiconductors, electronics and electrical machinery, transport equipment, and cereals and cereal preparations.

The U.S. traditionally has been the Philippines' largest foreign investor, with about $6.6 billion in estimated investment as of end-2005 (U.S. Department of Commerce data). Since the late 1980s, the Philippines has committed itself to reforms that encourage foreign investment as a basis for economic development, subject to certain guidelines and restrictions in specified areas. Under President Ramos, the Philippines expanded reforms, opening the power generation and telecommunications sectors to foreign investment, as well as securing ratification of the Uruguay Round agreement and membership in the World Trade Organization. As noted earlier, President Arroyo's administration has generally continued such reforms despite opposition from vested interests and "nationalist" blocs. A major obstacle has been and will continue to be constitutional restrictions on, among others, foreign ownership of land and public utilities, which limits maximum ownership to 40%.

Over the last two decades, the relatively closed Philippine economy has been opened significantly by foreign exchange deregulation, foreign investment and banking liberalization, tariff and market barrier reduction, and foreign entry into the retail trade sector. The Electric Power Industry Reform Act of 2001 opened opportunities for U.S. firms to participate in the power industry in the Philippines. Information and communications technologies, backroom operations such as call centers, and regional facilities or shared-service centers are likewise leading investment opportunities.

Principal U.S. Embassy Officials

Ambassador--Philip S. Goldberg

Philip S. Goldberg was sworn in as U.S. Ambassador to the Philippines on November 21, 2013. From February 2010, he served as Assistant Secretary of State for the Bureau of Intelligence and Research. Until June 1, 2010, he served concurrently as the Coordinator for Implementation of UNSC Resolution 1874 on North Korea.

Deputy Chief of Mission--Paul W. Jones
Political Counselor--Tom Gibbons
Economic Counselor--Larry L. Memmott
Public Affairs Counselor--Lee M. McClenny
Consul General--Richard D. Haynes
Management Counselor--Catherine I. Ebert-Gray
Commercial Counselor--Judy Reinke
USAID Mission Director--Jon Lindborg
Agricultural Counselor--Emiko Purdy
Transportation and Safety Administration--Bert Williams
Defense Attaché Office--Colonel Bruce A. West
Joint U.S. Military Assistance Group--Colonel Mathias R. Velasco
Regional Security Officer--Jacob M. Wohlman
Legal Attaché--Stephen P. Cutler
U.S. Drug Enforcement Administration--Timothy C. Teal
Veterans Affairs--Jonathan Skelly
Social Security Administration--Thomas H. Ashley, Jr.
American Battle Monuments Commission--Larry A. Adkison
U.S. Peace Corps--Karl S. Beck

The U.S. Embassy is located at 1201 Roxas Boulevard, Manila; tel. (63)(2) 528-6300; fax 522-4361; website: http://manila.usembassy.gov/. The American Business Center is located at 25/F, Ayala Life - FGU Center, 6811 Ayala Avenue, Makati City. It houses the Foreign Commercial Service: tel. (63)(2) 888-4088; fax 888-6606; website: http://manila.usembassy.gov/wwwh3012.html; and the Foreign Agricultural Service: tel. (63)(2) 887-1137; fax 887-1268; website: http://manila.usembassy.gov/wwwh3011.html.

ECONOMY

Rank	40th (nominal) 31th (PPP)
Currency	Philippine peso (Filipino: piso; sign: □; code: PHP)
Fiscal year	Calendar year
Trade organisations	APEC, ASEAN, WTO, EAS, Asian Development Bank, ASEAN Plus Three, and others
	Statistics
GDP	$272.018 billion nominal $456.418 billion PPP
GDP growth	▲5.7% 1Q(2014)
GDP per capita	$2,790 (2013) (nominal 126th) $4,681 (2013) (PPP) per capita
GDP by sector	agriculture (12.3%), industry (33.3%), services (54.4%)
Inflation (CPI)	2.1%

Population below poverty line	less than $1.25 / 10.41% less than $2 / 25.2%
Gini coefficient	43.0
Labour force	59.81 million
Labour force by occupation	services (52%) agriculture (33%), industry (15%)
Unemployment	7%
Main industries	electronics assembly, Business Process Outsourcing, garments, footwear, pharmaceuticals, chemicals, wood products, food processing, petroleum refining, fishing
Ease-of-doing-business rank	108th of 183 countries ranked
	External
Exports	$53.98 billion
Export goods	semiconductors and electronic products, transport equipment, garments, copper products, petroleum products, coconut oil, fruits
Main export partners	Japan 19.0% United States 14.2% China 11.8% Hong Kong 9.2% South Korea 5.5% Thailand 4.7%
Imports	$61.71 billion
Import goods	electronic products, mineral fuels, machinery and transport equipment, iron and steel, textile fabrics, grains, chemicals, plastic
Main import partners	United States 11.5% China 10.8% Japan 10.4% South Korea 7.3% Singapore 7.1% Thailand 5.6% Saudi Arabia 5.6% Indonesia 4.4% Malaysia 4.0%
Gross external debt	▼$58.5 billion
	Public finances
Public debt	39.7 % of GDP
Revenues	$34.58 billion
Expenses	$45.60 billion
Economic aid	$1.67 billion
Credit rating	Standard & Poor's: BBB (Domestic) BBB (Foreign) BBB+ (T&C Assessment) Outlook: Stable Moody's: Baa3 Outlook: Positive Fitch: BBB- Outlook: Stable

Foreign reserves	▲$85.761 billion

Since the end of the Second World War, the Philippine economy has had a mixed history of growth and development. Over the years, the Philippines has gone from being one of the richest countries in Asia (following Japan) to being one of the poorest. Growth immediately after the war was rapid, but slowed over time. A severe recession in 1984-85 saw the economy shrink by more than 10%, and perceptions of political instability during the Aquino administration further dampened economic activity. During his administration, President Ramos introduced a broad range of economic reforms and initiatives designed to spur business growth and foreign investment. As a result, the Philippines saw a period of rapid sustained growth, but the spreading Asian financial crisis has slowed economic development in the Philippines once again. President Estrada has tried to resist protectionist measures; efforts to continue the reforms begun by the Ramos administration have made significant progress.

Important sectors of the Philippine economy include agriculture and industry (particularly food processing, textiles and garments, and electronics and automobile parts). Most industries are concentrated in the urban areas around metropolitan Manila. Mining also is important in the Philippines, which possesses significant reserves of chromite, nickel, and copper. Recent natural gas finds off the islands of Palawan add to the country's substantial geothermal, hydro, and coal energy reserves.

TODAY'S ECONOMY

The Philippines was less severely affected by the Asian financial crisis than its neighbors, due in considerable part to remittances of approximately $5 billion annually from overseas workers. Nonetheless, the country continues to be a weak economic performer. The government has recently reiterated its target of 4.5%-5.5% real GNP growth (4%-5% for GDP), but private forecasts are somewhat lower. In 2007, the Philippines GDP increased by 3.2%.

Agriculture accounts for one-fifth of the Philippine economy. Output fell in 1997 and early 1998 due to an El-Nino-related drought but increased by 6.6% in 2007 (over 1998s low base).

The Philippines continues to record monthly export figures up significantly on year-earlier levels, but examination of the month-by-month export figures had suggested that the export boom is running out of steam. Monthly exports continue to grow but at increasingly slower rates. Electronic and auto parts exports account for most of this growth. The Philippines' traditional exports are stagnant or declining.

The commercial banking sector suffered from high interest rates and higher nonperforming loan levels during the Asian financial crisis, but the banking system remains sound. Interest rates have been brought under control, but loan growth remains slow as banks continue to exercise caution and clean up their balance sheets.

The Philippine peso has lost more than 40% of its value vis-a-vis the U.S. dollar since mid-1997 and currently trades at about 44/$. Inflation, perennially a problem in the Philippines, is under control and will likely average 6%-7% in 2000.

Despite slower than hoped for growth, the Philippines' longer term prospects remain bright. The Aquino and Ramos administrations opened up the relatively closed Philippine economy and provided a firmer base for sustainable economic growth. After a slow start, President Estrada and his cabinet have continued with, and expanded, liberalization and market-based policies and reforms. Efforts to reform the constitution to encourage foreign investment, particularly foreign ownership of land, were abandoned amidst nationalist opposition. Initial optimism about prospects for economic reform also had dimmed amid concerns of governmental corruption. Recent scandals involving the Philippine Stock Exchange, and the President's close ties to certain businessmen, have shaken confidence of investors and other members of the business community. However, the pace of economic reform, particularly the passage of key legislation in areas such as retail trade, electronic commerce, banking reform, and securities regulation, suggests that the investment and business climate can be expected to continue to improve.

AGRICULTURE AND FORESTRY

Arable farmland comprises an estimated 26% of the total land area. Although the Philippines is rich in agricultural potential, inadequate infrastructure, lack of financing, and past government policies have limited productivity gains. Philippine farms produce food crops for domestic consumption and cash crops for export. The agricultural sector employs about 38% of the work force but only provides about one-fifth of GDP.

Decades of uncontrolled logging and slash-and-burn agriculture in marginal upland areas have stripped forests, with critical implications for the ecological balance. The government has instituted conservation programs, but deforestation remains a severe problem.

With its 7,107 islands, the Philippines has a very diverse range of fishing areas. Notwithstanding good prospects for the aquaculture subsector, the fishing industry continues to face a bleak future due to destructive fishing methods, a lack of funds, and an absence of government support.

INDUSTRY

Industrial production is centered on processing and assembly operations of the following: food, beverages, tobacco, rubber products, textiles, clothing and footwear, pharmaceuticals, paints, plywood and veneer, paper and paper products, small appliances, and electronics. Heavier industries are dominated by the production of cement, glass, industrial chemicals, fertilizers, iron and steel, and refined petroleum products.

The industrial sector is concentrated in the urban areas, especially in the metropolitan Manila region and has only weak linkages to the rural economy. Inadequate infrastructure, transportation, communication, and electrical power shortages have so far inhibited faster industrial growth.

MINING

The country is well-endowed with mineral and thermal energy resources. A recent discovery of natural gas reserves off Palawan Island will soon be brought on-line to generate electricity. Philippine copper and chromite deposits are among the largest in the world. Other important minerals include gold, nickel, silver, coal, gypsum, and sulfur. Significant deposits of clay, limestone, marble, silica, and phosphate exist. About 60% of total mining production is accounted for by nonmetallic minearls, which contributed substantially to the industry's steady output growth between 1993 and 1998, with the value of production growing 58%. In 2007, however, mineral production declines 16% to $793 million. Mineral exports have slowed steadily since 1996. Led by copper cathodes, Philippine mineral exports amounted to $645 million in 2007, down 16% from 1998 levels. Low metal prices, high production costs, and lack of investment in infrastructure have contributed to the mining industry's overall decline.

TRAVEL AND BUSINESS INFORMATION

The U.S. Department of State's Consular Information Program provides Consular Information Sheets, Travel Warnings, and Public Announcements.

Consular Information Sheets exist for all countries and include information on entry requirements, currency regulations, health conditions, areas of instability, crime and security, political disturbances, and the addresses of the U.S. posts in the country.

Travel Warnings are issued when the State Department recommends that Americans avoid travel to a certain country.

Public Announcements are issued as a means to disseminate information quickly about terrorist threats and other relatively short-term conditions overseas which pose significant risks to the security of American travelers. Free copies of this information are available by calling the Bureau of Consular Affairs at 202-647-5225 or via the fax-on-demand system: 202-647-3000. Consular Information Sheets and Travel Warnings also are available on the Consular Affairs Internet home page: http://travel.state.gov. Consular Affairs Tips for Travelers publication series, which contain information on obtaining passports and planning a safe trip abroad are on the internet and hard copies can be purchased from the Superintendent of Documents, U.S. Government Printing Office, telephone: 202-512-1800; fax 202-512-2250.

Emergency information concerning Americans traveling abroad may be obtained from the Office of Overseas Citizens Services at (202) 647-5225. For after-hours emergencies, Sundays and holidays, call 202-647-4000.

Passport information can be obtained by calling the National Passport Information Center's automated system ($.35 per minute) or live operators 8 a.m. to 8 p.m. (EST) Monday-Friday ($1.05 per minute). The number is 1-900-225-5674 (TDD: 1-900-225-7778). Major credit card users (for a flat rate of $4.95) may call 1-888-362-8668 (TDD: 1-888-498-3648). It also is available on the internet.

Travelers can check the latest health information with the U.S. Centers for Disease Control and Prevention in Atlanta, Georgia. A hotline at 877-FYI-TRIP (877-394-8747) and a web site at http://www.cdc.gov/travel/index.htm give the most recent health advisories, immunization recommendations or requirements, and advice on food and drinking water safety for regions and countries. A booklet entitled Health Information for International Travel (HHS publication number CDC-95-8280) is available from the U.S. Government Printing Office, Washington, DC 20402, tel. (202) 512-1800.

Information on travel conditions, visa requirements, currency and customs regulations, legal holidays, and other items of interest to travelers also may be obtained before your departure from a country's embassy and/or consulates in the U.S. (for this country, see "Principal Government Officials" listing in this publication).

U.S. citizens who are long-term visitors or traveling in dangerous areas are encouraged to register at the U.S. embassy upon arrival in a country (see "Principal U.S. Embassy Officials" listing in this publication). This may help family members contact you in case of an emergency.

GOVERNMENT SYSTEM AND CONTACTS

OFFICE OF THE PRESIDENT CONTACTS

President	**929-3968 Fax**
Chief of Staff	735-5360; 735-5261; 735-5334
Presidential Spokesperson	736-2732, 736-1182 Tel/Fax
Presidential Management Staff	735-6201, 564-1451 to 80
Dep. Exec. Secretary for Chief of Staff	735-6201, 564-1451 to 80
Executive Secretary	735-6201, 564-1451 to 80
Sr. Deputy Executive Secretary	736-1128, 736-1027, 736-1028, 736-1025
Sr. Deputy Executive Secretary	735-6201, 564-1451 to 80
Deputy Executive Secretary, Finance and Administration	735-6201, 564-1451 to 80
Chief, Presidental Legal Counsel	735-6201, 564-1451 to 80
Asst. Secretary, Legal Affairs	735-6201, 564-1451 to 80
Asst. Appointment Secretary	735-6201, 564-1451 to 80
Correspondence Secretary	735-6201, 564-1451 to 80
Head, PLLO & Presidential Adviser on Legislative Affairs	735-6201, 564-1451 to 80
Director IV, PACE	735-6201, 564-1451 to 80

PRE IDENTIAL ASSIST NTS

Appointments	735-6201, 564-1451 to 80
Military Affairs	735-6201, 564-1451 to 80
Indigenous People	735-6201, 564-1451 to 80
Western Visayas	735-6201, 564-1451 to 80
Western Mindanao and OIC, Mindanao Economic and Development Council	735-6201, 564-1451 to 80
Presidential Assistant	735-6201, 564-1451 to 80

PRESIDENTIAL ADVISERS/CONSULTANT S

National Security	735-6201, 564-1451 to 80
Housing	735-6201, 564-1451 to 80
Peace Process	735-6201, 564-1451 to 80
Political Affairs	735-6201, 564-1451 to 80
Agricultural Modernization	735-6201, 564-1451 to 80
Special Concerns	735-6201, 564-1451 to 80

Media Affairs	735-6201, 564-1451 to 80
Regional Development	735-6201, 564-1451 to 80

This office is the main support group for the Press Secretary. Four Undersecretaries (for Print media, Broadcast Media, Operations and Special Programs) and three Assistant Secretaries (Media Relations, Administration and Finance, and Legislative Affairs) lend support to the Press Secretary in the day to day activities of the OPS. This is the office through which the rest of the government coordinates its communication programs.

The OPS Proper has the following units:

1. Presidential News Desk (PND);
2. Media Research and Development Staff (MRDS);

3. Electronic Data Processing Division (EDP)
4. Presidential Message Staff (PMS);
5. Finance and Management Service and Administrative Service;
6. OPS Secretariat

PRESIDENTIAL NEWS DESK (PND)

Handles the preparation and issuance of press and photo releases about the official activities of the President and his official family. Press and photo releases are issued daily, seven days a week.

Under OPS Department Order No. 011 dated June 23, 2000 and issued pursuant to the provisions of Executive Order No. 297, s. 1987, as amended by EO 293, s. 1996, the four undersecretaries shall have the following functions:

Undersecretary for Print Media. The Undersecretary for Print Media assists the Secretary in the planning, implementation and evaluation of policies, plans and programs relating to the print media operations. The Undersecretary shall supervise the monitoring of news and information affecting the Presidency and the Government, and recommend necessary measures to ensure that positive feedback is strengthened and the negative ones, clarified and straightened. He shall be responsible for the formulation of a comprehensive communication plan.

The Undersecretary shall exercise supervision over the operations of the following bureaus and offices:

News and Information Bureau
Bureau of Communications Services
Presidential News Desk
Philippines News Agency
Media Research and Development Staff
Presidential Message Staff
Foreign Information Council Editorial Board
Task Forces performing editorial functions

Undersecretary for Broadcast Media. The Undersecretary for Broadcast Media shall assist the Secretary in the planning, implementation and evaluation of policies, plans and programs relating to broadcast media operations.

The Undersecretary shall exercise supervision over the news operations and documentation of the Bureau of Broadcast Services and the RTVM respectively, and ensure that news information regarding the activities, policies and directions of the government and the Presidency are implemented through the use of broadcast media, throughout the country.

Likewise, the Undersecretary shall assist the Press Secretary in the supervision of the Philippine Administrative Network Project under the French foreign-assisted project and the Electronic Data Processing Division.

Undersecretary for Operations. The Undersecretary for Operations shall assist the Secretary in the formulation and implementation of office objectives, policies and programs related to all projects and operations involving publicity campaign to be undertaken by the Office.

He shall exercise supervision and control over the operations of the Philippine Information Agency, including its provincial information centers and the National Printing Office.

Undersecretary for Special Programs. The Undersecretary for Special Programs shall be responsible for coordinating/implementing all matters related to the activities of or instructions from the President requiring direct assistance of the Office of the Press Secretary.

Assistant Secretary for Administration and Finance. The Assistant Secretary for Administration and finance shall report directly to the Press Secretary. He shall assist the Secretary in the planning, implementation and evaluation of policies and standards for an efficient, effective and cost-control oriented administration pursuant to the objectives of the Office. He shall exercise direct supervision over the administrative and financial operations of all operating units and bureaus under the Office of the Press Secretary.

Assistant Secretary for Media Relations. The Assistant Secretary for Media Relations shall report directly to the Press Secretary. He shall assist the Secretary in ensuring that liaison with representatives of local and foreign media is effectively coordinated and maintained. He shall also be responsible in providing assistance to media representatives on matters relating to the activities of the President, including the policies, programs, and activities of the Government. Likewise, he shall exercise direct supervision over the Press Working Area.

Assistant Secretary for Legislative Affairs. The Assistant Secretary for Legislative Affairs shall report directly to the Press Secretary and shall serve as the Office's link with the Senate and House of Representatives, including establishment of linkages with other government agencies and instrumentalities. He shall provide a forum for coordination and mutual support on matters relating to legislation.

The Press Secretary shall exercise direct supervision and control over the Media Accreditation and Relations Division and the Presidential Photo Section. Likewise, he shall continue to maintain administrative supervision over the People's Television Network, Inc., RPN-9 and IBC-13.

Contact: Secretariat, Kalayaan Hall, Malacanang, Manila
Telephone Numbers: (632) - 7333624, 7338674
In 1986, a government-wide reorganization was effected which abolished Office of Media Affairs-National Media Production Center (OMA-NMPC) among others to streamline government bureaucracy and redirect and reorient the government information system. The Philippine Information Agency (PIA) was then formed out of the defunct OMA-NMPC through Executive Order No. 100 promulgated on Dec. 24, 1986.

Under the new orientation and thrust of the government, **the PIA mission is geared towards creating conditions that will allow the free flow of accurate, timely and relevant information to and from the Filipino people**. The goal is to create an enlightened citizenry which can participate meaningfully in democratic processes.

The PIA is organized into 11 divisions, 15 regional information offices, 74 provincial information centers, 911 community development information centers (CDIC).

The present organization of PIA followed the same pattern as that of OMA-NMPC except for the establishments of CDICS. But PIA's information efforts are now geared to development communication goals rather than propaganda, image building and media control.

PIA information centers serve as access centers on information particularly on government programs, projects and policies. They serve as one-stop shops which ensure two-way flow of communication between the government and the people. This nationwide network is the focal point for disseminating information on government programs and gathering of feedback on popular opinions, people's aspirations and expectations.

The **Motion Pictures Division/Film Laboratory** is considered a leading one-stop shop for film processing in the country.

The **Public Opinion Polls Division** monitors the public pulse with respect to government programs and policies.

The **Media Studies Division**, another research arm, conducts regular media monitoring and content analysis studies on government issues as perceived by columnists/editors as well as studies on media infrastructure, and access to information. It publishes communication monographs, Philippine Media Factbook, Media Profile, government directory, facts and figures. Results of studies are used as data base for policy formulation, project development and evaluation.

The **Media Infrastructure Division and Human Resources Development Division** have looked after the broadening of people's access to media and the upgrading of skills and ethical standards among communication personnel, particularly those in government. Training programs and values orientation seminars are held for communication personnel and services in the PIA as well as in other government and non-government organizations.

In the ICON, the PIA is the lead agency in the region in line with the policy for strengthening information coordination among the different line departments in the countryside. In the same spirit, PIA is an active member of other government organizations such as the PROP, RDC, AGPIO, AREX and its regional counterparts with an estimated outreach of 40% or 24 million of the total population.

The PIA has also established working relationships with international organizations like the ASEAN Committee on Culture and Information (COCI), UNICEF, UNESCO, Asian Mass Media Information Center, Institutional Development Research Center, WHO, JICA, UNDP, IRRI and UNHCR. PIA undertakes information related projects for these agencies.

Contact: USEC Roberto Capco (OIC)
Telephone Numbers: (632) - 9204386, 9204345
The Bureau of Communication Services (BCS) conceptualizes and implements programs that

project the activities, policies, and directions of the overnment in general, and the presidency in particular. In the 1989 review of agency mandates, the BCS was directed to **"provide services relating to policy formulation, communication planning, project development, research and evaluation, creating and production functions, coordination of information dissemination for the OPS and its bureaus and attached agencies."**

The Bureau **conducts polls and surveys** that serve as inputs to policy formulation, communication planning services, production and printing of information materials for special events such as EDSA anniversary, Independence Day, Alay Lakad, state visits and other state events. It also has its own in-house publications.

Contact: Usec. Roberto Capco (OIC)
Telephone Number: (632) - 7342119
The Presidential Broadcast Staff (RTVM) is an attached agency of the Office of the Press Secretary. It is tasked primarily with the video and audio documentation of the President's daily activities. Operating 24 hours daily, seven days a week, it also provides the President's office with prompt and efficient broadcast services. RTVM was organized on July 16, 1986.

Thrusts

The Presidential Broadcast Staff continues to create the broadest public awareness of the efforts and measures undertaken by the President toward national development; provides mechanisms for public interaction with the President that allow and encourage people's participation in the discussion and resolution of issues relating to their community, municipality, city, or province, as well as other of national concern.

RTVM is the first media institution in government that has provided, and continues to provide, regular television and radio coverage programs throughout a President's term, thereby setting a precedent and standard by which succeeding administrations may assess the extent and depth of private media's access to the Executive Branch.

RTVM has successfully laid the foundation for expanded Presidential archives that includes the most modem media forms (magnetic tapes and laser discs). The staff maintains complete audio and video archives of Presidential activities, as well as major governmental programs of the last eleven years: a rich lode on Philippine Government Data preserved for posterity in state-of-the-art technology.

RTVM also pioneered in mobilizing private broadcast media to reinforce broadcast media coverage of Presidential activities and major state events. Through the establishment of the Philippine Broadcast Pool (PBP), private and public sector media continue to cooperate and strengthen each other's information gathering and dissemination capability by sharing their material, technical and human resources.

The staff also undertakes regular radio-television programs on the Presidency, presidential activities and current issues. These are shown weekly or monthly.

RTVM likewise contributes to the development of Philippine radio and television as a whole, specifically, in its information and educational aspects. Special features on topics of national significance and documentaries on historical themes conceptualized and executed by the Staff have won widespread acceptance.

Contact: Director Jesus Terry Adevoso

Telephone Number: (632) - 7422371 local 6001, 6002

Primarily, Bureau of Broadcast Services (BBS), as a radio network, exists to reach the audiences that private broadcasters are not interested in. From only 14 stations of 1-kilowatt average power rating output in 1986, the government radio facility is now a network of 34 radio stations nationwide with an average power output rating of 10 kilowatts. Its stations in Manila, Cebu and Naga operate on 50 kilowatts output ratings. In terms of audience reach, where in 1986, government radio reached only 25% of the total population, now its reach is 50%.

The BBS continuously provides accurate and objective information and undertakes communication strategies that help bring the government closer to the people.

News and public affairs have always been the centerpiece of its programming operations. Cultural and educational features complete a well-balanced fare for the BBS audience.

Production work has been dedicated to accuracy, clarity and objectivity. However, as a matter of policy, emphasis is placed on broadcast materials that promote awareness of official government activities, projects, priorities, including regular presidential, pronouncements, legislative concerns, and virtually every single important event in the various agencies and instrumentalities of government that are addressed to the public welfare.

Radio Network

BBS has a vast radio network that reaches the whole nation with a collective transmitting power of 406.50 kilowatts. It has four Metro Manila stations namely: DZRB-Radyo ng Bayan, DWBR-the Business Radio, DZRM and DZFM Sports Radio and 30 provincial stations that are committed to serve the development thrusts of the government.

Of the 34 BBS stations, 30 are AM stations and 4 are FM stations. Twenty-one (21) stations have ten (10) kilowatt power output, three (3) have 50 kilowatt power output, four (4,) have one (1) kilowatt power output, one has 25 kilowatt power output and two, 0.25 kilowatt power output on FM. Many of the locations served by the BBS has a radio station for the first time, other areas have been abandoned by private radio stations.

Thus, in order to be an effective and responsible instrument of development, BBS steadily evaluates its radio programs and subsequently institutes the necessary changes in form and substance. Personnel undergo continuing programs to enhance their skills while equipment and facilities are regularly upgraded.

Contact: Dante A. Cruz

Telephone Number: (632) - 9203968

The National Printing Office (NPO) is a creation of Executive Order No. 285 dated July 25, 1987. The said E.O. abolished the General Services Administration (GSA) and transferred its functions to appropriate government agencies. In answer to the need for an effective government printing and publication system the relevant printing units of the Philippine Information Agency (PIA) were merged with the Government Printing Office which was then an agency of the GSA resulting in the creation of the NPO. NPO is mandated by Executive Order No. 285 with the exclusive printing jurisdiction of government standard and accountable forms, the official ballots, public documents and development information materials.

PIA was subsequently placed under the supervision and control of the Office of the Press Secretary under Administrative Order No. 49 dated November 20, 1987 thereby making NPO an attached agency of OPS.

NPO had 36 printing machines in operation in 1986, out of a total of 65 consisting mostly of pre-war vintage printing machines. The latest acquisition was in 1979. With the rehabilitation program initiated in 1990, it has now a total of 52 machines in operation including the merged printing units.

Although Executive Order No. 285, was issued on July 25, 1987 mandating the National Printing Office with exclusive printing jurisdiction on the printing, binding, and distribution of all standard and accountable forms, among others, it was only during the middle part of 1990 that the new management has fully complied with the mandate of E.O. No. 285 and started instituting changes.

The NPO management concentrated on the printing of standard and accountable forms after a nationwide survey has been conducted to determine the demands of said forms, thereby enabling this Office to program its projects and activities in proper operational perspective.

Contact: Dir. Melanio Torio

Telephone Number: (632) - 9252187

Television is the most effective medium for relaying messages to various publics and the People's Television Network (PTV-4) is proud to be on the air to bring news and information to the nation. PTV-4 is doubly proud to be present and serving right from the start - on February 24, 1986 - the third day of the EDSA Revolution. The station was on the air bringing much awaited news to an information-hungry Filipino nation.

Immediately upon taking over a heavily damaged broadcast facility, the People Power volunteers found an MBS-4 looted of equipment, with no program inventory, and with only one hundred fifty-four pesos (PI54.00) left in cash from a 1986 budget of sixty million pesos (P60M) and a few millions in debt. Worse, it had no official standing and no organization structure. There were only employees and equipment to do Malacañang's bidding. Even the employees had no tenure. The new PTV-4 was able to rise, phoenix-like, from the ruins of its predecessor, and in the span of six years, achieved many things.

PTV-4 has never been, officially, a government station. No money from the national government has even funded the station. PTV-4 has never had any allocation in the General Appropriations Act. All its funds are self-generated.

Innovative Public Information

1. Maintained a balance of views -- a complete turn around from the heavily handed censorship of its predecessor MBS-4 during the Marcos regime.

2. Carved out innovations in news programming as the only TV station with three major newscasts and daily and hourly breaks.

3. Led in public affairs programming with pioneers such as: Tinig ng Bayan, Headline, Talakayan sa Makati, Woman Watch, Dighay Buhay and Congress Forum which became forerunners of public affairs programs in Philippine television.

4. Provided models for public service and educational programs such as Damayan, Infoline, Tele-Aralan and Ating Alamin.

5. Provided leadership in sports programming.

6. Broke the dominance of commercial television networks, when in 1989, it ranked number two in TV ratings among five networks in Metro Manila. It was proven, therefore, that a government TV station can have a sizeable share of the viewing audience with a programming that is balanced and credible.

7. Became the first Hall of Fame awardee of the Catholic Mass Media Awards (CMMA) by winning the Best Station with Most Balanced Programming for three consecutive years, among other awards.

8. Provided longer daily broadcast hours to news and public affairs information including coverage during natural disasters.

From an MBS-4 with poor ratings, a small outreach and looted-of-equipment network in 1986, PTV-4 now ranks among the top networks in terms of nationwide reach and coverage. The Network embarked on a Facilities Upgrading Project with assistance from the French Government. Under the Second and Third French Protocols of 1990 between the Philippine and French Governments, PTV-4 was recipient of FF74.2 million (P28 M) in the form of transmitter facilities, studio, video and audio equipment.

PTV-4 now broadcasts from its new headquarters at the Philippine Information Agency compound in Visayas Avenue, Quezon City.

PTV-4 launched its satellite-simulcast broadcast programming last February 14, 1992 for nationwide outreach. With the acquisition of the uplink equipment to match the Transponder 54 of the Palapa B2P Satellite lease from Telkom, Indonesia, PTV-4 operates on a full-time satellite broadcast 24 hours a day.

Programming is 11 % News: 13% Public Affairs; 16% Educational; 19% Sports; 36% Entertainment and 5% Religious.

Contact: Gen. Manager : Jose S. Isabelo
Telephone Numbers: (632) - 9204389, 9215081

The News and Information Bureau (NIB) is composed of the following divisions: 1) Administrative and Financial Division; 2) Presidential Press Staff; 3) Media Accreditation and Relations Division; 4) Philippines News Agency. The Administrative and Finance Division attends to the general administrative and financial requirements of the Bureau and its line/operating divisions.

The Presidential Press Staff documents all of the utterances of the Presidency primarily for print media. A team of reporters join the Malacañang Press Corps in its interviews to provide a permanent record of whatever took place. The PPS reporters transcribe speeches and write out the necessary news reports, which form the basic documents of a particular event. Under the PPS is the Clipping Section which organizes all articles, columns and editorials on the Presidency.

The Media Accreditation and Relations Division, has two sections under it namely: Media Accreditation and Relations Office (MARO) and the International Press Center (IPC). The Media Accreditation and Relations Office handles media coverage arrangements of Presidential events, both here and abroad. Its Media Relations Officers make sure that media has a proper place in these events. They accompany media during out-of-town coverages, making sure that they have transportation and facilities for covering the events.

The International Press Center accredits foreign and local media whose IPC identification cards help them to cover individual officials and to enter events that are open for coverage. Although there has been some criticism from foreign advocates of Press Freedom, the arrangements that the IPC has made, including their helping foreign media to get their working permits from the Bureau of Immigration and Deportation, their helping them in the event that they have to deal with the policy on coverage matters and facilitating the entry of equipment through the NAIA has been favorably accepted and even endorsed by the foreign media who are working here.

The Philippine News Agency (PNA), provides daily news service to both local and foreign publics. The PNA has been transformed from a government propaganda arm to a professional news agency. It underwent reorganization to improve and professionalize news service delivery to its various media clients.

The Agency has a 24-hour computer-linked news exchange arrangement with 24 other news agencies in ASEAN and the Asia-Pacific region. The swapping of news, features, and special reports is part of the multilateral agreement among members of the ASEAN News Exchange (ANEX) and the Organization of Asia-Pacific News Agencies (OANA). ANEX comprises ANTARA of Indonesia, BERNAMA of Malaysia, the TNA of Thailand and the PNA. Although Brunei Darussalam and Singapore have no national news agencies, some of their media facilities are linked to the ANEX system through BERNAMA, the regional communications center of the exchange. OANA is a broader international news exchange framework which includes, among others, KYODO of Japan, YONHAP of South Korea, PTI and UNI of India, XINHUA of China, VNA of Vietnam, AAP and PPI of Pakistan, KPL of Laos, KCNA of North Korea, LANKAPUVATH of Sri Lanka, MONTSAME of Mongolia, IRNA of Iran, RSS of Nepal, TASS of Russia and ANADOLU of Turkey.

Contact: Usec Roberto Capco (OIC)

Telephone Numbers: (632) - 5278201 local 236

CABINET

OFFICE OF THE EXECUTIVE SECRETARY

Profile :: Executive Secretary Alberto "BERT" Romulo
Tel#: 736-1075 TO 76; 736-1010 | Email: agromulo@op.gov.ph

Executive Secretary Alberto "BERT" G. Romulo, through hardwork, discipline, dedication, and deep concern for every Filipino, has already carved for himself his own special niche in the Philippine politics not only as an economic manager but as a respected statesman as well.

OFFICE OF THE PRESS SECRETARY

Profile :: The Honorable Ignacio "Toting" Bunye
Tel#: 733-8658; 733-3629; 735-616; 735-6170
http://www.ops.gov.ph

Former Muntinlupa Congressman Ignacio "Toting" Bunye formally assumed the post of press secretary and presidential spokesman today (July 16, 2002).

Before he joined politics in l986, Bunye had been a reporter of DZMT, the radio station of the old Manila Times, and later as reporter of the Daily Star

DEPARTMENT OF AGRARIAN REFORM

Profile :: The Honorable Hernani Agsalud Braganza
http://www.dar.gov.ph
Tel#: 927-9287; 929-3088; 929-3968
Email: nani@dar.gov.ph

Born on 7 August 1964, Secretary Braganza is one of the youngest members of the Cabinet.

Sec. Braganza took his primary education at the Alaminos Central School before transferring to Claret School of Quezon City where he also took his secondary education. He went to De La Salle University (DLSU) in college where he graduated with a degree in AB History-Political Science in 1984.

DEPARTMENT OF AGRICULTURE

Profile :: The Honorable LEONARDO Q. MONTEMAYOR
Tel#: 920-4323; 920-4358; 929-8183 | Email: seclqm@da.gov.ph
Website: http://www.da.gov.ph

Newly appointed Agriculture Secretary Leonardo Q. Montemayor comes from a landed family in Pangasinan, but was born in Manila on 9 October 1949.

DEPARTMENT OF BUDGET AND MANAGEMENT

Profile :: The Honorable EMILIA T. BONCODIN
Tel#: 735-4926; 735-1959; 735-4927 | Email: etb@dbm.gov.ph
Website: http://www.dbm.gov.ph

OFFICE OF THE PRESS SECRETARY

Tel#: 633-7207; 633-7228; 632-0805
Website: http://www.deped.gov.ph

DEPARTMENT OF ENVIRONMENT AND NATURAL RESOURCES

Tel#: 928-0691 ; 929-6633 to 35 | Email: sechta@denr.gov.ph
Website: http://www.denr.gov.ph

DEPARTMENT OF FINANCE

Tel#: 523-4355; 523-6051; 521-2948 | Email: camacho@dof.gov.ph
Website: http://www.dof.gov.ph

DEPARTMENT OF HEALTH

Tel#: 711-9502 to 03; 743-1829; 743-1786 | Email: osec@doh.gov.ph
Website: http://www.doh.gov.ph

DEPARTMENT OF THE INTERIOR AND LOCAL GOVERNMENT

Tel#: 925-0320; 925-0323; 925-0032 | Email: osec@dilg.gov.ph
Website: http://www.dilg.gov.ph

DEPARTMENT OF JUSTICE

Tel#: 521-8344; 521-3721; 521-1614; 524-8794; 526-2746 | Email: sechbp@info.com.ph
Website: http://www.doj.gov.ph

DEPARTMENT OF LABOR AND EMPLOYMENT

Tel#: 527-2116; 527-2118; 527-3494; 527-2131; 527-3586 | Email: doleosec@info.com.ph
Website: http://www.dole.gov.ph

DEPARTMENT OF NATIONAL DEFENSE

Tel#: 911-6183; 911-6192; 911-6213 | Email: osnd@philonline.com

DEPARTMENT OF PUBLIC WORKS AND HIGHWAYS

Tel#: 527-4111; 527-5616; 527-5635 | Email: secdatumanong@dpwh.gov.ph
Website: http://www.dpwh.gov.ph

DEPARTMENT OF SCIENCE AND TECHNOLOGY

Tel#: 837-2939; 837-2937 | Email: efa@dost.gov.ph
Website: http://www.dost.gov.ph

DEPARTMENT OF TOURISM

Tel#: 524-1751; 525-4102; 521-7374; 525-3832; 521-7375 | Email: dotrjg@info.com.ph
Website: http://www.wowphilippines.com.ph

DEPARTMENT OF TRANSPORTATION AND COMMUNICATIONS

Tel#: 726-7125; 723-4698; 726-1111 | Email: dotc@i-next.net
Website: http://www.oksnaoks.dotc.gov.ph

NATIONAL ECONOMIC AND DEVELOPMENT AUTHORITY

Tel#: 631-3747 | Email: dbcanlas@neda.gov.ph
Website: http://www.neda.gov.ph

DEPARTMENT OF ENERGY

Tel#: 8401401-21 | Email: v_perez@doe.gov.ph

DEPARTMENT OF NATIONAL DEFENSE

DEPARTMENT OF NATIONAL DEFENSE DIRECTORY

OFFICE	NAME of CHIEF of Office/Resource Officers	OFC TEL NOS	OFC ML NOS	E-MAIL ADD
USND	Usec Feliciano M Gacis Jr Ma Cecilia N Reasonda	911-3300 911-6192		mcnreasonda@dnd.gov.ph
USCR	Usec Edgardo E. Batenga Bgen Nestor Castillo Cpt Nicolas J Quemado Jr	911-1651 911-6246 911-6246	8130/8011 8207/8484 8207/8484	
USO	Exec Dir, COC-IS, OPCEN/OHEA Usec Antonio C Santos Ms. Marita I Yoro (OUSO) Col Jose F Gamos (OPCEN) Col Benjamin Asuncion (OPCEN) 1LT Rex Banjo Q Bumanglag (OHEA)	911-6261 911-7935 911-6561 912-7386 912-7608 912-7422 912-7608 911-6183 911-6193	8226/8206 8206/3392 loc 130 3392 loc 131 8110/8100	rbumanglag@dnd.gov.ph
ASIL	OIC, ASCOM Asec Cesar H Bello Ms Roseadel H Yambao Engr Fidel Burgos BGen Victor Obillo AFP (Ret)	911-6244 911-6227 911-6244 911-6227 911-6244 911-6227 911-6244 8410/8402 8410/8402		
ASPP	Asec Ruben F Ciron Dir Ramon EL Martinez Jr Dir Joji V Aragon Maj Ferozaldo Paul T Regencia	911-6460 911-6517 9116262 911-6460 913-9450 911-4579 911-6460 8350/8200 8350/8350		benciron@yahoo.com benciron@mydestiny.net cdimo_dnd@yahoo.com phil-er-jva@pacific.net.ph fptr86@hotmail.com
ASPER	OIC, OLEG Asec Ricardo R Blancaflor Dir Regina D	911-4396 421-3531 911-6397 911-4396		gdabaron@yahoo.com jturga@r2Net.com

	Cabaron Maj Hernando Caraig Capt Allan Borlasa Mr Jerome Turga	911-4396 911-6546 8320/8455 8055/8055		
OASLA	Asec Leticia A Gloria	911-7188 8300		ALECON@I.Mla.com.ph
OASSAIP	Asec Alejandro P Melchor III Maj Benito A Madarang Maj Leouel A Santos	911-7171 911-7171 911-7171		Amelchor@zpdee.net dndbenjie@yahoo.com
NDCC	MGen Melchor P Rosales AFP (Ret) Col Ma Nina Q Dritsopoulou, MNSA Maj Ronaldo George Reario PN (M)	912-2424 912-6675 911-5061 loc 101 421-3237 912-3044 911-5061 loc 105 911-5061 loc 113 912-2665 911-1406		cda@ndcc.gov.ph cdexo@ndcc.gov.ph opcen@ndcc.gov.ph
NDCP	Commo Carlos Agustin AFP (Ret) Atty Pedro G Banzon	911-8469 911-8857 912-6016		cla@ndcp.edu.ph cla@issti.com pgbanzon@ndcp.edu.ph
PVAO	Commo Artemio Arugay AFP (Ret) Atty Dennis P Dinglasan Ms. Gina E Ballesfin	912-4526 912-4869 912-1895 421-1349 421-1340		PVAO@veteran.PVAO.gov.ph
GA	Radm Eriberto C Varona AFP (Ret) Engr Pepito A Bauto Engr Romeo C Fabian	911-4580 (GAMLO) (047)244-5625 (Batn) (047)244-5625 (Batn) (047)244-5625 loc347 8434		gammlo@mozcom.com bertvar@pacific.net.ph arsenal@batn.pworld.net.ph
VMMC	Dr Salvador P Flores Dr Elisa S Cariaso Dr. L.A. Casison	927-1873 920-2487 927-5918 927-6426 927-2250		
OSMA	Col Pedro Ike I Inserto PAF	912-4212 911-4583 8255		osma_dnd@yahoo.com
DICTO	Dir Ramon EL	911-6262		cdimo@dnd.gov.ph

	Martinez Jr CESO III Mr Andres D Navarro	911-4782 911-6262 911-4782 8200		
OPA	Dir Rosulo L Manlangit Mr Salvador Manuel Z Reyes Mr. Primitivo S Berunia	911-2882 911-3339 911-3339	8444/8445 8444/8445 8444/8445	psb108@hotmail.com
AS	Dir Mac G Orendain Ms. Gladys Cagadoc	911-7992 911-8118 8107/8344		gladyscagadoc@yahoo.com
MSS	Ms. Teresita Cuevas Ms Catalina C Orito Ms Sally Rosall Ms Lily Biscocho	911-4335 911-4296 911-4335 911-4335 911-4335 8326		mss_chief@hotmail.com lily@flash.net.ph
DISG	Maj Roy T Devesa PA Maj Louis B Binwag Jr Maj Alexander C Sañosa	911-2387 911-2387 911-5255 8120		rtdevesa@yahoo.com lbjr85cav@yahoo.com tig06bas@yahoo.com

DIPLOMATIC AND INTERNATIONAL CONTACTS IN PHILIPPINES

HEADS OF DIPLOMATIC MISSIONS

COUNTRY	HEAD OF MISSION	DATE OF ACCREDITATION
Holy See	H.E. Archbishop Antonio Franco	11 Jun. 1999
[SE]Colombia	H.E. Miguel Duran Ordonez	19 Nov. 1992
[KL]Palestine	H.E. Ahmad Muhammad Al-Fara	10 Apr. 1995
Qatar	H.E. Saleh Ibrahim Al-Kuwari	26 Feb. 1997
[TK]Ethiopia	H.E. Mahdi Ahmed Ali-Gadid	11 Apr 1997
[KL]Oman	H.E. Salim Bin Mohammed bin Salim Al-Wahaibi	23 Jul. 1997
Papua New Guinea	H.E. Graham John Ainui	05 Sep. 1997
[TK]Djibouti	H.E. Rachad Ahmed Saleh Farah	13 Mar. 1998
Venezuela	H.E. Milena Santana-Ramirez*	16 Apr. 1998
Saudi Arabia	H.E. Saleh Mohammad Al-Ghamdi	21 May 1998
Sri Lanka	H.E. P.G. Karunasiri	15 Sep. 1998
Netherlands	H.E. Theo Arnold	03 Nov. 1998

[TK]Bulgaria	H.E. Petar Andonov	02 Dec. 1998
[JK]Slovak Republic	H.E. Milan Lajciak	25 May 1999
Czech Republic	H.E. Stanislav Slavicky	06 Sep. 1999
[BK]Nepal	H.E. Janak Bahadur Singh	11 Oct. 1999
Cambodia	H.E. EK Sereywath	25 Oct. 1999
Iran	H.E. Gholamreza Yousefi	16 Nov.1999
Myanmar	H.E. U Tin Htun	24 Jan. 2000
Nigeria	H.E. Ray O.O. Inije	24 Jan. 2000
Libya	H.E. Salem M. Adam	24 Jan. 2000
[BE]Ireland	H.E. Declan Connolly	24 Jan. 2000
Panama	H.E. Juan Carlos Escalona	16 Feb. 2000
United Arab Emirates	H.E. Mohammed Ebrahim Abdullah Al-Jowaid	16 Feb. 2000
[TK]Belarus	H.E. Petr Krauchanka	16 Feb. 2000
[HN]Mongolia	H.E. Agvaandorjiin Tsolmon	27 Mar. 2000
Sweden	H.E. Ulf Håkansson	12 May 2000
[TK]Morocco	H.E. Mohammed Tangi	12 May 2000
Chile	H.E. Carmen Lynam Narvaez*	28 Aug. 2000
Israel	H.E. Irit Ben-Abba*	28 Aug. 2000
Finland	H.E. Raimo Antolla	28 Aug. 2000
China	H.E. Wang Chungui	28 Aug. 2000
Canada	H.E. Robert L. Collette	20 Sept. 2000
Norway	H.E. Pål Moe	20 Sept. 2000
[KL]Kenya	H.E. James Kihiu Karuga	24 Oct. 2000
[TK]Zambia	H.E. Elias Marko Chipimo	24 Oct. 2000
Germany	H.E. Herbert Jess	14 Dec. 2000
[HN]Ukraine	H.E. Rostyslav Mitrofanovitch Bilodid	14 Dec. 2000
Portugal	H.E. Joao Caetano Da Silva	28 Feb. 2001
Cuba	H.E. Ramon Domingo Alonso Medina	01 Mar. 2001
[BK]North Korea(DPRK)	H.E. Jo In Chol	10 Apr. 2001
[BK]Poland	H.E. Jerzy Surdykowsky	10 Apr. 2001
Italy	H.E. Umberto Colesanti	18 Apr. 2001
New Zealand	H.E. Terence Charles Baker	06 Jun 2001
Laos	H.E. Phiane Philakone	08 Jun 2001

Austria	H.E. Christian Krepela	11 Jun 2001
Brazil	H.E. Claudio Maria Henrique Do Couto Lyra	11 Jun 2001
[KL]Sudan	H.E. Mohammed Adam Ismail	16 Jul. 2001
[TK]Lebanon	H.E. Jaafar Moawi	17 Jul. 2001
Mexico	H.E. Enrique Hubbard	30 Jul. 2001
[KL]Swaziland	H.E. Mabili David Dlamini	01 Oct. 2001
Korea	H.E. Son Sang-ha	09 Oct. 2001
[TK]Ecuador	H.E. Marcelo Avila-Orejuela	10 Oct. 2001
India	H.E. Navrekha Sharma*	08 Nov. 2001
[BE]Eritrea	H.E. Mohammed Nur Ahmed	26 Nov. 2001
[TK]Tanzania	H.E. Elly Elikunda Elineema Mtango	28 Nov. 2001
Malaysia	H.E. Mohd. Taufik Mohd. Noor	05 Jan. 2002
[JK]Croatia	H.E. Boris Mitrovic	25 Jan. 2002
Kuwait	H.E. Ibrahim Muhanna Al-Muhanna	13 Feb. 2002
Thailand	H.E. Busba Bunnag*	13 Feb. 2002
Peru	H.E. Jorge Chavez	21 Feb. 2002
U.S.A.	H.E. Francis Joseph Ricciardone	21 Feb. 2002
[TK]Nicaragua	H.E. Harry Bodan Shields	21 Mar. 2002
United Kingdom	H.E. Paul Stephen Dimond	12 Apr. 2002
[BE]Yemen	H.E. Abdulwhab Mohamed Al-Shawkani	18 Apr. 2002
France	H.E. Renee Veyret*	28 May 2002
Australia	H.E. Ruth Lorraine Pearce*	28 May 2002
[BE]Lesotho	H.E. Lefa Joseph Mokotjo	13 Jun. 2002
[KL]South Africa	H.E. Abraham S. Nkomo	25 Jun. 2002
Turkey	H.E. Tanju Sümer	26 Jun. 2002
Japan	H.E. Kojiro Takano	26 Jun. 2002
Bangladesh	H.E. M. Munir-uz-Zaman	06 Aug. 2002
Brunei Darussalam	H.E. Hajah Maimunah Dato Paduka Haji Elias*	06 Aug. 2002
[ND]Angola	H.E. Eliseo Avila De Jesus Figuieredo	07 Aug. 2002
[KL]Algeria	H.E. Rachid Bladehane	07 Aug. 2002
[TK]Lithuania	H.E. Algirdas Kudzys	18 Sep. 2002

Belgium	H.E. Christiaan Tanghe	30 Sep 2002
TKJordan	H.E. Samir Issa Al-Naouri	30 Sep 2002
Pakistan	H.E. Iftikhar Hussain Kazmi	25 Nov 2002
Switzerland	H.E. Lise Favre*	25 Nov 2002
Egypt	H.E. Saber Abder Mansour	25Nov. 2002
Russia	H.E. Anatoli Vladimirovich Nebogatov	27 Nov 2002
Vietnam	H.E. Dinh Tich	27 Nov 2002
BEBahrain	H.E. Karim Ebrahim al-Shakar	27 Nov 2002
KLGhana	H.E. John Bentum-Williams	18 Dec 2002
JKHungary	H.E. Gyorgy Busztin	18 Dec 2002
KLDenmark	H.E. Leif Mogens Reimann	18 Dec 2002
Romania	H.E. Radu HOMESCU	30 Jan 2003
Spain	H.E. Ignacio Saqaz	30 Jan 2003
. .		
European Union	H.E. Johannes De Kok	26 Jun. 2002
Sovereign Military Order of Malta	H.E. Enrique Syquia	13 May 1996

CHARGE D'AFFAIRES, A.I.

Colombia	Mrs. Stella Marquez de Araneta*
Iraq	Mr. ASamir A.M. Bolus
Singapore	Mr. Paul Koh
Indonesia	Mr. Alexander Laturiuw

INTERNATIONAL ORGANIZATIONS

United Nations Development Programme	Mr. Terence Jones
Asian Development Bank	Mr. Tadao Chino
Food and Agriculture Org. of U.N.	Mr. Sang Mu Lee
International Committee of the Red Cross	Mr. Dominique Dufour
International Finance Corporation	Mr. Vipul Bhagat
International Labor Organization	Dr. Werner Konrad Blenk
International Monetary Fund	Mr. Sean Nolan
International Organization for Migration	Mr. Bruce Reed
International Rice Research Institute	Dr. Ronald P. Cantrell
United Nations Children's Fund	Dr. Terrel Hill
United Nations High Commissioner for Refugees	Mr. Thamrongsak Meechubot

United Nations Population Fund	Mr. Zahidul Duque
World Bank/IBRD	Mr. Robert Vance Pulley
World Health Organization	Dr. Shigeru Omi

LEGEND: Ambassadors based in:
BK = Bangkok * Female Ambassadors/CDA's
BE = Beijing
HN = Hanoi
JK = Jakarta
KL = Kuala Lumpur
SE = Seoul
TK = Tokyo
ND = New Delhi
SG = Singapore

PHILIPPINE CONSULATES

1. AGANA	PHILIPPINE CONSULATE GENERAL Hon. (Mr.) BAYANI S. MERCADO Consul General Suite 601-2, ITC Building, Marine Drive Tamuning, GUAM 96911, PO Box 9880 Tel. Nos. (671) 646-4620; 646-4630 Fax No. 00-671-6491868 Email: pcgagana@ite.net (Jurisdiction: Guam, Marshall Islands, Micronesia, Wake Island)
2. CHICAGO	PHILIPPINE CONSULATE GENERAL Hon. (Ms.) EMELINDA LEE PINEDA Consul General 30 North Michigan Avenue, Suite 2100 Chicago, Illinois, 60602 U.S.A. Tel. Nos. (1312) 332-6458/59 Fax No. 00-1312-3323657 Email: phchi@moon.igcom.net Website: http://www.pcgchicago.com (Jurisdiction : Arkansas, Indiana, Kansas, Minnesota, Michigan, Missisippi, Missouri, Nebraska, North Dakota, South Dakota, Ohio, Illinois, and Wisconsin)
3. GUANGZHOU	PHILIPPINE CONSULATE GENERAL Hon. (Mr.) ISAIAS F. BEGONIA Consul General Rm 709-711, 7th Flr., Guangdong International Hotel 339 Huanshi Dong Lu, Guangzhou, Guangdong Province 510130, PEOPLE'S REPUBLIC OF CHINA Tel. Nos. 8620-833-11461, 833-10996; 833-11888 Fax No. 00-8620-833-30573 Email: gzphcggz@public1.guangshou.gd.cn konjen@public.guangzhou.gd.cn Website: http://pcggz.bizhosting.com
4. HAMBURG	PHILIPPINE CONSULATE GENERAL Hon. (Ms.) MINERVA JEAN A. FALCON Consul General

	Jungfrauental 13, 20149 Hamburg, GERMANY Tel. Nos. (040) 442-952 & 442-953 Fax No. 00-040-459987 Email: hamburgpcg@t-online.de
5. HONG KONG	PHILIPPINE CONSULATE GENERAL Hon. (Ms.) VICTORIA S. BATACLAN Consul General Room 602, 6th Floor, United Centre Bldg., 95 Queensway, Admiralty, HONGKONG Tel. Nos. (852) 2823 8500, 2823-8501, 2823-8510 Fax No. 00-852-28669885, 2866 8559 Email: pcg@philcongen-hk.com prhk@asiaonline.net
6. HONOLULU	PHILIPPINE CONSULATE GENERAL Hon. (Mr.) ROLANDO S. GREGORIO Consul General 2433 Pali Highway, Honolulu, HAWAII 96817 Tel. Nos. (1808) 595-6316 to 19 Fax No. 00-1808-5952581 Email: honolulupc@hawaii.rr.com (Jurisdiction: hawaii, American Samoa, Kiribati, tonga, French Polynesia)
7. JEDDAH	PHILIPPINE CONSULATE GENERAL Hon. (Mr.) KADATUAN P. USOP Consul General Al-Sayeddah Kaddija Street, Al Faisaliyah District 1 P.O. Box 4794, Jeddah 21412, KINGDOM OF SAUDI ARABIA Tel.Nos.(9662) 6600-348, 6670-925, 6600-354 Fax No. 00-9662-6630838 Email: jeddahpc@sps.net.sa jeddah_pc@dfa.gov.ph (Jurisdiction: Western Region of the Kingdom including the Governorates of Makkah, Madinah, Asir, Abha, Al Baha, Khamis Mushayt, Gizan, Rabigh, Taif & Yanbu.)
8. LOS ANGELES	PHILIPPINE CONSULATE GENERAL Hon. (Mr.) MARCIANO A. PAYNOR, JR. Consul General 3600 Wilshire Boulevard, Suite 500, Los Angeles, California 90010, U.S.A. Tel. No. (1213) 639-0989 Fax No. 00-1213-639-0990 Email: losangelpc@aol.com Website: http://www.philcongenla.org/ (Jurisdiction: Southern California, Arizona, Southern Nevada, Texas, New Mexico)
9. MANADO	PHILIPPINE CONSULATE GENERAL Hon. (Mr.) REYNALDO C. MARTINEZ Consul General J1n. Tikala Satu No. 12, Tikala Ares Lingkungan I 95124 Manado City, Indonesia, P.O. Box 1079 Tel. No. (062431) 861178 & 862181 Fax No. 00-62431-862365 Email: manadopc@manado.wasantara.net.id

10. MILAN	PHILIPPINE CONSULATE GENERAL Hon. (Ms.) MILAGROS R. PEREZ Consul General Via Santa Maria Segreta 6, 20123 Milan, ITALY Tel. Nos. (392) 805-14-00; 8051 270 & 8752 90 Fax No. 00-392-878797 Email: milanpcg@libero.it
11. NEW YORK (PCG)	PHILIPPINE CONSULATE GENERAL Hon. (Ms.) LINGLINGAY F. LACANLALE Consul General 556 Fifth Avenue, New York, New York 10036-5095, U.S.A. Tel. Nos. (1212) 764-1330 & 575-4774 Fax No. 00-1212-3821146 Email: philconsulateny@mindspring.com Website: http://philconsulateny.home.mindspring.com/ (Jurisdiction: Connecticut, Delaware, Louisiana, Maine, Massachusetts, New Hampshire, New Jersey, Pennsylvania, Rhode Island, Vermont)
12. OSAKA	PHILIPPINE CONSULATE GENERAL Hon. (Mr.) ANTONIO P. VILLAMAYOR Consul General Twin21 MID Tower, 24F 2-1-61 Shiromi, Chuo-ku, Osaka, JAPAN Tel. Nos. (06) 6-910-7881 Fax No. 06-6-910-8734 Mobile No. (090) 4036-7984 Email: osakapc@osk.3web.ne.jp Website: http://www4.osk.3web.ne.jp/~osakapc/ (Jurisdiction: Honshu, Toyama, Aichi & West thereof, Shikoku & Khushu areas)
13. SAIPAN	PHILIPPINE CONSULATE GENERAL Hon. (Ms.) JULIA C. HEIDEMANN Consul General 5th Floor, Nauru Building Susupe P.O. Box 500731 CK Saipan MP 96950 COMMONWEALTH OF NORTHERN MARIANA ISLANDS Tel. Nos. (670) 234-1848 & 235-8360; 234-1850; 1851 Fax No. 00-670-2341849 Email: saipanpcg@vzpacifica.net (Jurisdiction: Island of Saipan, Tinian, Rota and The Northern Islands)
14. SAN FRANCISCO	PHILIPPINE CONSULATE GENERAL Hon. (Mr.) DELIA MENEZ-ROSAL Consul General 447 Sutter Street, 6th Floor, Philippine Center Building, San Francisco, California 94108, U.S.A. Tel. Nos. (1415) 433-6666 to 68; 433-6675; 433-6680 Fax No. 00-1415-4212641 Email: SanFranciscoPC@aol.com
15. SHANGHAI	PHILIPPINE CONSULATE GENERAL

	Hon. (Mr.) JESUS I. YABES Consul General Suite 368, Shanghai Centre, 1376 Nanjing West Road, Shanghai 200040 China Tel: (86-21) 62798337 Fax: (86-21) 62798332 Emails: ShanghaiPC@dfa.gov.ph Website: http://www.philcongenshanghai.org
16. SYDNEY	PHILIPPINE CONSULATE GENERAL Hon. (Ms.) MARIA ZENEIDA A. COLLINSON Consul General Philippine Center, Level 1, 27-33 Wentworth Ave. Sydney, NSW 2000, AUSTRALIA Tel. No.(612) 9262-7377 Fax No. 00-612-9262-7355 Email: phsydpc@ozemail.com.au Website: http://www.emanila.com/phconsul
17. TORONTO	PHILIPPINE CONSULATE GENERAL Hon. (Ms.) SUSAN O. CASTRENCE Consul General 151 Bloor Street West, Suite 365, Toronto, Ontario, M5S 1S4 CANADA Tel. Nos. (1416) 922-7181 Fax No. 00-1416-9222638 Email: torontopc@philcongen-toronto.com Website: http://www.philcongen-toronto.com
18. VANCOUVER	PHILIPPINE CONSULATE GENERAL Hon. (Ms.) ZENAIDA TACORDA-RABAGO Consul General 700 West Pender, Suite 1405, Vancouver, B.C., CANADA, V6C 1G8 Tel. Nos. (1604) 685-1619; 685 7645 / 8576 Fax No. 00-1604-6859945 Email: VancouverPC@dfa.gov.ph
19. XIAMEN	PHILIPPINE CONSULATE GENERAL Hon. (Ms.) MA. CORAZON Y. BAHJIN Consul General No. 2 Ling Xiang Li, Lian Hua District, Xiamen City 361009, PEOPLE'S REPUBLIC OF CHINA Tel. Nos. (592) 513-0355; 513 0366 Fax No. (0086) (592) 5530803 Email: xiamenpc@public.xm.fj.cn (Jurisdiction: Prov. of Fujian, Zhejiang & Jiangxi, PROC)

PHILIPPINES EMBASSY IN THE US

Office of the Ambassador Contact numbers: Telephone: (202) 467-9366 and (202) 467-9364 Fax: (202) 467-9417	Office of the Deputy Chief of Mission Contact numbers: Telephone: (202) 467-9378
Cultural Section Contact numbers:	Political Section Contact numbers:

Telephone: (202) 467-9399 and (202) 467-9398 RSVP line: (202) 467-9318 Email: Cultural@philippineembassy-usa.org	Telephone: (202) 467-9313 and (202) 467-9314
Economics Section Contact numbers: Telephone: (202) 467-9393 and (202) 467-9317	Press and Information Section Contact numbers: (202) 467-9432
Consular Section Contact numbers: Telephone: (202) 467-9312Fax: (202) 466-6288 Email: Consular@philippineembassy-usa.org	

Defense and Armed Forces Affairs Office Contact numbers: Telephone: (202) 467-9329, (202) 467-9381, (202) 467-9328 and (202) 467-9407 Fax: (202) 467-9436 and (202) 467-9437	Police Attaché's Office Contact numbers: Telephone: (202) 467-9394 and (202) 467-9395 Fax: (202) 467-9415
Veterans Affairs Office Contact numbers:Telephone: (202) 467-9410 Fax: (202) 986-5336	Labor Attaché's Office Contact numbers: Telephone: (202) 467-9425 and (202) 467-9426 Fax: (202) 887-5830
Agricultural Attaché Office Contact numbers: Telephone: (202) 467-9422 and (202) 467-9423 Fax: (202) 467-9421	Commercial Attaché Office Contact numbers: Telephone: (202) 467-9394 and (202) 467-9395 Fax: (202) 467-9428 and (202) 467-9322

IMPORTANT STRATEGIC AND BUSINESS CONTACTS

FIRST CONTACTS

Information on Passport and Visa
at http://travel.state.gov/visa_services.html

US Embassy
Address:
1201 Roxas Boulevard - Ermita 1000 - Manila - The Philippines
Tel: (63-2) 523-1001
Website:http://usembassy.state.gov/posts/rp1/wwwhmain.html
The United States has Embassies in most countries in Asia. These Embassies are headed by an U.S. Ambassador who is named by the President and subject to the approval of the U.S. Senate. Typically Ambassador's are a mix of career and non career government employees. All of these report to the U.S. State Department in Washington, DC. The State Department has directed that development of trade and expansion of business are prime responsibilities of each Ambassador and his Embassy. U.S. Embassies can therefore be an ally in helping you learn more about the market in their country, research opportunities and act as a last resort in case of problems that need political support.

Embassy in the U.S.
Address:Embassy of the Philippines
1600 Massachusetts Avenue, NW, Washington DC 20036
Telephone: (202) 467-9300
Fax: (202) 467-9417
Website:http://www.embassyonline.com/main.html
Foreign embassies also view promotion of trade and investment as major goals. You should contact the country's Embassy, particularly the country's Commercial Counselor for help on researching your business plan.

U.S. Foreign Commercial Offices
Street Address: 395 Senator Gil Puyat Ave. Extension Makati
Mailing Address: APO AP 96440
E-mail Address: OManila@doc.govTelephone: 011-632-890-9362 Fax: 011-632-895-3028
Website: http://www.ita.doc.gov/uscs/philippines/philipp.html
Most U.S. Embassies have at least one representative and in many cases a whole office that is sent to the target country by the U.S. Department of Commerce. The goal of these offices is to increase U.S. business with the target country. These offices can be helpful in assisting you in researching opportunities in a target country.

American Chamber of Commerce
E-mail: amcham@mozcom.com
Most countries in Asia have U.S. Chambers of Commerce made up of member U.S. companies doing business in that country. Typically large Chambers of Commerce have a hired staff person who acts as the Executive Director. Smaller Chambers may have only a volunteer staff. American Chambers of Commerce often are good sources of information on the ease or difficulty in doing business in the target country. Oftentimes they can refer you to members who have detailed insight into set-up problems, the incidence of corruption in the host country or other challenges. Oftentimes the target country will have its own chamber of commerce which is seeking to promote business and investment in their country. These Chambers which represent the target country can also be helpful.

US-ASEAN Business Council
Website: http://www.us-asean.org
The US-ASEAN Business Council is a non-profit organization based in Washington, DC, that promotes business, trade, and investment with the ASEAN countries. Their website includes economic and business information on each ASEAN country and links to numberous other useful websites.

Minister of Commerce
[see Embassy in USA]
Address:Embassy of the Philippines
1600 Massachusetts Avenue, NW, Washington DC 20036
Telephone: (202) 467-9300
Fax: (202) 467-9417
Website:http://www.embassyonline.com/main.html
Most Asian countries have Ministries of Commerce which are the equivalent of the U.S. Department of Commerce. These Ministries attempt to promote their countries products, attract investment and regulate business. Generally most Asian countries seek investment and the opening of foreign manufacturing and other projects because it expands employment, increases trade and tax revenues. You may want to use the Ministry to check the information you are getting from other sources and to contact as a source of further data.

Minister of Industry
[see Embassy in USA]
Address:Embassy of the Philippines
1600 Massachusetts Avenue, NW, Washington DC 20036
Telephone: (202) 467-9300
Fax: (202) 467-9417
Website: http://www.embassyonline.com/main.html
The U.S. does not have a Department of Industry but many Asian countries do. These Ministries goal is to encourage local and foreign firms to establish factories in the host country. If you are interested in manufacturing, you may want to contact them. If your target country does not have a Ministry of Industry, their embassy in Washington, DC may be helpful in connecting you with the correct government offices in the target country.

Minister of Agriculture
[see Embassy in USA]
Address:Embassy of the Philippines
1600 Massachusetts Avenue, NW, Washington DC 20036
Telephone: (202) 467-9300
Fax: (202) 467-9417
Website: http://www.embassyonline.com/main.html
The U.S. government has a Department of Agriculture with offices around the nation. Additionally, most States also have a State Agriculture office. Agriculture production is central to virtually all Asian nations. Most countries in Asia have a national Ministry of Agriculture. This Ministry is a key source for data on agriculture production in the country, restrictions on agriculture operation and many other issues. If your business idea involves Agriculture we recommend you contact both the U.S. Agricultural Attaché at the U.S. Embassy and also the target country Ministry of Agriculture to help you fully research your project.

GOVERNMENT

ORGANIZING FOR EXPORTS

Bureau of Internal Revenue
East Triangle, Diliman, QUEZON CITY, METRO MANILA
Contact Number/s : (63-2) 922-3293/921-4324
Fax : 922-4894
Email : bir-net@mailstation.net

Bureau of Trade Regulation and Consumer Protection
2nd Floor, Trade and Industry Bldg. 361 Sen. Gil J. Puyat Avenue, MAKATI, METRO MANILA
Contact Number/s : (63-2) 896-5785
Fax : 890-4949
Email : btrcp@dti.gov.ph

U.P. Institute for Small Scale Industries
Enrique Virata Hall, U.P. Campus Diliman, QUEZON CITY, METRO MANILA
Contact Number/s : 927-9238, 920-6923
Fax : 927-1034
Email : do@upissi.ph.net

Securities and Exchange Commission
SEC Bldg. EDSA, MANDALUYONG, METRO MANILA
Contact Number/s : 726-0931 to 39
Fax : 725-4399, 725-8141

Philippine Trade Training Center
PTTC Bldg., Sen. Gil J. Puyat Ave., cor. Roxas Blvd, PASAY CITY, METRO MANILA
Contact Number/s : (63-2) 834-1344, 834-1341
Fax : (63-2) 834-1343
Email : pttc@dti.gov.ph

Bangko Sentral Ng Pilipinas Institute
Rm. 1101, 11th Floor, Multi-Storey Bldg. Mabini St., Malate, MANILA, METRO MANILA
Contact Number/s : (63-2)536-0102

Fax : 536-0080

IMPORT PROCEDURES AND DOCUMENTATION

- **Air Transportation Office**
Old MIA Road, PASAY CITY, METRO MANILA
Contact Number/s : (63-2) 831-8078
Fax : 834-01-43

- **Bureau of Domestic Trade Promotion**
2/F, Trade and Industry Bldg.361 Sen. Gil J. Puyat Avenue, MAKATI, METRO MANILA
Contact Number/s : (63-2) 890-49-01to 05, 897-76-17
Fax : 890-48-58
Email : bdtp@dti.gov.ph

- **Bangko Sentral ng Pilipinas- Dept. of Loans and Credit**
A. Mabini, Ermita, MANILA, METRO MANILA
Contact Number/s : (63-2) 536-6061, 523-7848
Fax : 536-6061

- **Bangko Sentral ng Pilipinas - International Operation Dept.**
Rm. 313, 5-Storey Bldg. Mabini St. Malate, MANILA, METRO MANILA
Contact Number/s : (63-2) 523-7792, 536-6077
Fax : 521-8162

- **Board of Investments**
Industry and Investments Bldg. 385 Sen. Gil J. Puyat Ave., MAKATI, METRO MANILA
Contact Number/s : (63-2) 895-3638, 895-3518
Fax : 895-3512

- **Bureau of Animal Industry**
Visayas Ave., Diliman, QUEZON CITY, METRO MANILA
Contact Number/s : (63-2) 927-0971, 926-6883
Fax : 928-1778, 928-2836

- **Burea of Customs**
Port Area, MANILA, METRO MANILA
Contact Number/s : (63-2) 527-4511, 527-4517, 527-4570
Fax : 527-1953

- **Bureau of Export Trade Promotion**
5th-8th floors, New Solid Bldg. 357. Sen Gil J. Puyat Ave.,, MAKATI, METRO MANILA
Contact Number/s : (63-2) 896-3658, 890-4683, 759-3381, 899-0133
Fax : 890-4716, 890-4707

- **Bureau of Fisheries and Aquatic Resources**
860 Quezon Ave., QUEZON CITY, METRO MANILA
Contact Number/s : (63-2) 373-7452, 372-5057
Fax : 372-5048, 372-5056
Email : philfish@vlink.net.ph

- **Bureau of Food and Drugs**
Alabang, MUNTINLUPA, METRO MANILA
Contact Number/s : (63-2) 807-0751, 807-0721
Fax : 807-0721, 807-0725, 807-0751

- **Bureau of Forest Management**
Visayas Ave., Diliman, QUEZON CITY, METRO MANILA
Contact Number/s : (63-2) 927-4788, 925-2136, 925-2138
Fax : 920-0374

- **Bureau of Import Services**
3/F OPPEN Bldg. Sen. Gil J. Puyat, MAKATI, METRO MANILA
Contact Number/s : (63-2) 895-7466
Fax : 895-7466
Email : bisdti@pdx.rpnet.com

- **Bureau of International Trade Relations**
3/F DTI Bldg. 361 Sen. Gil J. Puyat Ave., MAKATI, METRO MANILA

Contact Number/s : 890-5148, 890-4670, 897-8290, 897-8292
Fax : 890-4812
Email : bitr@dti.gov.ph

Burea of Mines and Geosciences
North Ave., Diliman, QUEZON CITY, METRO MANILA
Contact Number/s : 920-9120, 928-8642
Fax : 920-1635
Email : denr-min@gaia.psdn.org.ph

Burea of Plant Industry
692 San Andres Malate, MANILA, METRO MANILA
Contact Number/s : 525-7909, 525-7857, 525-2987, 523-9132
Fax : 521-7650

Bureau of Product Standards
3/F Trade and INdustry Bldg. 361 Sen. Gil J. Puyat Ave., MAKATI, METRO MANILA
Contact Number/s : 890-4859, 890-4924
Fax : 890-5129
Email : dtibpsrp@mnl.sequel.net

Bureau of Small and Medium Business Development
3/F OPPEN Bldg., 349 Sen. Gil J. Puyat Ave., MAKATI, METRO MANILA
Fax : 896-7916
Email : bsmbd@mnl.sequel.net

Bureau of Trade Regulation and Consumer Protection
2/F DTI Bldg. 361 Sen. Gil J. Puyat Ave., MAKATI, METRO MANILA
Contact Number/s : 890-4949, 896-5785
Fax : 890-4949
Email : btrcp@dti.gov.ph

Center for International Trade Expositions and Missions
International Trade Center Complex, Roxas Blvd. cor. Sen. Gil J. Puyat, PASAY CITY, METRO MANILA
Contact Number/s : 832-3956, 831-2382, 831-2201
Fax : 832-3965, 834-0177
Email : info@citem.com.ph

Center for Industrial Competitiveness
2/F Trade and Industry Bldg. 361 Sen. Gil J. Puyat Ave., MAKATI, METRO MANILA
Contact Number/s : 890-4860, 890-4853
Fax : 897-5554
null

Civil Aeronautics Board
CAB Bldg., MIA Road, PASAY CITY, METRO MANILA
Contact Number/s : 833-7259, 833-7266, 833-7248
Fax : 833-6911

Clark Development Corporation
Clark Special Economic Zone Bldg., 2127 Dorst Ave., cor. Weston Clark Field, PAMPANGA
Contact Number/s : (63-45) 599-2042, 599-2092
Fax : (045) 599-2507

Cooperative Development Authority
5/F BENLOR Bldg., 1184 Quezon Ave., QUEZON CITY, METRO MANILA
Contact Number/s : (63-2) 372-3801 to 24
Fax : 371-2077

Cottage Industry Technology Center
20 Russet St., SSS Village, MARIKINA, METRO MANILA
Contact Number/s : (63-2) 948-2875
Fax : 942-0107

Dangerous Drugs Board
5/F, CHAMP Bldg. Bonifacio Drive, Port Area, MANILA, METRO MANILA

Department of Agriculture
Elliptical Rd. Diliman, QUEZON CITY, METRO MANILA
Contact Number/s : (63-2) 928-8741 to 65, 920-4358
Fax : 929-8183, 928-5140

Department of Environment and Natural Resources
DENR Bldg., Visayas Ave., Diliman, QUEZON CITY, METRO MANILA
Contact Number/s : (63-2) 928-0691, 929-6633
Fax : 920-4352

Department of Finance
Department of Finance Bldg., BSP Complex, Roxas Blvd. Malate, MANILA, METRO MANILA
Contact Number/s : (63-2) 523-4955
Fax : 526-7516

Department of Foreign Affairs
2330 Roxas Blvd., PASAY CITY, METRO MANILA
Contact Number/s : (63-2) 834-4254
Fax : 834-4266

Department of Science and Technology
Gen. Santos Ave., Bicutan, TAGUIG, METRO MANILA
Contact Number/s : (63-2) 837-2071, 837-2939
Fax : 837-2937
Email : wgp@agham.dost.gov.ph

Department of Tourism
Dept. of Tourism Bldg. T.M. Kalaw St., Rizal Park, MANILA, METRO MANILA
Contact Number/s : (63-2) 524-1751, 523-8411, 524-4760, 524-5402
Fax : 521-7374
Email : dotgca@mnl.sequel.net

Department of Finance - Mabuhay Lane
Executive Tower Bldg., BSP Complex Malate, MANILA, METRO MANILA
Contact Number/s : (63-2) 526-5989
Fax : 526-0519

Deaprtment of Finance - One-Stop shop Inter-Agency Tax Credit and Duty Drawback Center
3/F Executive Tower Bldg., BSP Complex Malate, MANILA, METRO MANILA
Contact Number/s : (63-2) 526-2281
Fax : 526-1515

Department of National Defense
Camp General Emilio Aguinaldo, QUEZON CITY, METRO MANILA
Contact Number/s : (63-2) 911-6227, 911-6244
Fax : 911-6227

Energy Regulatory Board
Pacific Center Bldg., San Miguel Ave., Ortigas Ave., PASIG, METRO MANILA
Contact Number/s : 631-5879
Fax : 631-5879

Export Develoment Council
6/F New Solid Bldg., 357 Sen. Gil J. Puyat Ave., MAKATI, METRO MANILA
Contact Number/s : 890-4645, 890-4809
Fax : 890-4645
Email : edc@dti.gov.ph

Fertilizer and Pesticide Authority
4/F Bldg. B, NIA Complex, EDSA, QUEZON CITY, METRO MANILA
Contact Number/s : 922-3364, 922-3668
Fax : 922-3355
Email : pmdpspa@skyinet.net

Fiber Industry Development Authority
Asiatrust Annex Bldg. 1424 Quezon Ave., QUEZON CITY, METRO MANILA
Contact Number/s : 373-9236
Fax : 373-9238

Food Development Center
FTI Complex, TAGUIG, METRO MANILA
Contact Number/s : 838-4014 to 16, 838-4478, 838-4601
Fax : 838-4016, 838-4692
Email : fdcadmin@mnl.sequel.net

Garments and Textile Export Board

New Solid Bldg. 357 Sen. Gil J. Puyat,
MAKATI, METRO MANILA
Contact Number/s : 890-4651, 890-4647
Fax : 890-4653

□ **Industrial Technology and Development Institute**
Dept. of Science and Technology, DOST Compound, Gen. Santos Ave., Bicutan, TAGUIG, METRO MANILA
Contact Number/s : 837-3171, 837-6157
Fax : 837-3167

□ **Intellectual Property Office**
IPO Bldg. 351 Sen. Gil J. Puyat Ave., MAKATI, METRO MANILA
Contact Number/s : 890-4862
Fax : 890-4936
Email : ipo@dti.gov.ph

□ **International Coffee Organization Certifying Agency**
5/F New Solid Bldg. 357 Sen. Gil J. Puyat Ave., MAKATI, METRO MANILA
Contact Number/s : 890-4663, 890-4672
Fax : 759-6955
Email : icoca@dti.gov.ph

□ **Maritime Industry Authority**
PPL Bldg. 1000 United Nations Ave., Ermita, MANILA, METRO MANILA
Contact Number/s : 521-0107, 523-8651 to 60
Fax : 524-2746

□ **Metals Industry Research and Development Center**
MIRDC Compound Gen. Santos Ave., Bicutan, TAGUIG, METRO MANILA
Contact Number/s : 837-0431 to 38, 837-0613
Fax : 838-7878, 837-0430
Email : rtv@sun1.dost.gov.ph

□ **Movie and Television Review and Classification Board**
Francisco Bldg. 1373 E. Rodriguez Ave., QUEZON CITY, METRO MANILA
Contact Number/s : 721-4952, 721-3106, 721-3103
Fax : 725-9151

□ **National Bureau of Investigation**
Taft Avenue, MANILA, METRO MANILA
Contact Number/s : 525-3673
Fax : 536-3535

□ **National Economic and Development Authority**
NEDA sa Pasig, Amber Ave., PASIG, METRO MANILA
Contact Number/s : 634-3734
Fax : 631-3734
Email : tius-td@mail.neda.gov.ph

□ **National Food Authority**
Matimyas Bldg. E. Rodriguez Ave., QUEZON CITY, METRO MANILA
Contact Number/s : 712-1719, 721-1705
Fax : 712-1110

□ **National Meat Inspection Commission**
Dept. of Agriculture, Visayas Ave., Diliman, QUEZON CITY, METRO MANILA
Contact Number/s : 924-3119, 924-7971, 924-3118
Fax : 924-7980

□ **National Museum**
Executive House, P. Burgos St., MANILA, METRO MANILA
Contact Number/s : 527-1215, 527-1242
Fax : 527-0306

□ **National Statistics Office**
Solicarel Bldg. I, Ramon Magsaysay Blvd., Sta. Mesa, MANILA, METRO MANILA
Contact Number/s : 713-7074, 716-0734, 716-0807
Fax : 713-7073, 715-6503

□ **National Subcontractors' Exchange (Subconex)**
2/F Trade and Industry Bldg., 361 Sen. Gil J. Puyat Ave., MAKATI, METRO MANILA
Contact Number/s : 890-4901, 892-9965, 890-4855, 813-0563, 892-7709

Fax : 890-4858, 892-9961
Email : bdtp@dti.gov.ph

National Telecommunications Commission
NTC Bldg., BIR Rd., East Triangle, Diliman, QUEZON CITY, METRO MANILA
Contact Number/s : 924-4024
Fax : 924-3787

National Tobacco Administration
NTA Bldg. Panay Ave., cor Scout Reyes St., QUEZON CITY, METRO MANILA
Contact Number/s : 374-2505, 374-3987
Fax : 374-2505

Office of Legal Affairs
Dept. of Trade and Industry 4/F, Trade and Industry Bldg., 361 Sen Gil J. Puyat Ave., MAKATI, METRO MANILA
Contact Number/s : 897-7614
Fax : 890-4908

Office of the President of the Philippines
Malaca?ang, MANILA, METRO MANILA
Contact Number/s : 735-6201
Fax : 736-1064

Philippine Coconut Authority
Elliptical Rd. Diliman, QUEZON CITY, METRO MANILA
Contact Number/s : 928-7011, 928-8741
Fax : 921-6173
Email : nmbpmdp@ibahn.net

Philippine Economic Zone Authority
Roxas Blvd. cor San Luis St., PASAY CITY, METRO MANILA
Contact Number/s : 551-3455, 551-3454
Fax : 891-6380
Email : peza@webquest.com

Philippine Institute for Development Studies
NEDA sa Makati Bldg., 106 Amorsolo St. Legaspi Village, MAKATI, METRO MANILA
Contact Number/s : 893-9592
Fax : 893-9591

Philippine International Trading Corporation
Philippines International Center, 46 Sen. Gil J. Puyat Ave., MAKATI, METRO MANILA
Contact Number/s : 845-4376, 845-4466
Fax : 845-4476
Email : pitc@mnl.sequel.net

Philippine Ports Authority
22 Maulle de San Francisco St., Marsman Bldg., South Harbor, Port Area, MANILA, METRO MANILA
Contact Number/s : 523-4633
Fax : 527-4853
Email : jopena@ppa.gov.ph

Philippine Shippers' Bureau
5/F DTI Bldg., 361 Sen. Gil J. Puyat Ave., MAKATI, METRO MANILA
Contact Number/s : 890-5133
Fax : 890-4901 local 358
Email : psb@dti.gov.ph

Philippine Textile Research Institute
Dept. of Science and Technology, Gen. Santos Ave., Bicutan, TAGUIG, METRO MANILA
Contact Number/s : 837-1325, 837-1157
Fax : 837-1325

Philippine Trade Training Center
PTTC Bldg., Sen. Gil J. Puyat Ave., cor Roxas Blvd., PASAY CITY, METRO MANILA
Contact Number/s : 834-1341, 834-1444 to 49
Fax : 834-1343
Email : pttc@dti.gov.ph

Product Development and Design Center of the Philippines
CCP Complex, Roxas Blvd., MANILA, METRO MANILA
Contact Number/s : 832-1112, 832-3646
Fax : 832-3649
Email : pddcp@mozcom.com

□ **Protected Areas and Wildlife Bureau**
Ninoy Aquino Parks and Wildlife Nature Center Quezon Ave., Diliman, QUEZON CITY, METRO MANILA
Contact Number/s : 924-6031, 928-6397
Fax : 924-0109
Email : pawb-plan@psdn.org.ph

□ **Quarantine Office National**
25th and Chicago St., Port Area, MANILA, METRO MANILA
Contact Number/s : 527-4678, 527-4655
Fax : 527-4678

□ **Radiation Health Service**
San Lazaro Compound, Rizal Ave., MANILA, METRO MANILA
Contact Number/s : 838-3415
Fax : 711-6016

□ **Subic Bay Metropolitan Authority**
Bldg. 229, Waterfront Rd., Subic Bay Freeport Zone 222, PAMPANGA
Contact Number/s : (047) 252-4381, 252-4382, 252-4999
Fax : (047) 252-3014
Email : payumo/SBMA@SBMA.com

□ **Sugar Regulatory Commission**
Philippine Sugar Center Bldg., North Ave., Diliman, QUEZON CITY, METRO MANILA
Contact Number/s : 920-4367, 926-1933
Fax : 920-4325

□ **Tariff Commission**
5/F PHC East Ave., Diliman, QUEZON CITY, METRO MANILA
Contact Number/s : 921-7960, 926-2805
Fax : 921-7960
Email : tarcm@mail.neda.gov.ph

□ **Technology and Livelihood Resource Center**
709 City State Center, Shaw Blvd., PASIG, METRO MANILA
Contact Number/s : 637-4108
Fax : 633-5860

□ **Trade and Industry Information Center**
4/F Industry and Investments Bldg., 385 Sen. Gil J. Puyat Ave., MAKATI, METRO MANILA
Contact Number/s : 895-3611
Fax : 895-6487
Email : tiic@boi.gov.ph

□ **The Guarantee Fund for Small and Medium Enterprises**
7/F One Corporate Plaza, 845 Arnaiz Ave., MAKATI, METRO MANILA
Contact Number/s : 816-1294
Fax : 816-1293
Email : ag@mislinux.dost.gov.ph

□ **Trade and Investment Development Corporation of the Philippines**
5/F Executive Bldg., Center, Sen. Gil J. Puyat Ave., cor. Makati Ave., MAKATI, METRO MANILA
Contact Number/s : 896-4515, 897-5108, 896-4515
Fax : 895-4454

□ **U.P. Institute for Small-Scale Industries**
Enrique Virata Hall, U.P. Campus Diliman, QUEZON CITY, METRO MANILA
Contact Number/s : 927-9238, 920-6923
Fax : 927-1034
Email : do@upissi.ph.net

□ **Videogram Regulatory Board**
2nd and 3rd Floors, CSP Bldg., 815 Quezon Ave., QUEZON CITY, METRO MANILA
Contact Number/s : 374-1391
Fax : 373-0540

EXPORT MARKETING AND PROMOTION

□ **Bureau of Export Trade Promotion**
5th-8th Floors, New Solid Bldg., 357 Sen. Gil J. Puyat Ave,, MAKATI, METRO MANILA
Contact Number/s : 896-3658, 890-4683, 899-0133
Fax : 890-4716, 890-4707

□ **Center for International Trade Expositions and Missions**
International Trade Center Complex, Roxas Blvd., cor. Sen. Gil J. Puyat Ave., PASAY CITY, METRO MANILA
Contact Number/s : 832-3956, 831-2382, 831-2201
Fax : 832-3965, 834-0177
Email : citem@info.com.ph

□ **Garments and Textile Export Board**
New Solid Bldg., 357 Sen. Gil J. Puyat Ave., MAKATI, METRO MANILA
Contact Number/s : 890-4651, 890-4647
Fax : 890-4653

□ **Philippine International Trading Corporation**
Philippines International Center, 46 Sen. Gil J. Puyat Ave., MAKATI, METRO MANILA
Contact Number/s : 845-4376, 845-4466
Fax : 895-4476
Email : pitc@mnl.sequel.net

TECHNICAL SERVICES AND QUALITY CONTROL

□ **Bureau of International Trade Relations**
3/F DTI Bldg., 361 Sen. Gil J. Puyat Ave., MAKATI, METRO MANILA
Contact Number/s : 890-5148, 890-4670, 897-8290, 897-8292
Fax : 890-4812
Email : bitr@dti.gov.ph

□ **Bureau of Product Standards**
3/F Trade and Industry Bldg., 361 Sen. Gil J. Puyat Ave., MAKATI, METRO MANILA
Contact Number/s : 890-4859, 890-4924
Fax : 890-5129
Email : dtibpsrp@mnl.sequel.net

□ **Center for Industrial Competitiveness**
2/F Trade and Industry Bldg., 361 Sen. Gil J. Puyat Ave., MAKATI, METRO MANILA
Contact Number/s : 890-4860, 890-4853
Fax : 897-5554
null

□ **Cottage Industry Technology Center**
20 Russet St., SSS Village 1811, MARIKINA, METRO MANILA
Contact Number/s : 948-2875
Fax : 942-0107

□ **Export Development Council**
6/F New Solid Bldg., 357 Sen. Gil J. Puyat Ave., MAKATI, METRO MANILA
Contact Number/s : 890-4645, 890-4809
Fax : 890-4645
Email : edc@dti.gov.ph

□ **Intellectual Property Office**
IPO Bldg., 351 Sen. Gil J. PUyat Ave., MAKATI, METRO MANILA
Contact Number/s : 890-4862
Fax : 890-4936
Email : ipo@dti.gov.ph

□ **Metals Industry Research and Development Center**
MIRDC Compound, Gen. Santos Ave., Bicutan, TAGUIG, METRO MANILA
Contact Number/s : 837-0431 to 38, 837-0613
Fax : 838-7878, 837-0430
Email : rtv@sun1.dost.gov.ph

□ **Office of Legal Affairs**
Dept. of Trade and Industry 4/F, Trade and Industry Bldg., 361 Sen. Gil J. Puyat Ave., MAKATI, METRO MANILA
Contact Number/s : 897-7614
Fax : 890-4908

□ **Philippine Shippers' Bureau**
5/F DTI Bldg., 361 Sen. Gil J. Puyat Ave., MAKATI, METRO MANILA
Contact Number/s : 890-5133
Fax : 890-4901 loc. 358
Email : psb@dti.gov.ph

□ **Philippine Textile Research Institute**
Dept. of Science and Technology, Gen. Santos Ave., Bicutan, TAGUIG, METRO MANILA

Contact Number/s : 837-1325, 837-1157
Fax : 837-1325

□ **Philippine Trade Training Center**
PTTC Bldg., Sen. Gil J. Puyat Ave. cor. Roxas Blvd., PASAY CITY, METRO MANILA
Contact Number/s : 834-1344, 834-1341
Fax : 834-1343
Email : pttc@dti.gov.ph

PRODUCT DESIGN AND DEVELOPMENT

□ **Intellectual Property Office**
IPO Bldg., 351 Sen. Gil J. Puyat Ave., MAKATI, METRO MANILA
Contact Number/s : 890-4862
Fax : 890-4936
Email : ipo@dti.gov.ph

□ **Product Development and Design Center of the Philippines**
CCP Complex, Roxas Blvd., MANILA, METRO MANILA
Contact Number/s : 832-1112, 832-3646
Fax : 832-3649
Email : pddcp@mozcom.com

EXPORT FINANCING AND INCENTIVES

□ **Bangko Sentral ng Pilipinas-Department of Loans and Credit**
A. Mabini Street, Ermita, MANILA, METRO MANILA
Fax : (63-2)536-6061; 523-7848
Email : 536-6061

□ **Board of Investments**
Industry and Investments Bldg., 385 Sen. Gil J. Puyat Avenue, MAKATI, METRO MANILA
Contact Number/s : (63-2)895-3638;895-3518
Fax : 895-3512

□ **Philippine Economic Zone Authority**
Roxas Blvd., cor. San Luis Street,, PASAY CITY, METRO MANILA
Contact Number/s : 551-3455;551-3454
Fax : 891-6380
Email : peza@webquest.com

□ **Philippine International Trading Corp.**
Philippines International Centre, 46 Sen. Gil Puyat Avenue,, MAKATI, METRO MANILA
Contact Number/s : 845-4376;845-4466
Fax : 845-4476
Email : pitc@mnl.sequel.net

□ **Technology & Livelihood Resource Center**
#709 City State Centre, Shaw Boulevard,, PASIG, METRO MANILA
Contact Number/s : 637-4108
Fax : 633-5860

□ **The Guarantee Fund For Small and Medium Enterprises**
7/F One Corporate Plaza, 845 Arnaiz Avenue,, MAKATI, METRO MANILA
Contact Number/s : 816-1294
Fax : 816-1293
Email : ag@mislinux.dost.gov.ph

□ **Trade and Investment Develoment Corporation of the Philippines (TIDC)**
5/F Executive Bldg. Center, Sen Gil J. Puyat Ave., cor Makati Ave.,, MAKATI, METRO MANILA
Contact Number/s : 896-4515;897-5108;896-4515
Fax : 895-4454

EXPORT-ASSISTANCE CENTER

DEPARTMENT OF TRADE AND INDUSTRY
385 Industry and Investments Bldg., Sen. Gil Puyat Ave., Makati City, Philippines 1200
Telephone: (63-2) 895-3611 Fax: (63-2) 895-6487 Email: web@dti.dti.gov.ph

The Department of Trade and Industry aims to serve the needs of both business and consumers. Specifically, its services are aimed at creating a business-friendly environment that promotes and facilitates the growth of investments, trade and industry in the country. At the same time, by promoting competition and enforcing fair trade laws, DTI protects the welfare of consumers and enables them to get value for their money.

Consumer Protection

- Consumer Center/Consumer Welfare Desks
- i-Reklamo
- Consumer Education
- Price Monitoring/Guide
- Formation of Consumer Groups
- Product Standards
- Import Commodity Clearance (ICC)

Investment Facilitation

- Locator Services (Economic Zone Authority)
- One-Stop Action Center (0SAC)
- Investment Marketing
- Build-Operate-Transfer

Elmer H. San Pascual
Department Manager
Promotions and Press Relations Group
Philippine Economic Zone Authority
PEZA Building, Roxas Blvd. cor. San Luis St., Pasay City
Tel. no. (632) 891-6381
Fax: (632) 890-9307
Email: peza@i-next.net

Trade Promotion

- Export Procedure
- Trade Information
- Export Assistance
- Local fairs and missions
- The National Trade Fair
- International Fairs and Missions
- Export Facilitation
- Shipping
- Import Procedures
- Trade Dispute Resolution

Export Policy Development and Advocacy

- Trade Policies and Procedures Simplification
- Agricultural Policies
- Material Supply Chain
- Quality and Productivity

Local Government Units
Legislative Advocacy and Monitoring
Financing

Training

Construction Management Skills
Industrial Skills
Training for Exports
SME Training
Facilities
Labor Management Relations

SME Development

Financing / Guarantee Programs
HRD
Marketing
Product Design and Packaging Assistance

DTI's helps clients through its assistance centers:

i-Reklamo

Consumers can now lodge their complaints online through i-Reklamo. The facility's complaints verification enables consumers to know the status of their complaints.

One-Stop Action Center

The Board of Investment's (BOI) frontline unit, the One-Stop Action Center (OSAC) assists investors do business in the Philippines under one roof. It houses representatives from different government agencies who answer investors' inquiries and the process of investors' business registration.

These representatives come from the Bureau of Immigration (BI), Bangko Sentral ng Pilipinas (BSP) or the Central Bank of the Philippines, Department of Labor and Employment (DOLE), Securities and Exchange Commission (SEC), and the Philippine Industrial Estate Association (PHILEA).

OSAC offers the following service:

Conducts business counseling
Monitors the status of investors' registration applications
Informs investors of the action taken on their application within the shortest possible time

Business counseling covers the following:

Licenses to multinational companies operating Regional Headquarters in the Philippines
Alien Employment Permits
Endorsement of conversion of tourist visas to special non-immigrant visas, working visas and Special Investment Resident Visa (SIRV)

Employment of foreign nationals in BOI-registered firms
Travel tax exemptions for personnel of BOI-registered regional headquarters of multinational companies
Tax and duty-free importation of household goods, personal effects, training and conference materials
Seminars, consultations and counseling on investment-related subjects

BOI-OSAC Contact Details:
Dennis R. Miralles
Director
One-Stop-Action Center
Board of Investments
Industry & Investments Building
385 Sen. Gil Puyat Ave., Makati City
Tel. No.: (0632) 899-3586
Fax No.: (0632) 895-8322
E-mail: DRMiralles@boi.gov.ph

Export Assistance Network
The Bureau of Export and Trade Promotion's (BETP) Export Assistance Network (EXPONET) helps exporters and prospective exporters access information and resolve specific problems related to exporting.

Its network consists of over 128 agencies within and outside DTI, including the Bureau of Customs (BoC), Bangko Sentral ng Pilipinas (BSP) or the Central Bank of the Philippines, and other export-related agencies including those represented at the One-Stop Export Documentation Center. Advisers are stationed in all DTI regional and provincial offices.

EXPONET provides information on:

Export seminar schedules
Export organizing
Export procedures and documentation
Import facilities for exporters
Buyer linkages
Export financing and incentives
Product raw material sourcing
Statistical information

The agency also assists exporters in export-related problems / trade complaints.

Contact Details:

Sonia L. Rodriguez
Division Chief
Export Trade Facilitation Division
Bureau of Export Trade Promotion
5F New Solid Building
357 Sen. Gil J. Puyat Ave.
Makati City
Directline: (632) 890-46-40
Fax: (632) 890-47-07

Email: betpetfd@dti.gov.ph

IT Help Desk

The IT Help Desk assists the public and responds to queries on:

- Doing business in the Philippines especially IT investment opportunities
- E-Commerce Act of the Philippines
- Provides facility for
    - Library research
    - IT discussion
    - Showcase for IT products

Contact Details:

Dita Maralit
Director
IT Help Desk, Office of Special Concerns
5F Trade and Industry Building
361 Sen. Gil J. Puyat Ave., Makati City
Tel. No.: 890-51-23/897-17-13
Fax No.: 890-48-16
Email: DitaMaralit@dti.gov.ph, Osc@dti.gov.ph

INVESTMENT MARKETING

Ms. Florina A. Vistal
Executive Director
Board of Investments
Industry & Investments Building
385 Sen. Gil Puyat Ave., Makati City
Phone Number: (0632)896-9212
Fax Number : (0632) 897-2181
E-mail : FAVistal@boi.gov.ph

Investment Marketing Department
Ms. Celestina B. Ilagan
Director
Board of Investments
Industry & Investments Building
385 Sen. Gil Puyat Ave., Makati City
Phone Number : (0632) 896-9212
Fax Number : (0632) 895-3521
E-mail : CBIlagan@boi.gov.ph

Asia Division
Ms. Araceli Y. Clor
Chief
Board of Investments
Industry & Investments Building
385 Sen. Gil Puyat Ave., Makati City

Phone Number : (0632) 895-3991
Telefax Number : (0632) 895-3991
E-mail : AYClor@boi.gov.ph

Americas Division
Lolit B. Reyes
Officer-in-Charge
Board of Investments
Industry & Investments Building
385 Sen. Gil Puyat Ave., Makati City
Phone Number : (0632) 899-6206
Fax Number : (0632) 895-3521
E-mail : MDBReyes@boi.gov.ph

Europe Division
Ms. Ellorence D. Cruz
Senior Investments Specialist
Board of Investments
Industry & Investments Building
385 Sen. Gil Puyat Ave., Makati City
Phone Number : (0632) 8958372/8973082/896-9201
Fax Number : (0632) 895-3521
E-mail : EDCruz@boi.gov.ph

INVESTMENT CENTER

It is advisable to seek the assistance and prior briefing from the Board of Investments' ONE-STOP-ACTION CENTER, the Bureau of Trade Regulation and Consumer Protection (BTRCP), the Philippine Economic Zone Authority (PEZA) and the Securities and Exchange Commission (SEC).

Following are the contact details of the above agencies:

One-Stop-Action Center 5/F Industry and Investments Bldg., 385 Sen. Gil J. Puyat Ave., Makati City MM PHILIPPINES Tel: (63 2) 895-8322; 895-3656; 895-3657; 896-7342 Fax: (63 2) 895-3521 DENNIS R. MIRALES, Officer-in-Charge, Investments Assistance (Tel: 896-7884; Fax: 895-8322; Email: boisac@mnl.sequel.net) ADELINA E. BATALLONES, Chief, One-Stop-Action Center (Tel: 896-7342, local 205)

Philippine Economic Zone Authority Roxas Blvd., cor. San Luis St., Pasay City MM PHILIPPINES Tel: (63 2) 551-3454 to 55; 551-3432; 551-3438 Fax: (63 2) 891-6380; 891-6382 www.peza.gov.ph Director General: LILIA B. DE LIMA (dg@peza.gov.ph)

Bureau of Trade Regulations and Consumer Protection 2/F Trade and Industry Bldg., 361 Sen. Gil J. Puyat Ave., Makati City MM PHILIPPINES Tel: (63 2) 890-5124; 890-4949; 890-4901 locals 448, 441 Fax: (63 2) 890-4872 Email: btrcp@dti.gov.ph Director: Atty. Ma. Teresa S. Arao-Mahiwo (Tel: 890-4932; 890-5124)

Securities and Exchange Commission SEC Bldg., EDSA near Ortigas Ave., Greenhills, Mandaluyong City 1550 MM PHILIPPINES Tel: (63 2) 726-0931 to 39 Fax: (63 2) 726-8459 Email: sec1997@webquest.com www.sec.gov.ph Chairperson: Atty. LILIA R. BAUTISTA

Board of Investments 5/F Industry and Investments Bldg., 385 Sen. Gil J. Puyat Ave., Makati City, Metro Manila (MM) PHILIPPINES Tel: (63 2) 890-9332; 895-3638; 895-3640 Fax: (63 2) 895-3512 Email: useciig@dti.gov.ph Governor: THOMAS G. AQUINO (Tel: 895-3518; 895-3993; Fax: 899-9232; Email: boigov1@mnl.sequel.net Governor: JOSE ANTONIO LEVISTE (Tel: 897-2830; Fax: 895-4024; Email: boigov2@mnl.sequel.net Governor: OFELIA V. BULAONG (Tel: 896-5167; Fax: 895-3981; Email: boigov3@mnl.sequel.net

U.S. AND PHILIPPINE CONTACTS

U.S. EMBASSY CONTACTS:

U.S. Embassy Manila
Thomas Hubbard, Ambassador
Eugene Martin, Deputy Chief of Mission
1201 Roxas Blvd., Manila
Phone : (632) 523-1001 ext. 2276
Fax : (632) 522-4361
E-mail: thomas.c.hubbard@dos.us-state.gov
eugene.martin@dos.us-state.gov

U.S. & Foreign Commercial Service (US & FCS)
Carmine D'Aloisio, Counselor for Commercial Affairs
Robert Bannerman, Commercial Attache
2nd Floor, 395 Sen. Gil Puyat Ave., Makati City
Phone : (632) 890-9717; 895-3002; 890-9362
Fax : (632) 895-3028
E-mail: cdaloisio@cs.doc.gov
Omanila@cs.doc.gov

Foreign Agricultural Service (FAS)
Charles Alexander, Agricultural Counselor
Kevin Sage-el, Agricultural Attache
4th Floor, 395 Sen. Gil Puyat Ave., Makati City
Phone : (632) 523-1001 ext. 2270; 895-9536; 895-4708
Fax : (632) 890-2728
E-mail: agmanila@fas.usda.gov

Joint U.S. Military Assistant Group to the Republic of the Phils. (JUSMAG)
Col. Roy Adams, Jr., Chief
1201 Roxas Boulevard, Manila
Phone : (632) 523-1319
Fax : (632) 522-4356; 523-1296
E-mail: jusmag@qinet.net

U.S. Agency for International Development (USAID)
Patricia K. Buckles, Director
Ramon Magsaysay Center, 1680 Roxas Blvd., Manila
Phone : (632) 522-4411
Fax : (632) 521-5241
E-mail: pbuckles@usaid.gov

U.S. - Asian Environmental Partnership (US-AEP)

Office of Technology Cooperation
Alma Bella P. Madrazo, Ph.D., Director
c/o U.S. & Foreign Commercial Service
2nd Floor, 395 Sen. Gil Puyat Ave., Makati City
Phone : (632) 896-5128; 896-2877
Fax : (632) 890-9361
E-mail: amadrazo@cs.doc.gov

Asian Development Bank - FCS Liaison (FCS-ADB)
Denny Barnes, Senior Commercial Officer
3rd Floor, 395 Sen. Gil Puyat Ave., Makati City
Phone : (632) 523-1001 ext. 2019; 890-9364; 895-3020
Fax : (632) 890-9713
E-mail: dbarnes@cs.doc.gov

U.S. Trade and Development Agency (TDA)
John Herrman, Deputy Regional Director
Asia Office:
c/o U.S. & Foreign Commercial Service
395 Sen. Gil Puyat Ave., Makati City
Phone : (632) 895-1152
Fax : (632) 890-8960
E-mail: jherrman@cs.doc.gov
U.S. Headquarters:
1621 N. Kent, Room 309
Rosslyn, VA 22209
Phone : (703) 875-4357
Fax : (703) 875-4009

Defense Attache Office (DAO)
Col. Robert Worthington, Defense Attache
1201 Roxas Blvd., Manila
Phone : (632) 523-1001
Fax : (632) 522-1774
E-mail: usdaomanila@netasia.net

Economic Section
Terry Breese, Economic Counselor
1201 Roxas Blvd., Manila
Phone : (632) 523-1001 ext. 2280/2003
Fax : (632) 522-3569
E-mail: breeseta@manilwpoa.us-state.gov

AMCHAM AND BUSINESS COUNCILS:

The American Chamber of Commerce of the Phils., Inc. (AMCHAM)
Carlos Contreras, President
Robert Sears, Executive Director
2nd Floor, Corinthian Plaza, Paseo de Roxas, Makati City
Phone : (632) 811-3192
Fax : (632) 811-3081; 811-3184; 811-3241
E-mail: amchamrp@mozcom.com

RP-U.S. Business Council
Ramon del Rosario, Sr., Chairman
7th Floor, Phinma Bldg., 166 Salcedo St.
Legaspi Village, Makati City
Phone : (632) 818-8205; 810-9526
Fax : (632) 817-9807
E-mail: phinma@bworldonline.com.ph

U.S.-Asean Council for Business & Technology, Inc.
Philip Gielczyk, Executive Director
4th Floor, 395 Sen. Gil Puyat Ave., Makati City
Phone : (632) 895-4333; 895-3008
Fax : (632) 895-3007
E-mail: usbc@mozcom.com

TRADE AND INDUSTRY ASSOCIATIONS:

Association of Firearms and Ammunition Dealers of the Philippines
(AFAD)
Nereo Dionisio, President
c/o P.B. Dionisio
27 A. Roces Ave., Quezon City
Phone : (632) 373-3088
Fax : (632) 414-9951

Chamber of Real Estate & Builders Associations, Inc. (CREBA)
Charlie Gorayeb, President
3rd Floor, CREBA Center
Don Alejandro Roces Ave. corner South "A" St., Quezon City
Phone : (632) 373-2265 to 70
Fax : (632) 373-2271 and 74

Computer Distributors and Dealers Association of the Philippines
(COMDDAP)
Jimmy D. Go, Director and President
7th Floor, SEDCCO I Bldg., Rada corner Legaspi St.
Legaspi Village, Makati City
Phone : (632) 810-3814; 892-7947
Fax : (632) 815-6531

Confederation of Filipino Consulting Organizations, Inc.
(COFILCO)
Angel Lazaro, Jr., President
160 Panay Avenue cor. Edsa
Phone : (632) 734-6902
Fax : (632) 735-3170

Council of Engineering Consultants of the Philippines (CECOPHIL)
Isaac S. David, President
2nd Floor, PNCC Bldg.
Edsa cor. Reliance St. Mandaluyong City
Phone : (632) 638-8618
Fax : (632) 638-8618
E-mail: fildravo@tri-isys.com

Hospital, Medical, Laboratory Equipment & Supply Importers
Association of the Philippines, Inc. (HOMLESIAP)
Enrique Lim, President
c/o 3-I Philippines, 704 Aurora Blvd., Quezon City
Phone : (632) 721-5211; 721-8352
Fax : (632) 721-7012

Hotel and Restaurant Association of the Philippines (HRAP)
Lorenzo J. Cruz, President
Rm. 205, Regina Bldg., Aguirre St.
Legaspi Village, Makati City
Phone : (632) 815-4659 or 61
Fax : (632) 815-4663
E-mail: hrap@mnl.sequel.net

Integrated Telecommunications Suppliers Association of the
Philippines (ITESAP)
Rodrigo Jose B. Pau, President
7th Floor Rm 711 Sen. Gil Puyat cor. Tindalo St. Makati City
Phone : (632) 759-3869 or 813-6398
Fax : (632) 813-6397
E-mail: msdcno@mnl.sequel.net

Institute of Integrated Electrical Engineers of the Philippines,
Inc. (IIEEP)
Amador Callado, President
IEEE National Headquarters, IIEE Bldg.
41 Monte de Piedad St., Cubao, Quezon City
Phone : (632) 721-6442
Fax : (632) 721-6442; 412-5772
E-mail: iiee@pworld.net.ph

Kapisanan ng mga Brodkaster sa Pilipinas (KBP)
(Association of Broadcasters of the Philippines)
Butch S. Canoy, President
6th Floor, LTA Bldg., #118 Perea St.
Legaspi Village, Makati City
Phone : (632) 892-4129; 815-1990 to 93
Fax : (632) 815-1989; 815-1993
E-mail: kbp@pacific.net.ph

National Confederation of Constructors Association of the Philippines (NCCAP)
Wilfredo Castro, President
Rm. 210, Eagle Court Condominium
26 Matalino St., Diliman, Quezon City
Phone : (632) 922-9094; 920-9449
Fax : (632) 928-3187

Philippine Chamber of Commerce and Industry (PCCI)
Alberto P. Fenix, Jr., President
Ground Floor, East Wing, Secretariat Bldg.
PICC, CCP Complex, Roxas Blvd., Pasay City
Phone : (632) 833-8591; 833-8592
Fax : (632) 833-8895
E-mail: pcciintr@mozcom.com

Philippine Chamber of Food Manufacturers, Inc. (PCFMI)
Vicente H. Lim, President
Rm. 1216, Cityland 10, Tower II
6817 Ayala Ave. corner H.V. dela Costa St.
Salcedo Village, Makati City
Phone : (632) 894-0388; 892-4163
Fax : (632) 893-3893

Philippine Constructors Association (PCA)
Jaime H. Pajara, President
3rd Floor, Padilla Bldg., Emerald Ave.
Ortigas Complex, Pasig City
Phone : (632) 631-3135; 631-2778
Fax : (632) 631-2788
E-mail: philcon@skynet.net

Philippine Electronics and Telecommunications Federation (PETEF)
Ma. Corazon M. Acol, President
7th Floor, Unit 11, PS Bank Tower
Tindalo corner Sen. Gil J. Puyat Ave., Makati City
Phone : (632) 813-6398; 759-3869
Fax : (632) 813-6397
E-mail: petef@mailstation.net

Philippine Food Processors & Exporters Confederation (PHILFOODEX)
Jesus Tanchanco, Sr., President
Rm. 304, JS Contractor Bldg.
423 Magallanes St., Intramuros, Manila
Phone : (632) 527-5811
Fax : (632) 527-5811

Philippine Franchise Association (PFA)
Vicente Paterno, Chairman
2nd Floor, Collins Bldg., 167 EDSA, Mandaluyong City
Phone : (632) 532-5677; 531-3894
Fax : (632) 532-5644
E-mail: pra@snap.portalinc.com

Philippine Hospital Association (PHA)
Dr. Rico M. Medina, President
14 Kamias Road, Quezon City
Phone : (632) 922-7675; 922-7674
Fax : (632) 921-2219

Philippine Hotel Owners Association (PHOA)
Bryan Cockrell, President
12th Floor, BA Lepanto Bldg.
Paseo de Roxas St., Makati City
Phone : (632) 818-5160; 818-9377
Fax : (632) 818-4143

Philippine Independent Power Producers Association (PIPPA)
Jose Alejandro, President
c/o Ganda Energy and Holdings
6th Floor, Westmont Bldg.
411 Quintin Paredes St., Binondo, Manila
Phone : (632) 243-0685; 243-1132
Fax : (632) 243-0644

Philippine Industrial Estates Association (PHILEA)
Vigor D. Mendoza II, Executive Director
Suite 52, Legaspi Suites
178 Salcedo Village, Makati City
Phone : (632) 894-5736; 894-5737; 892-0290
Fax : (632) 813-6709

Philippine Institute of Architects (PIA)
Francisco G. Flameno, Jr., President
#65 East Capitol Drive
Barrio Kapitolyo, Pasig City
Phone : (632) 631-9715; 634-2512
Fax : (632) 631-9715

Philippine Medical Association (PMA)
Modesto Llamas, President
PMA Bldg., North Ave., Quezon City
Phone : (632) 928-2132; 929-3514
Fax : (632) 929-4974

Philippine Retailers Association (PRA)
Manuel M. Siggaoat, Chairman
2nd Floor, Collins Bldg., 167 EDSA, Mandaluyong City
Phone : (632) 532-5677; 531-3894
Fax : (632) 532-5644
E-mail: pra@snap.portalinc.com

Renewable Energy Association of the Philippines (REAP)
Olegario Serafica, President
#11 Liamzon St., Midtown, Marikina, Metro Manila
Phone : (632) 645-8167
Fax : (632) 645-8167
E-mail: renergy@compass.com.ph

Society of Philippine Electrical Contractors & Suppliers, Inc.
(SPECSI)
Engr. Edward L. Mendoza, President
2nd Floor, IIEE Bldg., 41 Monte de Piedad St.
Cubao, Quezon City
Phone : (632) 722-4725; 413-9177; 413-0787
Fax : (632) 722-4725

United Architects of the Philippines (UAP)
Emmanuel P. Cuntapay, National President
Folk Arts Theater, CCP Complex
Roxas Blvd., Pasay City
Phone : (632) 551-4329; 5514350 to 51; 551-4233
Fax : (632) 832-7850
E-mail: uniarki@compass.com.ph

Water Environment Association of the Philippines (WEAP)
Porthos Almajose, President
#67 E-F Bansalangin cor. Saleng St.
Veterans Village Proj. 7 Quezon City
Phone : (632) 410-1119; 413-3739
Fax : (632) 374-0250
E-mail: mendoza@qinet.net

GOVERNMENT AGENCIES:

Air Transportation Office (ATO)
Carlos F. Ta¤ega, Assistant Secretary
MIA Road, Pasay City
Phone : (632) 832-3308; 833-0125; 831-8078
Fax : (632) 833-0125

Armed Forces of the Philippines (AFP)
Roberto Sabularse, Deputy Chief of Staff for Logistics (J4)
Gen. Headquarters, AFP, Camp Crame, Quezon City
Phone : (632) 911-6365
Fax : (632) 911-7924
E-mail: oj4_jhq@epic.net

Bangko Sentral ng Pilipinas (BSP)
(Central Bank of the Philippines)
Gabriel C. Singson, Governor
A. Mabini St., Malate, Manila
Phone : (632) 524-7011
Fax : (632) 522-3987

Bureau of Customs (BOC)
Pedro Mendoza, Commissioner
South Harbor, Port Area, Manila
Phone : (632) 527-1982; 527-4570; 527-4511
Fax : (632) 527-1953

Bureau of Food and Drugs (BFAD)
Quintin Kintanar, Director
Filinvest Corporate City Compound
Alabang, Muntinlupa, Metro Manila
Phone : (632) 807-0721
Fax : (632) 807-0751
E-mail: bfadmis@itdgate.stii.dost.com.ph

Bureau of Internal Revenue (BIR)
Beethoven L. Rualo, Commissioner
BIR Bldg., East Triangle, Diliman, Quezon City
Phone : (632) 926-5771; 926-3803
Fax : (632) 922-9345
E-mail: blrualo@mailstation.net

Bureau of Product Standards (BPS)
Jesus L. Motoomull, Director
Trade and Industry Bldg.
361 Sen. Gil Puyat Ave., Makati City
Phone : (632) 890-4901; 890-4965; 890-4926; 890-5130
Fax : (632) 890-4926; 890-5130
E-mail: dtibpsrp@mnl.sequel.net

Clark Development Corporation (CDC)
Head Office:
Bldg. 2127, CP Garcia corner E. Carino St.
Clark Special Economic Zone, Pampanga
Phone : (63-45) 599-2042; 599-2092
Fax : (63-45) 599-2507
Liaison Office:
15th Floor, JMT Corporate Condominium
ADB Ave. corner Do¤a Julia Vargas Ave.
Ortigas Center, Pasig City
Phone : (632) 633-8671; 634-1626
Fax : (632) 633-8672

Coordinating Council of the Philippine Assistance Program -
BOT Center (CCPAP-BOT)
Jorge Briones, Deputy Executive Director
Podium Level, Executive Tower Bldg.
BSP Complex, A. Mabini St.
Ermita, Manila
Phone : (632) 526-2237
Fax : (632) 525-7126; 521-4263
E-mail: bot@ccpap.admu.edu.ph

Construction Industry Authority of the Philippines (CIAP)
Kathryn dela Cruz, Officer in Charge
7th Floor, Peninsula Court Bldg.
8375 Makati Ave. corner Paseo de Roxas, Makati City
Phone : (632) 750-2273/2283
Fax : (632) 750-2270
E-mail: ciapinfonet@pdx.rpnet.com

Department of Energy (DOE)
Mario Tiaoqui, Secretary
Energy Center, Merritt Road
Fort Bonifacio, Taguig, Metro Manila
Phone : (632) 844-1021 to 29; 844-2850

Fax : (632) 817-8603
E-mail: mtiaoqui@DOE.gov.ph

Department of Environment and Natural Resources (DENR)
Antonio Cerilles, Secretary
DENR Bldg., V6isayas Ave., Diliman, Quezon City
Phone : (632) 928-0691-93
Fax : (632) 920-4352
E-mail: osec@denr.gov.ph; webmaster@denr.gov.ph

Department of Health (DOH)
Felipe Estrella, Secretary
San Lazaro Compound, Sta. Cruz, Manila
Phone : (632) 711-9502/03; 743-1786; 743-8301
Fax : (632) 743-1829
E-mail: osec@doh.gov.ph

Department of Interior and Local Government (DILG)
Ronaldo Puno, Undersecretary
17th Floor, Francisco A. Gold Condominium
EDSA corner Mapagmahal St., Quezon City
Phone : (632) 925-0320; 438-3170 to 71
Fax : (632) 925-0332
E-mail: punorv@dilg.gov.ph

Department of National Defense (DND)
Orlando Mercado, Secretary
3rd Floor, DND Bldg., Camp Aguinaldo, Quezon City
Phone : (632) 911-6183, 911-6193
Fax : (632) 911-6213

Department of Public Works and Highway (DPWH)
Gregorio R. Vigilar, Secretary
Bonifacio Drive, Port Area, Manila
Phone : (632) 527-4111; 527-5616
Fax : (632) 527-5635

Department of Trade and Industry (DTI)
Jose Pardo, Secretary
4th Floor, Industry and Investment Bldg.
385 Sen. Gil Puyat Ave., Makati City
Phone : (632) 895-3778; 895-3515; 897-6734
Fax : (632) 896-1166
E-mail: dtiosec@mnl.sequel.net

Department of Transportation and Communications (DOTC)
Vicente Rivera, Jr., Secretary
17th Floor, Columbia Tower
Ortigas Ave., Mandaluyong City
Phone : (632) 726-7105 to 06; 726-7125
Fax : (632) 726-7104
E-mail: dotc@webquest.com

Environmental Management Bureau (EMB)
Marlito Cardenas, Director
Topaz Bldg., 99-101 Kamias Road, Quezon City
Phone : (632) 924-7540; 929-5698
Fax : (632) 929-5698
E-mail: emb@psdn.org.ph

Housing and Urban Development Coordinating Council (HUDCC)
Karina David, Chairman
6th Floor, Atrium Bldg.
Makati Ave., Makati City
Phone : (632) 811-4168; 811-4170
Fax : (632) 811-4158

Intellectual Property Office
Emma C. Francisco, Director-General
1st Floor, 361 Trade & Industry Bldg.
Sen. Gil Puyat Ave., Makati City
Phone : (632) 890-4862; 890-4950
Fax : (632) 890-4936
E-mail: ipo@dti.gov.ph

Manila International Airport Authority (MIAA)
Antonio Gana, General Manager
4th Floor, Office of the General Manager
New Administration Bldg., MIA Road, Pasay City
Phone : (632) 833-1176
Fax : (632) 833-1180

Metropolitan Waterworks and Sewerage System (MWSS)
Reynaldo Vea, Administrator
Katipunan Road, Balara, Quezon City
Phone : (632) 922-3757; 922-2969
Fax : (632) 921-2887
E-mail: mwssrvea@info.com.ph

National Computer Center (NCC)
Cynthia A. Topacio, Acting Managing Director
NCC Bldg., C.P. Garcia Ave.
U.P. Diliman, Quezon City
Phone : (632) 920-7420; 920-7444
Fax : (632) 920-7444
E-mail: ncccat@mnl.sequel.net
ncegpa@mnl.sequel.net

National Economic and Development Authority (NEDA)
Felipe Medalla, Secretary of Socio-Economic Planning & NEDA
Director-General
NEDA sa Pasig, Amber Ave., Pasig City
Phone : (632) 631-3716
Fax : (632) 631-3747
E-mail: fmm@nedamis.neda.gov.ph

National Power Corporation (NPC)
Federico Puno, President

BIR Road corner Quezon Ave., Diliman, Quezon City
Phone : (632) 924-5420; 921-2998
Fax : (632) 922-4339
E-mail: fepuno@napocor.com.ph

National Telecommunications Commission (NTC)
Ponciano Cruz, Commissioner
NTC Bldg., BIR Road, East Triangle
Diliman, Quezon City
Phone : (632) 924-4042; 921-3251
Fax : (632) 921-7128

Philippine Coast Guard (PCG)
Manuel de Leon, Rear Admiral, Commandant
139 25th Street, Port Area, Manila
Phone : (632) 527-3868; 527-3907
Fax : (632) 527-3907

Philippine Contractors Accreditation Board (PCAB)
Froilan Castro, Executive Director
7th Floor, Peninsula Court Bldg.
8735 Makati Ave. corner Paseo de Roxas, Makati City
Phone : (632) 750-2271/72
Fax : (632) 750-2274

Philippine National Police (PNP)
Roberto Lastimosa, Chief
Camp Crame, Quezon City
Phone : (632) 723-8108; 724-8819; 722-0802
Fax : (632) 722-5443

Philippine National Railways (PNR)
Rafael Mosura, Jr. General Manager
PNR Management Compound Center
Torres Bugallon St., Caloocan City
Phone : (632) 362-2406; 362-3491; 287-3062
Fax : (632) 362-0824

Philippine Ports Authority (PPA)
Carlos L. Agustin, General Manager
22 Muelle de San Francisco St.
South Harbor, Manila
Phone : (632) 527-4844; 527-8356; 527-4856
Fax : (632) 527-4853
E-mail: cla@ppa.gov.ph

Subic Bay Metropolitan Authority (SBMA)
Bldg. 229, Waterfront Road, Subic Bay Free Port
Olongapo City, Philippines
Phone : (63-47) 222-3721; 384-6780
Fax : (63-47) 222-3573

Tariff Commission
Emmanuel T. Velasco, Chairman
5th Floor, Philippine Heart Center Bldg.
East Ave., Quezon City
Phone : (632) 921-7960; 433-5899; 923-1301 x3509
Fax : (632) 921-7960
E-mail: tarcm@nedamis.neda.gov.ph

OTHER PRIVATE SECTOR CONTACTS

Board of Investments-American Desk
Robert W. Blume, Investment Promotions Manager
385 Sen. Gil Puyat Ave., Makati City
Phone : (632) 895-8851; 895-3918
Fax : (632) 896-2315
E-mail: amdeskboi@vasia.com

SGS Far East Limited
Economic Affairs Division - Manila Liaison Office
David W. Robinson, Chief Executive Officer
20th Floor, Citibank Tower
8741 Paseo de Roxas, Makati City
Phone : (632) 848-0777
Fax : (632) 848-0755
SGS New York City Office
Phone : (212) 482-8700
Fax : (212) 363-3316

MARKET RESEARCH FIRMS

Applied Marketing Research, Inc.
Pat Barretto, Jr., President and General Manager
#8 2nd St., Barrio Kapitolyo, Pasig City
Phone : (632) 632-7668
Fax : (632) 635-2419

Asia Pacific Centre for Research
Aniceto P. Fontanilla, President
Rm. 411, Marbella I Condominium
2223 Roxas Blvd., Pasay City
Phone : (632) 831-5390
Fax : (632) 833-3831
E-mail: acreinc@tworld.net.ph

Feedback, Inc.
Fidela Z. Zaballa, President
Suite 114, Limketkai Bldg., Ortigas Ave.
Greenhills, San Juan, Metro Manila
Phone : (632) 721-4456; 721-4458; 726-9624
Fax : (632) 725-8727
E-mail: feedback@world.net.ph

Frank Small & Associates
Darrah Estrada, Managing Director
Ground Floor, Republic Glass Bldg.
196 Salcedo corner Aguirre Sts.
Legaspi Village, Makati City
Phone : (632) 818-1150
Fax : (632) 818-4587
E-mail: fsaphil@fc.emc.com.ph

FSA (Philippines), Inc.

Melchor Gadi, General Manager
3rd Floor, Philippine Social Science Center Bldg.
Commonwealth Ave., Diliman, Quezon City
Phone : (632) 929-8741
Fax : (632) 929-6846
E-mail: fsa@gaia.psdn.iphil.net

Joaquin Cunanan & Co.
Jose P. Lavares, Senior Partner
14th Floor, Multinational Bancorp Center
6805 Ayala Ave., Makati City
Phone : (632) 845-2728
Fax : (632) 845-2806
E-mail: cisaudit@mozcom.com
manila.note.pw.com

Leverage International (Consultants), Inc.
Cecilia Sanchez, Chair
Suite 84, Legaspi Suites
178 Salcedo St., Legaspi Village, Makati City
Phone : (632) 810-1389; 818-6828
Fax : (632) 810-1594
E-mail: lvrge@netasia.net

Philippine Survey and Research Center, Inc.
Carmencita Esteban, President
PSRC Bldg., Calbayog corner Kanlaon Sts.
Highway Hill, Mandaluyong City
Phone : (632) 532-4001
Fax : (632) 532-1233
E-mail: psrcri@webquest.com

Research Philippines - Unisearch, Inc.
Eduardo N. Roa, Managing Director
3rd Floor, Gloria Bldg., 109 Aguirre St.
Legaspi Village, Makati City
Phone : (632) 810-6057; 893-4105
Fax : (632) 893-4104

Smart Research Services Inc.
Waldomar E. Canales, President
Rm. 309, Vi-La Bldg., 598 EDSA
Cubao, Quezon City
Phone : (632) 911-2178
Fax : (632) 911-2178

Sycip, Gorres and Velayo
Ma. Luz V. Balmaceda, Marketing Director
6760 Ayala Ave., Makati City
Phone : (632) 891-0307; 894-8364
Fax : (632) 819-0872
E-mail: maria.l.balmaceda@arthurandersen.com

Summit Research and Consultancy, Inc.
Marcelo E. de la Cruz, President
2601 Century Citadel Building
5007 P. Burgos St., Bel-Air, Makati City
Phone : (632) 897-2665; 897-2370 loc. 2601
Fax : (632) 897-2705
E-mail: mdc205@vlink.net.ph

Trends-MBL
Mercedes R. Abad, President and General Manager
Total Research Needs-MBL, Inc.
2nd Floor, Culmat Bldg.
E. Rodriguez Ave., Quezon City
Phone: (632) 721-8510; 721-8548
Fax : (632) 721-8645

University of Asia and the Pacific
School of Economics
Dr. Roberto de Vera, Director
Pearl Drive, Ortigas Commercial Center
Pasig City
Phone: (632) 635-3146; 637-0912 to 26
Fax : (632) 631-1305
E-mail: rdevera@sec.uap.edu.ph

COMMERCIAL BANKS:

Al-Amanah Islamic Investment Bank of the Philippines
Farouk A. Carpizo, Director
2nd Floor, Unit D and E Classica Condominium
112 H.V. Dela Costa St., Salcedo Village, Makati City
Phone: (632) 816-4258
Fax : (632) 819-5249

Allied Banking Corp.
Federico C. Pascual, President
6754 Ayala Ave. corner Legaspi St., Makati City
Phone : (632) 810-2448; 816-5531
Fax : (632) 810-2362

Asianbank Corp.
Ramon F. Del Rosario, Jr., Chairman and CEO
Asianbank Center, Sen. Gil Puyat Ave.
Salcedo Village, Makati City
Phone : (632) 819-0611; 819-3151
Fax : (632) 810-7018
E-mail: francisv@mnl.sequel.net

Australia and New Zealand Banking Group Ltd.
F.W. Michael La Brooy, General Manager
Tower 1, Ayala Triangle, Ayala Ave.
corner Paseo de Roxas, Makati City
Phone : (632) 848-5091
Fax : (632) 848-5086

Banco de Oro Commercial Bank
Jesus A. Jacinto, Jr., Vice Chairman
#12 ADB Ave., Benguet Center
Ortigas Complex, Mandaluyong City
Phone : (632) 631-7812; 636-6060; 631-7810
Fax : (632) 631-7810

Banco Santander Philippines, Inc.
Vicente B. Castillo, President

27th Floor, Tower I, Ayala Triangle
Ayala Ave., Makati City
Phone : (632) 848-5847; 848-6270
Fax : (632) 759-4193
E-mail: vbcastillo.manila@sinvest.es

Bangkok Bank PCL
Preyamit Hetrakul, Vice President and General Manager
25th Floor, Far East Bank Center
Sen. Gil Puyat Ave., Makati City
Phone : (632) 891-4011 to 19
Fax : (632) 891-4037

Bank of America
Jose Querubin, Country Manager
BA Lepanto Bldg., 8747 Paseo de Roxas, Makati City
Phone : (632) 815-5450; 815-5451; 815-5000
Fax : (632) 815-5895

Bank of Commerce
Raul B. de Mesa, President
Bankers' Centre, 6764 Ayala Ave., Makati City
Phone : (632) 810-0672; 817-4906
Fax : (632) 812-4395

Bank of the Philippine Islands
Xavier P. Loinaz, President
19th Floor BPI Bldg., Ayala Ave., Makati City
Phone : (632) 816-9600; 818-5541
Fax : (632) 891-0183

Bank of Southeast Asia
Pascual M. Garcia III, President
ASB Center, 114 Benavidez St.
Legaspi Village, Makati City
Phone : (632) 840-4790; 892-7777
Fax : (632) 813-1235

Bank of Tokyo-Mitsubishi, Ltd.
Hisako Sakashita, General Manager
5th Floor, 6750 Ayala Ave., Makati City
Phone : (632) 818-7253; 892-1976 to 78
Fax : (632) 816-0413

Chase Manhattan Bank
James R. Boardman, Managing Director and Senior Country Officer
4th Floor Corinthian Plaza, 121 Paseo de Roxas, Makati City
Phone : (632) 878-1100; 811-3362; 811-3348 to 55
Fax : (632) 878-1297

China Banking Corporation
Peter S. Dee, President and CEO
8745 Paseo de Roxas corner Villar St., Makati City
Phone : (632) 818-5038; 814-2423; 816-4179
Fax : (632) 892-7486

Chinatrust (Philippines) Banking Corp.
William B. Go, President
Tower 1, Ayala Triangle
corner Paseo de Roxas and Ayala Ave., Makati City
Phone : (632) 759-4996; 848-5519
Fax : (632) 759-4982

Citibank, N.A.
Suresh Maharaj, Senior Vice President & Country Corporate Officer
8741 Paseo de Roxas, Makati City
Phone : (632) 813-9177; 894-7700 to 01
Fax : (632) 894-7703

Dao Heng Bank
Ricardo Balvido, Jr., EVP/OIC
146 Valero St., Salcedo Village, Makati City
Phone : (632) 812-8110; 840-3003 to 3016
Fax : (632) 817-8794

Deutsche Bank AG
Peter Verhoeven, General Manager
26th Floor, Tower 1, Ayala Triangle
Paseo de Roxas corner Ayala Ave., Makati City
Phone : (632) 894-6801; 894-6800
Fax : (632) 894-6809
E-mail: peter.verhoeven@ap.deuba.com

Development Bank of the Philippines
Alfredo C. Antonio, Chairman
8th Floor, DBP Bldg., Makati Ave., corner Sen. Gil Puyat Ave.
Makati City
Phone : (632) 892-3988; 818-9511 loc. 3801 or 3802
Fax : (632) 818-5528
E-mail: DBPchairman@ibm.net

Development Bank of Singapore, Ltd.
Sadasivan Vijayakumar, SVP & Country General Manager
32nd Floor, Citibank Tower, Valero Street
Salcedo Village, Makati City
Phone : (632) 848-0470; 848-0461; 848-0468
Fax : (632) 848-0478

East West Banking Corp.
Elrey T. Ramos, President
349 Sen. Gil Puyat Ave., Makati City
Phone : (632) 890-5644; 890-5571
Fax : (632) 890-5479

Equitable Banking Corporation
Wilfrido V. Vergara, President
262 Juan Luna St., Binondo, Manila
Phone : (632) 242-7101; 243-0311; 241-5963; 897-2971; 897-2982

Fax : (632) 241-6091

Export and Industry Bank
Benjamin P. Castillo, President
#30 Paseo de Roxas corner Jupiter St., Makati City
Phone : (632) 896-3296; 896-3311
Fax : (632) 896-3310

Far East Bank & Trust Company
Octavio V. Espiritu, President
Far East Bank Center
Sen. Gil Puyat Ave. corner Makati Ave., Makati City
Phone : (632) 845-9043; 891-4000
Fax : (632) 891-4088

Fuji Bank, Ltd.
Takuji Iwasaki, General Manager and CEO
26th Floor, Citibank Tower
Valero corner Villar St., Salcedo Village, Makati City
Phone : (632) 848-0071; 848-0001; 848-0010
Fax : (632) 815-3770

Hongkong and Shanghai Banking Corp.
Brian Fredrick, CEO
6780 Ayala Avenue, Makati City
Phone : (632) 810-1661; 814-5200
Fax : (632) 818-2718

International Commercial Bank of China
Herman Chen, Senior Vice President and General Manager
3rd Floor, Pacific Star Bldg.
Sen. Gil Puyat Ave. corner Makati Ave., Makati City
Phone : (632) 811-5807 to 14
Fax : (632) 811-5774

International Exchange Bank
Ramon Y. Sy, President & CEO
Salcedo Towers 169 H.V. Dela Costa, Salcedo Village
Makati City
Phone : (632) 810-3310; 753-3000
Fax : (632) 840-4640
E-mail: ramonsy@ibank.com.ph

Internationale Nederlanden Bank N.V.
Renato T. De Guzman, Country Manager
21st Floor, Tower 1, Ayala Triangle
Ayala Ave., Makati City
Phone : (632) 840-8862; 840-8888
Fax : (632) 848-5229
E-mail: ingbphmm@globe.com.ph

Korea Exchange Bank
Bong Heui Yang, General Manager
33rd Floor, Citibank Towers
8741 Paseo de Roxas, Makati City
Phone : (632) 848-1988; 848-0101
Fax : (632) 818-0074

Land Bank of the Philippines
Jesli A. Lapus, President
319 Sen. Gil Puyat Ave., Makati City
Phone : (632) 818-9411; 844-5064; 843-8824
Fax : (632) 817-2536
E-mail: jalapus@webquest.com

Metropolitan Bank and Trust Co.
Antonio S. Abacan, Jr., President
Metrobank Plaza, Sen. Gil Puyat Ave., Makati City
Phone : (632) 810-3311
Fax : (632) 813-4068; 817-6248
E-mail: metrobnk@mnl.sequel.net

Philippine Banking Corp.
Norberto C. Nazareno, President
6797 Ayala Ave., Makati City
Phone : (632) 815-4566; 817-0901
Fax : (632) 818-3779

Philippine Bank of Communication
Anthony Q. Chua , President and CEO
216 Juan Luna St., Binondo Manila
Phone : (632) 242-1787; 242-8701
Fax : (632) 241-3753
E-mail: aqchua@bancnet.net

Philippine Commercial International Bank
Rafael B. Buenaventura, President & CEO
21st Floor, PCI Bank Tower I, Makati Ave., Makati City
Phone : (632) 817-2424; 817-2240; 840-7000
Fax : (632) 818-3946
E-mail: paengb@mnl.sequel.net

Philippine National Bank
Daniel L. Lacson, Chairman
PNB Financial Center, Roxas Blvd., Pasay City
Phone : (632) 891-6301
Fax : (632) 526-3042

Philippine Trust Company
Dr. Emilio T. Yap, Chairman
Philtrust Bank Bldg., United Nations Ave. corner San Marcelino St., Paco, Manila
Phone : (632) 524-9061
Fax : (632) 521-7309

Philippine Veterans Bank
Sunday A. Lavin, President
PVB Bldg., 101 Herrera corner dela Rosa St.
Legaspi Village, Makati City
Phone : (632) 817-1237; 894-3919; 893-5766
Fax : (632) 813-0194

Pilipinas Bank
William S. Piotiosic, Chairman
111 Paseo de Roxas corner Legaspi St.
Legaspi Village, Makati City
Phone : (632) 816-1483; 819-1931; 815-3122
Fax : (632) 815-3140

PNB-Republic Bank
Wong Yong Tur, CEO
Legaspi Tower 300, Roxas Blvd.
corner Vito Cruz, Metro Manila
Phone : (632) 521-6169; 521-0096; 525-9134
Fax : (632) 521-8513; 521-8514

Prudential Bank
Jose L. Santos, President
Prudential Bank Bldg., Ayala Ave., Makati City
Phone : (632) 817-8981
Fax : (632) 817-5146
E-mail: pbank@prudential bank.com

Rizal Commercial Banking Corp.
Cesar E.A. Virata, Chairman
RCBC Bldg., 333 Sen. Gil Puyat Ave., Makati City
Phone : (632) 894-9988; 894-9000
Fax : (632) 891-0988

Security Bank Corp.
Maximo Madridejos, First Vice President
SBTC Bldg., 6776 Ayala Ave., Makati City
Phone : (632) 867-6788
Fax : (632) 813-2069
E-mail: secb@mnl.sequel.net
security.bank.library@usa.net

Solidbank Corporation
Deogracias N. Vistan, President & CEO
Solidbank Bldg., 777 Paseo de Roxas, Makati City
Phone : (632) 814-5560; 894-8888; 813-3964
Fax : (632) 893-5824
E-mail: dnvistan@solidbank.com.ph

Standard Chartered
Eirvin B. Knox, CEO
Bankmer Bldg., 6756 Ayala Avenue, Makati City
Phone : (632) 892-0961
Fax : (632) 810;6268; 810-6228

TA Bank of the Philippines, Inc.
Exequiel P. Villacorta, Jr., President and CEO
Octagon Center, San Miguel Ave.
Ortigas Center, Pasig City
Phone : (632) 637-6278; 910-1818
Fax : (632) 637-6279
E-mail: tabankop@pw.net

Traders Royal Bank
Roberto S. Benedicto, Chairman
TRB Towers, Roxas Blvd., Pasay City
Phone : (632) 831-2821 loc. 211; 831-9671
Fax : (632) 831-2494; 831-9671
E-mail: africa@mnl.sequel.net

Union Bank of the Philippines
Justo A. Ortiz, Chairman and CEO
SSS Makati Bldg., Ayala Ave. corner Herrera St., Makati City
Phone : (632) 892-0011; 811-3566
Fax : (632) 893-8590
E-mail: 104543.3146@compuserve.com

United Coconut Planters Bank
Tirso D. Antiporda, Jr., Chairman & CEO
15th Floor, UCPB Bldg., Makati Ave., Makati City
Phone : (632) 818-1908; 811-9000
Fax : (632) 818-0887
E-mail: tdaceo.ucpbibm.net

Urban Bank
Teodoro C. Borlongan, President
Urban Square, Urban Avenue, Makati City
Phone : (632) 843-0819; 843-0811
Fax : (632) 816-4668
E-mail: borlongan.tc@urbanvirtualbank.com

Westmont Bank
Edgardo B. Espiritu, President
411 Quintin Paredes St., Binondo, Manila
Phone : (632) 243-0970 or 72; 243-0951 to 60 loc. 200-201
Fax : (632) 243-0968

Multilateral Bank Offices in the Philippines:

Asian Development Bank (ADB)
Linda Tsao Yang, U.S. Executive Director
Asian Development Bank
6 ADB Ave., Mandaluyong City
Philippines 1099
Phone : (632) 632-6051
Fax : (632) 632-4003
E-mail: ltyang@mail.asiandebank.org

International Finance Corporation (IFC)
Vicul Prakash, Chief of Mission, Regional Mission in East Asia
and Pacific
3rd Floor, Corinthian Plaza
121 Paseo de Roxas, Makati City
Phone : (632) 811-3231; 811-3226; 811-3294
Fax : (632) 811-3293

World Bank
Vinay Bhargava, Country Director
23rd Floor, The Taipan Place
Emerald Ave., Pasig City
Phone : (632) 637-5855
Fax : (632) 637-5870; 917-3050

E-mail: vbhargava@worldbank.org

WASHINGTON-BASED U.S. GOVERNMENT CONTACTS:

Commerce Liaison Office (CLO)
Charles Kestenbaum, Director, Commerce Liaison Officer
Office of the U.S. Executive Director
World Bank
1818 H. Street, NW, Washington, D.C. 20433
Phone : (202) 458-0120; 458-0118
Fax : (202) 477-2967

Export - Import Bank of the United States
Fahmila Imam, Loan Officer
811 Vermont Ave., N.W.,
Washington, D.C. 20571
Phone : (202) 565-3700
Fax : (202) 565-3717
Email : fahmila.imam@imail.exim.gov

The Multilateral Development Bank Office
US&FCS, DOC
Janet Thomas, Acting Director
14th & Constitution Ave., NW, Washington, DC 20230
Phone : (202) 482-3399
Fax : (202) 273-0927

Overseas Private Investment Corporation (OPIC)
James Brache, Regional Manager
1100 New York Ave., N.W., Washington, D.C. 20527
Phone : (202) 336-8585
Fax : (202) 408-5142

TPCC - The Trade Information Center
International Trade Administration
U.S. Department of Commerce
14th & Constitution Ave., HCHB 7424
Washington, D.C.
Phone: 1-800-USA-TRADE
Fax: (202) 482-4473
Internet: http://www.ita.doc.gov/tic

E-mail: info@tda.gov

US DEPARTMENTS

U.S. Department of State
Office of the Coordinator for Business Affairs
E/CBA
2201 C Street, NW
Washington, D.C. 20250
Phone : (202) 647-1625
Fax : (202) 647-3953

U.S. Department of Commerce (USDOC)
Jean Kelly, Philippine Desk Officer
Herbert Hoover Bldg.
14th & Constitution Ave., N.W.
Washington, D.C. 20230 - 00011
Phone : (202) 482-3448
Fax : (202) 482-3316

U.S. Department of Agriculture (USDA)
Foreign Agricultural Service
Trade Assistance and Promotion Office
Phone : (202) 720-7420

U.S. Department of State
Philippine Desk
EAP/PIMBS
2201 C Street, NW
Washington, D.C. 20250
Phone : (202) 647-1221
Fax : (202) 736-4559

United States-Asia Environmental Partnership Program (US-AEP)
Jeremy Hagger, Managing Director
1720 Eye Street NW - Suite 700, Washington, D.C. 20006
Phone : (202) 712-0270
Fax : (202) 216-3379

U.S. Trade and Development Agency
Geoff Jackson, Regional Director - Asia/Pacific
U.S. Department of State
Room 309, SA-16, Washington, D.C. 20523-1602
Phone : (703) 875-4357
Fax : (703) 875-4009

REGIONAL DEVELOPMENT OFFICERS

BDTP OFFICIALS

RHODORA M. LEAÑO
Bureau Director
Tel. No. : (632)897-7617 Fax No. : (632) 890-4858
Email Address : RhodoraLeaño@dti.gov.ph

AGNES V. RAVELAS

Chief, Product Promotion Division
Tel. No. : (632)890-4877; (632) 890-4933; (632) 890-4901 to 40 local 450
Email Address : AgnesRavelas@dti.gov.ph

ROSANNA S. IBAÑEZ
OIC, Market Development Division
Tel. No. : (632)890-4855; (632)890-4901 to 40 locals 446 or 442
Email Address : RosannaIbañez@dti.gov.ph

FE C. BULAO
Chief, Market Information Division
Tel. No. : (632)890-4917; (632)890-4855
Email Address : FeBulao@dti.gov.ph

REGIONAL ACCOUNT OFFICERS

CORDILLERA ADMINISTRATIVE REGION (CAR)

GERARDO E. RAVELAS
Tel. No. : (632)890-4855; (632)890-4901 to 40 locals 446 or 442
E-mail Address: GerardoRavelas@dti.gov.ph

REGION 1

MA. LOURDES C. DE GUZMAN
Tel. No. : (632)890-4877; (632) 890-4933; (632) 890-4901 to 40 local 468
E-mail Address: MalouDeGuzman@dti.gov.ph

REGION 2

MARY JEAN S. GELLOR
Tel. No. : (632)890-4877; (632) 890-4933; (632) 890-4901 to 40 local 468
E-mail Address: JeanGellor@dti.gov.ph

REGION 3

CELIA M. GUINA
Tel. No. : (632)890-4877; (632) 890-4933; (632) 890-4901 to 40 local 468
E-mail Address: CeliaGuina@dti.gov.ph

REGION 4

ACHILLES G. CASTAÑEDA
Tel. No. : (632)890-4877; (632) 890-4933; (632) 890-4901 to 40 local 468
E-mail Address: AchillesCastañeda@dti.gov.ph

ROBERTO R. ZACARIAS
Tel. No. : (632)890-4855; (632)890-4901 to 40 locals 447 or 442
E-mail Address: RobertoZacarias@dti.gov.ph

REGION 5

RUBY C. AGUAS
Tel. No. : (632)890-4855; (632)890-4901 to 40 locals 446 or 442
E-mail Address: RubyAguas@dti.gov.ph

REGION 6

ANN B. ROPA
Tel. No. : (632)890-4917; (632)890-4855
E-mail Address: AnnRopa@dti.gov.ph

REGION 7

ARMANDO P. CANICULA
Tel. No. : (632)890-4877; (632) 890-4933; (632) 890-4901 to 40 local 468

REGION 8

GRACE M. MEDINA
Tel. No. : (632)890-4855; (632)890-4901 to 40 locals 446 or 442
E-mail Address: GraceMedina@dti.gov.ph

REGION 9

CARMELITA M. QUIRINO
Tel. No. : (632)890-4855; (632)890-4901 to 40 locals 446 or 442
E-mail Address: CarmelitaQuirino@dti.gov.ph

REGIONS 10, 12 & ARMM

SARAH JANE S. FAROLAN
Tel. No. : (632)890-4877; (632) 890-4933; (632) 890-4901 to 40 local 468
E-mail Address: SandeeFarolan@dti.gov.ph

REGION 11

CINDY CLAIRE C. SAQUING
Tel. No. : (632)890-4855; (632)890-4901 to 40 locals 446 or 442
E-mail Address: CindySaquing@dti.gov.ph

CARAGA

JOSE M. MULATO
Tel. No. : (632)890-4917; (632)890-4855
E-mail Address: JoseMulato@dti.gov.ph

NATIONAL CAPITAL REGION (NCR)

ACHILLES G. CASTAÑEDA
Tel. No. : (632)890-4877; (632) 890-4933; (632) 890-4901 to 40 local 468
E-mail Address:
AchillesCastañeda@dti.gov.ph

DTI DIRECTORS

- **Florencio G. Sison**
Construction Manpower Development Foundation
7F Prudential Bank Bldg.
2158 Pasong Tamo, Makati City
Contact Number/s : 815-11-51
Fax : 815-11-52
Email : cmdf@mydestiny.net

- **Kathryn Josephine dela Cruz**
Construction Industry Authority of the Philippines
4F Jupiter 1 Bldg.,56 Jupiter St.,
Bel Air, Makati City
Contact Number/s : 895-44-24/897-93-13
Fax : 897-93-36
Email : ciap@info.com.ph

- **Rhodora M. Leaño**
Bureau of Small and Medium Enterprise Development
3rd Floor, Oppen bldg.
349 Sen. Gil J. Puyat Avenue
Makati City
Contact Number/s : 890-53-33 loc. 3231/890-56-82
Fax : 896-79-16
Email : RhodoraLea?o@dti.dti.gov.

- **Jerry T. Clavecillas**
Bureau of Small and Medium Enterprise Development 3rd Floor, Oppen Bldg. 349 Sen. Gil J. Puyat Avenue, MAKATI, METRO MANILA
Contact Number/s : 8905682, 8905333 loc 3231
Fax : 8967916

- **Jose V. Hipolito**
Cagayan Economic Zone Authority (CEZA)
7F Weststar Bldg.
611 Shaw Blvd., Pasig City
Contact Number/s : 636-57-80 to 82
Fax : 631-39-97
Email : cagayanecozone@pacific.

- **Virgilio P. Fulgencio**
Center for Industrial Competitiveness
2nd Floor, Trade and Industry Bldg.
361 Sen. Gil J. Puyat Avenue,
Makati City
Contact Number/s : 890-48-89
Fax : 897-55-54
Email : cic@dti.dti.gov.ph

- **Jesus L. Motoomull**
Buroau of Product Standards
3F Trade and Industry Bldg.
361 Sen. Gil J. Puyat Avenue
Makati City
Contact Number/s : 890-49-65
Fax : 890-51-31
Email : bps@dti.dti.gov.ph

- **Ramon T. Kabigting**
Bureau of International Trade Relations
3F Trade and Industry Bldg.
361 Sen. Gil J. Puyat Avenue,
Makati City
Contact Number/s : 897-82-90 / 890-51-48 / 890-49-01 Loc. 416
Fax : 890-48-12
Email : bitr_mon@dti.dti.gov.ph

- **Luis M. Catibayan**
Bureau of Import Services
3F Oppen Bldg.
349 Sen. Gil J. Puyat Avenue
Makati City
Contact Number/s : 896-44-30
Fax : 895-74-66
Email : bis@dti.dti.gov.ph

- **Fernando P. Cala II**
Bureau of Export Trade Promotion
5F/8F New Solid Bldg.
357 Sen. Gil J. Puyat
Makati City,
Contact Number/s : 899-01-33/895-36-54/759-33-81
Fax : 890-47-05/890-47-16
Email : FPC@dti.gov.ph

□ **Meynard Orbeta**
Bureau of Domestic Trade
2F Trade and Industry Bldg.
361 Sen. Gil J. Puyat Avenue
Makati City
Contact Number/s : 890-48-77/ 890-49-01
Locs. 459/322
Fax : 890-48-58
Email : MOrbeta @yahoo.com

□ **Mary Jean T. Pacheco**
Office of Operational Planning
4F Board of Investments Bldg.
385 Sen Gil J. Puyat Avenue
Makati City
Contact Number/s : 890-49-51 / 890-49-54 /
890-49-01 Loc. 319
Fax : 890-49-51
Email : oop@dti.dti.gov.ph

□ **Ma. Lourdes A. Yaptinchay**
Office of the Assistant Secretary for Policy, Planning, Special Concern and Communications
4F Industry and Investments Bldg.
385 Sen. Gil J. Puyat Ave.,
Makati City
Contact Number/s : 897-12-43
Fax : 896-78-89
Email : Layaptinchay@boi.gov.ph

□ **Virgilio A. Sevandal**
Office of Legal Affairs
4F Trade and Industry Bldg.
361 Sen. Gil J. Puyat Avenue
Makati City
Contact Number/s : 890-48-97
Fax : 890-49-01 Loc. 512

□ **Ofelia V. Bulaong**
National Development Company
2,3,7 & 8F NDC Building
116 Tordesillas Street
Salcedo Village, Makati City
Contact Number/s : 840-11-48/813-22-28
Locs. 202/203
Fax : 892-1982
Email : ofgenman@info.com.ph

□ **Vina Liza Ruth C. Cabrera**
Management Information Services
5F Trade and Industry Bldg.
361 Sen. Gil J. Puyat Avenue
Makati City
Contact Number/s : 890-48-65
Fax : 890-49-70
Email : mis@dti.dti.gov.ph

□ **Antonio R. Reyes**
International Coffee Organization Certifying Agency
5F New Solid Bldg.
357 Sen. Gil Puyat Avenue, Makati City
Contact Number/s : 759-69-55/890-47-50
Fax : 759-69-55
Email : icoca@dti.dti.gov.ph

□ **Ma. Lourdes T. Baua**
Human Resource Development Services
6F Trade and Industry Bldg.
361 Sen. Gil J. Puyat Avenue, Makati City
Contact Number/s : 890-49-27/890-59-36
Fax : 890-48-57
Email : LourdesBaua@dti.dti.gov.ph

□ **Adelaida L. Inton**
Philippine Trade Training Center
International Trade Center Complex
Roxas Blvd. Corner Sen. Gil J. Puyat Ave.
1300 Pasay City
Contact Number/s : 832-23-97/834-13-41/
834-13-44 to 49 Loc. 333
Fax : 834-13-43
Email : pttc@dti.dti.gov.ph

□ **Alfonso M. Valenzuela**
Press Relations Office
4F Industry and Investments Bldg.
385 Sen. Gil J. Puyat Avenue, Makati City,

□ **Lilia B. De Lima**
Philippine Economic Zone Authority
Roxas Boulevard, Cor. San Luis St.,
Pasay City
Contact Number/s : 551-34-32; 551-34-55
Fax : 891-63-80
Email : dglbl@peza.gov.ph

□ **Dita M. Maralit**

Office of Special Concerns
5F Trade and Industry Bldg.
361 Sen. Gil J. Puyat Avenue
Makati City
Contact Number/s : 890-51-23/ 897-17-13
Fax : 890-48-16
Email : DitaMaralit@dti.gov.ph

- **Minerva P. Franco**
Product Development and Design Center of the Philippines
CCP Complex, Roxas Blvd.,
Pasay City
Contact Number/s : 832-36-46
Fax : 832-36-49
Email : pddcp@mozcom.com

- **Zorayda Amelia C. Alonzo**
Small Business Guarantee and Finance Corporation
17F & 18F Flr. Antel Corporate Center
139 Valero St.,Salcedo Village, Makati City
Contact Number/s : 813-5720 / 81057-91 Loc. 333
Fax : 813-5726
Email : sbgfc@info.com.ph

- **Minerva R. Fajardo**
Trade & Industry Information Center
4F Industry and Investments Bldg.
385 Sen. Gil J. Puyat Avenue, Makati City
Contact Number/s : 895-36-11/ 890-13-32 Loc. 265
Fax : 895-64-87
Email : MRFajardo@boi.gov.ph

- **Anthony Abad**
Philippine International Trading Corporation
5F National Development Company
116 Tordesillas St., Makati City
Contact Number/s : 845-43-76
Fax : 845-44-73/76

- **Atty. Pedro Vicente C. Mendoza**
Philippine Shippers? Bureau
5F Trade and Industry Bldg.
361 Sen. Gil J. Puyat Avenue
Makati City,
Contact Number/s : 890-48-92/890-49-40
Fax : 890-51-34
Email : psb@dti.dti.gov.ph

- **Franklin P. Bunoan**
Cottage Industry Technology Center
20 Russet St., SSS Village
Marikina City
Contact Number/s : 942-45-61
Fax : 942-01-07
Email : citc@dti.gov.ph

- **Manuel B. Abad**
DTI-CARP National Program Office
4F Oppen Bldg., 349 Sen. Gil J. Puyat Avenue
Makati City
Contact Number/s : 890-49-66
Fax : 897-10-24
Email : Carp@dti.dti.gov.ph

- **Ireneo V. Vizmonte**
Financial Management Services
4F Trade and Industry Bldg.
361 Sen. Gil J. Puyat Avenue,
Makati City
Contact Number/s : 890-49-61
Fax : 890-48-86
Email : fms@dti.dti.gov.ph

- **Mauino T. Haresco**
Foreign Trade Service Corps Coordinating Office
5F New Solid Bldg.
357 Sen. Gil J. Puyat Avenue
Makati City
Contact Number/s : (632) 897-96-59 / 890-50-73/897-96-72/897-96-61
Fax : 890-47-47
Email : ftscmnl@dti.gov.ph

- **Carl John G. Matriano**
Contact Number/s : 896-51-67
Fax : 895-39-81 / 897-66-82 Loc. 321
Email : CJGCapistrano@boi.gov.ph

- **Gregory L. Domingo**
Board of Investments
5F Industry and Investments Bldg.

385 Sen Gil J. Puyat Avenue,
Makati City
Contact Number/s : 890-93-32 / 890-93-30 / 897-66-82 Loc. 248
Fax : 895-35-12
Email : GLDomingo@boi.gov.ph

TRADE ASSOCIATIONS

 SEAWEED INDUSTRY ASSOCIATION OF THE PHILIPPINES
Shemberg Marketing cor. Lapu-Lapu, Osme?a St., Cebu City
Contact Number/s : (63 32)346-0863
Fax : (63 32)346-0863

 PHILIPPINE SUGAR MILLERS ASSOCIATION, INC.
1402 Security Bank Centre, 6776 Ayala Ave., Makati City
Contact Number/s : (63 2)891-1138; 891-1202
Fax : (63 2)891-1144
Email : psma@netasia-mnl.net

 PHILIPPINE ASSOCIATION OF MEAT PROCESSORS, INC.
Suite 203-204 Sunrise Condominium, Ortigas Ave., Greenhills, San Juan, Metro Manila
Contact Number/s : (63 2)721-2674
Fax : (63 2)721-235

 PHILIPPINE ASOCIATION OF FLOUR MILLERS, INC.
Rm. 311, 3rd Floor, Atrium Bldg., Makati City
Contact Number/s : (63 2)892-1413; 812-1786; 893-2252
Fax : (63 2)810-9462

 PHILIPPINE COCONUT OIL PRODUCERS ASSOCIATION , INC.
c/o United Coconut Authority of the Philippines(UCAP), 2nd Floor, PCRDF Bldg., Pearl Drive cor. Lourdes St., Ortigas Complex, Pasig City
Contact Number/s : (63 2)633-8029; 633-9286 to 87
Fax : (63 2)633-8030

 INTEGRATED FOOD MANUFACTURERS ASSOCIATION OF THE PHILIPPINES
#62 19th St., New Manila Rolling Hills Village, New Manila, Quezon City
Contact Number/s : (63 2)721-1653; 721-9518
Fax : (63 2)721-0144

 COCONUT OIL REFINERS ASSOCIATION
c/o AFTA Corporation, 102 Agana Circle St., BF Homes, Paranaque City
Contact Number/s : (63 2)825-5105; 825-4480
Fax : (63 2)827-5105

 ASSOCIATION OF PHILIPPINE COCONUT DESSICATORS
c/o United Coconut Authority of the Philippines(UCAP), 2nd Floor, PCRDF Bldg., Pearl Drive cor. Lourdes St., Ortigas Complex, Pasig City
Contact Number/s : (63 2)633-9286 TO 87
Fax : (63 2)633-8030

 ASSOCIATION OF COCONUT BROKERS, INC.
c/o Eisellgen House of Trade, 4402 Bluebelle Road, Sunvalley, Paranaque City
Contact Number/s : (63 2)823-3631; 776-0496
Fax : (63 2)823-3631
Email : eisllgen@pworld.net.ph

 ASSOCIATION OF PROFESSIONAL CONGRESS EXHIBITION ORGANIZERS & SUPPLIERS PHILS., INC.
c/o WORLDEXCO, 433 Delegation Bldg., PICC, CCP Complex, Roxas Blvd., Pasay City
Contact Number/s : (63 2)834-0608
Fax : (63 2)834-0602

 PIPES AND TUBES MANUFACTURERS ASSOCIATION OF THE PHILIPPINES INCORPORATED
Bo. Domingo, Cainta, Rizal
Contact Number/s : (63 2)655-7534
Fax : (63 2)655-7534

 PHILIPPINE STEELMAKERS ASSOCIATION
25th Floor, Galleria Corporate Center, EDSA cor. Ortigas Ave., Ortigas, Quezon City
Contact Number/s : (63 2)633-8033
Fax : (63 2)633-8048

□ PHILIPPINE NAIL MANUFACTURERS ASSOCIATION
23 Kaingin Road, Brgy. A. Samson, Quezon City
Contact Number/s : (63 2)363-2339; 363-2385; 363-9599
Fax : (63 2)363-9499

□ PHILIPPINE CEMENT MANUFACTURERS CORPORATION
13 Economia St., Bagumbayan, Libis, Quezon City or 4 EDSA, San Juan, Metro Manila
Contact Number/s : (63 2)634-4492; 437-1961; 437-1992
Fax : (63 2)635-9772
Email : plcemcor@info.com.ph

□ PHILIPPINE IRON AND STEEL TRADERS ASSOCIATION
Suite 304 Sunrise Condominium I, Ortigas Ave., Greenhills, San Juan, Metro Manila
Contact Number/s : (63 2)727-0536
Fax : (63 2)721-3599

□ GALVANIZED IRON WIRE MANUFACTURERS ASSOCIATION, INC.
1174 A. Mabini ST., Caloocan City
Contact Number/s : (63 2)241-1497 to 98
Fax : (63 2)241-1659

□ PHILIPPINE OLEOCHEMICAL MANUFACTURERS ASSOCIATION
c/o United Coconut Chemicals, Inc., 17/F, UCPB Bldg., Makati Ave., Makati City
Contact Number/s : (63 2)816-0371 to 75; 815-4104
Fax : (63 2)817-1725; 817-2251

□ PHILIPPINE ASSOCIATION OF FEED MILLERS, INC.
Rm. 302 Maligaya Bldg. III, 430 E. Rodriguez Sr. Blvd., Cubao, Quezon City
Contact Number/s : (63 2)722-2912; 721-0906
Fax : (63 2)722-9206
Email : pafmi@pacific.net.ph

□ SINAMAY MANUFACTURERS
c/o Fiber Industry Development Authority (FIDA), Asiantrust Bank Annex Building, 1424 Quezon Avenue, Quezon City
Contact Number/s : (63 2) 373-7489; 373-7486
Fax : (63 2) 373-9238

□ SALAGO EXPORTERS & PROCESSORS
c/o Fiber Industry Development Authority (FIDA), Asiantrust Bank Annex Building, 1424 Quezon Avenue, Quezon City
Contact Number/s : (63 2) 373-7489; 373-7486
Fax : (63 2) 373-9238

□ RAFFIA PROCESSORS & EXPORTERS
c/o Fiber Industry Development Authority (FIDA), Asiantrust Bank Annex Building, 1424 Quezon Avenue, Quezon City
Contact Number/s : (63 2) 373-7489; 373-7486
Fax : (63 2) 373-9238

□ PI?A CLOTH & BY-PRODUCTS SUPPLIERS
c/o Fiber Industry Development Authority (FIDA), Asiantrust Bank Annex Building, 1424 Quezon Avenue, Quezon City
Contact Number/s : (63 2) 373 7489; 373-7486
Fax : (63 2) 373-9238

□ MAGUEY SUPPLIERS & PROCESSORS
c/o Fiber Industry Development Authority (FIDA), Asiantrust Bank Annex Building, 1424 Quezon Avenue, Quezon City
Contact Number/s : (63 2) 373-7489; 373-7486
Fax : (63 2) 373-9238

□ COIR PRODUCERS, PROCESSORS AND EXPORTERS
c/o Fiber Industry Development Authority (FIDA), Asiantrust Bank Annex Building, 1424 Quezon Avenue, Quezon City
Contact Number/s : (63 2) 373-7489; 373-7486
Fax : (63 2) 373-9238

□ BUNTAL FIBER PROCESSORS AND EXPORTERS
c/o Fiber Industry Development Authority (FIDA), Asiantrust Bank Annex Building, 1424 Quezon Avenue, Quezon City
Contact Number/s : (63 2) 373-7489; 373-7486
Fax : (63 2) 373-9238

□ ABACA FIBER AND PULP PROCESSORS AND EXPORTERS
c/o Fiber Industry Development Authority (FIDA), Asiantrust Bank Annex Building, 1424 Quezon Avenue, Quezon City
Contact Number/s : (63 2) 373-7489; 373-7486
Fax : (63 2) 373-9238

□ LAGUNA TECHNOPARK

Laguna Technopark, Sta. Rosa & Bi?an, Laguna
Contact Number/s : (049) 541-1476/77
Contact Person: Leonisa S. Suarez

 PHILIPPINE METALCASTING ASSOCIATION,INC.
Quezon City Polytechnic Compound, 673 Quirino Highway San Bartolome , Novaliches, Quezon City
Contact Number/s : (632)419-4278
Fax : (632)939-9320
Contact Person: Jerry Hui

 CALAMBA PREMIERE INDUSTRIAL PARK
Calamba Premiere Industrial Park
Contact Number/s : (049) 834-2567 to 69
Contact Person: Cecilia Z. Velena

 ANGELES INDUSTRIAL PARK
Angeles Industrial Park, Bacolor, Pampanga
Contact Number/s : (045) 323-4488
Contact Person: Zita Rubi

 AMKOR ANAM TECHNOLOGY ZONE
Amkor Anam Technology Zone, Muntinlupa City
Contact Number/s : (632) 850-7336
Contact Person: Napoleon V. Balingit

 MACTAN ECONOMIC ZONE II
Mactan Economic Zone II, Basak, Lapu-Lapu City
Contact Number/s : (032) 340-4694
Contact Person: Ralph Minoza

 LIGHT INDUSTRY & SCIENCE PARK OF THE PHILIPPINES 2
Light Industry &Science Park of the Philippines 2, Calamba, Laguna
Contact Number/s : (049) 244-5677
Contact Person: Jose Expedito Flores

 VICTORIA WAVE
Victoria Wave, Tala, Malaria, Caloocan City
Contact Number/s : (632) 939-7218
Contact Person: Ramon Abordo

 DAIICHI INDUSTRIAL PARK
DAIICHI Industrial Park, Silang Cavite
Contact Number/s : (046) 506-2653
Contact Person: Hipolito Bautista

 GATEWAY BUSINESS PARK
Gateway Business Park, General Trias, Cavite
Contact Number/s : (046) 433-0235
Contact Person: Miguel Manalo

 LAGUNA INTERNATIONAL INDUSTRIAL PARK
Laguna International Industrial Park, Bi?an, Laguna
Contact Number/s : (049) 539-0095
Contact Person: Cecilia Z. Velena

 COMPUTER MANUFACTURERS DISTRIBUTORS AND DEALERS AND DEALERS ASSOCIATION OF THE PHILIPPINES
7th Floor SEDCCO I Building, Rada corner Legaspi Streets Legaspi Village, Makati City
Contact Number/s : (632)810-3814/892-7947
Fax : (632)815-6531/7509456
Email : comddap1@info.com.ph
Contact Person: Gina D. Dimayuga

 LIGHT INDUSTRY & SCIENCE PARK OF THE PHILIPPINES 1
Light Industry & Science Prk of the Philippines I
Contact Number/s : (049) 543-0078
Contact Person: Ismael H. Itaas

 LIMA TECHNOLOGY CENTER
Lipa and Malvar, Batangas
Contact Number/s : (043) 981-4089
Contact Person: Gaudencio Lat

 FIRST PHILIPPINE INDUSTRIAL PARK
Tanauan, Batangas
Contact Number/s : (049) 834-2567 to 69
Contact Person: Expedito J. Flores

 FIRST CAVITE INDUSTRIAL ESTATE
Dasmari?as, Cavite
Contact Number/s : (046) 402-0641
Contact PErson: Hipolito Bautista

 CAVITE ECONOMIC ZONE
Cavite Economic Zone, Rosario, Cavite
Contact Number/s : (046) 437-6090
Contact Person: Digna Torres

 CARMELRAY INDUSTRIAL PARK 2
Brgys. Punto and Tulo, Calamba, Laguna
Contact Number/s : (049) 549-3282
Contact Person: Lorna Balite

□ CARMELRAY INDUSTRIAL PARK I
Canlubang, Laguna
Contact Number/s : (049) 549-3282
Contact Person: Lorna Balite

□ BATAAN ECONOMIC ZONE
Mariveles, Bataan
Contact Number/s : (047) 935-4009
Contact Person: Dante Quindoza

□ BAGUIO CITY ECONOMIC ZONE
Baguio City Economic Zone, Loakan Road, Baguio City
Contact Number/s : (074) 447-3931
Contact Person: Ma. Sansaluna A. Pinagayao

□ AUSTRALIAN-NEW ZEALAND CHAMBER OF COMMERCE (PHILIPPINES), INC.
Muelle de San Francisco St., South Harbor, Port Area, Manila
Contact Number/s : (632) 527-8251/86
Fax : (632) 527-2467
Email : rbarclay@asianterminals.com.ph
Contact Person: Richard Barclay

□ PHILIPPINE CHAMBER OF COMMERCE AND INDUSTRY
14th Floor, Multinational Bancorporation Centre, 6805 Ayala Ave., Makati City
Contact Number/s : (63 2) 843-3374; 843-4098; 843-4128; 843-3176;
Fax : (63 2)843-4102; 843-4103
Email : pcciintr@mozcom.com
Contact Person: Miguel B. Varela

□ FRENCH BUSINESS ASSOCIATION IN THE PHILIPPINES
Unit 1503 Medical Plaza Makati Bldg. Amorsolo cor. Dela Rosa Street Legaspi Village, Makati City"
Contact Number/s : (632)813-9005
Fax : (632)892-6114
Email : info@leclub-fba.org

□ TINCANS MANUFACTURERS ASSOCIATION OF THE PHILIPPINES
55 Amang Rodriguez Ave., Santolan, Pasig City
Contact Number/s : (632) 646-0840; 646-2476
Fax : (632) 645-2061

□ AMERICAN CHAMBER OF COMMERCE OF THE PHILIPPINES
2/F Corinthian Plaza, Paseo de Roxas St., Makati City
Contact Number/s : (632) 818-7911 to 13
Fax : (632) 811-3081
Email : amchamrp@mozcom.com

□ ASSOCIATION OF PAPER TRADERS OF THE PHILIPPINES INC.(APTP)
2205-A East Tower, Philippine Stock Exchange Center, Exchange Road, Ortigas Center, Pasig City
Contact Number/s : 638-7788
Fax : 638-1388
Contact Person: MR. PETE O. TAN

□ WOODEN GIFTS AND ACCESSORIES MANUFACTURERS ASSOCIATION INC. (WOODTAG)
51 Calumpit St., Veterans Village, Project 7, Quezon City
Contact Number/s : (632) 522-9787
Fax : (632) 522-0869
Contact Person: MR. MARIANITO R. ALCALA

□ HOME TEXTILE ASSOCIATION OF THE PHILIPPINES (HOMETEXTILE)
7 Col. Martelino Sat., Heroes Hill, 1100 Quezon City
Contact Number/s : 807-6007
Fax : 807-6007; 807-2805
Contact Person: MR. JOEY GUTIERREZ

□ TEXTILE MILLS ASSOCIATION OF THE PHILIPPINES (TMAP)
G/F, Alexander House, 132 Amorsolo St., Legaspi Village, Makati City
Contact Number/s : 818-6601/6605
Fax : 818-3107
Email : tmap@pacific.net.ph
Contact Person: MR. HERMENEGILDO ZAYCO

□ PULP AND PAPER MANUFACTURERS ASSOCIATION INC.(PULPAPEL)
11th Floor, ACE Building, 101 Rada Street, Legaspi Village, Makati City
Contact Number/s : 894-0053; 929-1396; 924-7985
Fax : 894-0055; 815-9480; 924-7985
Contact Person: MR. LAURO D. GUEVARRA

□ PHILIPPINE WOOD PRODUCERS ASSOCIATION(PWPA)

3rd Floor, LTA Building, Rm. 305, 118 Perea St., Legaspi Village, Makati City
Contact Number/s : (63 2) 817-6751; 817-6885
Fax : (63 2) 817-6884
Contact Person: MR. ANTONIO C. OLIZON

 PHILIPPINE RETAILERS ASSOCIATION (PRA)
Unit 2610 Jolibee Plaza, Emerald Avenue, Ortigas Center, Pasig City
Contact Number/s : 687-4180 to 81
Fax : 671-1566
Contact Person: MR. MANUEL SIGGAOAT, SR.

 PHILIPPINE ELECTRONICS & TELECOMMUNICATIONS FEDERATION (PETEF)
7/F, Unit 11 PS Bank Tower, Tindalo St., Sen. Gil Puyat Ave, Makati City
Contact Number/s : 813-6398
Fax : 813-6397
Email : petef@mailstation.net
Contact Person: MR. DAVID FERNANDO

 PHILIPPINE ELECTRICAL ELECTRONICS & ALLIED INDUSTRIES FEDERATION (PEEAIF)
2nd Floor, Union-Ajinomoto Building, 331 Sen Gil J. Puyat Avenue, Makati City
Contact Number/s : 895-6081 to 89 local 271
Fax : 890-6663
Contact Person: MR. RAUL JOSEPH CONCEPCION

 PHILIPPINE CHAMBER OF HANDICRAFT INDUSTRIES INC(PCHI)
Cityland Condominium 3, Room 516 Herrera corner Esteban St., Makati City 1229
Contact Number/s : 817-2243; 867-1321 to 22
Fax : 631-4631
Email : philcham@info.com.ph
Contact Person: MS. MILAGROS LACSON

 PHILIPPINE ASSOCIATION OF SUPERMARKETS INC. (PASI)
C/o Shoppersville Supermarket, 355 Katipunan Road, Loyola Heights, Quezon City
Contact Number/s : 426-1246
Fax : 929-1304
Contact Person: MR. JOSE A. ALBERT

 PHILIPPINE ASSOCIATION OF PEARL PRODUCERS/EXPORTERS
45 Don Vicente Madrigal Avenue, Corinthian Gardens, Quezon City
Contact Number/s : 810-0572
Fax : 818-9778
Contact Person: MS. CARMINA SANCHEZ

 PHILIPPINE AMALGAMATED SUPERMARKETS ASSOCIATION INC.(PAGASA)
C/o 2 Nicanor A Ramirez Street, Welcome Rotonda, Quezon City
Contact Number/s : 732-0509; 711-1290
Fax : 732-0509
Contact Person: MR. STEVEN T. CUA

 PHARMACEUTICAL AND HEALTHCARE ASSOCIATION OF THE PHILIPPINES(PHAP)
Unit 502, One Corporate Plaza, 845 Pasay Road, Makati City
Contact Number/s : 815-0325; 816-0618/7334; 819-2702
Fax : 819-2702
Email : phap7346@info.com.ph
Contact Person: MR. LEO WASSMER, JR.

 ILOILO FURNITURE MANUFACTURERS ASSOCIATION, INC. (IFMA)
RTESDC Regional Center, TESDA Compound, Zamora Street, Iloilo City
Contact Number/s : (033) 338-2791
Fax : (033) 338-2791
Email : ifmailo@skynet.net
Contact Person: MR. NOE O. GUMAYAO

 EUROPEAN CHAMBER OF COMMERCE OF THE PHILIPPINES
19/F PS Bank Tower, Sen Gil Puyat Ave. cor. Tindalo St., Makati City
Contact Number/s : (632) 759-6680, 845-1324
Fax : ((632) 759-6690, 845-1395
Email : info@eccp.com

 HOTEL AND RESTAURANT ASSOCIATION OF THE PHILIPPINES (HRAP)
Suite 200 Hotel Intramuros de Manila, Plaza San Luis Complex corner Cabildo & Ordante Sts., Intramuros, Manila
Contact Number/s : (632) 527-5113; 527-9926
Fax : (632) 527-9927
Contact Person: MR. EDUARD HOOGEWEEGEN

□ GARMENT BUSINESS ASSOCIATION OF THE PHILIPPINES (GBAP)
Rm. 1503 Cityland 10 Tower 2, H.V. Dela Costa St., Salcedo Village, Makati City
Contact Number/s : 841-0474; 810-3482
Fax : 841-0473
Contact Person: MS. VICTORIA REYES

□ FEDERATION OF HANDMADE PAPERMAKERSCONVERTER INC.(FEHPA)
C/o Kraffiti Co. Phil., 383 Do?a Enrique Subd. Baliuag, 3006 Bulacan
Contact Number/s : (097) 766-2946
Fax : (097) 766-2946
Contact Person: MS. TRELICITA RAMOS

□ FEDERATION OF ELECTRICAL & ELECTRONICS SUPPLIERS & MANUFACTURERS OF THE PHILIPPINES, INC.-CEBU
C/o Conching's Electrical Supply, 134 V. Gullas Street, Cebu City
Contact Number/s : 253-8605; 8763; 8791
Fax : 254-4284; 9250; 231-3845
Contact Person: MR. WILFREDO PO

□ FEDERATION OF ELECTRCIAL & ELECTRONICS SUPPLIERS & MANUFACTURERS OF THE PHILIPPINES, INC.-MANILA
3001 Ramon Magsaysay Blvd., cor. M. dela Fuente St., Sta. Mesa, Manila
Contact Number/s : 715-3002; 715-3184
Fax : 716-3789
Contact Person: MR. ROBINSON TANG

□ COOKING, HEATING AND ELECTRIC FAN MANUFACTURERS
3rd Floor, Union Ajinomoto Building, 331 Sen. Gil Puyat Avenue, Makati City
Contact Number/s : 895-6081 to 89 loc. 271
Fax : 890-6663
Contact Person: MS. FERNANDITAS MALIT

□ CONSUMER ELECTRONICS PRODUCTS MANUFACTURERS ASSOCIATION (CEPMA)
3rd Floor, Union Ajinomoto Building, 331 Sen. Gil Puyat Avenue, Makati City
Contact Number/s : 895-6081 to 89 loc. 271
Fax : 890-6663
Contact Person: MS. FERNANDITAS MALIT

□ CONFEDERATION OF GARMENT EXPORTERS OF THE PHILIPPINES (CONGEP)
Suite 609, 6/F, Executive Bldg. Center, Senator Gil Puyat Avenue, Makati City
Contact Number/s : 895-7614
Fax : 895-7614
Email : congep@vasia.com
Contact Person: MR. GEORGE SIY

□ CHAMBER OF FURNITURE INDUSTRYOF THE PHILIPPINES-VIGAN
c/o DTI-Ilocos Sur, 3/F A.R. Lahoz Bldg., Jose Singson St., Vigan, Ilocos Sur
Contact Number/s : (077) 722-2688/2046
Fax : (077) 722-2046
Contact Person: MR. HERNANI F. PLETE

□ CHAMBER OF FURNITURE INDUSTRYOF THE PHILIPPINES-TARLAC
125 Brgy. San Isidro, Tarlac City
Contact Number/s : (045) 982-0959
Fax : (045) 982-6125
Contact Person: MR. CLARO. M. LOPEZ

□ CHAMBER OF FURNITURE INDUSTRY OF THE PHILIPINES - ZAMBOANGA
c/o DTI-Zamboanga City, 2/F SKT Bldg., Rizal St., Zamboanga City
Contact Number/s : (062) 991-2701/2705
Fax : (062) 993-0594
Contact Person: MR. GLENN B. SALILIG

□ CHAMBER OF FURNITURE INDUSTRY OF THE PHILIPINES - ZAMBALES
c/o Walch's Furniture, National Hi-way, Brgy. San Antonio, Zambales
Contact Number/s : (047) 621-0037

□ CHAMBER OF FURNITURE INDUSTRIES OF THE PHILIPPINES-NEGROS
C/o DTI Bacolod 2nd Floor, Milagros Plaza Building,
Gatutlao-Rosario Street, Bacolod City 6100
Contact Number/s : (034) 434-2621; 433-8764
Fax : (034) 433-0250
Contact Person: ENGR. WOODRO L. GUANZON

□ CHAMBER OF FURNITURE INDUSTRIES OF THE PHILIPPINES-ILIGAN
C/o Crown Furnitureb 0025-D Diocesan Centrum, Lluch Street, Iligan City
Contact Number/s : (063) 221-3772; 221-6494

Fax : (063) 221-1761
Contact Person: ENGR. CIRIACO A. DARUNDAY, JR.

 CHAMBER OF FURNITURE INDUSTRIES OF THE PHILIPPINES-CAGAYAN
C/o Department of Trade & Industry - Cagayan Provincial Office
3rd Floor, Tony Go Bldg. Corner Luna & Burgos Sts., Tuguegarao City
Contact Number/s : (078) 844-1348; 846-4410
Contact Person: MR. ROLANDO VALENZUELA

 CHAMBER OF FURNITURE INDUSTRIES OF THE PHILIPPINES (CFIP-NATIONAL)
Unit H, 9th Floor, Strata 100 Building, Emerald Avenue, Ortigas Centre, Pasig City
Contact Number/s : 631-2834;632-9007; 637-2742 to 43
Fax : 631-2977
Email : ifo@cfipnet.com/pifs@cfipnet.com
Contact Person: MR. JOSE LEO CAPARAS

 CHAMBER OF FURNITURE INDUSTRY OF THE PHILIPPINES-DAVAO
c/o Nature's Eccentricities, 011 Pendatum St., Kidapawan City, North Cotabato
Contact Number/s : (064) 288-1817
Fax : (064) 288-1817

 CEBU FURNITURE INDUSTRIES FOUNDATION, INC. (CFIFI)
3rd Floor, LDM Building corner M.J. Cuenco Avenue & Legaspi Sts., Cebu City
Contact Number/s : (032) 253-3091; 253-0274
Fax : (032) 254-8246
Email : infocfif@nextmil.com
Contact Person: MR. CHARLES M. STREEGAN

 ASSOCIATION OF ACCESSORY MANUFACTURERS & EXPORTERS OF THE PHILIPPINES (AAMEP)
c/o UDD Exports, 14 Topside Alta Vista Village, Loyola Heights, Quezon City
Contact Number/s : 913-4685
Fax : 913-4647
Contact Person: MR. REY PAULINO

 ASSOCIATION OF HOME APPLIANCE MANUFACTURERS (AHAM)
3rd Floor, Union Ajinomoto Building, 331 Sen. Gil Puyat Avenue, Makati City
Contact Number/s : 895-6081 to 89 loc. 271
Fax : 890-6663
Contact Person: MR. RAUL JOSEPH CONCEPCION

 ADVERTISING BOARD OF THE PHILIPPINES, INC. (ADBOARD)
6/F DAO I Condominium, 189 Salcedo St., Legaspi Vill., Makati City,
Contact Number/s : 818-6158; 817-7724
Fax : 818-7109
Contact Person: MR. OSCAR T. VALENZUELA

 ALBAY FURNITURE MANUFACTURERS ASSOCIATION (AFMA)
C/o DTI Provincial Office, 2nd Floor, DBP Building, Legaspi City
Contact Number/s : (052) 480-7693; 480-7078
Fax : (052) 214-3226; 214-3176
Contact Person: MR. ROLANDO B. GUERINA

 LUISITA INDUSTRIAL PARK
Luisita Industrial Park, San Miguel, Tarlac
Contact Number/s : (0452) 985-0526; 985-1994
Contact Person: Reynaldo Guieb

 ASSOCIATION OF CONSOLIDATED AUTOMOTIVE PARTS PRODUCERS, INC.
2nd Floor, Guieb Bldg., Pres. Quirino Ave., Malate, Manila
Contact Number/s : (63 2)522-0533
Fax : (63 2)525-6664

 CHAMBER OF AUTOMOTIVE MANUFACTURERS OF THE PHILIPPINES
Suite 1206, 12th Floor, jollibee Center, San Miguel Ave., Pasig City
Contact Number/s : (63 2)632-9733 to 35
Fax : (63 2)632-9941; 631-5313

 PHILIPPINE AUTOMOTIVE FEDERATION , INC.
Suite 1206, 12th Floor, jollibee Center, San Miguel Ave., Pasig City
Contact Number/s : (63 2)632-9733 to 35
Fax : (63 2)632-9941; 631-5313

 PACKAGING INSTITUTE OF THE PHILIPPINES
Rm. 287, 2nd Floor, Comfoods Bldg., Sen. Gil Puyat Ave. cor. Chino Roces Ave., Makati City

Contact Number/s : (63 2)844-5661 to 69 ext. 290 / 361
Fax : (63 2)817-2936
Email : pipmlax@info.com.ph

□ DIRECT SELLING ASSOCIATION OF THE PHILIPPINES
3rd Floor Avon Corporate Center, 144 Legaspi Village, Makati City
Contact Number/s : (63 2)864-2672; 864-2673
Fax : (63 2)892-1179
Email : dsaphils@mozcom.com

□ COCOON PRODUCERS AND SILK MANUFACTURERS
c/o Fiber Industry Development Authority (FIDA), Asiantrust Bank Annex Building, 1424 Quezon Avenue, Quezon City
Contact Number/s : (63 2) 373-7489; 373-7486
Fax : (63 2) 373-9238

□ ROPE AND TWINE SUPPLIERS
c/o Fiber Industry Development Authority (FIDA), Asiantrust Bank Annex Building, 1424 Quezon Avenue, Quezon City
Contact Number/s : (63 2) 373-7489; 373-7486
Fax : (63 2) 373-9238

□ FIBERCRAFT MANUFACTURERS
c/o Fiber Industry Development Authority (FIDA), Asiantrust Bank Annex Building, 1424 Quezon Avenue, Quezon City
Contact Number/s : (63 2) 373-7489; 373-7486
Fax : (63 2) 373-9238

□ SEMICONDUCTOR ELECTRONICS INDUSTRY FOUNDATION, INC. (SEIFI)
Unit 1102 11/F Alabang Business Tower Acacia Avenue, Madrigal Business Park, Ayala Alabang, Muntilupa City

□ METALWORKING INDUSTRIES ASSOCIATION OF THE PHILIPPINES (MANILA CHAPTER)
TESDA Complex, PEVOTI Bldg., Est Service Road, South Expressway, Taguig, Metro Manila
Contact Number/s : (632) 817-4615
Fax : (632) 817-4615

□ FRENCH BUSINESS ASSOCIATION IN THE PHILIPPINES
Unit 1503 Medical Plaza Makati Bldg., Amorsolo cor. Dela Rosa Street, Legaspi Village, Makati City
Contact Number/s : (632)813-9005
Fax : (632)892-6114
Email : info@leclub-fba.org

□ SPANISH CHAMBER OF COMMERCE OF THE PHILIPPINES
Room 42 Zeta II Building. 191 Salcedo St.Legaspi Village. Makati. Metro Manila.
Contact Number/s : 632-8935966
Fax : 632-8926215.
Email : camara@la-camara.com

□ INFORMATION TECHNOLOGY ASSOCIATION OF THE PHILIPPINES
22nd Floor, PCI Equitable Tower, ADB Ave., cor. Poveda St., Ortigas Center, Pasig City
Contact Number/s : (632) 635-3737
Fax : (632) 635-3738
Email : miguel.uy@philippines.ncr.com

□ BEVERAGE INDUSTRY ASSOCIATION OF THE PHILIPPINES
Roco, Bunag, Kapunan, Migallos & Jardeleza Law Offices, 16/F Strata 200 Bldg., Emerald St., Pasig City
Contact Number/s : (632) 631-6171
Fax : (632) 631-9530; 631-6194
Email : rbkmlo@mnl.sequel.net
Contact Person: Atty. Lorna P. Kapunan

□ PHILIPPINE RUBBER INDUSTRIES ASSOCIATION, INC.
c/o Philippine Belt Mfg., Corp., 2nd Floor Siemkang Bldg., 280 Dasmari?as St., Binondo, Manila

□ PHILIPPINE LIQUEFIED PETROLEUM GAS ASSOCIATION OF THE PHILIPPINES
218 San Vicente St., Binondo, Manila
Contact Number/s : (632) 241-2668; 631-3363
Fax : (632) 633-7781
Contact Person: Joselito Asentero

□ NEW PETROLEUM PLAYERS ASSOCIATION OF THE PHILIPPINES
7TH Floor, Cityland Paong Tamo Tower, Km. 8, 2210 Don Chino Roces Ave., Makati City
Contact Number/s : (632) 817-6445
Fax : (632) 817-6421
Email : epc@I-manila.com
Contact Person: Fernando Martinez

□ SAMAHAN SA PILIPINAS NG MGA INDUSTRIYANG KEMIKA (CHEMICAL INDUSTRIES ASSOCIATION OF THE PHILIPPINES)
Unit 2201, Cityland Condominium 10 Tower 1, H.V. dela Costa St., 6815 Ayala Ave. North, Makati City
Contact Number/s : (63 2)812-9854
Fax : (63 2)814-0970
Email : spik@pacific.net.ph

□ SOAP AND DETERGENT ASSOCIATION OF THE PHILIPPINES
SGV I Bldg., 6760 Ayala Ave., Makati City
Contact Number/s : (63 2)891-0307
Fax : (63 2)819-0872; 818-1377

□ PHILIPPINE ASSOCIATION OF ELECTRICAL INDUSTRIES, INC.
Suite 712, Bank of the Philippine Islands Bldg., Plaza Cervantes, Binondo, Manila
Contact Number/s : (63 2)242-1144; 242-1145; 242-1161

□ INTEGRATED FOOD MANUFACTURERS ASSOCIATION OF THE PHILIPPINES
#62 19th St., New Manila Rolling Hills Village, New Manila, Quezon City
Contact Number/s : (63 2)721-1653; 721-9518
Fax : (63 2)721-0144

□ PHILIPPINE FOOD PROCESSORS AND EXPORTERS ASSOCIATION, INC.
Rm. 305, Bahay ng Alumni, Pres. Ramon Magsaysay Ave., University of the Philippines Campus, Diliman, Quezon City
Contact Number/s : (63 2)925-3519; 436-3556 to 57
Fax : (63 2)925-3518; 527-5810
Email : pfdexsec@philonline.com

□ MOTORCYCLE DEVELOPMENT PROGRAM PARTICIPANTS ASSOCIATION, INC.
Suite 1206, 12th Floor, Jollibee Center, San Miguel Ave., Pasig City
Contact Number/s : (63 2)632-9733 to 35
Fax : (63 2)632-9941; 631-5313
Email : mdppa@pacific.net.ph

□ FOREIGN BUYERS ASSOCIATION OF THE PHILIPPINES
Unit 1101 Cityland Condominium 10 Tower I, H. V. dela Costa St., Ayala North, Salcedo Village, Makati City
Contact Number/s : (63 2)892-8492; 813-0813
Fax : (63 2)893-5126

□ PHILIPPINE EXPORT CONFEDERATION, INC.
International Trade Center Complex, Roxas Blvd. Cor. Sen. Gil Puyat Ave., Pasay City
Contact Number/s : (63 2)833-2531 to 34; 833-2550
Fax : (63 2)831-3707; 831-0231

□ PHILIPPINE FRANCHISE ASSOCIATION
Unit 2610 jollibee Plaza, Emerald Ave., Ortigas Center, Pasig City
Contact Number/s : (63 2)687-4180; 636-0825
Fax : (63 2)687-4180; 636-0825

□ PHILIPPINE MARKETING ASSOCIATION, INC.
Suite 2414, Cityland 10, Tower I, 6815 Ayala Ave. cor. H.V. dela Costa, Makati City
Contact Number/s : (63 2)893-7127; 892-3144
Fax : (63 2)892-3261
Email : pma@philonline.com

□ PURCHASING AND MATERIALS MANAGEMENT ASSOCIATION OF THE PHILIPPINES
Unit 1706 A, Stock Exchange Center, East Tower, Exchange Road, Ortigas Center, Pasig City
Contact Number/s : (63 2)634-6632; 634-5942; 634-5955
Fax : (63 2)634-4348
Email : pmmap@info.com.ph
Contact Person: Ms. Imelda S. Carillo, C.P.M.

□ MOTOR VEHICLE PARTS MANUFACTURERS ASSOCIATION OF THE PHILIPPINES, INC.
1043 Zobel Roxas cor. Bautista Sts., Singalong, Metro Manila
Contact Number/s : (02) 521-1621 tro 25 loc. 105/109
Contact Person: Mr. Feliciano L. Torres

□ PRINTING INDUSTRIES ASSOCIATION OF THE PHILIPPINES, INC.
Suite 212 dela Rosa Condominium, 7648 dela Rosa St., Makati City

Contact Number/s : (632) 894-5224; 810-9754/9109
Fax : (632) 894-5224
Email : print@edsamail.com.ph
Contact Person: Atty. Jose Agaton R. Sibal

ACCREDITED FREIGHT FORWARDERS

□ Armi Cargo Express Philippines
Block 30 Lot 5 Golden City Subdivision, Canlalay, Biñan, LAGUNA
Contact Number/s : (6349) 411-1216 Cell No. : (0917) 397-2109
Fax : (6349) 411-1216
Email : armi_phil@yahoo.com
Contact Person: Armi T. Ridad - General Manager

□ CFDN Cargo Services
Block 8 Lot 4&6 Silcas Village, Biñan, LAGUNA
Contact Number/s : (6349) 529-3946
Fax : (6349) 529-3947
Contact Person: Teofila Dimayuga Nishuguchi - Proprietress; Irene D. Masangcay - Operations Manager

□ BJ Star Logistics, Inc.
G/F SGS Building, Humabon Avenue, North Reclamation Area, CEBU CITY, CEBU
Contact Number/s : (6332) 233-2941 (6332) 340-3157
Fax : (6332) 233-2943
Email : bjstar@cebu.pworld.net.ph; bjstar@skyinet.net
Contact Person: Brian S. Urdaneta - President; Ricardo V. Batoto, Jr. - VP for Operations

□ Cebu Logistics, Inc.
Room 208 Ybañez Building, Osmeña Boulevard, CEBU CITY, CEBU
Contact Number/s : (6332) 412-4015
Fax : (6332) 412-4015
Email : ceblogistics@pacific.net.ph
Contact Person: Ma. Rosela Inocencio Romeo - General Manager; Mae Martinez Omega - Operations Manager

□ Central Phils. Freight Forwarders
Room 203-B LDM Building, Legaspi Street, CEBU
Contact Number/s : (6332) 253-6993
Fax : (6332) 253-6991 (6332) 253-6993
Email : cpff@gsilink.com
Contact Person: Geronimo D. Sta. Ana - Managing Director; Antoniosky J. Wycoco - VP-Sales and Operations

□ Fastpak Global Express Corp.
FCTC Building, R. Palma Street, CEBU CITY, CEBU
Contact Number/s : (6332) 255-0912 (6332) 255-0067 (6332) 253-6986
Fax : (6332) 254-5844
Email : fgec@mozcom.com
Contact Person: Felipe O. Casing - Chief Executive Officer; Manuel S. Granada - President

□ PCM Express System, Inc.
PCM House, Patville Subdivision, Ayala Access Road, Banilad, CEBU CITY, CEBU
Contact Number/s : (6332) 231-0342 (6332) 231-0308
Fax : (6332) 231-0353 (6332) 232-0919
Email : golloncebu@nexus.com.ph; pcmcebu@pacific.net.ph
Contact Person: Corazon B. Gollon - General Manager/Finance Manager; Demetrio L. Dampios, Jr. - Operations Manager

□ Purcia Transport System, Inc.
Door #3 Ceniza Commercial Plaza, Highway, MANDAUE CITY, CEBU
Contact Number/s : (6332) 346-3770 (6332) 346-3633 (6332) 346-0144
Fax : (6332) 346-4041
Email : purcia@skyinet.net
Contact Person: Guilbert B. Purcia - President

□ Trusty Cargo, Inc.
Madrigal Compound cor. Legaspi Extension, S. Osmeña Blvd., CEBU CITY, CEBU
Contact Number/s : (6332) 254-2079 (6332) 262-1516
Fax : (6332) 262-1516
Contact Person: Carmelito C. Duterte - Manager

□ G&G Freight Phils., Inc.
Lot 1234 Block 2 Phase 3, Dagat-Dagatan Avenue, Kalookan City, KALOOKAN CITY, METRO MANILA
Contact Number/s : (632) 324-3517 (632) 324-3519 (632) 324-3518
Fax : (632) 324-3518
Contact Person: Augustus Caezar R. Gan - President/General Manager; Joseph J. Villanueva - VP/Marketing

□ OCW Brokerage Corp.
#150 4th Street, 11th Avenue, Grace Park, KALOOKAN CITY, METRO MANILA
Contact Number/s : (632) 366-3544
Fax : (632) 366-3544
Email : ocwbrokerage@pacific.net.ph
Contact Person: Artmar S. Aberin - General Manager

□ Firstline Integrated Resources Co.
Lot 30 Block 11 Mactan Country Homes, Timpolok, Babag 1, LAPU-LAPU CITY, CEBU
Contact Number/s : (6332) 340-6906
Fax : (6332) 340-6906
Email : 1stline@skyinet.net
Contact Person: Elizabeth V. Ybañez - President/General Manager

□ Aeroprime Cargo Forwarding Services, Inc.
#17 Chrysler Street, Greenview Park Subd., Pamplona, LAS PIÑAS, METRO MANILA
Contact Number/s : (632) 874-1547, 871-0851
Fax : (632) 874-5519
Email : aero@i-next.net
Contact Person: Brian R. Balo - President; Josephine R. Balo - Seafreight Supervisor

□ AML Europro International, Inc.
Block 6 Lot 28 America Avenue, Southland, Talon, LAS PIÑAS, METRO MANILA
Contact Number/s : (632) 568-9603
Fax : (632) 568-9603
Contact Person: Alexander M. Alatag - President/ General Manager; Nancy C. Bocalbos - VP/Operations Manager

□ BBM Freight Services, Inc.
#9 Mabolo corner Atis Street, Golden Acres Subdivision, LAS PIÑAS, METRO MANILA
Contact Number/s : (632) 806-7604
Fax : (632) 806-7604
Contact Person: Reynaldo Montemayor - President; Rosabel Quibal - Operations Head

□ Capital Cargo Company
#201 Lozada Street, Phase 2A, Gatchalian Subdivision, Manuyo Dos, LAS PIÑAS, METRO MANILA
Contact Number/s : (632) 825-7439
Fax : (632) 820-2858
Email : capitalcargo@edsamail.com.ph
Contact Person: Wilma A. Bautista - General Manager

□ DEA Brokerage Corporation
B-20 L-14 ML Vallejo St., BF Resort Village, LAS PIÑAS, METRO MANILA
Contact Number/s : (632) 875-3091 (632) 873-4192
Fax : (632) 873-4192
Dolora E. Agbulos-Quimio - President/General Manager

□ Kelsey Marie Int'l. Ltd. Co.
Vatican Drive, B.F. Homes, LAS PIÑAS, METRO MANILA
Contact Number/s : (632) 543-7417 (632) 801-8789 (632) 801-0263
Fax : (632) 801-0263
Email : philippinecargo@juno.com
Contact Person: Marie Pinky Rose P. Cabradilla - Gen. Partner; Girlie Padilla-Ramirez - Operations Manager

□ MC Plus, Inc.
#9 Mabolo cor. Atis Streets, Golden Acres Subdivision, Talon Uno, LAS PIÑAS, METRO MANILA
Contact Number/s : (632) 806-3631
Fax : (632) 806-3631
Email : cpmanila@compass.com.ph
Contact Person: Rebecca N. Vigal - President; Rosabel C. Quibal - Operations Head

□ Mika Customs Broker, Inc.

Blk.53 Lot 2 & 4, Melanie Marquez cor. Onelia Jose, BF Resort, LAS PIÑAS, METRO MANILA
Contact Number/s : (632) 874-3090
Fax : (632) 874-3090
Contact Person: Lolita L. Tadachi - President/General Manager; Benjamin S. Lampa - Operations Manager

□ Nes Cargo Express International Corporation
NES Cargo Building, Opal Road, Manuela Homes Subdivision, Talon V along Marcos Avenue, LAS PIÑAS, METRO MANILA
Contact Number/s : (632) 800-0031 (632) 806-1497
Fax : (632) 806-3450 (632) 806-4160
Email : forwarding@nescargo.com; sales@nescargo.com
Contact Person: Nestor E. Salvania - President/General Manager

□ Transpac Container Line, Inc.
G/F Azucena Building, 255 National Road, Pamplona, LAS PIÑAS, METRO MANILA
Contact Number/s : (632) 874-5357 (632) 871-0979
Fax : (632) 873-5937 (632) 871-0979
Email : transpac@qinet.net
Contact Person: Winfred A. Paler - President

□ Transpacific Cargo Transport Phils. (formerly Ramsey Cargo Express)
Block 26, Lot 8, Carolyn Masibay St., BF Resort Village, LAS PIÑAS, METRO MANILA
Contact Number/s : (632) 873-4107 (632) 874-3092 (632) 874-3628
Fax : (632) 874-8765
Contact Person: Efren G. Eugenio - President/General Manager

□ Airlift Asia, Inc. - Cebu Branch
Mactan Export Processing Zone, Mactan, Cebu, MACTAN AIRPORT, CEBU
Contact Number/s : (6332) 340-2866
Fax : (6332) 340-2911
Email : info@aai.com.ph
Contact Person: Eric R. Sanchez - Executive Director; Marivic E. Esmero - VP-Sales, Customer Service & Logistics

□ Aboitiz Orient Shipping Corporation
4/F Batungbacal Building, 7577 Dela Rosa St., near cor. Pasong Tamo, MAKATI, METRO MANILA
Contact Number/s : (632) 867-4546 to 52
Fax : (632) 867-4570
Stefan Schmitz - General Manager; Mario N. Hukom - Marketing Manager; Lani P. Amul - perations Supervisor

□ Accord CSA Shipping Philippines, Inc. (formerly Accord Shipping (NVOCC) Phils., Inc.)
3/F Pac-Atlantic Centre, 2917 Finlandia Street, San Isidro, MAKATI, METRO MANILA
Contact Number/s : (632) 843-9433
Fax : (632) 843-7060 (632) 887-0643
Email : accordph@i-next.net
Contact Person: Jose Antonio P. Castro - General Manager

□ Ace Navigation Co., Inc.
6/F King's Court Building 1, #2129 Chino Roces Avenue cor. Dela Rosa Street, MAKATI, METRO MANILA
Contact Number/s : (632) 811-2251 to 54
Fax : (632) 817-1117 (632) 811-1129
Email : acenav@i-next.net
Contact Person: Rodolfo F. Pamintuan - President/ General Manager; Rondel Jake B. Castillo - Forwarding Manager; Danilo I. Canete - VP-Marketing

□ Albatrax Philippines Forwarder
Suite 301, #5438 Don Tim Building, South Superhighway, Bangkal, MAKATI, METRO MANILA
Contact Number/s : (0916) 335-0869
Email : ph@aol.com
Contact Person: Ma. Doreen L. Betinol - Executive Director

□ Asia Pacific Express Corp.
10th Floor, Sterling Centre, De la Rosa corner Esteban Streets, Legaspi Village, MAKATI, METRO MANILA
Contact Number/s : (632) 810-7844 (632) 810-7855

Fax : (632) 893-2113
Email : nvocc@apexmnl.com.ph
Eun G. Chang - President/CEO; Amelita D. Semilla - Operations & Admin. Director

□ Asiaworld Transport Phils. Co., Inc.
1002 Cityland 10 Tower 2, H.V. Dela Costa Street, Salcedo Village, MAKATI, METRO MANILA
Contact Number/s : (632) 812-7707 (632) 812-7678
Fax : (632) 813-2701
Email : pafasiaworld@pacific.net.ph
Contact Person: Pedro A. Fernandez - President

□ Aweca Int'l. Forwarding Corp.
Room 314 Narra Building, 2276 Pasong Tamo Extension,, MAKATI, METRO MANILA
Contact Number/s : (632) 817-0814 (632) 817-0618
Fax : (632) 892-8533
Email : aweca@compass.com.ph
Contact Person: Eredito P. Feliciano - President; Vivian C. David - VP-Operations

□ C2K Express, Inc.
Stall 131 G/F Buendia Shopping Plaza, Buendia, MAKATI, METRO MANILA
Contact Number/s : (632) 817-3519 (632) 817-2466 (632) 817-2533 (632)
Fax : (632) 817-2533
Contact Person: Daniel B. Tamayo - General Manager

□ CDR Express International, Inc.
#1737B Dian Street, Palanan, MAKATI, METRO MANILA
Contact Number/s : (632) 834-6942 (632) 551-8350
Fax : (632) 551-8350
Contact Person: Alicia D. Ramos - President; Janeth R. Baldo - Manager

□ Daito Nan-Shin Shipping Co., Inc.
3/F, Princess Bldg., 104 Esteban Street, Legaspi Village, MAKATI, METRO MANILA
Contact Number/s : (632) 812-6481 (632) 892-1608 (632) 893-0636
Fax : (632) 817-2388
Contact Person: Mr. Kenji Abe - Managing Director; Marissa Remigio - Chief Executive Officer mariz@pworld.net.ph (mktg./proj. cargoes); impex@pworld.net.ph (impt./expt.) ; dnsbrokr@pworld.net.ph (customs brokerage) ; dnsacctg@pworld.net.ph (accounting)

□ Emerald Forwarding Corp.
2301 Lising Building, Pasong Tamo Extension, MAKATI, METRO MANILA
Contact Number/s : (632) 888-4770
Fax : (632) 888-4783
Email : emerald@compass.com.ph
Contact Person: Reynald G. Mata - Logistics Manager

□ EW Express International Services, Inc.
Soundtrack Building, 7447 Santillan Street, MAKATI, METRO MANILA
Contact Number/s : (632) 759-2645 (632) 759-2646
Fax : (632) 894-1295
Email : eweis@tri-isys.com; ewxpress@tri-isys.com
Contact Person: Rafaela N. Suplig - General Manager/Marketing; Walter A. Mamaradlo - Operations Manager

□ Fame Cargo International, Inc.
G-37 South Star Plaza, South Superhighway, Brgy. Bangkal, MAKATI, METRO MANILA
Contact Number/s : (632) 813-1937
Fax : (632) 813-1937
Contact Person: Edisa V. Serranilla - President/ General Manager; Gil T. Villarin - Operations Manager

□ Fame Express, Inc.
#2822 D&E Borneo Street, Brgy. San Isidro, MAKATI, METRO MANILA
Contact Number/s : (632) 729-7703
Fax : (632) 889-4740
Contact Person: Salvacion E. Gan - President

□ Famous Pacific Forwarding Phils., Inc.
Rms. 1805-1806 Cityland 10 Tower 2, Corner Valero & De la Costa Streets, Salcedo Village, MAKATI, METRO MANILA

Contact Number/s : (632) 812-2688 (632) 813-2904 (632) 893-9891 (632)
Fax : (632) 893-9892
Contact Person: Menchie A. Castillo - Import Director; Marina M. Rollan - Export Director

□ Freight Concepts Int'l., Inc.
Unit 1911 Herrera cor. Valero Streets, Salcedo Village, MAKATI, METRO MANILA
Contact Number/s : (632) 810-9498 (632) 810-9384
Fax : (632) 810-9420
Email : fcii@info.com.ph
Contact Person: Agnes Connie A. Tabligan - Managing Director

□ Freight Dynamics, Inc.
#98 Herrera Tower, Herrera St., Salcedo Village, MAKATI, METRO MANILA
Contact Number/s : (632) 524-2709
Fax : (632) 845-0735
Email : gracia@tri-sys.com
Contact Person: Alejandro B. Chua - President; Emmanuel P. Villote - VP-Operations

□ Freight Management Worldwide Services, Inc.
18/F Unit 1801, Antel 2000 Corporate Center, 121 Valero Street, Salcedo Village, MAKATI, METRO MANILA
Contact Number/s : (632) 887-5551
Fax : (632) 887-5539
Contact Person: Jose de Asis - President; Juan Miguel de Asis - Exec. Asst. for Operations & Finance

□ Freightbest Int'l., Inc.
1358 Apolinario cor. Lacuña, Bangkal, MAKATI, METRO MANILA
Contact Number/s : (632) 887-3010 (632) 843-2801
Fax : (632) 843-2801
Contact Person: Kennedy M. Dionisio - President; Mario M. Dela Rosa - General Manager

□ GAC Shipping & Cargo Systems Philippines, Inc.
G/F Zuellig Annex Building, Malugay Street, MAKATI, METRO MANILA
Contact Number/s : (632) 892-2713 to 26
Fax : (632) 893-4028 (632) 812-2628 (632) 867-3396
Email : manila.ops@gulfagencycompany.com
Contact Person: Jaime F. Cuerva - President; Cecilio B. De Leon - Seafreight Manager; Antonio R. Yu-Asensi - Airfreight Manager; Rommel H. Yuzon - Operations Manager (International Freight Forwarding/Brokerage)

□ General Signal Industries, Inc.
#2301 Lising Building, Pasong Tamo Extension, MAKATI, METRO MANILA
Contact Number/s : (632) 888-4770 to 76
Fax : (632) 813-3034
Email : gsii@compass.com.ph
Contact Persons: George Schulze, Jr. - President; Reynald G. Mata - Logistics Manager

□ Great Links Logistics Int'l. Corp.
2/F 3818 Mascardo Street, MAKATI, METRO MANILA
Contact Number/s : (632) 899-1107
Fax : (632) 896-0666
Contact Person: Jaime A. Roxas - President/Chief Exec. Officer; Ferdinand A. Roxas - Exec. Vice-President/Chief Operating Officer

□ Holy Spirit Freight Forwarder, Inc.
4495 Calatagan St., Palanan, MAKATI, METRO MANILA
Contact Number/s : (632) 831-0377 (632) 551-0195
Fax : (632) 551-0195
Carmencita Banzon - Managing Director; Ethel Baclig - Marketing Manager export-U.S. branch

□ Icon Reefer Corporation
Unit 526 Valero Plaza Building, 124 Valero Street, Salcedo Village, MAKATI, METRO MANILA
Contact Number/s : (632) 840-0581 (632) 840-0632
Fax : (632) 840-0632
Email : iconreefer@yahoo.com

Contact Person: Filomena M. Lim - President; Ma. Elena V. Dee - Vice-President

 ICS Translink (Phils) Inc.
Unit 439 Cityland Pasong Tamo Tower, #2210 Don Chino Roces Avenue, MAKATI, METRO MANILA
Contact Number/s : (632) 892-0961 to 66
Fax : (632) 892-1071 to 72
Email : tsimnl@translinkshipping.com.ph
Contact Person: Armi H. Laya - President; Carina R. Domingo - Executive Director

 ICS-Phils. Freight Logistics, Inc.
Unit 435 Cityland Pasong Tamo Tower, #2210 Don Chino Roces Avenue, MAKATI, METRO MANILA
Contact Number/s : (632) 892-0961 to 63
Fax : (632) 892-1071 to 72
Contact Person: Margarita A.L. Santero - President; Carina R. Domingo - Managing Director

 Intertranz Container Lines, Inc.
#906 88 Corporate Center, Sedeño cor. Valero Street, MAKATI, METRO MANILA
Contact Number/s : (632) 752-5721 to 24 Cell. No.: (0917) 521-2868
Fax : (632) 752-5724 (632) 752-6096 to 97
Email : atumibay@info.com.ph; tranzinc@info.com.ph
Contact Person: Josefina F. Tumibay - Managing Director

 Jugro Transport International Phils., Corporation (formerly Unsworth Transport Int'l. Phils.)
3818 A. Mascardo St., corner Pasong Tamo St., MAKATI, METRO MANILA
Contact Number/s : (632) 895-5515 (632) 896-0666
Fax : (632) 896-0666 (632) 896-6478
Email : jugro@jugro.com
Contact Person: Julio G. Roxas, Jr. - President/Chief Executive Officer; Jaime A. Roxas - Executive Vice-President/COO

 Konoike Transport (Philippines) , Inc.
Unit 1506 Medical Plaza, dela Rosa Street cor. Amorsolo Street, Legaspi Village, MAKATI, METRO MANILA
Contact Number/s : (632) 752-4727
Fax : (632) 812-3813
Email : ktcmnl@skyinet.net
Contact Person: Hirokazu Iwahashi - President; Marilou B. Macabenta - Operations Supervisor

 Kunawarra Logistics, Inc.
Unit 402 Heart Tower Condominium, Valero Street, Salcedo Village, MAKATI, METRO MANILA
Contact Number/s : (632) 893-0280
Fax : (632) 817-2528
Contact Person: Marilou M. Robles - General Manager

 Lima Logistics Services, Inc.
3/F Solid House Building, 2285 Don Chino Roces Ave. Extension (formerly Pasong Tamo), MAKATI, METRO MANILA
Contact Number/s : (632) 893-7170
Fax : (632) 893-7185
Contact Person: Tomas I. Alcantara - President/ Chairman; Lewis E. Ortega - Manager, Brokerage & Freight Forwarding

 Longway Lines Phils., Inc.
Suite 2D, Valuepoint Condominium, 227 Salcedo St., Legaspi Village, MAKATI, METRO MANILA
Contact Number/s : (632) 813-3707 (632) 894-4106 (632) 892-9085
Fax : (632) 818-0802
Email : longway@info.com.ph; lwyphile@info.com.ph
Contact Person: Rudy Valerio - President/General Manager

 Mac-Nels Shipping (Phils.) , Inc.
Unit 807 Herrera Tower, Herrera cor. Valero Street, Salcedo Village, MAKATI, METRO MANILA
Contact Number/s : (632) 843-4424
Fax : (632) 817-1506 (632) 753-3457
Email : macnels@access.net.ph; macnels@info.com.ph

Contact Person: Ma. Luz F. Caliwag - General Manager; Marcelina G. Castillo - Office Manager

 Macshop Distribution Co., Inc.
1193 Vito Cruz Extension, corner Zapote Street, MAKATI, METRO MANILA
Contact Number/s : (632) 897-1630 (632) 897-1631
Fax : (632) 897-1617
Contact Person: Cecilio P. Galang - President

 Manila Logistic, Inc.
Unit 1102 Cityland Pasong Tamo Tower, Pio del Pilar, MAKATI, METRO MANILA
Contact Number/s : (632) 757-3856
Fax : (632) 757-3855
Email : manilalog@pacific.net.ph
Apollo V. Petallano - Chief Operating Officer; Miguel M. Villamor - VP, Operations

 Master Container Lines Phils., Inc.
Room 309, 3/F, Executive Center Building, Sen. Gil Puyat Ave., MAKATI, METRO MANILA
Contact Number/s : (632) 750-2814 to 21
Fax : (632) 750-2710 to 11
Email : gina@master2002.com.ph
Contact Person: Gina S. Pacquing - Managing Director

 MBT Int'l. Freight Forwarder, Inc.
2nd Floor, Unit 3 NYS Building, 1156 Chino Roces Avenue, San Antonio Village, MAKATI, METRO MANILA
Contact Number/s : (632) 895-1158 (632) 897-1001 (632) 895-1288 (632)
Fax : (632) 895-1186
Email : mbt@i-next.net; lucille@fastmail.i-next.net
Contact Person: Melinda T. Gimmi - President/Gen. Manager; Lucille W. Dejaño - Operations Manager

 MD International Forwarding, Inc.
Unit 206 Abimir Place, Dian Street, Palanan, MAKATI, METRO MANILA
Contact Number/s : (632) 550-1061
Fax : (632) 550-1047
Email : mdifi@asia.com
Maria Teresa Francisco - President; Davis de Joya - General Manager & Operations Manager

 Miracle Container Lines Philippines, Inc.
Suite 204, Heart Tower Condominium, 108 Valero St., Salcedo Village, MAKATI, METRO MANILA
Contact Number/s : (632) 818-6567
Fax : (632) 818-2507
Lino T. Cabasag - General Manager

 Misaki Freight Logistics, Inc.
#209 Fedman Suites, 199 Salcedo St., Legaspi Village, MAKATI, METRO MANILA
Contact Number/s : (632) 893-1191
Fax : (632) 813-6405
Email : misakiinc@hotmail.com; misaki@edsamail.com.ph
Contact Person: Jed Patrick E. Mabilog - CEO and President; Brigido A. Tac-an - Operations Manager; Samuel C. Albania, Jr. - Administrative Manager

 Mission Movers, Inc.
Room 203 RS Building, 1190 Vito Cruz Extension, MAKATI, METRO MANILA
Contact Number/s : (632) 896-2497 (632) 896-2482 (632) 895-1817
Fax : (632) 897-0614 (632) 890-8768
Contact Person: Lourdes H. De Paz - General Manager

 Mitsui-Soko (Philippines) , Inc.
6th Floor King's Court II Building, 2129 Chino Roces Avenue, Legaspi Village, MAKATI, METRO MANILA
Contact Number/s : (632) 811-2716 to 21
Email : mitsoko@skyinet.net
Contact Person: Jonathan Fung - General Manager; Noli G. Valera - Administrative Manager

 Naigai Nitto Logistics Phils., Inc.
3rd Floor Princess Building, 104 Esteban Street, Legaspi Village, MAKATI, METRO MANILA

Contact Number/s : (632) 893-5495 (632) 812-8615
Fax : (632) 817-2388
Contact Person: Marissa E. Remigio - President; Dennis M. Ortega - Operations/Logistics Manager

 Nippon Express Phils., Corp.
15th Floor Valero Tower, 122 Valero Street, Salcedo Village, MAKATI, METRO MANILA
Contact Number/s : (632) 751-9308 (632) 812-5959
Fax : (632) 893-7969 (632) 750-5232 (632) 812-8850 (632)
Contact Person: Mr. Atsushi Kitayama - General Manager, Ocean Cargo Branch

 Pac-Atlantic Lines (Phils) , Inc.
2/F Pac-Atlantic Building, #2917 Finlandia Street, San Isidro, MAKATI, METRO MANILA
Contact Number/s : (632) 843-6689
Fax : (632) 843-7080 (632) 843-7095 (632) 843-6932
Email : customercare@pac-atlantic.com.ph
Ramon T. de Leon - President/Managing Director; Jose Alberto S. Garcia - General Manager

 Pelican Customs Brokerage Corporation
Room 900A Don V. Madrigal Building, Ayala Avenue, MAKATI, METRO MANILA
Contact Number/s : (632) 891-5984
Fax : (632) 891-5985
Contact Person: Antonio A. Tuazon - General Manager

 Penanshin Shipping Phils., Inc.
Unit 1710 Herrera Tower, Herrera corner Valero Street, Salcedo Street, Salcedo Village, MAKATI, METRO MANILA
Contact Number/s : (632) 817-2628
Fax : (632) 753-3650
Email : penmnl@access.net.ph
Contact Person: Helen B. Benitez - Vice President; Marcelina G. Castillo - Office Manager; Filicidad Gonzales - Export Supervisor; Lucil Umali - Import Supervisor

 Port Jersey Shipping Industries, Inc.
8061 Estrella Avenue, San Antonio Village, 1203 Makati City, MAKATI, METRO MANILA
Contact Number/s : (632) 895-9920 (632) 899-5462 (632) 899-4184
Fax : (632) 890-3665
Contact Person: Ramon C. Ungco - President/General Manager; Marianito A. Estal - Admin. & Operations Manager

 Pronto Express Distributions, Inc.
G/F 1195-C Doña Potenciana Building, Corner Pasong Tamo & Yakal Streets, MAKATI, METRO MANILA
Contact Number/s : (632) 812-3801 to 06 (632) 817-3379 (632) 817-7432
Fax : (632) 815-4642
Email : pronexdi@philonline.com.ph; babypedi@evoserve.com
Contact Person: Ms. Florita M. Deomampo - President/General Manager; Owen Y. Lee - Chairman of the Board

 PTC Agency & Transport, Inc.
First Maritime Place Building, 7458-7460 Bagtican Street, San Antonio Village, MAKATI, METRO MANILA
Contact Number/s : (632) 898-1111 (632) 898-1181 (632) 898-1182
Fax : (632) 898-1182
Email : ptccom@pacific.net.ph; ptcat@pacific.net.ph
Contact Person: Carlos C. Salinas - President; Divina M. Moises - Manager

 Roadrunner Global Transport Corporation
G6-7 South Star Plaza, South Superhighway, Bangkal, MAKATI, METRO MANILA
Contact Number/s : (632) 813-1356 (632) 867-1351 (632) 894-2227
Fax : (632) 894-2227
Email : rdunner@compass.com.ph
Contact Person: Maria Teresa R. Yusi - General Manager; Knowell Mercado - Operations Manager

 Sankyu Logistics Philippines, Inc.
8/F Salamin Building, Salcedo Street, Legaspi Village, MAKATI, METRO MANILA
Contact Number/s : (632) 759-3630
Fax : (632) 759-3625

Email : filsancs@globenet.com.ph
Contact Person: Juan F. Luces - General Manager/Operations Manager; Renato C. T. Leon - Administration Manager

 Sapphire Cargo Movers, Inc.
3/F Evekal Bldg., 855 Pasay City Road, Cor. Amorsolo St., MAKATI, METRO MANILA
Contact Number/s : (632) 817-8391 to 97 (632) 817-9913 to 14 (632) 81
Fax : (632) 819-1854 (632) 817-3444
Contact Person: Ernesto S. Levanza - President/General Manager

 Sealinkage International, Inc.
Room 408 Comfoods Building, Sen. Gil Puyat Avenue cor. Pasong Tamo, MAKATI, METRO MANILA
Contact Number/s : (632) 812-0125 (632) 812-0720
Fax : (632) 812-6039
Email : veeseal@info.com.ph
Contact Person: Luzviminda A. Natividad - President/General Manager

 Seaswift Int'l. Phils., Inc.
Room 408 Comfoods Building, Sen. Gil Puyat cor. Pasong Tamo Street, MAKATI, METRO MANILA
Contact Number/s : (632) 812-0720 (632) 812-0757
Fax : (632) 812-6039
Email : Seaswift@info.com.ph
Contact Person: Luzviminda A. Natividad - President/General Manager

 Sparrow Freight Phils., Inc.
Room 408 Comfoods Building, Sen. Gil Puyat Ave. corner Pasong Tamo, MAKATI, METRO MANILA
Contact Number/s : (632) 812-0690
Fax : (632) 812-6039
Email : mktg.sparrow@axti.com
Contact Person: Luzviminda A. Natividad - President & General Manager

 STAMM International Inc.
STAMM House, 3407 Gen. Lim Street, Bangkal, MAKATI, METRO MANILA
Contact Number/s : (632) 843-5521 to 24
Fax : (632) 887-7804 (632) 845-3115
Email : stamm@stamm.com.ph
Urs Hebersen - Managing Director; Doris P. Torres - General Manager

 Technotrans Express Logistics, Inc.
2/F Royal Regent Building, #5085 Filmore Street, Palanan, MAKATI, METRO MANILA
Contact Number/s : (632) 551-8369 to 72
Fax : (632) 834-2716
Email : techno@starnet.net.ph
Contact Person: Gualberto G. Abella - President; Hector A. Garcia - General Manager

 Tell Me Trans Corp.
4th Floor Alscophil Building, 2053 Edison Street, MAKATI, METRO MANILA
Contact Number/s : (632) 638-7557
Fax : (632) 637-0773
Email : tellmetrans@hanmail.net
Contact Person: Bernard A. Tumaman - General Manager and Chief Operating Officer; Catherine S. Trinidad - Assistant General Manager; Edwin S. Quind0 - Shipping Manager

 Three Star Forwarder
#4262 Emilia Street, Palanan, MAKATI, METRO MANILA
Contact Number/s : (632) 552-9375
Fax : (632) 552-9247
Contact Person: Lorna Collado-Nagashima - Owner/Proprietress

 Toyomizu Corporation
Room 202 CAEG Building, 7611 Dela Rosa Street, MAKATI, METRO MANILA
Contact Number/s : (632) 812-1882 (632) 812-1911 (632) 812-1913
Fax : (632) 812-1915
Email : toyomizu@compass.com.ph
Contact Person: Mercedita C. Manuel - Managing Director; Dolores J. Viray - Finance & Marketing Manager; Victoria C. Reyes - Operations Manager

 Transcend Cargo Express, Inc.

#2739 Heneral Capinpin Street, Bangkal, MAKATI, METRO MANILA
Contact Number/s : (632) 889-4955 to 57 (632) 889-3638 to 39
Fax : (632) 889-4847
Email : tcei@nsclub.net
Contact Person: Robin E. Tenefrancia - President; Placido E. Ramos - Operations Manager-Brokerage

- Wellcross Brokerage Corporation
Unit 806 8/F Cityland Herrera Tower, Herrera St., Salcedo Village, MAKATI, METRO MANILA
Contact Number/s : (632) 817-1404 (632) 813-0140
Fax : (632) 753-2655
Contact Person: Chris S. Bracamonte - President/General Manager; Ruel Francis L. Cabral - Vice-President/Operations Manager

- World Logistics Group, Inc.
Penthouse Unit, JMP Building, 1754 Nicanor Garcia Street, MAKATI, METRO MANILA
Contact Number/s : (632) 890-2682 (632) 890-2963
Fax : (632) 890-2681
Email : world@vasia.com
Contact Person: Antonio Leo P. Miguel - President/General Manager

- Worldwide Seafreight Agency, Inc.
S-219 South Star Plaza, South Superhighway, MAKATI, METRO MANILA
Contact Number/s : (632) 843-9133
Fax : (632) 840-2201
Email : veeseal@info.com.ph
Contact Person: Luzviminda A. Natividad - President & General Manager

- WSA Lines Phils., Inc.
Suite 304 Heart Tower Condominium, #108 Valero Street, Salcedo Village, MAKATI, METRO MANILA
Contact Number/s : (632) 892-3388
Fax : (632) 813-6981
Email : wsaphils@qinet.net
Contact Person: Jovencio Abila - Managing Director; Lino T. Cabasag - Asst. General Manager

- Bestway International Brokers Forwarders, Inc.
Unit 301 57-A Esteban Street, MANDALUYONG, METRO MANILA
Contact Number/s : (632) 749-9658 (632) 301-1052 (632) 301-1326
Fax : (632) 749-9675
Contact Person: Jon D. De Villa - President/General Manager

- Highlights Express Air and Ocean Cargo Co.
UG02 Cityland Pioneer, Pioneer Street, MANDALUYONG, METRO MANILA
Contact Number/s : (632) 746-7028 (632) 638-2936
Fax : (632) 746-4217
Contact Person: Josephine M. Capistrano - Manager

- Silver Duck Shipping Corp.
806 Globe Telecom Plaza, Pioneer Street, MANDALUYONG, METRO MANILA
Contact Number/s : (632) 636-4892 (632) 636-4899
Fax : (632) 636-4909
Contact Person: Abelardo Santos - President; Dominador Bautista, Jr. - Manager (Operations & Warehousing Division)

- Tai Ping Enterprises
#146 Pinatubo Street, MANDALUYONG, METRO MANILA
Contact Number/s : (632) 531-1505
Fax : (632) 531-2392
Contact Person: Eduardo Espiritu Ong - Owner/General Manager

- Admiral Overseas Shipping Corp. of Cebu
Room 208 NDI Commercial Complex, A.S. Fortuna Street, MANDAUE CITY, CEBU
Contact Number/s : (6332) 346-7958-59, 344-9622
Fax : (6332) 346-7950
Email : aosc@mozcom.com; aoscceb@mozcom.com

Contact Person: Romeo P. Dilla, Jr. - President & General Manager; Jocelyn P. Briones - Officer-in-Charge

□ Bluetrans Cargo Systems, Inc.
Room 317 N & N Cortes Arcade, A.C. Cortes Avenue, MANDAUE CITY, CEBU
Contact Number/s : (6332) 345-5803
Fax : (6332) 345-5804
Contact Person: Ma. Lourdes G. Buning - President

□ CFS Container Freight Services, Inc.
Suite 305 N & N Cortes Arcade, AC Cortes Avenue, MANDAUE CITY, CEBU
Contact Number/s : (6332) 344-7837 to 38 (6332) 420-1879
Fax : (6332) 344-7839
Email : pweecfs@cebu.weblinq.com
Amado Jose R. Garcia - President; Edith B. Demain - Customs Service Rep. - Export; Joy M. Enoroba - Customs Service Rep. - Import

□ FB Logistics Transport, Inc.
Suite 216 KRC Building, Subangdaku, MANDAUE CITY, CEBU
Contact Number/s : (6332) 345-2915
Fax : (6332) 345-2916
Contact Person: Bimbong O. Megio - President

□ Goodspeed Int'l. Forwarder, Inc.
Unit 2, Engineer Victor Yap Bldg., Hernan Cortes St., Wireless, MANDAUE CITY, CEBU
Contact Number/s : (6332) 346-3193 (6332) 345-6130
Fax : (6332) 345-6141
Email : gifi@cbu.skyinet.net
Contact Person: Stanley L. Uang - VP/General Manager; Ester C. Dela Pena - Sales & Operations Manager

□ Prestige Trading and Freight Services
Door 10 Villamor Arcade, S.B. Cabahug Street, Ibabao, MANDAUE CITY, CEBU
Contact Number/s : (6332) 345-8953 (6332) 345-8983 (6332) 422-5567
Fax : (6332) 345-6454
Email : presdcl@skyinet.net

Contact Person: Merlina G. Sen0 - Proprietress/Managing Director; Elma M. Jabil - Operations Manager

□ RMA Cargo Logistics, Inc.
No. 888 A.C. Cortes Avenue, MANDAUE CITY, CEBU
Contact Number/s : (6332) 343-6771 (6332) 343-6772
Fax : (6332) 343-6773
Email : rmaropo@pacific.net.ph
Contact Person: Romel M. Aropo - President & General Manager

□ 617 International Cargo Forwarders, Inc.
Room 303 Republic Supermarket Bldg., F. Torres Street, Sta. Cruz, MANILA, METRO MANILA
Contact Number/s : (632) 733-0681, 733-8186 loc. 27
Fax : (632) 733-6129
Contact Person: Erlinda U. Marinas - President/Licensed Customs Broker; Remedios A. Lopez - Operations Manager

□ 8 Kids International Logistics Corporation
Unit 108 Ledesma Building, Real cor. General Luna Streets, Intramuros, MANILA, METRO MANILA
Contact Number/s : (632) 527-4069
Fax : (632) 338-2240
Contact Person: Ma. Teresa R. Yusi - General Manager; Erlinda Sapo - Operations Manager

□ A & L Cargo Int'l Corp.
Room 468 Regina Building, 410 Escolta, MANILA, METRO MANILA
Contact Number/s : (632) 241-5666, 241-5857
Fax : (632) 243-1601
Contact Person: Ms. Ariadne M. Fulay - President; Lina W. Lim - Vice-President

□ ABG Transport Corporation
Room 520 FEMII Building, Aduana St., Intramuros, MANILA, METRO MANILA
Contact Number/s : (632) 527-6972, 527-5277, 301-1103 to 05, 527-6957
Fax : (632) 527-6957
Email : abgcustombro@eastern.com.ph

Contact Person: Arnulfo B. Garnica - General Manager; Vivencio T. Benavides, Jr. - Operations Manager

 ABI Customs Brokerage
Suite 405 Gedisco Terrace Bldg., 1148 Roxas Blvd., Ermita, MANILA, METRO MANILA
Contact Number/s : (632) 528-1567, 522-8235
Fax : (632) 528-1567
Contact Person: Abelardo T. Pineda - President

 Absolute Logistics Phils., Inc.
Ground Floor, Champ Building, Anda Circle, Port Area, MANILA, METRO MANILA
Contact Number/s : (632) 404-2254, 404-2147
Fax : (632) 404-2267
Email : absolutelog@edsamail.com.ph; rsalas@edsamail.com.ph
Contact Person: Ferdinand V. Ferrer - President; Rosalie L. Salas - General Manager

 Acestar Int'l. Service Corp.
5/F ECJ Condominium, cor. Real and Arzobispo Street, Intramuros, MANILA, METRO MANILA
Contact Number/s : (632) 527-3243 to 44, 527-1605
Fax : (632) 527-7324 to 25
Email : acestar@pacific.net.ph
Contact Person: Roderico F. SalutillO - President; Analyn A. SalutillO - General Manager; Edwin Abia - Operations/Export & Import

 Aduana International Freight Forwarding Services, Inc.
Suite 502 Metropolitan Tower, 1746 A. Mabini Street, Malate, MANILA, METRO MANILA
Contact Number/s : (632) 523-1580, 536-4689
Fax : (632) 303-2611
Email : aduana@skyinet.net; aduanaintl@skyinet.net
Contact Person: Ma. Lourdes M. Austria - President; Antonio V. Marfil - General Manager; Olivia M. DomingO - Operations Manager

 AJ&J Cargo Movers, Inc.
Unit-C G/F Ramagi Bldg., 1081 Pedro Gil St. Paco, MANILA, METRO MANILA
Contact Number/s : (632) 524-3829 (632) 525-3419
Fax : (632) 522-3381
Email : ajjcmi@vasia.com
Contact Person: Alfonso C. Obsum - President; Vicente C. Gloria - Operations Manager

 Anviro Forwarders, Inc.
Unit A 9&10 State Condominium III, 1148 Romualdez Street, Paco, MANILA, METRO MANILA
Contact Number/s : (632) 247-7833 (632) 524-2244 (632) 524-2291
Fax : (632) 525-6765
Contact Person: Angeles R. Robis - Chairman & CEO Director; Agresio Salvador - Marketing Manager

 APL Logistics Philippines, Inc. (formerly American Consolidation Services (Phils.) , Inc.)
Grd. Floor, Velco Center, Corner Chicago and 13th Streets, Port Area, MANILA, METRO MANILA
Contact Number/s : (632) 528-1021 to 29
Fax : (632) 528-0010
Contact Person: Tita R. Rivera-Lim - General Manager

 APM Int'l. Freight Forwarders, Inc.
2206 Jose Abad Santos corner Batangas St., Tondo, MANILA, METRO MANILA
Contact Number/s : (632) 251-6379 (632) 251-6384
Fax : (632) 256-8773
Email : apmff@I-manila.com.ph
Contact Person: Rolando P. Ilaga - General Manager

 Archon Cargo Express
2/F #22, 1007 P. Noval Street, Sampaloc, MANILA, METRO MANILA
Contact Number/s : (632) 736-0894 (632) 493-4312
Fax : (632) 736-0894

Contact Person: Vanessa M. Miclat - Proprietress/Manager

□ Asia Cargo Container Line, Inc.
Rooms 511, 5/F Phoenix Bldg., Recoletos St., Intramuros, MANILA, METRO MANILA
Contact Number/s : (632) 527-2337
Fax : (632) 527-5439
Email : acclimnl@pworld.net.ph
Contact Person: Armand S. Ng - General Manager; Richard S. Ng - Asst. General Manager

□ Asian Consolidation International Services, Inc.
Room 801 Ermita Center Bldg., 1350 Roxas Blvd., Ermita, MANILA, METRO MANILA
Contact Number/s : (632) 536-4555 (632) 536-4560 (632) 536-4621
Fax : (632) 536-2495 (632) 400-7054
Email : acis@compass.com.ph
Contact Person: Vivian Vocales - President/General Manager; Arlin Mae Rebustillo - VP-Operations

□ Asian Freeports, Inc.
2/F, Rm. 214 E.A. Fernandez Bldg., 2510 Taft Avenue, MANILA, METRO MANILA
Contact Number/s : (632) 525-5223 (632) 525-5390 (632) 525-5594 (632)
Fax : (632) 525-1880 (632) 523-5281
Email : afi@pworld.net.ph
Contact Person: Renato T. Pamintuan - President; Arturo C. Maloto - General Manager

□ Atiko Trans, Inc.
3rd Floor ECJ Building, Real corner Arzobispo Street, Intramuros, MANILA, METRO MANILA
Contact Number/s : (632) 536-8612 to 14
Fax : (632) 526-2490
Contact Person: Anna D. Llave - President; Bobit C. Aquino - General Manager; Arthur C. Sayson - Marketing & Operations Manager

□ Atlantic Globe Movers, Inc.
G/F CLP Building, 372 Cabildo St., Intramuros, MANILA, METRO MANILA
Contact Number/s : (632) 527-3131 (632) 527-3125 (632) 527-5384
Fax : (632) 527-5385
Contact Person: Atty. Leonides I. David - President; Grace M. Santos - Marketing Manager; Maria B. Geronimo - Operations Manager

□ Aviantrix Logistics Int'l., Inc.
Suite 702 Dasma Corporate Center, 321 Dasmariñas Street, Binondo, MANILA, METRO MANILA
Contact Number/s : (632) 247-4106 to 07 (632) 247-4109 (632) 247-4185
Fax : (632) 247-4105
Email : aviantrx@mozcom.com
Contact Person: Roxan L. Bayatan - VP-Sales and Operations; Noli Regio - Export Officer; Manny Balinbing - Import Officer

□ Beagle Cargo Forwarders
Room 805 1010 Building, A. Mabini Street, Ermita, MANILA, METRO MANILA
Contact Number/s : (632) 522-2382 (632) 526-7266
Fax : (632) 522-2481
Email : ecf@compass.com.ph
Contact Person: Ricardo G. Tubig - Proprietor

□ Beta Express Int'l. Cargo, Inc.
2525 Bautista cor. C. Ayala, Malate, MANILA, METRO MANILA
Contact Number/s : (632) 521-8406 (632) 521-8408
Fax : (632) 526-6175
Contact Person: Benjamin P. Ng - President/Managing Director

□ Bollard Chandlers International, Inc. (formerly Portman Terminals & Warehousing, Inc.)
Room 410 FEMII Building, A. Soriano Jr. Street, Intramuros, MANILA, METRO MANILA
Contact Number/s : (632) 527-2849
Fax : (632) 528-0404
Contact Person: Rogelio G. Soledad - President/General Manager; Emily S. Magabanua - VP for Marketing/Operations

□ Bookbridge International Corp.
5/F ECJ Condominium, Arzobispo cor. Real Sts., Intramuros, MANILA, METRO MANILA
Contact Number/s : (632) 527-7210 (632) 524-3252 (632) 524-3255
Fax : (632) 527-7211
Email : bookbridge@pacific.net.ph
Contact Person: Darleen S. Guillen - General Manager

□ BTI Courier Express Inc.
JL Building, Taft Ave., MANILA, METRO MANILA
Contact Number/s : (632) 522-4556/ (632) 524-4805
Contact Person: Bernardita S. Cabalza - President; Agapita D. Silava - Vice-President; Marie Jofflyn M. Digamon - VP-Operations

□ BVM Sanchez & Son Customs Broker & Freight Forwarding Co., Inc.
Suite 207 Ledesma Building, General Luna St., Intramuros, MANILA, METRO MANILA
Contact Number/s : (632) 527-8701 (632) 527-8703 (632) 527-8704 (632)
Fax : (632) 527-8598
Email : bvm.customs@skyinet.net
Contact Person: Bernardina M. Sanchez - President

□ CAM Int'l. Forwarding Corp.
Rm. # 225 Natividad Bldg., T. Pinpin St., Escolta, MANILA, METRO MANILA
Contact Number/s : (632) 243-0495 to 96
Fax : (632) 243-0592 (632) 241-4945
Email : camifi2000@hotmail.com
Contact Person: Carmelita M. Chua - President; Peterson Jason M. Pascual - General Manager

□ Cargo Quest Transport
Room 418 Noah's Ark Building, 303 Calle Escolta, MANILA, METRO MANILA
Contact Number/s : (632) 241-3092 (632) 244-4969
Fax : (632) 241-3372
Email : cargo@skyinet.net
Contact Person: Gina C. Ramos - President & General Manager; Lilibeth C. Ramos - Sales & Marketing Manager

□ CEL Consolidators and Freight Forwarders, Inc.
7/F, Carolina Building, 2106 Madre Ignacia Street, Malate, MANILA, METRO MANILA
Contact Number/s : (632) 526-2355 (632) 536-0391
Fax : (632) 526-2466
Email : celmktg@info.com.ph
Contact Person: Agapito D. Capistrano - President; Danilo C. Roque - General Manager

□ Centaur Maritime Services, Inc.
Rm. 9 Rear G/F, TRB Bldg., Aduana St., Intramuros, MANILA, METRO MANILA
Contact Number/s : (632) 527-3417 (632) 527-3398 (632) 528-0242
Fax : (632) 527-3402
Email : centaur@tri-sys.com
Contact Person: Daniel S. Gonzales - President & General Manager; Bayani H. Magalong - Operations Manager

□ Charter Quest Int'l. Phils. Corp.
Suite 409 Calvo Building, Escolta, MANILA, METRO MANILA
Contact Number/s : (632) 243-2944
Fax : (632) 243-5120
Email : charter_quest@hotmail.com
Contact Person: Arnel Dr. Mangaliman - President /General Manager; Oswald T. Lana - Freight Forwarding Manager

□ Cilberlift Freight Forwarders
Rm. 201 Ledesma Bldg., cor. Real & Gen. Luna Sts., Intramuros, MANILA, METRO MANILA
Contact Number/s : (632) 527-4067 (632) 527-4291 (632) 527-2276
Fax : (632) 527-2276
Email : cilber@tcs.com.ph
Contact Person: Gilbert L. Aquino - President; Cecilia G. Aquino - General Manager

□ Citadel Logistics, Inc.
2/F Citadel Building, 637 Bonifacio Drive, Port Area, MANILA, METRO MANILA
Contact Number/s : (632) 527-9921

Fax : (632) 527-5639
Email : leromero@citadel.com.ph
Contact Person: Erlinda E. Romero - General Manager; Alex F. Tanwangco - Chief Operating Officer

□ CNT Worldwide Transport Inc.
Cargo Center I & II, CNT Arcade, 3333 New Panaderos St., Sta. Ana, MANILA, METRO MANILA
Contact Number/s : (632) 534-7766 (632) 534-7772
Fax : (632) 534-7742 to 43
Email : cnt@fc.emc.com.ph
Contact Person: Jeffrey L. Tan - President & General Manager; Rolly Y. Yu - Asst. General Manager

□ COGSA Container Line Inc.
Rm. 411 First United Building Corporation, #413 Escolta St., Binondo, MANILA, METRO MANILA
Contact Number/s : (632) 243-4813 (632) 244-6498 Cell No.: (0917
Fax : (632) 244-6498
Email : cogsa@mindgate.net; Jgd@mindgate.net
Contact Person: Jocelyne G. Deveza - Managing Director

□ Commercial Freight Services, Inc.
G/F Shipping Center Bldg., 707 A. Soriano, Jr. Ave., Intramuros, MANILA, METRO MANILA
Contact Number/s : (632) 527-6031 to 49 (632) 527-5690 to 92 (632) 52
Fax : (632) 527-5454
Email : comfrt@pworld.net.ph
Contact Person: Jesse L. Contreras - General Manager

□ Consolidation Plus Frieght International, Inc.
Room 304 Madrigal Building, Escolta, MANILA, METRO MANILA
Contact Number/s : (632) 309-0621 to 22
Fax : (632) 309-0623
Email : cpfi@pacific.net.ph
Contact Person: Peter Leo C. Avestruz - General Manager; Mylene Desembrano - Export Coordinator; Shirley Mendoza - Admin. Officer

□ Cots Freight Int'l., Inc.
3/F Wallem Phils. Building, corner Beaterio & Legaspi Sts., Intramuros, MANILA, METRO MANILA
Contact Number/s : (632) 526-1327 (632) 526-1341
Fax : (632) 526-1351
Email : cots@compass.com.ph
Contact Person: Georgia B. Alviar - General Manager

□ CTSI Phils., Inc. (formerly PRO Cargo Forwarders Phils., Inc.)
5/F Times Plaza Building, Corner UN Avenue, Ermita, MANILA, METRO MANILA
Contact Number/s : (632) 536-3359
Fax : (632) 536-2481
Email : ctsiphils@ctsimnl.com
Contact Person: Dominador R. Estiva - President; Eleanor Paner - General Manager

□ Cubic Freight, Inc.
Rm. 406 A. Regina Bldg., Escolta Street, MANILA, METRO MANILA
Contact Number/s : (632) 243-9297 (632) 243-9640
Fax : (632) 242-0188
Email : cubic@skyinet.net
Contact Person: Ronaldo A. Rayo - President

□ Cyrus Logistics, Inc.
G/F Palm Plaza Hotel, Adriatico cor. P. Gil Streets, Malate, MANILA, METRO MANILA
Contact Number/s : (632) 526-1273 to 74
Fax : (632) 521-6378
Email : cyrus@mozcom.com
Contact Person: Estrella M. Dimaculangan - President/General Manager; Celso M. Dimaculangan - Vice President/Operations

□ Dalca Corporation
2/F Casa Maritima, 651 General Luna St., Intramuros, MANILA, METRO MANILA
Contact Number/s : (632) 527-7621 to 27 loc. 314, 310 & 237 (632) 527
Fax : (632) 527-1827

Email : dalca@bworldonline.com
Contact Person: Dante L. Catahay - President; Jeffrey Catahay - General Manager

 Dateline Cargo Express Int'l., Inc.
Rm. 306, East Wing Velco Center Bldg., corner Chicago & 13th Sts., Port Area, MANILA, METRO MANILA
Contact Number/s : (632) 528-1044 to 49
Fax : (632) 527-2550
Contact Person: Ma. Socorro D. Lim - President & Gen. Manager ; Lynn Buenviaje - Director

 Dero Logistic Services Corporation
Room 206 LCD & Co. Union Building, Bonifacio Drive, Port Area, MANILA, METRO MANILA
Contact Number/s : (632) 404-2070 to 72 (632) 404-2474 to 76
Fax : (632) 404-2071
Email : dero@broline.com
Contact Person: Delfin L. Caponpon - President; Bernard Tumanan - Forwarding Manager

 Dio-Rez Freight Services
#414 Capt. Luis Gonzaga Building, Rizal Avenue, Sta. Cruz, MANILA, METRO MANILA
Contact Number/s : (632) 733-2512 (632) 733-0217
Fax : (632) 734-1268
Contact Person: Diosdado M. Santiago - Owner/General Manager/Licensed Customs Broker

 Direct Container Lines, Inc.
5/F Section A Ramon Magsaysay Center, 1680 Roxas Boulevard, MANILA, METRO MANILA
Contact Number/s : (632) 524-8084 (632) 526-2322 to 23
Fax : (632) 521-8665
Contact Person: Juan Carlos Y. Aquias - Manager; Cristina O. Merin - Operations Manager

 Dors & Emmanuel Forwarding/Consolidation Services
#1044 A.C. Tabora Street, Brgy. 195 Zone 17, Tondo, MANILA, METRO MANILA
Contact Number/s : (632) 365-5271 Cell No. : (0912) 254-6165;
Contact Person: Ronald Allan A. Dizon - President

 DSF Consolidated Freight Services, Inc.
Room 460 Regina Building, Escolta, MANILA, METRO MANILA
Contact Number/s : (632) 244-5006 to 07 (632) 243-5039 (632) 244-5008
Fax : (632) 244-5008
Email : dsf_phils@pacific.net.ph
Contact Person: Manolo C. Manalo - President; Jennifer SG. Manalo - Vice-President; Johnny P. Quismundo - Operations Manager

 Dynatrans Freight Forwarding Services
Room 4C 4th Floor, 985 JEMMS Building, cor. Delpan & Zaragosa Street, Tondo, MANILA, METRO MANILA
Contact Number/s : (632) 243-9398
Fax : (632) 245-1956
Email : dyna@tri-sys.com; dfs@tri-sys.com
Contact Person: Edna G. Isabedra - General Manager; Michael M. Morales - Sales Manager; John Rovero - Operations Manager

 Eaglespeed Brokerage Corp.
Rm. 350-B Padilla Delos Reyes Bldg., 232 J. Luna Street, Binondo, MANILA, METRO MANILA
Contact Number/s : (632) 242-6596
Fax : (632) 243-2330
Contact Person: Virginia H. dela Paz - General Manager; Clemencio A. Cantero - Operations Manager

 Economical Transport Consolidators & Freight Forwarders
4/F Marine Central Building, Magallanes cor. Sta. Potenciana Sts., Intramuros, MANILA, METRO MANILA
Contact Number/s : (632) 523-8988 (632) 523-8990
Fax : (632) 527-0522
Email : ecotrans@broline.com

Contact Person: Jaime A. Gaytano - VP & General Manager

□ Ecu-Line Philippines, Inc.
Room 202 Focus Phils. Building, No. 200 2/F, Port Area, MANILA, METRO MANILA
Contact Number/s : (632) 527-2465
Fax : (632) 527-0653
Email : jra@qinet.net
Contact Person: Rolando R. Bay - General Manager

□ Elitsped Services, Inc.
G/F UY Tioco Bldg., 1906 Pilar Hidalgo Lim St., Malate, MANILA, METRO MANILA
Contact Number/s : (632) 523-1479 (632) 523-1489 (632) 525-6473 (632)
Fax : (632) 524-5197 (632) 765-2538
Email : esimnl97@virtual.unet.net.ph
Contact Person: Benjamin C. Pioquinto - Managing Director; Jazmin Papa - Operations Manager

□ En Gerdi Customs Brokerage & Forwarding Services, Inc.
Unit 7 2/F Casa Solanda, Anda Street, Intramuros, MANILA, METRO MANILA
Contact Number/s : (632) 526-1561 (632) 526-1575
Fax : (632) 527-3901
Email : en_gerdi@yahoo.com
Contact Person: Michael A. Limchunbin - President; Petronila A. Abad - Vice-President

□ Equitee Freight & Customs Brokerage
Room 405 Unlad Condominium, Malvar Street, Malate, MANILA, METRO MANILA
Contact Number/s : (632) 536-1486 (632) 536-3634 (632) 536-1623
Fax : (632) 536-1623
Email : equitee_frt@edsamail.com.ph
Contact Person: Michael V. Tenorio - General Manager

□ Euro-Asiatic Shipping, Inc.
12/F Victoria Building, 429 UN Avenue, Ermita, MANILA, METRO MANILA
Contact Number/s : (632) 525-5569 (632) 525-5572
Fax : (632) 526-8061
Email : euro@epic.net
Contact Person: Capt. Lou A. Atienza - President & CEO; Raquel C. Blanquera - General Manager

□ Far East Multi-Trans Agency Phils., Inc.
S-310 BF Condominium, A. Soriano Jr. Ave., cor. Solana St., Intramuros, MANILA, METRO MANILA
Contact Number/s : (632) 527-3338
Fax : (632) 527-3353
Email : femt@pacific.net.ph
Contact Person: Arnold A. Alano - General Manager

□ Filipinas Int'l. Transport Corp.
2nd Floor, TDG-NYK Harbor Centre Bldg., Railroad St. corner 23rd & 24th Streets, Port Area, MANILA, METRO MANILA
Contact Number/s : (632) 528-1050 (632) 527-7064
Fax : (632) 527-7064
Email : fitmnl@tdgworld.com
Contact Person: Ramon A. Villanueva - Business Coordination Manager; Eric Sta. Maria Asuncion - General Manager for Cooperate Affairs & Operations

□ First Associated Cargo Express, Inc.
Room 301 Mercantile Insurance Bldg., cor. Gen. Luna & Beaterio Sts., Intramuros, MANILA, METRO MANILA
Contact Number/s : (632) 527-7701 Loc. 285/219 (632) 527-5787
Fax : (632) 527-5789 (632) 825-2265
Email : faceimain@i-manila.com.ph; facei_cb@i-manila.com.ph
Contact Person: Junio O. Jose - President; Gerardo M. Supnet - VP-Logistics; Neil A. Nacpil - VP-Freight Forwarding

□ First Link Cargo Services
#110 Mercantile Insurance Building, Cor. General Luna and Beaterio Streets, Intramuros, MANILA, METRO MANILA
Contact Number/s : (632) 527-0608
Fax : (632) 527-6532

Contact Person: George G. So - Managing Director; Franklin A. Hernandez - Operations Manager

 First Rate Cargo Handlers, Inc.
1119-A San Andres, Malate, MANILA, METRO MANILA
Contact Number/s : (632) 484-1030 (632) 400-1990
Fax : (632) 400-1990
Email : reyrexie@skyinet.net; sandrie141294@yahoo.com
Contact Person: Alexandria A. Resurreccion - Managing Director

 Firstlink Container Lines, Inc.
14/F Marc Tower 2000, #1973 Taft Avenue cor. San Andres Street, Malate, MANILA, METRO MANILA
Contact Number/s : (632) 404-2890 to 93 (632) 400-4437
Fax : (632) 404-2450
Email : first_cl@pacific.net.ph
Contact Person: Edward J. Aguilar - President & General Manager; Arleen T. Francisco - Operations Manager

 Freight Connection Phils., Inc.
5th Floor ECJ Condominium, Corner Real & Arzobispo Sts., Intramuros, MANILA, METRO MANILA
Contact Number/s : (632) 527-6780 (632) 527-6783 (632) 527-6785 (632)
Fax : (632) 527-3928 (632) 528-0289
Contact Person: Ma. Victoria A Geniza - President; Marie Ann A. Javier - Operations Manager

 Freightmaster International Services
G/F FOCUS Philippines Compound, No. 200 2nd Street, Port Area, MANILA, METRO MANILA
Contact Number/s : (632) 527-2290 (632) 527-0653 (632) 527-0658
Fax : (632) 527-0653 (632) 527-0658
Email : freight@netgazer.com.ph
Contact Person: Jovencio R. Abila - President/Managing Director; Danilo C. Teofilo - General Manager

 Freightrans Cargo, Inc.
G/F Jose P. Laurel Memorial Foundation Bldg., Roxas Boulevard cor. Pedro Gil Street, Ermita, MANILA, METRO MANILA
Contact Number/s : (632) 522-9186 (632) 536-1254
Fax : (632) 450-1058
Contact Person: Reynaldo R. Platitas - General Manager

 Friends Logistics, Inc. (formerly Friends Brokerage Corporation)
Room 1002, Victoria Building, 429 UN Ave., Ermita, MANILA, METRO MANILA
Contact Number/s : (632) 528-4303 to 05 (632) 526-7244 to 45
Fax : (632) 521-7850
Email : friends@qinet.net
Contact Person: Rogelio C. De Guzman - President/General Manager; Reynaldo T. Moit - Operations Manager; Maria Vivian M. Erme - Forwarding Manager

 FSMS International Forwarder
#269 San Basilio Street, Zaragosa, Tondo, MANILA, METRO MANILA
Contact Number/s : (632) 245-1380
Fax : (632) 247-4249
Email : felyyyyy@hotmail.com
Contact Person: Felicidad C. Tolentino - President/General Manager; Jun Tiglao - Operations Manager

 FX Freight Forwarders, Inc.
Rm. 402-A, VIP Building, Roxas Boulevard, Ermita, MANILA, METRO MANILA
Contact Number/s : (632) 521-8875 (632) 521-9218
Fax : (632) 338-0599 (632) 521-9218
Email : fx_system@skyinet.net
Contact Person: Jorge C. Felix - President; Raymond B. Olaguera - General Manager

 G&U Logistics Philippines, Inc.
2/F Shipping Center Building, A. Soriano Avenue, Intramuros, MANILA, METRO MANILA
Contact Number/s : (632) 525-6879 (632) 525-6891

Fax : (632) 525-6894
Email : gu-loglr@compass.com.ph
Contact Person: Erlinda E. Romero - Manager, Business Development

□ Gateway Logistics, Inc.
5/F ECJ Condominium, Real cor. Arzobispo Streets, Intramuros, MANILA, METRO MANILA
Contact Number/s : (632) 525-9795
Fax : (632) 525-9856
Contact Person: Norman L. Forbes - President; Nell Armin De Pano Raralio - General Manager

□ GBQS Transport Phil., Inc.
Room 521 Phoenix Building, Recoletos St., Intramuros, MANILA, METRO MANILA
Contact Number/s : (632) 521-8501 to 10 loc.140 (632) 527
Fax : (632) 527-2336
Email : gbqs@pacific.net.ph
Contact Person: Vic O. Loresto - President/General Manager

□ GC Legend Freight Forwarder, Inc.
Room 209 Madrigal Building, Escolta, MANILA, METRO MANILA
Contact Number/s : (632) 243-4071 (632) 243-4008
Fax : (632) 243-4008
Email : gclegend@tri-isys.com; gcfrt@tri-isys.com
Contact Person: Emilio C. Gatacilo - President/ General Manager; Clifford U. Gatacil0 - Operations Manager

□ Global Era Logistics, Inc.
Room 218-B Regina Building, Escolta Street, MANILA, METRO MANILA
Contact Number/s : (632) 243-8349 (632) 243-7736
Fax : (632) 243-6218
Contact Person: Romeo A. Barrientos - President; Emma A. Diguangco - General Manager

□ Global Network Freight Phils., Inc.
Suite 300 DES Building, Remedios Street cor. Taft. Avenue, Malate, MANILA, METRO MANILA
Contact Number/s : (632) 536-3002
Fax : (632) 523-7798
Email : globenet@broline.com
Contact Person: Juan Romulo T. Eala - President & Gen. Manager

□ Global Philippines Container Line Corp.
#916-83 Sotto Yuvienco Bldg., Gonzales Street, U.N. Avenue, Ermita, MANILA, METRO MANILA
Contact Number/s : (632) 245-2432
Fax : (632) 245-2442
Email : global_phil@edsamail.com.ph; globalphil@pacific.net.ph
Contact Person: Mel C. Bulseco - President/GM/ Operations; Ana Nerissa A. Palileo - Assistant Operations Manager

□ Globeline Shipping Agencies, Inc.
Unit A 4/F Ramon Magsaysay Center, Roxas Boulevard, Malate, MANILA, METRO MANILA
Contact Number/s : (632) 526-9041 (632) 526-9046
Fax : (632) 526-6340
Contact Person: Felix C. Baltasar - Managing Director; Brenda C. Ramirez - Administrative Manager

□ GOC Customs Brokerage
Room 202 Torimar Building, Escolta, MANILA, METRO MANILA
Contact Number/s : (632) 242-5644
Fax : (632) 242-5643
Contact Person: Georgina O. Claridad - Owner/Manager

□ Gold Patch Link International, Inc.
Room 604 6/F GLC Building, TM Kalaw Street cor. Mabini Street, MANILA, METRO MANILA
Contact Number/s : (632) 404-1747
Fax : (632) 404-1459
Contact Person: Nelson G. Manahan - General Manager; Evita D. Luna - Operations Manager

 Goldbridge International Freight Forwarders, Inc.
Room 321 FUBC Building, Escolta Street, Binondo, MANILA, METRO MANILA
Contact Number/s : (632) 243-0827
Fax : (632) 247-3387
Email : goldbridge@pacific.net.ph
Contact Person: Fleurdeliz D. Santos - General Manager

 Good Success Forwarding Services
Room 205 Ledesma Building, Real corner Gen. Luna Sts., Real de Palacio, Intramuros, MANILA, METRO MANILA
Contact Number/s : (632) 527-8033
Fax : (632) 527-0567
Contact Person: Angelito G. Fernando - General Manager

 GST Ocean and Air Logistics Corp.
Room 906 Doña Victoria Building, 429 UN Avenue, Ermita, MANILA, METRO MANILA
Contact Number/s : (632) 526-7495
Fax : (632) 526-7495
Email : lorendg@info.com.ph
Contact Person: Danilo R. Sarayot - President; Lorena DB. De Guzman - Managing Director; Ma. Montaha V. Tecson - Director

 H & T Int'l. Freight, Inc.
Room 623 Roman Santos Building, Plaza Lacson, Sta. Cruz, MANILA, METRO MANILA
Contact Number/s : (632) 736-2657 (632) 734-4733
Fax : (632) 736-2658
Email : tonet@htphils.com.ph
Contact Person: Rose Antonette R. Reyes - President; Michelle Liza C. Malong - General Manager

 Haba-Sped Logistics Phils., Inc.
Room 312 Palacio Grande Building, General Luna cor. Anda Street, Intramuros, MANILA, METRO MANILA
Contact Number/s : (632) 527-7984 (632) 527-8018 (632) 536-1441
Fax : (632) 528-0329
Email : info@habasped.com.ph
Contact Person: Marites D. Dela Cruz - President

 Harvest Logistics, Inc.
3rd Floor ECJ Building, cor. Arzobispo & Real Sts., Intramuros, MANILA, METRO MANILA
Contact Number/s : (632) 523-3377
Fax : (632) 523-3448
Email : hlimnl@epic.net
Contact Person: Jae J. Jang - Chairman; Romulo C. Ordas - President

 Harvest World Express Phils., Inc.
Apt.304, 3/F Royal Bay Terrace Condominium, U.N. Avenue cor. Cortada, Ermita, MANILA, METRO MANILA
Contact Number/s : (632) 525-6612 (632) 525-6617 (632) 525-6619
Fax : (632) 400-9752
Email : hwephilars@pacific.net.ph
Contact Person: Arius R. Sobrevinas - Chief Executive Officer; Ruben B. Suarez - Operations Manager

 Hemisphere Brokerage Corp.
Unit 902 Dasmarinas Corporation Center, 321 Dasmarinas Street, Binondo, MANILA, METRO MANILA
Contact Number/s : (632) 244-5622 to 24 (632) 244-5624
Fax : (632) 244-5624
Contact Person: Rossendo C. Agulto, Sr. - President/General Manager

 Holen Industries Company Ltd.
Room 305 3/F VIP Building, #1140 Roxas Boulevard, Ermita, MANILA, METRO MANILA
Contact Number/s : (632) 302-2589 (632) 302-2591
Fax : (632) 302-2590
Email : babytiger@wildside.ph; meje-tiger@hotmail.com
Contact Person: Maria Elena Joy P. Eder - General Manager; Sixto G. Eder, Sr. - Operations Manager

 Intermarine Express Lines, Inc. (formerly Intermodal Express Lines)

Unit 302, 3/F, BF Condominium, A. Soriano Ave. cor. Solana St., Intramuros, MANILA, METRO MANILA
Contact Number/s : (632) 527-3410 (632) 527-3370 (632) 527-3383
Fax : (632) 527-3396
Email : imarine@amanet.net; leny_ieli@pacific.net.ph
Contact Person: Elenita A. Meman - President & General Manager; Oscar T. Meman, Jr. - EVP & Operations Manager

□ International Connection Logistics, Inc.
Room 316 FUBC Building, 413 Escolta, Binondo, MANILA, METRO MANILA
Contact Number/s : (632) 244-2509 (632) 241-0243 (632) 241-7005 loc.1
Fax : (632) 243-8441
Email : iclphil@skyinet.net
Contact Person: Zoraida V. Oledan - President; Pilita A. Fernandez - Sales & Operations Manager

□ Inter-Ocean Container Lines, Inc.
10th Floor MARC 2000 Tower, #1973 Taft Avenue corner Quirino Avenue, Malate, MANILA, METRO MANILA
Contact Number/s : (632) 404-0321 to 22 (632) 404-0325 (632) 404-0327
Fax : (632) 404-0329 (632) 404-0754
Email : iocl@inter-ocean.com.ph
Contact Person: Jovencio R. Abila - President/General Manager; Rolando R. Bay - Marketing Manager

□ Intraglobe Cargo Transport Corp.
Unit 502 Burke Building, Burke Street cor. Escolta St., Binondo, MANILA, METRO MANILA
Contact Number/s : (632) 247-6269
Fax : (632) 245-3568
Email : ictc@info.com.ph
Contact Person: Nilo Z. Insigne - President; Victor Gil Valdez - General/Operations Manager

□ Jade Bros. Freight Int'l., Inc.
Rm. 319-320 Calvo Building, Escolta, MANILA, METRO MANILA
Contact Number/s : (632) 245-7130 to 31 (632) 241-4488
Fax : (632) 243-3705
Email : jadebros@tri-sys.com
Contact Person: Emmanuel A. Santos - President; Bernard Guy R. Godoy - Operations Manager

□ Jade Logistic Services, Inc.
Ground Floor, Marine Central Bldg., cor. Sta. Potenciana & Magallanes Sts., Intramuros, MANILA, METRO MANILA
Contact Number/s : (632) 400-0021 (632) 400-0338 (632) 400-4440 to 42
Fax : (632) 527-8221
Email : jade@broline.com
Contact Person: Jaime A. Gaytano - General Manager; Ricardo G. Lisondra - Operations Manager

□ Jalien Int'l. Cargo Systems, Inc.
Rm. 650 Padilla Delos Reyes Bldg., 232 Juan Luna St., Binondo, MANILA, METRO MANILA
Contact Number/s : (632) 243-2328 (632) 243-6184 (632) 241-6643 (632)
Fax : (632) 243-3616
Email : jalien@rpl.net
Contact Person: Jacqueline C. Ambrosio - President; Perfecto B. Maestro - Operations Manager

□ JCIB Express Cargo Movers Corporation
Rm. 426 Calvo Building, Escolta, MANILA, METRO MANILA
Contact Number/s : (632) 243-2950
Fax : (632) 243-2944
Contact Person: Nelson F. Luciano - General Manager

□ JCM Cargo Network Corporation (formerly Cargonet Int'l. Corp.)
Rm. 338 Regina Building, Escolta, MANILA, METRO MANILA
Contact Number/s : (632) 243-1588 to 89 (632) 241-6366 (632) 241-5664
Fax : (632) 241-6346
Contact Person: Renato C. Ayson - Managing Director

 Jemara Int'l. Freight Services, Inc.
Room 202 Ledesma Building, Real corner General Luna St., Real de Palacio, Intramuros, MANILA, METRO MANILA
Contact Number/s : (632) 527-2277 (632) 527-5481 (632) 527-0531
Fax : (632) 527-2292 to 93
Email : jemara@skyinet.net
Contact Person: Cresauro C. Buensuceso - President; Elna VP. Inmenz0 - Operations Manager

 Jezzine Freight Services
Room 312 Regina Building, Escolta, MANILA, METRO MANILA
Contact Number/s : (632) 244-6922
Fax : (632) 243-6954
Contact Person: Perfecto V. Bautista - Manager/Licensed Customs Broker

 JRP Cargo Forwarding Corporation
Room 410 Champ Building, Bonifacio Drive, Port Area, Intramuros, MANILA, METRO MANILA
Contact Number/s : (632) 636-4910
Fax : (632) 747-8336
Contact Person: Dominador Bautista, Jr. - President

 Junna Forwarding and Brokerage, Inc.
JIC Bldg., #2419 Syquia cor. Calderon Sts., Sta. Ana, MANILA, METRO MANILA
Contact Number/s : (632) 563-5508 (632) 563-8347
Fax : (632) 563-5515 to 16
Email : junna@skyinet.net
Contact Person: Lamberto C. Almeda, Jr. - President

 Kawatetsu Pac-Atlantic Transport, Inc.
2/F Delgado Building, #637 Bonifacio Drive, Port Area, MANILA, METRO MANILA
Contact Number/s : (632) 527-1266 (632) 527-1263
Fax : (632) 526-1840
Email : dannyang@qinet.net
Contact Person: Danilo G. Ang - General Manager; Luis A. Alparan, Jr. - Operations Manager

 Keihin-Everett Forwarding Co., Inc.
Rm. 501 B.F. Condominium Bldg., Andres Soriano Ave. corner Solana Street, Intramuros, MANILA, METRO MANILA
Contact Number/s : (632) 527-8961 to 69
Fax : (632) 527-3354
Email : kefci@mozcom.com; kefci4@mozcom.com
Contact Person: Capt. Crisostomo Villanueva - Vice-President; Sally Rizada - Forwarding & NVOCC Asst. Mgr.

 Lebria Transport & Allied Services Corp.
2111-B M. Adriatico Street, Malate, MANILA, METRO MANILA
Contact Number/s : (632) 521-3749 (632) 521-3466 (632) 521-3688
Fax : (632) 521-3674 (632) 338-3862
Email : lebriaph@pworld.net.ph
Contact Person: Lope V. Lebria - President; Iluminada V. Lebria - General Manager; Elsie C. Esquill0 - Freight Forwarding Manager

 LMC Logistics & Allied Svcs. Inc.
Unit 3-A Shipping Center 707, Andres Soriano Jr. Ave., Intramuros, MANILA, METRO MANILA
Contact Number/s : (632) 524-6670
Fax : (632) 527-0860
Contact Person: Dario C. Cruz - President; Roberto M. Mesa - Vice-President; Jennifer P. Abesamis - Forwarding Manager

 Maersk Logistics Filipinas, Inc. (formerly Mercantile Filipinas, Inc.)
#900 Romualdez Street, Ermita, MANILA, METRO MANILA
Contact Number/s : (632) 527-9200
Fax : (632) 526-7415 (632) 522-4992
Email : philogmkt@maersk-logistics.com
Contact Person: Ramon H. Fuentes - General Manager; Patrick L. Perez - SCM/Corporate Development Manager

 Marine Cargo Brokerage
2808 R. Cruz Street, Hermosa Extension, Gagalangin, Tondo, MANILA, METRO MANILA
Contact Number/s : (632) 251-3123

Fax : (632) 251-1134
Email : marinecargo@pacific.net.ph
Contact Person: Marilou A. Furton - Owner

□ Mark Davies Int'l. Corp.
Suite 1408 Federal Tower Condominium, Dasmariñas cor. Muelle de Binondo Streets, Binondo, MANILA, METRO MANILA
Contact Number/s : (632) 244-6114 to 15
Fax : (632) 244-3143
Email : mrkdavis@evoserve.com
Contact Person: Editha P. Vaporoso - President; Susano C. Gemora, Jr. - General Manager; Conrado S. Mactal, Jr. - Operations Manager

□ Mark Ernest Brokerage Corporation
Rm. 518 FEMII Bldg., Andres Soriano Jr. St., Intramuros, MANILA, METRO MANILA
Contact Number/s : (632) 527-1672 (632) 527-1684
Fax : (632) 528-0460
Contact Person: Demosthenes M. Sanchez, Jr. - General Manager; Emmanuel N. Matugas - Operations Manager

□ Masuda Logistics Int'l. Corp.
Room 224 Calvo Building, Escolta Street, Binondo, MANILA, METRO MANILA
Contact Number/s : (632) 247-2347 (632) 245-1819
Fax : (632) 247-2355
Contact Person: Jacqueline Alvarado - General Manager

□ Maytrans Cargo Express, Inc.
Room 328 FEMII Building, A. Soriano Ave., Intramuros, MANILA, METRO MANILA
Contact Number/s : (632) 527-4316 (632) 527-9354
Fax : (632) 527-9332
Email : maytrans@pacific.net.ph
Contact Person: Elenita A. Meman - President

□ MD Express Manila, Inc.
Section A&B 11/F Ramon Magsaysay Ctr. Bldg., 1680 Roxas Boulevard, MANILA, METRO MANILA
Contact Number/s : (632) 536-2769 to 73
Fax : (632) 536-2774
Email : mdbroker@pworld.net.ph; tmplmdex@pworld.net.ph; mdemalou@pworld.net.ph
Contact Person: Ericson M. Marquez - President/General Manager; Antonio M. Puda - Operations Manager

□ Mecafor Cargo Specialist, Inc.
Room 302 Padilla de los Reyes Building, 232 Juan Luna Street, Binondo, MANILA, METRO MANILA
Contact Number/s : (632) 243-0775 (632) 243-0711
Fax : (632) 242-6604
Contact Person: Melody R. Carnaje - General Manager; Florencio R. Carnaje. Jr. - Operations Manager

□ Meister Transport, Inc.
HHC Building, 636 Victoria cor. Basco Streets, Intramuros, MANILA, METRO MANILA
Contact Number/s : (632) 527-8307 to 10
Fax : (632) 527-3946
Email : mti@meister.com.ph
Contact Person: Veronica Dar Santos - Pres./General Manager; Lou Javier - VP/Asst. General Manager

□ Meyo Door to Door Services
#2626 T. Ayala Street, P. Ocampo, Malate, MANILA, METRO MANILA
Contact Number/s : (632) 307-1791
Fax : (632) 522-6697
Contact Person: Maria Luz C. Oshida - Owner/Manager; Leonisa Aculina - Supervisor; Richard C. Casilagan - Sub.Supervisor

□ Mobility Express International Freight, Inc.
Room 402 Champ Building, Anda Circle, Port Area, MANILA, METRO MANILA
Contact Number/s : (632) 527-4943
Fax : (632) 527-4943
Email : mobility@mobility.com.ph
Contact Person: Cristina A. De Los Santos - General Manager; Ever D. Encarnacion - Import & Sales Manager; Henry M. Daguman - Operations Manager

 Monlu Int'l. & Domestic Forwarders Corporation
Room 408 FUBC 413 Escolta Street, MANILA, METRO MANILA
Contact Number/s : (632) 241-1831 (632) 241-1834 (632) 243-4814
Fax : (632) 243-4814
Email : monlu@mindgate.net
Contact Person: Senencio S. Luna - President; Irene S. Luna - General Manager

 MOV Int'l. Forwarders, Inc.
Rm 315 FEMII Bldg. Annex A, A. Soriano St., Intramuros, MANILA, METRO MANILA
Contact Number/s : (632) 527-2916 (632) 527-2897 (632) 527-2893
Fax : (632) 527-2932
Email : movgrp@mnl.sequel.net
Contact Person: Miguel O. de Villa - President; Noel L. Francisco - Operations Manager

 Mutual Fortune Express, Inc.
Unit 306, The Centennial Bldg., No. 375 Escolta Street, Binondo, MANILA, METRO MANILA
Contact Number/s : (632) 242-1168 (632) 242-1176 (632) 243-1968 (632)
Fax : (632) 242-1273 (632) 309-0365
Email : mfsi@tri.isys.com; mfeimanila@eastern.com.ph
Contact Person: Wang Chi Wei - General Manager; Jose O. Rivera - Asst. General Manager

 Nautilus Logistics & Maritime Services Co., Inc.
Unit 4 Arquiza Trade Center, Ermita, MANILA, METRO MANILA
Contact Number/s : (632) 522-8944 (632) 522-8939
Fax : (632) 522-8939
Email : nlams@egis.net
Contact Person: Raul D. Evangelista - President; Danilo M. Velasquez - Shipping Manager

 New Century Link Freight Forwarding Services, Inc.
Room 409 Manufacturers' Bldg., Sta. Cruz Plaza, Sta. Cruz, MANILA, METRO MANILA
Contact Number/s : (632) 736-9114 (632) 733-7693
Fax : (632) 733-7693
Contact Person: Wilhemina I. Taguinod - General Manager; Gina T. Regalado - Operations Manager

 New Star Cargo Forwarding, Inc.
Rm. 304 Burke Bldg., Escolta, MANILA, METRO MANILA
Contact Number/s : (632) 244-6634 (632) 242-6428 (632) 244-6633
Fax : (632) 244-6633
Contact Person: Roberto C. Borja, Jr. - President

 New Wave Transport Phils., Inc.
2/F Mary Bachrach Building, A.C. Delgado cor. 25th Sts., Port Area, MANILA, METRO MANILA
Contact Number/s : (632) 527-7058 (632) 527-7057
Fax : (632) 527-7059
Contact Person: Jose Roberto C. Delgad0 - Chairman & CEO; Isao Niimi - President; Akihiro Azuma - Director and General Manager; Melissa M. Balatbat - Asst. General Manager

 Nonpareil Int'l. Freight and Cargo Services, Inc.
#960-964 San Andres corner San Marcelino Sts., Malate, MANILA, METRO MANILA
Contact Number/s : (632) 526-8077 (632) 525-5552
Fax : (632) 526-1020
Email : nifcs@tri-isys.com
Contact Person: Rolando E. Quiambao - President & General Manager; Cynthia S. Pacuan - VP for Brokerage & Int'l. Operations

 Ocean Eagle Container Lines Corp.
12th Floor Ramon Magsaysay Center, 1680 Roxas Boulevard, Malate, MANILA, METRO MANILA
Contact Number/s : (632) 524-8209 (632) 524-9102 (632) 524-8081 (632)
Fax : (632) 524-8568

Email : oecl@philonline.com
Contact Person: Dr. Arturo C. Llorin - General Manager; Theodore M. Gonzaga - Operations Manager

□ Ocean Hawk Cargo Services
Room 3A Sotto-Yuvienco Building, #910 Gonzales Street, Ermita, MANILA, METRO MANILA
Contact Number/s : (632) 522-5889 (632) 525-3216
Fax : (632) 525-3216
Contact Person: Iluminado L. Ramos - General Manager; Ma. Elisa Montalvo - Documentation Manager

□ Ocean Pearl International
Suite 208 Burke Building, W. Burke Street cor. Escolta, MANILA, METRO MANILA
Contact Number/s : (632) 243-1149 (632) 247-0629
Fax : (632) 243-6509
Email : opearl@pworld.net.ph
Contact Person: Editha N. Manimtim - President; Cecilio M. Manimtim - General Manager

□ Oceanlink Forwarders & Services Phils., Inc.
3/F Marine Central Building, cor. Magallanes & Sta. Potenciana Sts., Intramuros, MANILA, METRO MANILA
Contact Number/s : (632) 523-8998 (632) 527-3757
Fax : (632) 528-0215 (632) 338-1728 (632) 338-1729
Email : ocealink@i-next.net
Contact Person: Romeo M. Dino, Jr. - General Manager

□ One Asia Resources Worldwide, Inc.
Room 222 Madrigal Building, Escolta Street, MANILA, METRO MANILA
Contact Number/s : (632) 244-9384
Fax : (632) 244-9385
Contact Person: Romeo M. Escareal, Jr. - General Manager; Maranao O. Aguir - Operations Manager

□ OOCL (Philippines) , Inc.
4-5/F Dy Int'l. Bldg., San Marcelino, cor. Malvar Sts., Malate, MANILA, METRO MANILA
Contact Number/s : (632) 536-7085 (632) 536-7158
Fax : (632) 536-8551
Contact Person: Enrico R. Sanchez - President/GM; Wilfredo A. Hans - Finance/AGM; Wenefredo P. Naagas - Cargo System Manager

□ Orient Freight Int'l., Inc.
Bldg. 2 Warehouse No. 1, Ground Floor, 2071 Marbella Manila II Bldg., 2071 Roxas Blvd., Malate, MANILA, METRO MANILA
Contact Number/s : (632) 521-2336 to 39 (632) 551-2336 to 39
Fax : (632) 522-3637 (632) 536-0264
Email : administrator@orientfreight.com; martingarcia@orientfreight.com
Contact Person: Jose Ramon R. Garcia - President; Luis V. Casal - VP-Forwarding Services

□ Orientstar Freight International, Inc.
Unit C 18th Floor Ramon Magsaysay Center, 1680 Roxas Boulevard, Malate, MANILA, METRO MANILA
Contact Number/s : (632) 404-2067 (632) 404-2069
Fax : (632) 404-2080
Email : website: www.orientstargroup.com
Contact Person: Marilou Z. Barajan - General Manager

□ Overseas Container Transport System, Inc.
513 Phoenix Bldg., Recoletos Street, Intamuros, MANILA, METRO MANILA
Contact Number/s : (632) 527-2337 local 18 & 41 (632) 527-548
Fax : (632) 527-5439 (632) 527-5487
Contact Person: Laurentino E. Morta, Jr. - General Manager

□ Pacific Charter Forwarders, Inc.
Room 604, Allied Bank Building, 410 Quintin Paredes Street, Binondo, MANILA, METRO MANILA

Contact Number/s : (632) 241-9134 (632) 242-0192 (632) 241-8238
Fax : (632) 243-0697
Email : pcharter@compass.com.ph
Contact Person: Stella Chua - General Manager

□ Pacific Concord Container Lines, Inc.
2/F PCIC Building, Atlanta Street, corner 14th and 15th Streets, Port Area, METRO MANILA
Contact Number/s : (632) 526-2040 (632) 526-2011 (632) 526-1988 (632)
Fax : (632) 526-1987 (632) 526-2072
Email : paccord@compass.com.ph
Contact Person: Barbie B. Rivadeneira - Marketing Director/General Manager; Reynaldo G. Mata - Operation In-Charge

□ Phil. Genesis Freight Unlimited, Inc.
Room 203 Mercantile Insurance Bldg., General Luna cor. Beaterio Sts., Intramuros, MANILA, METRO MANILA
Contact Number/s : (632) 527-8749 (632) 527-8769 (632) 527-7701
Fax : (632) 527-8766 (632) 527-1333
Email : philgen@mozcom.com
Contact Person: Josephina Capulong Yap - President; Mel C. Bulseco - Vice-President

□ Phil. Ocean Air Int'l. Corp.
Room 604 6/F Madrigal Bldg., 286 Escolta, MANILA, METRO MANILA
Contact Number/s : (632) 241-6469 (632) 241-6283 (632) 241-0809
Fax : (632) 241-6466
Email : oceanair@skyinet.net
Contact Person: Conrado E. Valmores - President/Gen. Manager

□ Phil. Pioneer Forwarding Corp.
Suite 900 Ermita Center Bldg., 1350 Roxas Blvd., Ermita, MANILA, METRO MANILA
Contact Number/s : (632) 526-7416 to 24 (632) 521-9008
Fax : (632) 521-9125
Contact Person: Reynaldo B. Gonzales - Forwarding Manager

□ Philkosa Sea & Air Freight Services, Inc.
3/F Omi Building, 20th Street, Port Area, MANILA, METRO MANILA
Contact Number/s : (632) 527-6071 to 75 (632) 301-9253 (632) 301-925
Fax : (632) 522-7585
Email : stktrading@phil.com; kr.stazurinc@yahoo.com
Contact Person: Josefina B. Santos - President; Kim Nam Yi - Senior Vice President; Jhayson P. Igual - General Manager

□ Port Consolidators, Inc.
Suite 1109 Ermita Center Building, 1350 Roxas Boulevard, Ermita, MANILA, METRO MANILA
Contact Number/s : (632) 526-7953 (632) 526-7957 (632) 526-2358
Fax : (632) 526-0276
Email : pcimnl@nsclub.net
Contact Person: Marsha Joy U. Castillo - President

□ Port Net Transport Services, Inc.
Unit 308-A The Centennial Bldg., 375 Calle Escolta, Binondo, MANILA, METRO MANILA
Contact Number/s : (632) 309-0350 (632) 309-0352 to 53
Fax : (632) 309-0355
Email : portnet@nsclub.net
Contact Person: Marsha Joy U. Castillo - President; Daisy B. Sotelo - Managing Director; Byrne P. Bajao - Operations Manager

□ Powerhaus Logistics Corporation
G/F Unlad Condominium, #1665 General Malvar Street, cor. Taft Avenue, Malate, MANILA, METRO MANILA
Contact Number/s : (632) 526-2150 (632) 521-2291
Fax : (632) 521-5350
Email : powerlog@the.net.ph
Contact Person: Rowena Z. De Guzman - General Manager

□ Precious Door to Door Delivery Services
#1933-G Otis Street, Paco, MANILA, METRO MANILA

Contact Number/s : (632) 562-3570 (632) 564-8742
Fax : (632) 564-8742
Contact Person: Sonny A. Carillo - Owner/Manager

□ President Container Line, Inc.
#518 Phoenix Building, Recoletos Street, Intramuros, MANILA, METRO MANILA
Contact Number/s : (632) 301-0056
Fax : (632) 301-0055
Email : acclimnl@pworld.net.ph
Contact Person: Octavio de Leon - General Manager; Evelyn A. Yambao - Operations Manager

□ Prime Cargo Handlers, Inc. (formerly Prime Service Customs Brokerage Corp.)
G/F RBAP Bldg., A. Soriano Ave., Cor. Arzobispo St., Intramuros, MANILA, METRO MANILA
Contact Number/s : (632) 527-2976
Fax : (632) 527-2970
Contact Person: Manolo G. Sy - President/General Manager; Marichu A. Misa - Operations

□ Pyxis Services, Inc.
2/F R&L Building, 1607 Alavarez St., Sta. Cruz, MANILA, METRO MANILA
Contact Number/s : (632) 749-6324
Fax : (632) 338-1932
Contact Person: Roberto T. Lim - President

□ Quantum Freight, Inc.
Unit 308 The Centennial Bldg., 375 Calle Escolta, Binondo, MANILA, METRO MANILA
Contact Number/s : (632) 309-0359 (632) 309-0360 (632) 309-0142
Fax : (632) 309-0181
Email : quantum@nsclub.net
Contact Person: Arnel R. Buenavides - President; Marsha Joy U. Castillo - Vice-President; Mary Joy Tarrosa - Business Dev't. Manager

□ R&E International Freight Forwarders, Inc.
Room 8 Jefferson Bldg., 13th Street, cor. Atlanta St., Port Area, MANILA, METRO MANILA
Contact Number/s : (632) 527-7566 (632) 527-7570
Fax : (632) 527-6723
Contact Person: Emelinda A. Guzman - President/General Manager; Perlita F. Bautista - Operations Manager

□ REJ Freight Services
Room 321 First United Building, 413 Escolta Street, Binondo, MANILA, METRO MANILA
Contact Number/s : (632) 243-0827
Fax : (632) 247-3387
Contact Person: Enrico T. David - General Manager

□ RFC Freight Corporation
Rm. 108 Homerson Bldg., Bataan Ext., Bagumbayan St., Sta. Mesa, MANILA, METRO MANILA
Contact Number/s : (632) 714-6411
Fax : (632) 716-0848
Contact Person: Hanson So - General Manager; Larcy Marichi Y. So - Asst. General Manager/Finance Manager

□ RGV Container Lines Inc.
4/F Trinidad Building, UN Avenue cor. A. Mabini Street, Ermita, MANILA, METRO MANILA
Contact Number/s : (632) 526-8031 (632) 526-8239
Fax : (632) 526-8238
Email : rgv@pacific.net.ph
Contact Person: Willy C. Uy, Jr. - General Manager; Elna V. Perfas - Vice President/Operations

□ RO Ilagan Customs Brokerage
G/F, Champ Building, Bonifacio Drive, Port Area, MANILA, METRO MANILA
Contact Number/s : (632) 527-3054 (632) 527-3050 (632) 527-3218
Fax : (632) 527-3218
Email : roi@nwave.net
Contact Person: Rener O. Ilagan - Licensed Customs Broker/Gen. Manager

□ Roadwat Shipping & Allied Services, Inc.
Suite 208 Ledesma Building, Cor. Real & General Luna Streets, Intramuros, MANILA, METRO MANILA
Contact Number/s : (632) 526-2155 (632) 526-2156
Fax : (632) 526-2156
Contact Person: Felomino I. Gregorio - General Manager; Jesus J. Oredina - Operations Manager

□ RV Marzan International Forwarders, Inc.
23rd Street, A.C. Delgado Street, Port Area, MANILA, METRO MANILA
Contact Number/s : (632) 527-4669 (632) 524-7732 (632) 527-4737 (632)
Fax : (632) 527-4666 (632) 527-4756
Email : jpmarzan@pacific.net.ph
Contact Person: Jose Vicente G. Umali - VP-General Manager

□ Safeway Phils. Freight Co.
Room 322 Calvo Building, Escolta, MANILA, METRO MANILA
Contact Number/s : (632) 243-2945
Fax : (632) 241-4554
Contact Person: Aurora K. Santos - Managing Partner

□ Sea Net Int'l. Phil. Inc.
425 Regina Building, Calle Escolta, Binondo, MANILA, METRO MANILA
Contact Number/s : (632) 247-0841 (632) 243-7867
Fax : (632) 243-7867
Contact Person: Arnel R. Buenavides - President

□ Sea Star Express Corp.
6/F Ramon Magsaysay Center, 1680 Roxas Boulevard, MANILA, METRO MANILA
Contact Number/s : (632) 522-7788
Fax : (632) 522-7787
Email : seastar@seapineship.com
Contact Person: Ma. Cecilia S. Zeta - General Manager; Abraham A. Bentulan, Jr. - Operations Manager; Gyu Cho Lee - Marketing Director

□ Seahawk Transport, Inc.
Suite 206 Ledesma Building, cor. G. Luna & Real Streets, Intramuros, MANILA, METRO MANILA
Contact Number/s : (632) 400-0051 (632) 338-5500 to 02
Fax : (632) 527-8786
Email : seahawk@compass.com.ph
Contact Person: Arlin Mae E. Rebustillo - President/General Manager; Ma. Theresa D. Cabral - Managing Director

□ Sealark Customs Services
4F Champ Building, Bonifacio Drive, Port Area, MANILA, METRO MANILA
Contact Number/s : (632) 527-7018
Fax : (632) 527-7018
Contact Person: Segismundo R. Alarcon - Licensed Customs Broker/Manager

□ Sen Tek International Freight Forwarding Corporation
12A 12th Floor Legaspi Tower 300, Roxas Blvd., cor. Vito Cruz St., MANILA, METRO MANILA
Contact Number/s : (632) 521-1934
Fax : (632) 522-6175
Email : sentek@pacific.net.ph
Contact Person: Josephine Gallardo - Forwarding Manager; Rolando De Miguel - Operations Manager

□ Seven Seas International Cargo Svcs. Co.
#1058 Antipolo St., Sampaloc, MANILA, METRO MANILA
Contact Number/s : (632) 338-4556 (632) 338-4558
Fax : (632) 338-4558
Contact Person: Joy O. Motel - President & General Manager

□ Shelleson-Kase Phils. Corp.
Room 402 MNA Corp. Building, 186 2nd Street, cor. Bonifacio Drive, Port Area, MANILA, METRO MANILA
Contact Number/s : (632) 527-6153 (632) 527-9852
Fax : (632) 527-9840
Email : shelesonkase@edsamail.com.ph

Contact Person: Franklin Roger L. Sun - President

□ Shin Yang Forwarding & Brokerage Corporation
Rm. 206 Ermita Center Building, Roxas Blvd., Ermita, MANILA, METRO MANILA
Contact Number/s : (632) 522-2040 to 41 (632) 526-4846
Fax : (632) 526-4849
Contact Person: Remedios del Valle - General Manager; Marilyn Calderon - Operations Manager

□ Shuttle Cargo Int'l. Phil. Inc.
S-110 Mercantile Insurance Building, Cor. Gen. Luna & Beaterio Streets, Intramuros, MANILA, METRO MANILA
Contact Number/s : (632) 527-0603 (632) 527-0608
Fax : (632) 527-6532 (632) 527-6533
Contact Person: George G. So - Managing Director

□ SK Guiamano Cargo Services Corporation
TIPSI Bldg., MD Tacoma & 2nd Streets, Port Area, MANILA, METRO MANILA
Contact Number/s : (632) 527-2777
Fax : (632) 524-1907
Email : guiamano@amanet.net
Contact Person: Mr. Silay K. Guiamano - Pres. & Gen. Manager; Dolores S. Guiamano - EVP/ Finance

□ Sky Land Brokerage Inc.
Sky Land Building, Cabildo Street, Intramuros, MANILA, METRO MANILA
Contact Number/s : (632) 527-8321 to 26 (632) 527-1607
Fax : (632) 527-1698
Contact Person: Dominador L. De Guzman - President/General Manager; Oliver C. De Guzman - VP-Operations

□ Skylink Company Inc.
#59 Dasmariñas Street, Binondo, MANILA, METRO MANILA
Contact Number/s : (632) 243-3747 (632) 241-3194
Fax : (632) 241-6965 (632) 242-2056
Email : skylink@skyint'l.com.ph
Contact Person: Macario C. Yu - President; Mary Ann P. Yu - Vice-President

□ Solex Express Phils., Inc.
Room 106 Ledesma Building, Real cor. General Luna Street, Intramuros, MANILA, METRO MANILA
Contact Number/s : (632) 527-6992 to 93
Fax : (632) 528-0054
Email : solexph@pworld.net.ph
Contact Person: Eduardo C. Tolentino - President & Managing Director; Rannie D. del Mundo - Finance and Admin. Manager

□ Solid Hub Cargo Express, Inc.
Room 208 Phoenix Building, Recoletos Street, Intramuros, MANILA, METRO MANILA
Contact Number/s : (632) 404-1766
Fax : (632) 724-3102 (632) 404-1766
Email : solidhub@asia.com
Contact Person: Diana Yap - Managing Director & Accounting Head; Lysander Salas - Operations Officer for Freight Forwarding

□ Speedtrans Int'l. Inc.
Room 1207 Federal Tower Condominium, Dasmariñas cor. M. De Binondo Streets, Binondo, METRO MANILA
Contact Number/s : (632) 241-3558
Fax : (632) 241-3157 (632) 244-5257
Contact Person: Editha V. Muñoz - President; Marco U. Pagaduan - Seafreight Manager

□ Springer Int'l. Inc.
118C Mercantile Insurance Building, corner General Luna & Beaterio St., Intramuros, MANILA, METRO MANILA
Contact Number/s : (632) 527-7082 to 84 (632) 527-7701 loc. 275
Fax : (632) 527-7069
Email : springer@philonline.com.ph
Contact Person: Edwin S. Guillarte - General Manager; Ms. Rely Tan - Airfreight Manager

□ St. Patrick Int'l. Forwarders, Inc.
R-317 Padilla delos Reyes Bldg., 232 Juan Luna St., Binondo, MANILA, METRO MANILA

Contact Number/s : (632) 241-5380 (632) 243-0403
Fax : (632) 243-0403
Email : spi_fi@tri-sys.com
Contact Person: Ricardo Manuel Z. Manrique - President

 Starlite Cargo Xpress, Inc.
Warehouse 1, Tabacalera Compound, Correa Street, UN Avenue, MANILA, METRO MANILA
Contact Number/s : (632) 525-9154 to 65
Fax : (632) 528-4623 (632) 528-4625
Contact Person: Alfonso G. Cusi - President; Karl Wozniak - Managing Director; Shirley L. Francisco - VP-Marketing & Business Dev't.

 Sun East Asia Transport Inc.
Room 101 Mercantile Insurance Building, cor. Gen. Luna & Beaterio Sts., Intramuros, MANILA, METRO MANILA
Contact Number/s : (632) 527-0918 (632) 527-0930 to 31 (632) 527-0928
Fax : (632) 338-6445 (632) 527-0931
Contact Person: Virgilio S. Veneracion - President & Chairman of the Board; Marieta D. Veneracion - VP for Admin. & Finance

 SYL Forwarders, Inc.
G1 Gochangco Bldg., 610 TM Kalaw St. Manila, MANILA, METRO MANILA
Contact Number/s : (632) 525-0495 (632) 524-6362
Fax : (632) 524-6376
Contact Person: Angel Jose L. Ramos - President

 Teamtrans Cargo Services, Inc.
#636 Victoria corner Basco Street, HHC Building, Intramuros, MANILA, METRO MANILA
Contact Number/s : (632) 525-7626 (632) 526-6473
Fax : (632) 525-7629
Email : tcsi-air@compass.com.ph; tcsi@compass.com.ph
Contact Person: Teresita B. Estiva - President & Gen. Manager

 TER International Line
Suite 411, EBA Building, 239 Juan Luna St., Binondo, MANILA, METRO MANILA
Contact Number/s : (632) 252-2379
Fax : (632) 255-6597
Contact Person: Terence Allen Go - Managing Director/Chief Operations Manager; Jesse Van King Go - Assistant Manager

 Total Solution Freight & Allied Services, Inc.
Room 502-504 Ferguson Park Tower, MH Del Pilar cor. Flores Street, Ermita, MANILA, METRO MANILA
Contact Number/s : (632) 522-6562 to 64
Fax : (632) 526-5429
Email : tsf@pacific.net.ph
Contact Person: Hanlon C. Monteverde - General Manager

 Trancy Logistics (Phils.) , Inc.
Ramon Magsaysay Center, No. 1680 Roxas Boulevard, Malate, MANILA, METRO MANILA
Contact Number/s : (632) 521-1681
Fax : (632) 522-3597
Contact Person: Hori Masayoshi - Vice President; Reynon M. Jayag - General Manager

 Transcontainer (TCL) Philippines, Inc. (formerly TCL-NAIGAI Phils., Inc.)
2nd Floor, TDG-NYK Harbor Centre Bldg., Railroad, corner 23rd & 24th Streets, Port Area, MANILA, METRO MANILA
Contact Number/s : (632) 527-7060 to 62 (632) 527-9888
Fax : (632) 524-4573 (632) 527-5779
Email : tclphils@i-next.net
Contact Person: Hidetake Yoshizuka - President; Ma. Luisa P. Gregorio - Administrative Officer; Mildred A. Santos - Manager, Freight & Customer Service Dept.

 Transilver Freight Services
Rm. 517 First United Building Corp., Escolta, MANILA, METRO MANILA
Contact Number/s : (632) 244-0962 (632) 244-6001 (632) 245-2851
Fax : (632) 245-3119
Email : transilver@mindgate.net

Contact Person: Remegio N. Lacsa - Owner/Proprietor

□ Trans-Marine 2000, Inc.
#102 Ledesma Building, Real cor. General Luna Streets, Intramuros, MANILA, METRO MANILA
Contact Number/s : (632) 338-4241 to 43 (632) 527-0358
Fax : (632) 338-2240
Email : tn2000@yesmynet.com
Contact Person: Danny V. Gonzales - Asst. Gen. Manager/Operations Manager; Venus Z. Cunanan - Finance Manager

□ Transmodal Int'l. Inc.
2/F, Palacio Grande Bldg., Corner Gen. Luna and Anda Streets, Intramuros, MANILA, METRO MANILA
Contact Number/s : (632) 528-0292
Fax : (632) 528-0303 (632) 528-0328
Email : info@transmodalphil.com
Contact Person: Irene Manguiat - President/General Manager; Elma P. Simbahan - Seafreight Export Manager; Marcelo P. Bucod - Seafreight Import Manager

□ Trans-Union Express Phils., Inc.
Room 303A Mercantile Insurance Bldg., Gen. Luna Street, Intramuros, MANILA, METRO MANILA
Contact Number/s : (632) 338-7091 (632) 527-7701 loc. 212
Fax : (632) 527-1764
Email : tue@pacific.net.ph
Contact Person: Corazon R. O'Hara - President

□ Trans-World Brokerage Corporation
Suite 226 Regina Building #410 Escolta, MANILA, METRO MANILA
Contact Number/s : (632) 241-5676 (632) 243-5145
Fax : (632) 241-6589 (632) 243-4851
Contact Person: Gonzalo D. Roque, Jr. - President; Ruth A. Bathan - General Manager-Freight Forwarding

□ Triple "A" Customs Services, Inc.
Room 308 FEMII Building, A. Soriano Ave., Intramuros, MANILA, METRO MANILA
Contact Number/s : (632) 527-7287 (632) 528-0385
Fax : (632) 528-0385
Contact Person: Fortunato Dela Cruz - President/GM; Marlyn T. Dela Cruz - VP-Finance

□ Troika Freight International, Inc.
3/F Peterson Building, 352 T. Pinpin Street cor. Escolta, Binondo, MANILA, METRO MANILA
Contact Number/s : (632) 243-8829
Fax : (632) 243-8828
Email : tficmnl@tri-sys.com
Contact Person: Joel P. Mascariña - Managing Partner/Operations Manager; Julius A. Almendral - Partner & Marketing Manager

□ Ultrafreight, Inc.
Movers and Managers Compound, 2nd Street cor. Tacoma, Port Area, MANILA, METRO MANILA
Contact Number/s : (632) 527-0519 (632) 527-0492 (632) 527-0458
Fax : (632) 527-0785
Email : ultra@mozcom.com
Contact Person: Reynaldo P. Garcia - President; Ma. Teresa Garcia - General Manager; Othelo N. Dayrit - Operations Manager

□ Unicargo Int'l. Forwarding
Rm. 103 Mercantile Insurance Bldg., Gen. Luna cor. Beaterio Streets, Intramuros, MANILA, METRO MANILA
Contact Number/s : (632) 528-0283 to 84 (632) 536-1431 to 34
Fax : (632) 528-0310
Email : unicargo@compass.com.ph
Contact Person: Angelo I. Carpena - Pres. & General Manager; Lorie T. Carpena - VP for Marketing; Rowena F. dela Cruz - Customer Service Dept.

□ United Container Int'l. Lines, Inc.
Rm. 513, Phoenix Building, Recoletos St., Intramuros, MANILA, METRO MANILA

Contact Number/s : (632) 527-2324
Fax : (632) 527-5439
Email : acclimnl@pworld.net.ph
Contact Person: Richard S. Ng - General Manager; William Hofer - Import Supervisor

 United Logistics Corp.
Cargo Center 2, CNT Arcade, No. 3333 New Panaderos Street, Sta. Ana, MANILA, METRO MANILA
Contact Number/s : (632) 534-7766 loc. 130 & 131 (632) 533-2554
Fax : (632) 533-2554
Email : ulc@pacific.net.ph
Contact Person: Eugenio S. Ynion, Jr. - General Manager; Pepito V. Go - Asst. General Manager; Alvin G. Tasic - Operations Supervisor

 United Pacific Forwarder Corp.
Room 205 Ledesma Building, Gen. Luna cor. Real Street, Intramuros, MANILA, METRO MANILA
Contact Number/s : (632) 527-8726 to 28
Fax : (632) 522-9655
Email : ictc@info.com.ph
Contact Person: Luzviminda C. Siguenza - President & General Manager

 Unitrans Int'l. Forwarders, Inc.
3/F OFSI Building, 555 Cabildo/Urdaneta Sts., Intramuros, MANILA, METRO MANILA
Contact Number/s : (632) 527-8586 to 90
Fax : (632) 527-8591
Email : unitrans@pworld.net.ph; uifimla@pworld.net.ph
Contact Person: Nelson A. Calimoso - Managing Director; Nicerio A. Noriega - General Manager

 Universal Consolidation Management Phils., Inc.
2/F Palacio Grande, Gen. Luna cor. Anda St., Intramuros, MANILA, METRO MANILA
Contact Number/s : (632) 527-1414 (632) 528-0292
Fax : (632) 528-0303
Contact Person: Irene M. Manguiat - President/General Manager; Elma P. Simbahan - Operations Manager

 Uniwide Express Brokerage Inc.
Suite 603 Plywood Industries Bldg., Corner T.M. Kalaw & A. Mabini Streets, Ermita, MANILA, METRO MANILA
Contact Number/s : (632) 521-1443 (632) 521-1445
Fax : (632) 521-1445
Contact Person: Ms. Africa L. Alfonso - President/General Manager; Diosdado Red - Operations Manager

 Uppercity Multimodal Forwarder
Rm. 304, 3rd Floor, A & T Building, # 244 Escolta, MANILA, METRO MANILA
Contact Number/s : (632) 242-1481 (632) 247-6701 (632) 244-5951
Fax : (632) 242-1492
Contact Person: Romeo P. Ilaga - President/Owner; Milagros A. Ilaga - Finance Officer

 Valuefreight International Forwarding Corporation
Room 302 MNA Building, 186 2nd Street, cor. Bonifacio Drive, Port Area, MANILA, METRO MANILA
Contact Number/s : (632) 527-0468 (632) 527-0461
Fax : (632) 527-0461
Email : valuefreight@edsamail.com.ph
Contact Person: Kendrick Sy - General Manager; Maria Cristina P. Parra - Operations Manager

 Victories Freight Forwarding Int'l., Inc.
Room 612 Manufacturer Building, Sta. Cruz, MANILA, METRO MANILA
Contact Number/s : (632) 734-0766 (632) 734-0746
Fax : (632) 734-0740
Contact Person: Efren V. Carbungco - President & General Manager

 Virtual Logistics, Inc.
Rm. 312 Herald Building, 61 Muralla Street, Intramuros, MANILA, METRO MANILA
Contact Number/s : (632) 527-0379 (632) 527-0221 (632) 527-0224

Fax : (632) 527-0209
Email : virtual@compass.com.ph
Contact Person: Mary Elizabeth L. Hernandez - President/General Manager; Manolito Adriano - Operations Manager

□ Walkers Freight Forwarder, Inc.
6/F Madrigal Building, 286 Escolta Street, Binondo, MANILA, METRO MANILA
Contact Number/s : (632) 243-7525 (632) 247-4714 (632) 244-6028
Fax : (632) 243-7425
Email : walkers@pacific.net.ph
Contact Person: Ramon L. Olgado - President & Chief Executive Officer

□ WC Freight System, Inc.
Room 704 Pacific Bank Building, 460 Quintin Paredes Street, Binondo, MANILA, METRO MANILA
Contact Number/s : (632) 243-7994 to 95
Fax : (632) 243-7991
Email : country@pworld.net.ph
Contact Person: Eduardo C. Tolentino - President

□ Westport Line, Inc.
Unit 4A & 4B, Osmeña Building, 1991 A. Mabini Street, Malate, MANILA, METRO MANILA
Contact Number/s : (632) 524-6532 (632) 524-6538 (632) 524-3523
Fax : (632) 526-5627
Email : wplimnl@compass.com.ph
Contact Person: Joseph Ernie Camua - President; Editha F. Manansala - Station Manager

□ WLJ Cargo Forwarding Corporation
#410 Champ Building, A. Bonifacio Drive, Port Area, MANILA, METRO MANILA
Contact Number/s : (632) 526-0511
Fax : (632) 526-6552
Contact Person: Jeremiah Ancheta - General & Operations Manager

□ World Cargo Container Inc.
2/F Royal Bay Terrace, U.N. Avenue cor. Cortada Street, Ermita, MANILA, METRO MANILA
Contact Number/s : (632) 526-8031 (632) 526-5815
Fax : (632) 526-8238 to 39
Email : rgv@pacific.net.ph
Contact Person: Willy C. Uy, Jr. - President; Edgardo I. Ilejay - Marketing Manager

□ World Consolidation Phils., Inc.
G/F Elena II Building, No. 1036-38, J. Nakpil Street, Ermita, MANILA, METRO MANILA
Contact Number/s : (632) 536-2114 to 20 (632) 522-5303 to 07
Fax : (632) 536-2117
Email : wcpi@compass.com.ph; worldcon@compass.com.ph
Contact Person: Gina S. Pacquing - General Manager; Alma G. Quiambao - VP for Sales & Marketing; Judy B. Quiambao - Operations Supervisor

□ World Expert Logistics, Inc.
G/F Doña Mercedes Building, 584 San Andres Street, Malate, MANILA, METRO MANILA
Contact Number/s : (632) 522-6861 to 62
Fax : (632) 522-6863
Contact Person: Josephine R. Oquialda - General Manager; Junelyn C. Cardenas - Sales and Marketing

□ WTO Logistics Phils., Inc.
Artes Tower, #1956 Pilar Hidalgo Lim Street, Malate, MANILA, METRO MANILA
Contact Number/s : (632) 525-4113
Fax : (632) 524-1758
Contact Person: Ma. Theresa F. Esquivel - Chairman of the Board; Cynthia L. Garcia - Operations Manager

□ Yatari Express Phils., Inc.
Room 415 Federation Center Bldg., Muelle de Binondo, MANILA, METRO MANILA
Contact Number/s : (632) 242-2449
Fax : (632) 242-2482
Email : yatari@tri-sys.com
Contact Person: Estrelita C. Lim - Station Manager; Roda Ignacio - Export

Documentation Officer; Florenda I. Ramirez - Operations Supervisor

 Zeal Cargo International, Inc.
Room 1404 Victoria Building, #429 United Nations Avenue, MANILA, METRO MANILA
Contact Number/s : (632) 400-6949 (632) 522-8688
Fax : (632) 404-1005
Email : zealcargo@pacific.net.ph
Contact Person: Pedro Ronald S. Pamatmat - President; Jonas T. Ventura - Forwarding Manager

 Forex Cargo (Phils.) Inc.
#181 Ipil Street cor. Ipil Extension, Marikina Heights, Marikina City, MARIKINA, METRO MANILA
Contact Number/s : (632) 941-9167 (632) 941-4212
Fax : (632) 941-8716
Email : fcphil@forexworld.com; westpac@forexworld.com
Contact Person: Benjamin M. Cariño - Chairman; Luzviminda C. Mendia - Exec. Vice President

 Tristar Express Phils. Co.
#50 Dragon Street, Midtown Subdivision, San Roque, Marikina City, MARIKINA, METRO MANILA
Contact Number/s : (632) 645-0583
Fax : (632) 682-8145
Email : tristarmnl@skyinet.net
Contact Person: Enrique Mendoza - General Manager

 RABM International Cargo Services
87 Arandia Street, Tunasan, Muntinlupa City, MUNTINLUPA, METRO MANILA
Contact Number/s : (632) 868-3316 (632) 565-6381
Fax : (632) 565-6381
Contact Person: Ruben N. Argame - Manager

 MOF Company (Subic) , Inc.
Building 1460 Argonaut Highway, Cubi Point, SBMA, Olongapo City, OLONGAPO CITY, ZAMBALES
Contact Number/s : (6347) 252-6346 (6347) 252-7526 (632) 892-5749
Fax : (6347) 252-7456
Email : info@mof-subic.com
Contact Person: Fernando Martin O. Peña - President; Oscar Talisaysay - Manager-Forwarding Division

 Nishiyoshi Forwarding, Inc.
Room 119, Charlie Building, Subic International Hotel, Subic Bay Freeport Zone, Zambales, OLONGAPO CITY, ZAMBALES
Contact Number/s : (6347) 252-3052
Fax : (6347) 252-3053
Contact Person: Teruo Nishida - President/Managing Director; Rosini C. Reyes - Operations Manager

 4K Express Consolidators, Inc.
Unit 11 G/F Cargo Village Complex cor. Multinational Village & NAIA Ave., Sto. Niño, PARAÑAQUE, METRO MANILA
Contact Number/s : (632) 854-3865
Fax : (632) 854-0681
Email : fourk@pworld.net.ph
Contact Person: Ms. Rosemarie D. Pangilinan - President; Mascardo C. Pangilinan - Vice-President; Santiago P. Zacarias - Operations Manager

 A & S Channel Express Phils., Inc.
Room 218 Salud-Dizon Bldg., #5 MIA Road, PARAÑAQUE, METRO MANILA
Contact Number/s : (632) 832-2847
Fax : (632) 832-2847
Email : a-schaneexprs@pacific.net.ph
Contact Person: Francisca B. Aglipay - President/General Manager

 A.T.E. Freight Phils., Inc.
#505 Quirino Avenue, Tambo, PARAÑAQUE, METRO MANILA
Contact Number/s : (632) 510-9215 to 20
Fax : (632) 833-0150
Email : atfrt@pacific.net.ph
Contact Person: Mr. Koki Sone - President; Mary Christine S. Adriano - General Manager; Mario C. Lacerona - Administration Manager

□ AB Cargo Lift Services Co.
#6570 J. de Leon Street, Gatchalian I Subdivision, PARAÑAQUE, METRO MANILA
Contact Number/s : (632) 829-8011
Fax : (632) 826-6373 (632) 829-3990
Email : abclift@pacific.net.ph
Contact Person: Luisa A. Baluyot - General Manager

□ Activair Incorporated
#1015 G MIA Townhouse, Sunrise Street, Concorde Subdivision, Tambo, PARAÑAQUE, METRO MANILA
Contact Number/s : (632) 851-1941, 851-1945 to 46, 854-6422
Fax : (632) 851-1942 (632) 854-6423
Email : activair@philonline.com
Contact Person: Arnel M. Pacheco - President; John Patrick M. Leyble - Vice-President

□ AE Eagle Philippines, Inc.
#9583 Maria Street, Airport Village, Brgy. Vitalez, PARAÑAQUE, METRO MANILA
Contact Number/s : (632) 854-5396
Fax : (632) 854-5398
Email : rfevill@compass.com.ph
Contact Person: Jose E. Clemente - President & CEO; Wilfredo M. De Leon - Seafreight & Project Manager

□ Aeroworld Logistics Phils., Inc. (formerly AWC-Aerotrans Worldwide Corp.)
Unit A-111 G/F Sky Freight Building, Ninoy Aquino Avenue, PARAÑAQUE, METRO MANILA
Contact Number/s : (632) 851-1111, 851-6923 to 24
Fax : (632) 851-6921 (632) 851-6818
Email : aeroworld@pacific.net.ph
Contact Person: Rivelyn C. Palabrica - Exec. Vice President ; Nellyn L. Manzano - Forwarding Supervisor

□ Afreight Int'l. Forwarders, Inc. (Formerly: Luzaf Forwarders, Inc.)
8530 Juanita De Leon Street, Dr. A. Santos Ave., San Dionisio, PARAÑAQUE, METRO MANILA
Contact Number/s : (632) 820-0624 to 25, 825-7170, 825-7110
Fax : (632) 820-0622
Contact Person: Edgardo J. S. Feliciano - Vice President

□ Afreight Phils., Inc.
#8530 Juanita de Leon Street, Olivarez Compound, Brgy. San Dionisio, PARAÑAQUE, METRO MANILA
Contact Number/s : (632) 820-8181, 820-6652
Fax : (632) 820-8180
Contact Person: Linda E. Acebuche - VP/General Manager

□ Air Power Int'l. Express
Air Power Bldg., Veronica de Leon St., corner Delbros Ave., Bo. Ibayo, Sto. Niño, PARAÑAQUE, METRO MANILA
Contact Number/s : (632) 852-4366
Fax : (632) 851-4181
Email : airpower@airpowermnl.com
Contact Person: Ernesto Ng - President; Rogelio Ng - Vice-President; Annabel Ng - Export Manager

□ Air Tiger Express Companies, Inc. (formerly Unique Int'l. Forwarders Phils., Inc.)
L6 B2 F2B Door2, Pacific Ave., Sto. Niño, PARAÑAQUE, METRO MANILA
Contact Number/s : (632) 853-4276, 512-1251 to 54
Fax : (632) 853-4277
Email : airtiger@mnl.airtiger.com.ph; atemnl@pacific.net.ph
Contact Person: Jose G. Mercado - General Manager; Helen Sunega - Export Seafreight Coordinator; Victorino Guilles, Jr. - Seafreight Import Coordinator

□ Airspeed International Corporation
GGB Bldg., Pascor Drive, Sto. Niño, PARAÑAQUE, METRO MANILA
Contact Number/s : (632) 852-7328 to 39
Fax : (632) 852-7377
Email : ephesian@globe.com.ph; airspeed@globe.com.ph
Contact Person: Rosemarie P. Rafael - President Emperatriz C. Regis - VP & General Manager; Dominador R. Eugenio - VP for

Sales-Seafreight; Edwin Quindo - Seafreight Manager

□ Al Mohr Customs Brokers, Inc.
L6 B2 F2B Pacific Ave., Sto. Niño, 1700, PARAÑAQUE, METRO MANILA
Contact Number/s : (632) 851-5990 (632) 551-4420
Fax : (632) 851-5989
Contact Person: Darwin R. Manalansan - President & General Manager; Beatriz P. Pamintuan - EVP/Operations Manager

□ Al-Atlas International Forwarders, Inc.
Dr. A. Santos Avenue corner Gatchalian I, San Dionisio, PARAÑAQUE, METRO MANILA
Contact Number/s : (632) 829-3603 to 05 (632) 829-0210 to 11
Fax : (632) 829-3990
Email : alatlas@pw.net
Contact Person: Charlie C. Fuentes - President; Maricar L. Gonzales - Air/Sea Port Operations Coordinator

□ All Continent Int'l. Freight Services, Inc.
L6-B OCS Bldg., Pascor Drive, Sta. Agueda St., Brgy. Sto. Niño, PARAÑAQUE, METRO MANILA
Contact Number/s : (632) 852-6194 (632) 853-5421 (632) 852-6195
Fax : (632) 852-6194
Email : allcontinents@netasia.net
Contact Person: Florentino E. Zapanta, Jr. - President & General Manager; Julito I. Ismael - Principal Broker/Operations Manager

□ All Systems Logistics (formerly All Systems Transport, Inc.)
3/F MTE Properties, Inc., No. 3, Sta. Agueda Avenue, Pascor Drive,, PARAÑAQUE, METRO MANILA
Contact Number/s : (632) 551-4614 to 20
Fax : (632) 551-4621
Email : ast@epic.net
Contact Person: Mary Lou T. Estrada - Chairman; Jose Ma. Sarasola II - President

□ All Trans-Link Network Phils., Inc.
#3 Sta. Agueda Avenue, Pascor Drive, PARAÑAQUE, METRO MANILA
Contact Number/s : (632) 551-4648 to 51
Fax : (632) 551-4652
Email : alltranslink@pacific.net.ph
Contact Person: Mary Lou T. Estrada - President; Antonio Lim Baliton - Executive Int'l. Freight

□ All Transport Network, Inc.
Delbros Ave. corner Sta. Agueda Ave., Pascor Drive, PARAÑAQUE, METRO MANILA
Contact Number/s : (632) 551-4646
Fax : (632) 831-3054 (632) 831-7400
Email : alltrans@atnmnl.e-d-i.net
Contact Person: Ms. Mary Lou T. Estrada - Chief Executive Officer; Antonio G. Estrada - Chief Operating Officer

□ Alliance Freight International, Inc.
AMDG Building, Int. 3 Mayuga Street, Tambo, PARAÑAQUE, METRO MANILA
Contact Number/s : (632) 833-7854 (632) 831-8851 (632) 532-0405
Fax : (632) 833-7849 (632) 853-6669
Contact Person: Joel M. Sia - President

□ Allnations Freight Forwarders, Inc.
#606 Quirino Avenue, Tambo, PARAÑAQUE, METRO MANILA
Contact Number/s : (632) 831-9806 (632) 832-0184
Fax : (632) 833-7650 (632) 832-0039
Email : allntns@pworld.net.ph
Contact Person: Arnel A. Merilleno - Vice-President

□ Allport Freight Consolidator, Inc.
Room 306-B GGB Building, Pascor Drive, Bgy. Sto. Niño, PARAÑAQUE, METRO MANILA
Contact Number/s : (632) 852-7374 (632) 854-1282
Fax : (632) 852-7374
Email : allport@pacific.net.ph
Contact Person: Ingrid R. Aprieto - General Manager

□ AMDG Freight Corporation

AMDG Bldg., Int. 3 P. Mayuga cor. MIA Road, Tambo, PARAÑAQUE, METRO MANILA
Contact Number/s : (632) 833-7854
Fax : (632) 833-7849
Email : amdgfrt@tri-sys.com
Contact Person: Reynaldo I. Atos - General Manager; Cesar M. Hontiveros - Operations Manager

 American Freight Forwarders, Inc.
JJM Bldg. 1, Kaingin Road, Multinational Village, PARAÑAQUE, METRO MANILA
Contact Number/s : (632) 822-1525 to 29
Fax : (632) 822-2774 (632) 822-1535
Email : affi3456@mnl.vlink.net.ph
Contact Person: Juanito G. Violeta - President & General Manager

 Anseri Forwarder
Unit 14 Ed and Joe Commercial Arcade, 153 Quirino Avenue, Baclaran, PARAÑAQUE, METRO MANILA
Contact Number/s : (632) 853-8780
Fax : (632) 853-8780
Email : anseri@compass.com.ph
Contact Person: Nancy C. Argañoza - General Manager

 Asia Ocean Services, Inc.
AAI Building, Kaingin Road, Multinational Drive, PARAÑAQUE, METRO MANILA
Contact Number/s : (632) 822-2481 to 87
Fax : (632) 822-2490
Contact Person: Conrad U. Puentes - President

 Asia Overseas Transport Co., Inc.
Unit S1 & S2 Gedcor Bldg., Irasan Complex, N. Aquino Ave., PARAÑAQUE, METRO MANILA
Contact Number/s : (632) 829-0340
Fax : (632) 829-0373 (632) 829-0377
Contact Person: Cynthia Reyes-Tsui - President & General Manager; Leonor M. Pano - Seafreight Operations Manager; Beth A. Diaz - Airfreight Operations Manager

 Asian Wings Express, Inc.
Room 306-B GGB Building, Cor. Queensway Avenue, Pascor Drive, Sto. Niño, PARAÑAQUE, METRO MANILA
Contact Number/s : (632) 852-7345
Fax : (632) 852-7344
Email : a_wexinc@pacific.net.ph
Contact Person: Corazon O'Hara - President; Amy Barrameda - Operations Manager

 ASPAC Int'l Airfreight, Inc.
Kaingin Road, Multinational Village, PARAÑAQUE, METRO MANILA
Contact Number/s : (632) 776-0888
Fax : (632) 776-4920 (632) 776-4624
Email : seafreight@aspacmanila. com.ph
Contact Person: Monico "Chito" E. David, Jr. - President/General Manager; Troy V. Panganiban - Supervisor-Int'l. Seafreight

 Associated Freight Consolidators, Inc.
Kaingin Road, Multinational Avenue, PARAÑAQUE, METRO MANILA
Contact Number/s : (632) 822-1027 to 29
Fax : (632) 822-1051
Email : afci@afciphil.com
Contact Person: Danilo L. Belgado - President/General Manager; Cornelio A. Pedro - Director, Sales and Services; Ma. Cecilia B. Jardin - Manager, Logistics & Special Projects

 Awards Cargo Agency Phils., Inc. (formerly HK-Awards Consolidation Services Phils., Inc.)
Unit 7 Bldg. A Cargo Village Complex, NAIA Road, PARAÑAQUE, METRO MANILA
Contact Number/s : (632) 852-6834
Fax : (632) 852-1828
Email : mam-awards@hkawards.com.ph; arv-awards@hkawards.com.ph
Contact Person: Hipolito B. Macaspac, Jr. - President/General Manager; Alfonso R. Villaverde III - Export Sales Manager; Ma. Victoria A. Montero - AVP-Import

 Baker Bros. Inc.
#14 Iraq St., Bgy. Don Bosco, Better Living, PARAÑAQUE, METRO MANILA
Contact Number/s : (632) 821-5463 to 64
Fax : (632) 824-0460
Email : bcfs-mal@epic.net

Contact Person: Lloyd S. Baker - Chairman/CEO/ COO; Susan R. Digal - Finance/Accounting Officer; Ma. Rosa A. Pangan - Forwarding Manager

□ Bermont Express Int'l., Inc.
Rm. 304-305, Doña Eusebia Rodriguez Bldg., 0611 Quirino Ave., San Dionisio, PARAÑAQUE, METRO MANILA
Contact Number/s : (632) 820-4348
Fax : (632) 825-2405
Email : brmont98@i-next.net
Contact Person: Rogelio B. Bermas - President; Mary Jane C. Bermas - EVP & General Manager; Rodel B. Llaneta - Operations Manager

□ Birkart-East West Freight Phils., Inc.
Bldg. B., Cargo Village Complex, NAIA Rd. cor. Multinational Ave., Sto. Niño, PARAÑAQUE, METRO MANILA
Contact Number/s : (632) 852-7123 to 25
Fax : (632) 852-7126
Email : bewmnl@birkart.com.ph
Contact Person: Franz Josef Christen - President/General Manager; Ed Panganiban - Sales Manager & Seafreight; Rommel Bernales - Airfreight/ Seafreight Manager

□ BIT Worldwide Phils., Inc.
XDE Building, 808 Villaver Compound, Quirino Avenue, Tambo, PARAÑAQUE, METRO MANILA
Contact Number/s : (632) 853-2075 to 78
Fax : (632) 852-1302 (632) 852-1254
Email : mcp@globe.com.ph
Contact Person: Manuel C. Protacio - President/ General Manager; Jerome S. Ibañez - VP-Sales

□ Brighten Freight International, Inc.
Unit 21 # 22 Cargo Complex Village, Multinational cor. Ninoy Aquino Ave., PARAÑAQUE, METRO MANILA
Contact Number/s : (632) 851-8345 to 47
Fax : (632) 851-8498
Email : bfi@pworld.net.ph
Contact Person: Ms. Victoria A. Geniza - President

□ Brilliant Eagle Freight, Inc.
Unit 106 Doña Eusebia Bldg., No. 0611 Quirino Ave., San Dionisio, PARAÑAQUE, METRO MANILA
Contact Number/s : (632) 825-0121 (632) 826-6871
Fax : (632) 829-3981
Email : befi@compass.com.ph
Contact Person: Susana S. Espiritu - Managing Director; Dominador Sandigan, Jr. - Operations Supervisor/Customs Broker

□ Cargo Bridge Phils., Inc.
8108 Dr. A. Santos Avenue, PARAÑAQUE, METRO MANILA
Contact Number/s : (632) 826-0959 to 62
Fax : (632) 826-0946
Email : cbridge@skyinet.net
Contact Person: Bernhard Ashauer, Jr - President; Mario I. Martos - Operations Manager

□ Cargo Marketing & Moving Corporation
ACM Building, P. Mayuga Street, MIA Road, Tambo, PARAÑAQUE, METRO MANILA
Contact Number/s : (632) 853-1410 (632) 851-9033
Fax : (632) 853-6294
Contact Person: Patrocinio H. Flores, Jr. - President/ General Manager

□ Cargoaire Maritime Corporation
Suite 1 & 2 JJM Bldg., Kaingin Road, Multinational Village, PARAÑAQUE, METRO MANILA
Contact Number/s : (632) 822-1537 to 38
Fax : (632) 822-1530 (632) 822-1536
Email : caroair@pworld.net.ph
Contact Person: Alfredo Mendoza - Managing Director; Edward Santillan - Seafreight Operations Manager

□ Cargofactors, Inc.
3/F ASA Building, Sta. Agueda Ave., Pascor Drive, Sto. Niño, PARAÑAQUE, METRO MANILA
Contact Number/s : (632) 852-7541
Fax : (632) 852-7543
Email : cargofactors@pacific.net.ph

Contact Person: Reynaldo A.D. Manlucu - President; Bonifacio V. Ebina - VP-Operations

□ Cargomatic International, Inc.
Isabelle Mansion, Penthouse I, Km. 14 Edison Ave., PARAÑAQUE, METRO MANILA
Contact Number/s : (632) 542-9155 to 56 (632) 542-9187 (632) 824-3868
Fax : (632) 776-5271
Email : cargonet@pworld.net.ph
Contact Person: Gladys Anima-Concon - General Manager

□ Cargotranz Trucking Services
L6 OCS Building, Pascor Compound, Sta. Agueda Street, Sto. Niño, PARAÑAQUE, METRO MANILA
Contact Number/s : (632) 851-5338 (632) 851-6856 (632) 851-5994
Fax : (632) 851-5994
Email : cargotranz@edsamail.com.ph
Contact Person: Lilia V. Zapata - General Manager

□ Cityfreight Int'l. Services, Inc.
Unit 12 G/F Cargo Village Complex, cor. Ninoy Aquino Ave. & Multinational Village, PARAÑAQUE, METRO MANILA
Contact Number/s : (632) 851-6726 (632) 851-7961
Fax : (632) 852-3053
Email : ctfreight@skyinet.net
Contact Person: Mascardo C. Pangilinan - President; Salvador Olanga - Operations Manager

□ Confederated Cargo Services, Inc.
Unit 24 Olive's Plaza, Ninoy Aquino Ave., PARAÑAQUE, METRO MANILA
Contact Number/s : (632) 829-9428 (632) 829-7933
Fax : (632) 829-7933
Email : ccsi@compass.com.ph
Contact Person: Rechilda T. Oquias - President & General Manager; Elizabeth E. Oquias - Vice-President; Evelyn E. Oquias - Operations Manager

□ Conor Express International Brokerage Corp.
9587 Maria Street, Airport Village, (Baltao), PARAÑAQUE, METRO MANILA
Contact Number/s : (632) 854-1725 (632) 854-1727 (632) 832-2353 to 55
Fax : (632) 832-1958
Email : conorintl@pacific.net.ph
Contact Person: Eduardo L. Callera - VP-Operations and General Manager

□ Container Bridge Phils., Inc.
Unit D-2 G/F Echelon Tower, Mabini St., Malate, PARAÑAQUE, METRO MANILA
Contact Number/s : (632) 536-7623 to 26 (632) 523-7109 to 10
Fax : (632) 523-7120
Email : manila@containerbridge.com.ph
Contact Person: Norman Fulgencio - President; Gino Gonzalo - General Manager; Joanna Beato - CS/Operations-in-Charge

□ CPI Transport, Inc.
Dragon Bldg., Pascor Drive, Sto. Niño, PARAÑAQUE, METRO MANILA
Contact Number/s : (632) 852-5707
Fax : (632) 852-9601 (632) 512-1327
Email : cpi.mnl@cpitransport.com.ph
Contact Person: Patrick Chen - President; Roy A. Raralio - EVP and General Manager

□ CWW Cargo Express
8252 Raymundo Bldg. Complex, Dr. A. Santos Ave., San Isidro, PARAÑAQUE, METRO MANILA
Contact Number/s : (632) 820-5670 to 72
Fax : (632) 825-4831
Email : cwwcargo@mnl.cyberspace.com.ph
Contact Person: Rodel S. Pante - General Manager

□ Danzas AEI, Inc. (formerly Royal Cargo Corporation)
Danzas Building, Sta. Agueda Avenue, Cor. Pascor Drive, 1704, PARAÑAQUE, METRO MANILA
Contact Number/s : (632) 852-4546 (632) 852-4553
Fax : (632) 551-4470 (632) 551-4471
Email : benjie.murro@ph.danzas.com

Contact Person: Michael K. Raeuber - President; Flora A. Evangelista - Seafreight Manager

 Danzas Intercontinental, Inc.
Rm. 127 Skyfreight Bldg., Ninoy Aquino Avenue, PARAÑAQUE, METRO MANILA
Contact Number/s : (632) 831-9520 (632) 831-1902 (632) 852-6560
Fax : (632) 853-1689
Contact Person: Elizabeth Gotiam - Ocean Freight Manager

 Dimerco Express Phils., Inc.
0170 Quirino Avenue, Tambo, PARAÑAQUE, METRO MANILA
Contact Number/s : (632) 854-0141 (632) 854-0146
Fax : (632) 854-1755
Contact Person: Leticia S. Palao - Ocean Frt. & Brok. Manager; Tagumpay I. Maayo - Asst. Sales Manager

 E2 Logistics Phils., Inc.
Oyster Industrial Complex Bldg. I, San Dionisio, PARAÑAQUE, METRO MANILA
Contact Number/s : (632) 829-2753
Fax : (632) 829-0132 to 33
Email : e2phil@skyinet.net
Contact Person: Eileen C. Garcia - President; Emmanuel R. Ibasco - Exec. Vice-President; Marites M. Martinez - Airfreight/Seafreight Manager

 Eagle Express Lines, Inc.
Cargo Village Complex Bldg. A, Cor. Multinational & Ninoy Aquino Avenues, PARAÑAQUE, METRO MANILA
Contact Number/s : (632) 852-3445 (632) 852-6446 (632) 852-6822 (632)
Fax : (632) 852-2857 (632) 852-6821
Email : eagle@aec.com.ph; aecolona@eaglegroup.com.ph
Contact Person: Angelito E. Colona - President & General Manager; Tomas de Vega - VP/Sales & Marketing; Nelson M. Mendoza - Assistant Vice-President

 EGL Eagle Global Logistics Phil. Inc. (formerly Circle Freight International (Phils.) Ltd., Inc.)
EGL Building, Johann Street, Cor. Pascor Drive, Bo. Ibayo, Sto. Niño, PARAÑAQUE, METRO MANILA
Contact Number/s : (632) 831-4631
Fax : (632) 831-5090
Email : grace.yap@eaglegl.com
Contact Person: Grace A. Yap - President & Managing Director; Rody F. Alborte - VP-Operations

 Elisha International Freight Forwarder, Inc.
Room 302 La Azalea Building, No. 8262 Dr. A. Santos Avenue, Sucat Road, PARAÑAQUE, METRO MANILA
Contact Number/s : (632) 826-1496
Fax : (632) 826-1496
Email : elisha@compass.com.ph; aes@compass.com.ph
Contact Person: Alberto E. Solomon - General Manager; Mary Ann A. Solomon - Operations Manager

 EMCS Philippines, Inc.
G/F Unit 8, Bulding A, Cargo Village Complex, Ninoy Aquino Ave., Sto. Niño, PARAÑAQUE, METRO MANILA
Contact Number/s : (632) 852-3445 (632) 852-6446
Fax : (632) 852-2857 (632) 852-6821
Contact Person: Angelito E. Colona - President; Nelson M. Mendoza - General Manager

 Emery Transnational Air Cargo Corp.
Rm. 108 Skyfreight Building, Ninoy Aquino Ave., PARAÑAQUE, METRO MANILA
Contact Number/s : (632) 852-7001 to 18 (632) 826-0986
Fax : (632) 852-7019 to 20 (632) 829-4059
Contact Person: Arthur P. Tugade - President; Benny B. Donsol - General Manager; Evelyn C. Abreu - Seafreight Manager

 EXCEL Cargo Systems, Inc.
Rm 126-B, Skyfreight Bldg., NAIA Avenue, PARAÑAQUE, METRO MANILA
Contact Number/s : (632) 852-3575 to 76

Fax : (632) 852-3577
Email : excel@skyinet.net
Contact Person: Mauricio G. Bermudez, Sr. - General Manager; Mauricio C. Bermudez, Jr. - Manager

□ Exel Philippines, Inc. (formerly MSAS Global Logistics Corporation)
ZEALCOR Business Center, Lot 5, Sta. Agueda Ave., Pascor Compound Bo. Ibayo, PARAÑAQUE, METRO MANILA
Contact Number/s : (632) 852-4323
Fax : (632) 852-4560 (632) 852-4313
Email : systems.mnloi@msas.com
Contact Person: Mr. Ole Ringheim - General Manager; Eva C. Dimapindan - Airfreight Manager; Ma. Elena F. Ampil - Seafreight Manager

□ Expeditors Philippines, Inc.
Pascor Building III, Pascor Drive, Sto. Niño, PARAÑAQUE, METRO MANILA
Contact Number/s : (632) 833-5571 (632) 891-6458
Fax : (632) 552-7096 to 97
Contact Person: Manuel B. Comanda - General Manager; Flora S. Datu - Accounting Manager

□ Explorer Freight Corporation
#707-D Columbia Airfreight Complex, N. Aquino Avenue, PARAÑAQUE, METRO MANILA
Contact Number/s : (632) 853-5841 to 42 (632) 852-0191 to 93
Fax : (632) 853-5843
Email : efcgsc@compass.com.ph
Contact Person: Guido S. Cuerda - President & General Manager

□ Fair Freight International Corporation
Unit 26-29, Cargo Village Complex, N. Aquino cor. Multinational Ave., PARAÑAQUE, METRO MANILA
Contact Number/s : (632) 852-7274 (632) 852-9678 to 79
Fax : (632) 852-5939
Email : fair@i-next.net
Contact Person: Feliciano S. Pimentel - President & General Manager; Albert Z. Jardin - Operations Manager; Nenita S. Colcol - Adminstrative Manager

□ Fast Brokerage Consolidators, Inc.
Oyster Industrial Complex Bldg. 1 cor. Kabihasnan Rd., NAIA Ave., Brgy. San Dionisio, Pque. City, PARAÑAQUE, METRO MANILA
Contact Number/s : (632) 820-8470 (632) 825-8486
Fax : (632) 825-7208
Contact Person: Stewart Y. Marquez - General Manager; Felipe O. Casing - President

□ Fast Info Link Cargo, Inc.
Unit 24 Cargo Village Complex, Ninoy Aquino Avenue, Brgy. Sto. Niño, PARAÑAQUE, METRO MANILA
Contact Number/s : (632) 854-0879 (632) 854-0882
Fax : (632) 854-0878
Email : filcimnl@mozcom.com
Contact Person: Juanito C. Hipolito - President/General Manager

□ FETA Freight Systems Phils., Inc.
S9/208 & 209 GEDCOR Square Bldg., Irasan cor. N. Aquino Avenue, Sto. Niño, PARAÑAQUE, METRO MANILA
Contact Number/s : (632) 829-8858 (632) 825-3836
Fax : (632) 829-2752 (632) 829-8985
Email : fetaphi@csi.com.ph; fetaphgm@csi.com.ph
Contact Person: Bernard Dan F. Angeles - President; Ramon G. Machica - EVP & General Manager

□ Firav Freight Int'l. Phils., Inc.
Lot 19 Cooperative Village, Juanita de Leon Street, San Dionsio, PARAÑAQUE, METRO MANILA
Contact Number/s : (632) 541-6866 (632) 820-5939
Fax : (632) 541-6867
Contact Person: Mr. Sun Taek Kim - President; Carina M. Consignado - General/Operations Manager

 First Imperial Cargo, Inc.
113 Roxas Blvd., Baclaran, PARAÑAQUE, METRO MANILA
Contact Number/s : (632) 833-1289
Fax : (632) 831-2557
Email : ficimnl@skyinet.net
Contact Person: Adrian B. Jimenez - General Manager; Eduardo S. Samson - Personnel/Admin. Manager

 Flying "A" Int'l. Freight Forwarder, Inc.
Unit F 8102 R&S Building, Dr. A. Santos Ave., Sucat Road, PARAÑAQUE, METRO MANILA
Contact Number/s : (632) 820-6467 (632) 820-6483
Fax : (632) 820-8076
Email : flying111a@skyinet.net
Contact Person: Ireneo A. Arbues - President/General Manager

 Fort Logistics Phils., Inc.
Unit 23, Ed & Joe's Commercial Arcade, 153 Quirino Avenue, Baclaran, PARAÑAQUE, METRO MANILA
Contact Number/s : (632) 851-3430 (632) 851-3431
Fax : (632) 833-8723
Email : fortlog@pacific.net.ph
Contact Person: Samuel C. Bautista - Maanging Director; Aldrin H. Perez - Forwarding Officer; Marilou de Ocampo - Customer Service Officer

 Freight Facilitators Corporation
S-11 GEDCOR Square Building, Irasan Street, San Dionsio, Sucat, PARAÑAQUE, METRO MANILA
Contact Number/s : (632) 826-8673 (632) 820-6911 (632) 829-0632
Fax : (632) 826-1521
Email : ffcmla@I-manila.com.ph
Contact Person: Christopher B. Almanzor - General Manager

 Freight Net Int'l. Phils., Inc.
Unit 302 Centennial Bldg., #325 Calle Escolta, Binondo, PARAÑAQUE, METRO MANILA
Contact Number/s : (632) 244-6221 (632) 243-7170 (632) 243-7168 (632)
Fax : (632) 309-0355
Email : fnimnl@skyinet.net
Contact Person: Marsha Joy Castillo - President; Romy Barrientos - Assistant General Manager; Loi Lim - Financial & Administrative Manager

 Freight Options, Inc.
S8-Gedcor Square Bldg., NAIA Avenue, PARAÑAQUE, METRO MANILA
Contact Number/s : (632) 829-9157 (632) 820-0116 to 17
Fax : (632) 829-9153
Email : frtoptns@info.com.ph; frtoptns@mozcom.com; perrymv@info.com.ph
Contact Person: Perfecto M. Villanueva - President; Thelma V. Flores - Vice-President

 Fritz Logistics Phils., Inc.
Queensway Avenue corner Sta. Agueda Street, Sto. Niño, PARAÑAQUE, METRO MANILA
Contact Number/s : (632) 851-1023
Fax : (632) 851-5196 (632) 851-1031
Email : mnl.general@fritz.com
Contact Person: Jerry H. Stehmeier - Managing Director; Manny Comanda - General Manager; Elsie P. Rosete - Operations Manager (Inbound); Belinda Mira - Operations Manager (Ocean Export)

 FTS Logistics, Inc.
Unit 30 Cargo Village Complex, Multinational Village cor. NAIA Avenue, Sto Niño, PARAÑAQUE, METRO MANILA
Contact Number/s : (632) 854-3865 to 66
Fax : (632) 854-0682
Email : ftsmnl@pacific.net.ph
Contact Person: Rosemarie D. Pangilinan - President & General Manager; Warlito S. Roberto - Operations Manager

 Gatelink Sea & Air Int'l. Phils. Co.
Room 310-A Gedcor Square Building, Corner Irasan Complex & Ninoy Aquino Avenue, San Dionisio, PARAÑAQUE, METRO MANILA
Contact Number/s : (632) 826-8586
Fax : (632) 826-8586
Email : gatelink@tri-sys.com

Contact Person: Roslyn R. Gabriel - General Manager; Woody Fajardo - Forwarding Manager

□ Geologistics, Inc. (formerly LEP International Phils., Inc.)
Geologistics Bldg., Ninoy Aquino Ave., PARAÑAQUE, METRO MANILA
Contact Number/s : (632) 852-7031 to 70
Fax : (632) 833-3790
Contact Person: Gil F. Cruz - President and CEO; Jade A. Posadas, Sr. - VP-Airfreight; Joselito B. Ilagan - VP-Seafreight

□ Gold Cargo Express Ventures, Inc.
Unit N Times Square Building, Dr. A. Santos Avenue, Sucat, PARAÑAQUE, METRO MANILA
Contact Number/s : (632) 825-0410
Fax : (632) 829-3869
Email : goldexpress@hotmail.com; jude@aimonline.org
Contact Person: Maria Judey C. Santamaria - President; Edison D. Ong - General Manager

□ GPS Logistics, Philippines Inc. (formerly USF Worldwide Philippines, Inc.)
Unit 112 Skyfreight Building, N. Aquino Ave., Sto. Niño, PARAÑAQUE, METRO MANILA
Contact Number/s : (632) 852-4866 to 70
Fax : (632) 852-4873
Contact Person: Medardo L. Medina - General Manager

□ Grandlink Freight International, Inc.
Unit 3 OCS Building, L6 Sta. Agueda St., Pascor Compound, Sto. Niño, PARAÑAQUE, METRO MANILA
Contact Number/s : (632) 853-5394 to 95
Fax : (632) 853-5396
Email : grandlink@i-next.net
Contact Person: Aurora Q. Tumang - President & General Manager; Leticia C. Cutaran - Seafreight Manager

□ GRM International, Inc.
Unit P,Q&R Columbia Airfreight Complex Bldg., 707 N. Aquino Avenue, PARAÑAQUE, METRO MANILA
Contact Number/s : (632) 832-2761 to 66
Fax : (632) 833-0224 (632) 832-3106
Email : grm@mnl.sequel.net
Contact Person: Rodrigo A. Anabu - General Manager; Antonio V. Cancio - General Manager -Ecozone; Antonio P. Marquez - Seafreight Operations Manager

□ Hankyu International Transport Philippines, Inc.
Unit 1, Cargo Forwarders & Consolidators Bldg., Ninoy Aquino Avenue cor. A. Bonifacio Street, Barangay San Dionisio, PARAÑAQUE, METRO MANILA
Contact Number/s : (632) 825-3636 (632) 825-7355 to 60
Fax : (632) 825-7046 (632) 825-7359
Contact Person: Manuel A. Barcelona, Jr. - President; Cristina M. Amio - Operations Manager

□ Harbor Logistics Customs Brokerage Company
Blk. 4, Lot 21 Saint Catherine Subdivision, San Isidro, PARAÑAQUE, METRO MANILA
Contact Number/s : (632) 541-7337 (632) 820-1082
Fax : (632) 820-1082
Email : harbor_logistics_inc@yahoo.com
Contact Person: Rosalie L. Adlao - General Manager; Sancho G. Almeda, Jr. - AGM/In-Charge of Operations

□ IFE Forwarding, Inc.
Unit 23 Cargo Village Complex, cor. Multinational Village, PARAÑAQUE, METRO MANILA
Contact Number/s : (632) 852-3043 (632) 854-0232 (632) 852-6310
Fax : (632) 854-0883
Email : ifemnl@info.com.ph
Contact Person: Vic M. Del Rosario - General Manager; Reynaldo I. Morada - VP for Operations

□ Intercontinental Freight Facilitators, Inc.
Unit T, 707 Columbia Airfreight Complex I, N. Aquino Ave., PARAÑAQUE, METRO MANILA
Contact Number/s : (632) 832-3910 (632) 851-3926 (632) 551-9744

Fax : (632) 851-3905
Email : iffi@skyinet.net; iffi@mozcom.com
Contact Person: Ma. Theresa F. Esquivel - President; Victor B. Borja - VP/Sales & Marketing

 Interdome Freight Specialist, Inc.
#581-C Quirino Avenue, Tambo, PARAÑAQUE, METRO MANILA
Contact Number/s : (632) 851-6402
Fax : (632) 851-6403
Email : intrdome@info.com.ph
Contact Person: Benjamin P. Yeh - President; Mario M. Dela Rosa, Jr. - Vice-President

 International Consolidator Phils., Inc
Unit 10 Cargo Village Complex, Ninoy Aquino Ave. cor. Multinational Ave., PARAÑAQUE, METRO MANILA
Contact Number/s : (632) 852-2587 (632) 852-9690 to 91
Fax : (632) 852-2577
Email : cs-impex@icpimnl.com
Contact Person: Marlon M. Villanueva - President; Erich H. Lingad - General Manager

 International Freight Forwarders Phils., Inc.
Rm. 114, Skyfreight Building, Ninoy Aquino Ave. corner Pascor Drive, Sto. Niño, PARAÑAQUE, METRO MANILA
Contact Number/s : (632) 833-4541 to 42 (632) 832-1213
Fax : (632) 832-5670 (632) 819-6430
Email : iffphilsmnl@qinet.net; lfsshipmnl@qinet.net
Contact Person: Juan B. Ferrer - Pres./Gen.Manager; Atty. Emmanuel Ariston V. Ferrer - Asst. Gen. Manager

 Interoute Freight Forwarder, Inc.
8252 E. Raymundo Building, Dr. A. Santos Avenue, Sucat, PARAÑAQUE, METRO MANILA
Contact Number/s : (632) 825-7919
Fax : (632) 825-0375
Email : interoute@surfershop.net.ph
Contact Person: Elinor C. Policarpio - Executive Vice-President; Danilo C. Pineda - Operations Manager

 Intership Marine Services, Inc.
#9756 Felicidad St., Gatchalian Housing Area, Brgy. Vitalez, PARAÑAQUE, METRO MANILA
Contact Number/s : (632) 851-3228 to 29 (632) 851-3230
Fax : (632) 852-1488 (632) 851-3230
Email : admllc@pacific.net.ph; monalfaro@pacific.net.ph
Contact Person: Loreto L. Cabasar, Sr. - President/General Manager; Alfredo L. Cabasar - Operations Manager

 Intertraffic Transport Corporation
0650 Quirino Avenue, San Dionisio, PARAÑAQUE, METRO MANILA
Contact Number/s : (632) 826-5412 (632) 826-7113 (632) 829-7667
Fax : (632) 826-5269
Contact Person: Rolando B. Rivera - President & General Manager; Teodoro D. Perdigon - Operations Manager

 JMC Door to Door Service Co.
#22 Don Bosco Street, Better Living Subdivision, PARAÑAQUE, METRO MANILA
Contact Number/s : (632) 776-0977 (632) 824-0149
Fax : (632) 824-0149
Contact Person: Medina A. Carlobos - General and Operations Manager; Fernando A. Carlobos - Asst. Manager

 Kawamura International Freight, Inc.
Room 304 Gedcor Square Building, Ninoy Aquino Ave. cor. Irasan St., San Dionsio, PARAÑAQUE, METRO MANILA
Contact Number/s : (632) 826-7929 (632) 826-8579 (632) 826-8663
Fax : (632) 826-8009
Email : 0214vra@webquest.com
Contact Person: Virginia R. Abella - President/Managing Director

 Kestrel Philippines, Inc.
Unit 2C Oyster Plaza Building, Kabihasnan Road cor. NAIA Ave., PARAÑAQUE, METRO MANILA

Contact Number/s : (632) 825-2978 (632) 829-9733
Fax : (632) 829-7173
Email : kestrel@info.com.ph; cbauca@info.com.ph; saleskestrel@mail.netasia.net
Contact Person: Cristina D. Bauca - General Manager; Myles Morales - Operations Manager

□ Kintetsu World Express (Phils.) , Inc.
Units 103 & 104 JJM Building II, NAIA Avenue, PARAÑAQUE, METRO MANILA
Contact Number/s : (632) 852-9220 to 29
Fax : (632) 852-9212 to 13
Email : kwemnl@ccsmtp.kwejp.co.jp
Contact Person: Keisuke Kamoto - President; Marilyn C. Alborto - General Manager/Operations

□ KSN Air & Sea Freight Co., Inc. (formerly KSN Airfreight Co., Inc.)
Room 113 Skyfreight Building, NAIA Avenue, PARAÑAQUE, METRO MANILA
Contact Number/s : (632) 852-4807 to 09 (632) 852-4814 to 15
Fax : (632) 852-4817
Email : ksnair@pacific.net.ph; acaneja@hotmail.com
Contact Person: Allan F. Caneja - President; Myla T. Dawal - Operations Manager

□ Kuehne & Nagel (Phils.) , Inc.
JJM Building 5, Ninoy Aquino Avenue, San Dionisio, PARAÑAQUE, METRO MANILA
Contact Number/s : (632) 820-4237
Fax : (632) 829-6295 (632) 829-6574
Email : mnlptgb@mail.kuehne-nagel.com
Contact Person: Mr. Burkhard Daeumich - President; Honesto M. Raquipiso - Corporate Secretary & Treasurer

□ Lambert Williams Logistics, Inc.
J1 Ninoy Aquino Avenue, San Dionisio, PARAÑAQUE, METRO MANILA
Contact Number/s : (632) 825-1219
Fax : (632) 825-1228
Contact Person: Joel F. Ortillo - President; Oscar Y. Quintana - Vice-President

□ LIBCAP Marketing Corp./LIBCAP Super Express
#10 Pildera St., MIA Road, Tambo, PARAÑAQUE, METRO MANILA
Contact Number/s : (632) 853-6306 to 13
Fax : (632) 853-1576
Email : libcapho@skyinet.net
Contact Person: Jose G. Mondragon - President/ General Manager; Ma. Lucia G. Mondragon - VP for Administration; Romeo Gilay - Brokerage Manager

□ Manila Int'l. Freight Forwarders, Inc.
Consolidators and Forwarders Building Center, Dr. A. Santos Avenue corner Bonifacio Street, Kabihasnan, San Antonio, PARAÑAQUE, METRO MANILA
Contact Number/s : (632) 825-3182 to 86
Fax : (632) 825-3609
Contact Person: Lucila C. Javina - Accounting Manager

□ Manzen Air & Sea Freight Forwarding & Trading
S-14 Irasan Complex, N. Aquino Avenue corner Irasan St., San Dionisio, PARAÑAQUE, METRO MANILA
Contact Number/s : (632) 825-0825
Fax : (632) 825-0825
Contact Person: Manuel G. Tan - Proprietor/General Manager; Michael S. Tan - Sales Manager

□ Mariano F. Castro & Sons, Inc.
#28 Doña Eva Street, Ireneville Subdivision, PARAÑAQUE, METRO MANILA
Contact Number/s : (632) 825-2611 (632) 820-3173 to 74
Fax : (632) 820-9612
Email : mfcsons@manilaforwarders.com; castr03@ibm.net
Contact Person: Mariano F. Castro - President; Jose Ma. J. Castro - Operations Manager; Emmanuel J. Castro - Administrative Officer

□ Mercury Freight Int'l, Inc.

Mercury Freight Int'l. Building, Ninoy Aquino Ave. cor A. Bonifacio St., San Dionisio, PARAÑAQUE, METRO MANILA
Contact Number/s : (632) 820-2033
Fax : (632) 829-1938
Email : mercury.frt@pacific.net.ph
Contact Person: Bayani C. Coching - President & General Manager

□ MOL Logistics Philippines, Inc. (formerly Cougar Logistics Phils., Inc.)
#6 Sta. Agueda Street, Brgy. Sto. Niño, Bo. Ibayo, PARAÑAQUE, METRO MANILA
Contact Number/s : (632) 852-4467 (632) 851-3144 (632) 851-2881 (632)
Fax : (632) 852-4477 (632) 852-4469 (632) 851-2868
Email : mlg-ph@molphil.co.ph; moamnl@skyinet.net; navarra@pacific.net.ph
Contact Person: Fernando V. Navarra, Jr. - President

□ Multi Freight Consolidator System, Inc.
Room 210 Gedcor Building, Irasan Street, San Dionisio, PARAÑAQUE, METRO MANILA
Contact Number/s : (632) 826-8414 (632) 826-8056
Fax : (632) 826-8056
Email : mfcs@compass.com.ph
Contact Person: Eileen T. Bautista - General Manager; Ninieza Edano - Marketing Manager

□ Multifreight Cargo Services, Inc.
8194-B Dahlia Street, Sto. Niño, PARAÑAQUE, METRO MANILA
Contact Number/s : (632) 853-4048
Fax : (632) 853-5822
Email : mfcsi@pacific.net.ph
Contact Person: Aquilina T. Duran - President/General Manager

□ Neutral Logistics and Warehouse, Inc.
Ninoy Aquino Avenue, San Dionisio, PARAÑAQUE, METRO MANILA
Contact Number/s : Cell No.: (0917) 448-8964
Contact Person: Rafael M. Garcia - President/General Manager; Mariven M. Romero - Customs Clearance Supervisor

□ Nissin Transport Phils. Corp.
#14 Cargo Village Complex, Ninoy Aquino Avenue, PARAÑAQUE, METRO MANILA
Contact Number/s : (632) 851-5625 (632) 851-5621 to 22
Fax : (632) 851-5637
Email : nissin@pacific.net.ph
Contact Person: Hiroshi Umino - General Manager; Erlindo M. Salvador - President; Aurora V. Nunez - Operations Manager

□ On-Board International Cargo Phils., Inc.
#3B ACM Bldg., P. Mayuga St., Tambo, PARAÑAQUE, METRO MANILA
Contact Number/s : (632) 833-4897 (632) 853-7954
Fax : (632) 832-2896
Contact Person: Analyn Cesa Cabero - General Manager

□ Options Logistics, Inc.
Unit 7 Columbia Airfreight Complex, 707 Ninoy Aquino Ave., Sto. Niño, PARAÑAQUE, METRO MANILA
Contact Number/s : (632) 831-5266
Fax : (632) 833-9592
Email : manila@optionslogistics.com.ph
Contact Person: John C. Sio - President; Emmanuel N. Pascual - General Manager

□ Oriental Air Transport Service Phils., Inc.
Time Square Unit N, 8145 Dr. A. Santos Ave., Sucat, PARAÑAQUE, METRO MANILA
Contact Number/s : (632) 851-8314 (632) 851-8306 Cell No.: (0918
Fax : (632) 820-1550
Email : oatsmnl@info.com.ph
Contact Person: Virgilio F. Cabrillas - Station Manager

□ Pacific Shipping and Distribution, Inc.
S206 Gedcor Square Building, Ninoy Aquino Ave. cor. Irasan St., San Dionisio, PARAÑAQUE, METRO MANILA
Contact Number/s : (632) 820-7456 (632) 820-6908
Fax : (632) 820-0284
Email : psdmnl@pacific.net.ph

Contact Person: Jose Roberto Adriano - General Manager

 Pak-Prime Logistics Int'l., Inc.
Unit 16 Building B Cargo Village, Ninoy Aquino Avenue, PARAÑAQUE, METRO MANILA
Contact Number/s : (632) 851-7228 to 29
Fax : (632) 851-7230
Contact Person: Ma. Merilea S. Primavera - President; Jean Paolo S. Primavera - Sales Manager

 Pan Globe Cargo Express, Inc.
Eraldi Building, 2A Johanne Street, Bo. Ibayo, PARAÑAQUE, METRO MANILA
Contact Number/s : (632) 852-9250 to 54 (632) 852-5526
Fax : (632) 852-9312
Email : inquiries@abxpanglobe.com.ph
Contact Person: Eddie Dufrenne - President; Ramon G. Alegre - VP & Corporate Treasurer; Leandro Mulle - Seafreight Manager

 Phil. Connection, Inc. (formerly Rey Langit Brokerage Services)
Lot 3,4 & 5 South St. Palanyag Road, Gatchalian Subdivision, PARAÑAQUE, METRO MANILA
Contact Number/s : (632) 546-8229
Fax : (632) 825-6140
Contact Person: Estrellita D. Langit - General Manager

 Platinum Logistics, Inc.
Building #3 Gedcor Square Compound, Irasan Street, San Dionisio, PARAÑAQUE, METRO MANILA
Contact Number/s : (632) 820-6341
Fax : (632) 820-6341
Email : platinum_logs@compass.com.ph
Contact Person: Joyce C. Angara - President/General Manager; Johnald R. Janoya - Operations Manager

 Primex Int'l. Phils., Inc.
ASA Bldg. Veronica de Leon Ave., cor. Delbros Ave., Sto. Niño, PARAÑAQUE, METRO MANILA
Contact Number/s : (632) 852-4352
Fax : (632) 853-8333
Email : info@primex.com.ph
Contact Person: Carmencita O. Ramoy - Pres. & Gen. Manager

 Pro-Log Philippines, Inc.
Unit 3 JJM Building, Kaingan Road, Multinational Village, PARAÑAQUE, METRO MANILA
Contact Number/s : (632) 776-9581 to 85
Fax : (632) 776-9587
Email : mnl_fernandoa@pro-logistics.com; mnl_mgt@pro-logistics.com
Contact Person: Silay K. Guiamano - President; Fernando Martin Juan Caro de Achaval - General Manager

 Quickflo Forwarders, Inc.
S-13 Gedcor Square, Ninoy Aquino Ave. cor. Irasan Street, San Dionisio, PARAÑAQUE, METRO MANILA
Contact Number/s : (632) 829-9158 to 59 (632) 513-6253 (632) 829-7270
Fax : (632) 829-7270
Email : qfmnl@pacific.net.ph
Contact Person: Corazon D. Kalinga - President; Romeo A. Martinez - VP-Seafreight Optns.

 RAF Int'l. Forwarding (Phils.) , Inc.
RAF Airborne House, Irasan Street, San Dionisio, PARAÑAQUE, METRO MANILA
Contact Number/s : (632) 820-2920 to 25
Fax : (632) 820-2917
Contact Person: Judith R. Azarcon - President; Amarna N. Manaligod - Operations Director; Luisito R. Ramos - Freight Operations Manager

 RCS Logistics Phils., Inc. (formerly Expresslane System Phils., Inc.)
Oyster Industrial Complex Bldg. 1, Ninoy Aquino Ave., San Dionisio, PARAÑAQUE, METRO MANILA
Contact Number/s : (632) 829-2753
Fax : (632) 829-0132
Email : espimnl@skyinet.net
Contact Person: Emily M. Rodriguez - General Manager

□ Royal Cargo Combined Logistics, Inc.
G/F RCC Building, Sta. Agueda Avenue, Pascor Drive, PARAÑAQUE, METRO MANILA
Contact Number/s : (632) 514-1339
Fax : (632) 852-4470
Contact Person: Michael K. Raeuber - President

□ Sagawa Express Phils., Inc.
505 Quirino Avenue, Tambo, PARAÑAQUE, METRO MANILA
Contact Number/s : (632) 510-8484
Fax : (632) 510-8485 to 86
Contact Person: Kiyoyuki Yamada - Deputy General Manager; Hanzel Leonardo D. Leaño - Operations Manager

□ Sea Air Dragon Express, Inc.
Unit 26, Ed & Joe's Commercial Arcade, 153 Quirino Ave., Tambo, PARAÑAQUE, METRO MANILA
Contact Number/s : (632) 831-5883
Fax : (632) 833-1615 (632) 831-5883
Contact Person: Mary Eileen C. Garcia - Managing Director; Grace V. Navarro - Operations Manager

□ Sea Quest Int'l. Freight Forwarders, Inc.
#1716 Luis Maria Guerrero Street, Malate, PARAÑAQUE, METRO MANILA
Contact Number/s : (632) 526-2405 (632) 523-5369 (632) 523-5375
Fax : (632) 526-2406 (632) 526-2408
Contact Person: Louis L. Cu - Exec. Vice-Pres./Gen. Manager; Marissa Valencia - Director

□ Sea-Jet Int'l. Forwarders Inc.
Unit 7 & 8 JJM Building 2, Ninoy Aquino Avenue, Sto. Niño, PARAÑAQUE, METRO MANILA
Contact Number/s : (632) 852-9001 to 04
Fax : (632) 852-9007
Email : info@seajetintl.ph; seajet@manila-online.net
Contact Person: Bienvenido C. Anunciacion - President; Chris Reyes - Seafreight Manager; Jhun L. Simon - Operations Manager

□ Seojeong Shipping & Air Cargo Forwarders, Inc.
Unit 3B D'Metz Building, 5004 P. Burgos Street, Poblacion, PARAÑAQUE, METRO MANILA
Contact Number/s : (632) 899-3662 to 63
Fax : (632) 897-2610
Contact Person: Joon Hyeok Lee - President; Ma. Antonieth N. Cipriano - Operations Manager

□ SFE-Scanwell Freight Express (Phils.) , Inc.
707 Unit M, Columbia Airfreight Complex, Ninoy Aquino Ave., PARAÑAQUE, METRO MANILA
Contact Number/s : (632) 831-1447 (632) 831-5786 (632) 833-5628
Fax : (632) 852-1002 (632) 831-6288
Email : mnl-ed-miranda@scanwell.com
Contact Person: Edmund M. Miranda - President & General Manager; Edwin Atienza - Operations Manager

□ Sincerity Int'l. Cargo Services Corp.
9485 Elizabeth St., Airport Village, PARAÑAQUE, METRO MANILA
Contact Number/s : (632) 853-8949 (632) 853-8951 (632) 851-1209
Fax : (632) 851-3259 (632) 851-9717 (632) 823-3878
Email : sincer@mozcom.com
Contact Person: Mrs. Tai Su-Mien Wang - General Manager

□ Sino Freight Forwarding & Services, Inc.
Unit 4 ASA Bldg. Delbros Ave., Sto. Niño, PARAÑAQUE, METRO MANILA
Contact Number/s : (632) 853-5619 (632) 853-5621
Fax : (632) 852-4355
Email : sinofreight@pacific.net.ph
Contact Person: Ma. Luz M. Miranda - President

□ Sky Freight Forwarders, Inc.

Sky Freight Building, Ninoy Aquino Ave, Bo. Sto. Niño, PARAÑAQUE, METRO MANILA
Contact Number/s : (632) 851-7092 to 99
Fax : (632) 833-1886
Contact Person: Alfredo L. de Guzman - General Manager; Eduardo G. De Guzman - Exec. Vice-Pres.

□ Skytraders Cargo Int'l., Inc.
No. 6 MIA Road, Tambo, PARAÑAQUE, METRO MANILA
Contact Number/s : (632) 832-1825
Fax : (632) 832-2836
Email : skytraders@mindgate.net; dhel@mindgate.net; skycarl@mindgate.net
Contact Person: Leopoldo P. De Ocampo - President & General Manager

□ Smart Choice Freight Forwarder
Suite 301 Doña Eusebia Bldg., #0611 Quirino Ave., San Dionisio, PARAÑAQUE, METRO MANILA
Contact Number/s : (632) 825-8575 (632) 825-8547
Fax : (632) 825-8547
Contact Person: Florenda M. Sanchez - Proprietress

□ SSE Cargo Forwarders Corp.
303 McDivitt Street, Phase II, Moonwalk, PARAÑAQUE, METRO MANILA
Contact Number/s : (632) 822-5572 (632) 821-0938 (632) 524-6376
Fax : (632) 524-6376
Contact Person: Clementino M. Perez - President; Lolita V. Perez - VP/General Manager; Myrna Bahala - Principal Broker

□ Star Consolidators Phils., Inc.
S.T.I.L. Building, Sta. Agueda cor. Delbros Avenue, Pascor Drive, Sto. Niño, PARAÑAQUE, METRO MANILA
Contact Number/s : (632) 852-9230 to 34
Fax : (632) 852-9149
Email : scpi@startrans.com.ph
Contact Person: Peter M. Kairuz - President; Arleen M. Manalo - Seafreight Manager

□ Straight Air & Ocean Services Phils., Inc.
#4397 Katigbak Drive, Tambo, PARAÑAQUE, METRO MANILA
Contact Number/s : (632) 854-0946 to 47
Fax : (632) 854-0945
Contact Person: Wilson Minguez - General Manager; Reymundo J. Arago - Export Manager; Grace Minguez - Import Officer

□ Sunfreight Forwarders & Customs Brokerage, Inc.
Sunfreight Building, 9422 Urma Drive, Airport Village, Brgy. Vitalez, PARAÑAQUE, METRO MANILA
Contact Number/s : (632) 853-7617 (632) 853-7619
Fax : (632) 852-9479 (632) 852-9425
Email : sunfrt@compass.com.ph
Contact Person: Jose Alex L. Wolcott - President; Danilo P. Gipulan - Vice-President

□ Target Airfreight Phil. Int'l., Inc.
Room 202 GEDCOR Square Building, Irasan Street, Ninoy Aquino Ave., PARAÑAQUE, METRO MANILA
Contact Number/s : (632) 829-9156 (632) 513-6639 to 41
Fax : (632) 829-9156 (632) 820-3072
Email : tafphil@mozcom.com
Contact Person: Alice S. Mayo - President; Emmanuel Thomas A. Sanchez - Operations-in-Charge

□ Tranfex Brokerage, Inc.
Roligon Cargo Complex, #505 Quirino Avenue, Tambo, PARAÑAQUE, METRO MANILA
Contact Number/s : (632) 832-5435 (632) 854-8318 to 21
Fax : (632) 551-2091 (632) 551-2098
Email : tranfex@pworld.net.ph
Contact Person: Napoleon M. Cagas - President/General Manager

□ Trans Air Corporation
9584 Jaime St. Airport Village, Baltao, PARAÑAQUE, METRO MANILA
Contact Number/s : (632) 853-7775 to 79
Fax : (632) 851-3276
Email : tacphil@starnet.net.ph

Contact Person: Joseph Gabriel C. Nocum - President; Rhodora V. Castillo - Operations Manager

 Trans-Aeromar Brokerage and Forwarding, Inc.
718-B Quirino Ave., Tambo, PARAÑAQUE, METRO MANILA
Contact Number/s : (632) 851-6056 (632) 852-8746 to 47 (632) 852-8739
Fax : (632) 852-8739
Contact Person: Alexander P. Solis - President & General Manager

 Transpacific International Consolidator, Inc.
Unit 302 G.G.B. Building, Pascor Drive, Sto. Niño, PARAÑAQUE, METRO MANILA
Contact Number/s : (632) 852-7376 (632) 854-1291 to 92 (632) 852-7359
Fax : (632) 852-7359
Email : tici@compass.com.ph
Contact Person: Marissa G. Elinon - President/ General Manager; Renato Del Rosario - Operations Supervisor

 Transway Freight International Corporation
#505 Quirino Avenue, Roligon Compound, Tambo, PARAÑAQUE, METRO MANILA
Contact Number/s : (632) 833-8650 (632) 833-9916
Fax : (632) 833-1492
Contact Person: Roger G. Tan - President; Ernesto Velado - Operations Manager; Wilfredo Velado - Sales Manager

 Twins International Freight Express, Inc.
Room 502 Excelsior Tower, 161 Roxas Boulevard, Baclaran, PARAÑAQUE, METRO MANILA
Contact Number/s : (632) 879-8022 (632) 879-8026
Fax : (632) 879-8026
Email : twinsph@tri-sys.com
Contact Person: Edgardo C. Lopez - President/General Manager; Eduardo C. Lopez - Operations Manager

 Unik CBS Phils., Inc.
Unit 11 & 12 Cargo Village Complex Bldg., Cor. Multinational Vill. & Ninoy Aquino Ave., Sto. Niño, PARAÑAQUE, METRO MANILA
Contact Number/s : (632) 852-3012 (632) 852-1884
Fax : (632) 851-6717 (632) 852-5963
Email : unikcbs@compass.com.ph
Contact Person: Christina M. Amio - General Manager; Andres Jolejole - Import/Export Manager

 Universal Freight, Inc.
600-A Quirino Avenue, Tambo, PARAÑAQUE, METRO MANILA
Contact Number/s : (632) 853-1479 (632) 851-1303
Fax : (632) 851-2740
Contact Person: Agnes H. Marquez - General Manager

 U-Ocean, Inc.
4/F Cargohaus Building, NAIA Complex, Brgy. Vitalez, PARAÑAQUE, METRO MANILA
Contact Number/s : (632) 879-4695 to 98
Fax : (632) 854-0374
Email : uocean@i-manila.com.ph
Contact Person: Glorioso R. Martinez - President

 UTI (Global Logistics) , Inc. (formerly Union Transport, Inc.)
707-C Columbia Airfreight Complex, Ninoy Aquino Avenue, PARAÑAQUE, METRO MANILA
Contact Number/s : (632) 833-1570 (632) 833-2953
Fax : (632) 833-9895
Email : mnl@go2uti.com.ph
Contact Person: Rosemary N. Su - General Manager; Veronica C. Lorenzana - Finance Manager

 VCF Int'l. Freight Forwarders Corp.
Unit 8&9 Irasan Center, NAIA Ave., San Dionisio, Sucat, PARAÑAQUE, METRO MANILA
Contact Number/s : (632) 826-1253 (632) 826-4477
Fax : (632) 820-9601
Email : vcfelite@skyinet.net

Contact Person: Danilo N. Ebojo - President/General Manager; Jose B. Isong - Operations Manager

□ Vigour Freight Phils., Inc.
No. 317 GEDCOR Bldg. Irasan St., cor. Ninoy Aquino Ave., PARAÑAQUE, METRO MANILA
Contact Number/s : (632) 829-0134
Fax : (632) 826-7978
Contact Person: Fabian A. Suzara - President

□ Wingspeed Shipping Corporation
G/F Mercury Freight Int'l. Building, Ninoy Aquino Ave. cor. A. Bonifacio, San Dionisio, PARAÑAQUE, METRO MANILA
Contact Number/s : (632) 820-4475 (632) 820-4478 to 79 (632) 825-1854
Fax : (632) 820-4463
Email : wingspd@info.com.ph
Contact Person: Bayani C. Coching - President

□ World Int'l. Cargo Transfer, Inc.
S-105 Doña Eusebia Rodriguez Bldg., Quirino Ave., San Dionisio, PARAÑAQUE, METRO MANILA
Contact Number/s : (632) 825-0114
Fax : (632) 829-6672
Email : wicti@skyinet.net
Contact Person: Augusto G. Santos - President & General Manager

□ Worldgate Logistic Services, Inc.
Suite 409 Burke Building, Burke St., Binondo, PARAÑAQUE, METRO MANILA
Contact Number/s : (632) 243-8331 to 33
Fax : (632) 243-8330
Email : wgate@pworld.net.ph
Contact Person: Antonio M. De Guzman - President; Remigio M. De Guzman - Vice-President

□ Worldwide Consolidated Freight Corp.
8145 Unit T Times Square Building, Dr. A. Santos Ave., PARAÑAQUE, METRO MANILA
Contact Number/s : (632) 829-5211 to 12 (632) 829-0663
Fax : (632) 829-5208
Email : worldfrt@skyinet.net
Contact Person: Hermenegildo D. Saranillo - President; Teodoro D. Perdigon - Export Manager

□ Worldwide Logistics Phils., Inc.
#86 Multinational Avenue, Multinational Village, PARAÑAQUE, METRO MANILA
Contact Number/s : (632) 776-3087 to 89
Fax : (632) 776-3086
Email : wwac@fastmail.i-next.net
Contact Person: Ditas C. Cabañez - General Manager; Nilo M. Marcelino - Operations Supervisor

□ Yusen Air & Sea Service Phils., Inc.
Ground Floor, PAMCOR Bldg., PASCOR Drive, Sto. Niño, PARAÑAQUE, METRO MANILA
Contact Number/s : (632) 852-7101 (632) 527-8888 loc. 273 to 281
Fax : (632) 832-3066 (632) 527-8733 (632) 527-8732
Email : yasps@yusen.co.jp; yaspm@yusen.co.jp
Contact Person: Atty. Arthur P. Tugade - President; Atty. Artemio U. Tuazon - General Manager; Rustico C. Arvesu - Division Manager, Operations; T. Kamiya - Division Manager, Seafreight; Joel D. Domingo - Asst. Div. Manager, Seafreight

□ AA&A Freight Express, Inc.
224 Dancel Street, Cartimar, PASAY CITY, METRO MANILA
Contact Number/s : (632) 831-9161, 831-5352
Fax : (632) 831-9161
Contact Person: Linda V. Pamplona - General Manager

□ ACK Freight Express, Inc.
CMC Building, Aurora Boulevard, cor. Andrews Avenue, PASAY CITY, METRO MANILA
Contact Number/s : (632) 854-8525
Fax : (632) 854-8523
Email : ackfrtex@I-next.net
Contact Person: Jerry Stehmeier - President; Raul Ch. Rabe - Chairman of the Board; Emmanuel L. Intia - Operations Manager; Miriam B. Baroma - Customs Service Officer

 Airtropolis Consolidators Phil. Inc.
3/F Pair-Pags Center, NAIA Compound, Ninoy Aquino Ave., PASAY CITY, METRO MANILA
Contact Number/s : (632) 853-9447 (632) 853-9448
Fax : (632) 853-9448
Contact Person: Mr. Seah Siew Kiong - President; Leticia D. Jimenez - Admin. & Operations Manager

 CCM Express, Inc.
Room 204 Doña Generosa Bldg., EDSA Extension, PASAY CITY, METRO MANILA
Contact Number/s : (632) 853-2069 (632) 853-1874 (632) 513-0268 to 70
Fax : (632) 891-7678
Email : ccm@philonline.com.ph
Contact Person: Manuel C. Protacio - President / General Manager

 Clipper Cargo Corporation
#2256 Aurora Boulevard, Tramo, PASAY CITY, METRO MANILA
Contact Number/s : (632) 851-5704 (632) 851-1842
Fax : (632) 851-1842
Contact Person: Felino R. Espinosa - President; Nenit Espinosa - Manager; Armand Lipar - Seafreight Manager

 Columbia Transport, Inc.
2253 Aurora Boulevard, PASAY CITY, METRO MANILA
Contact Number/s : (632) 833-2551 to 55
Fax : (632) 833-2358 (632) 831-8173
Email : coltrans@skyinet.net
Contact Person: Robert Lim Joseph - President; Veneracion Catacutan - Sales Manager

 Corwen Airfreight Int'l.
G-27 Miramar House, Domestic Drive, PASAY CITY, METRO MANILA
Contact Number/s : (632) 831-2072 (632) 831-2630
Fax : (632) 831-0903
Email : corcosca@cnl.net
Contact Person: Thelma Ruby A. Cosca - Managing Director

 Dolphin Logistics Int'l., Inc.
Rm. 403, 3JS Building, Sta. Monica St. cor. F.B. Harrison, PASAY CITY, METRO MANILA
Contact Number/s : (632) 551-0132
Fax : (632) 831-8459
Contact Person: Rondel Jake B. Castillo - President

 Elite Brokerage Corporation
Rm. 208 Ding Velayo Sports Center Bldg., Domestic Road, PASAY CITY, METRO MANILA
Contact Number/s : (632) 833-0297 (632) 831-0501
Fax : (632) 551-3517
Contact Person: Jose C. Paraiso - President; Ricardo C. Paraiso - Operations Manager

 Fastlane Freight International Corporation
Rm. 208 C.K. Sy Diamond Bldg., 156 Libertad St., PASAY CITY, METRO MANILA
Contact Number/s : (632) 551-0893 (632) 831-0229 (632) 833-8798
Fax : (632) 833-8798
Contact Person: Lilia M. de Leon - General Manager

 Greatway Int'l. Freight Forwarders, Inc.
G/F Ding Velayo Sports Centre, Domestic Road, PASAY CITY, METRO MANILA
Contact Number/s : (632) 831-1438 (632) 551-3696 (632) 551-3701
Fax : (632) 831-1438
Email : greatway@pworld.net.ph; greatway_iata@hotmail.com;
Contact Person: William Russell L. Sobrepeña - President & CEO; Leonida P. De Leon - Operations Manager

 Hecny Forwarders, Inc.
30 San Luis Street, PASAY CITY, METRO MANILA
Contact Number/s : (632) 833-2561 to 68
Fax : (632) 831-0084
Email : hecnymnl@globe.com.ph; hfiph@ibm.net

Contact Person: Spencer M. W. Li - General Manager

□ Intercontinental Forwarders Philippines, Inc.
No. 30 San Luis Street, PASAY CITY, METRO MANILA
Contact Number/s : (632) 834-7561 to 63
Fax : (632) 834-7560
Email : iffi@attglobal.net
Contact Person: Eileen Consuelo Abustan - General Manager

□ LBC Express, Inc.
Gen. Aviation Center, Domestic Road, PASAY CITY, METRO MANILA
Contact Number/s : (632) 832-1414 (632) 817-4273 (632) 817-4248
Fax : (632) 832-1911 (632) 832-1775 (632) 832-1841 (632)
Contact Person: Marilou Olan - President

□ M.L.A. World Transport, Inc.
Unit 601 IPI Buendia Tower, Sen. Gil Puyat Avenue, PASAY CITY, METRO MANILA
Contact Number/s : (632) 512-2442 (632) 887-2062 to 63 Cell. No.: (0
Fax : (632) 512-2443
Contact Person: Manuel L. Alejandrino - President & General Manager; Enrico A. Alejandrino - Operations Manager

□ Makati Transforwarder Corporation
2nd Floor Ding Velayo Building, Domestic Road, PASAY CITY, METRO MANILA
Contact Number/s : (632) 513-2431
Fax : (632) 833-3883 (632) 851-0286
Email : maktrans@impactnet.com
Contact Person: Julio Ma. Jaucian - President/General Manager; Jeffrey H. Jaucian - Forwarding Manager

□ Natural Logistics, Inc.
Room 307 Marbella 1, #2223 Roxas Boulevard, PASAY CITY, METRO MANILA
Contact Number/s : (632) 834-2365 (632) 834-2362
Fax : (632) 834-7465
Email : natural@philonline.com

Contact Person: Juliet Orayle-Bernardo - President

□ Ocean Phoenix Int'l. Corp.
Suite 402, Doña Generosa Building, EDSA Extension, PASAY CITY, METRO MANILA
Contact Number/s : (632) 891-7677 (632) 853-0891 (632) 853-0901 (632)
Fax : (632) 513-0356
Email : opicorp@vlink.net.ph
Contact Person: Arabello S. Andres - President & General Manager

□ Pentagon Cargo Brokerage, Inc.
1872 Tramo St., PASAY CITY, METRO MANILA
Contact Number/s : (632) 844-8766 (632) 812-2106
Fax : (632) 512-2119
Contact Person: Conrado Z. Liwanag - President; Ma. Compasion Rodriguez - Shipping-in-Charge

□ Phil. European Balikbayan Services, Inc.
Room 6 2/F Sky Dragon Building, Domestic Drive, PASAY CITY, METRO MANILA
Contact Number/s : (632) 832-3731 (632) 834-0588
Fax : (632) 834-0588
Contact Person: Mae Angeline R. Guerrero - General Manager

□ Rapid Air Freight, Inc.
6-Eleven Bldg., NAIA Road, PASAY CITY, METRO MANILA
Contact Number/s : (632) 831-7281 to 85 (632) 851-9190
Fax : (632) 832-2876 (632) 804-0412
Email : headq@rapidairfreight.com.ph; seafreight@rapidairfreight.com.ph
Contact Person: Ramon S. Monzon - President; Ma. Theresa T. Farro - General Manager; Liza M. Mercado - Administrative Supervisor

□ Resources Freight Philippines, Inc.
6-11 Building, NAIA Road, Pildera I, PASAY CITY, METRO MANILA
Contact Number/s : (632) 854-0277 to 78

Fax : (632) 833-0533
Email : rfpirobs@info.com.ph
Contact Person: Roberto R. Castillano - President; Felipe Yago - Overall Operations Manager

- Sakuma Brokerage International Services, Inc.
#2125 Alvarez Street, PASAY CITY, METRO MANILA
Contact Number/s : (632) 832-3070 (632) 833-2409
Fax : (632) 887-7571
Contact Person: Leonora R. Tirona - Owner/General Manager

- Summit Air Express Corp.
G/F Unit L Ding Velayo Sports Complex, Domestic Airport Drive, PASAY CITY, METRO MANILA
Contact Number/s : (632) 833-3444 (632) 833-8172 (632) 514-4181 (632)
Fax : (632) 831-7345
Email : sumair@surfshop.net.ph
Contact Person: Ernesto B. Adrales - President

- Syn Expeditors International, Inc.
Room 433 Central Park II Condominium, D. Jorge Street, PASAY CITY, METRO MANILA
Contact Number/s : (632) 889-5968 (632) 889-5973 (632) 889-1268 (632)
Fax : (632) 889-4248
Contact Person: Restituto P. Bachar - General Manager

- THI Phils. Corp.
4/F 2301 Taft Ave., PASAY CITY, METRO MANILA
Contact Number/s : (632) 510-4514 to 17
Fax : (632) 551-3639
Email : judykeh@pacific.net.ph
Contact Person: Judy Keh - President; Mary Khoe - Vice-President; Winefredo D. Penaflorida - Operations Manager

- Fillright, Inc.
#244 Sta. Monica Street, Capitol 8 Subdivision, Bo. Kapitolyo, PASIG, METRO MANILA
Contact Number/s : (632) 631-4908
Fax : (632) 637-7092
Contact Person: Wilfredo C. Wijangco - President/Gen. Manager

- Foxboro Express Cargo Systems Corp.
Unit 2307 Jolibee Plaza, Emerald Avenue, Ortigas Center, PASIG, METRO MANILA
Contact Number/s : (632) 687-4670 (632) 637-6526 to 29
Fax : (632) 687-4672
Email : keylogs@info.com.ph; mccfoxboro@yahoo.com
Contact Person: Roberto A. Sison - President; Miguelina C. Cabreros - EVP/General Manager; Francisca D. Guirigay - Seafreight/Airfreight Head; Ma. Victoria Villaruz - Operations Manager

- H & Y Draco International Corp.
Suite 1006 Taipan Place, Emerald Avenue, PASIG, METRO MANILA
Contact Number/s : (632) 632-1787 (632) 632-1785
Fax : (632) 632-1950
Email : dracoinc@pacific.net.ph
Contact Person: Young Doo Kim - General Manager; Tenny F. Tang - Marketing & Operations Manager

- Integrated Logistics Phils., Inc.
11 E.O. Building, United Street cor. 2nd Street, Barrio Kapitolyo, PASIG, METRO MANILA
Contact Number/s : (632) 637-2098 (632) 746-5304 (632) 746-7681
Fax : (632) 637-2097
Contact Person: Patricia A. Jose - President; Ma. Lourdes R. Balagtas - General Manager

- Pilipinas Kargamento, Inc.
#47 San Agustin Street, Capitol 8, PASIG, METRO MANILA
Contact Number/s : (632) 672-0964 (632) 671-4978 (632) 626-8015
Fax : (632) 672-0964

Contact Person: Jose Federico B. de Joya, Jr. - President & CEO

□ Cirera Express Corporation
#85-B K8th Street, Kamias, QUEZON CITY, METRO MANILA
Contact Number/s : (632) 928-2402 (632) 928-2424
Fax : (632) 928-2424
Email : cirera_express@pacific.net.ph
Contact Person: Marie Christine Cirera-Tantoco - President/General Manager; Noel Mabansag - Operations Manager

□ Farochilen Forwarders & Travel
#46 King Ferdinand Street, Kingspoint Subdivision, Bagbag, Novaliches, QUEZON CITY, METRO MANILA
Contact Number/s : (632) 937-8720 (632) 937-8960 (632) 419-1925
Fax : (632) 937-8975
Contact Person: Col. Leonardo N. Farochilen (Ret.) - Owner

□ FDX Forwarding Services
#131 Stanford Street, Cubao, QUEZON CITY, METRO MANILA
Contact Number/s : (632) 913-6097 (632) 438-8319
Fax : (632) 438-1067
Email : fdxmanila@yahoo.com
Contact Person: Agustina P. Dulay - President; Fred A. Dulay - Operations Manager

□ Foremost Dealing International Freight Forwarders, Inc. (formerly Foremost Dealing International, In
#102 West Avenue, QUEZON CITY, METRO MANILA
Contact Number/s : (632) 412-2494 (632) 412-2519 (632) 411-5181
Fax : (632) 411-5179
Email : foremost@skyinet.net
Contact Person: Danton D. Lucenario - President; Flora J. Lucenario - General Manager; Ma. Rosario M. Velasquez - Managing Director, NVOCC; Imelda T. Catapang - Import/Export Manager

□ Hienrich Forwarders Services
116-C Road 20 Street, Bahay Toro, Project 8, QUEZON CITY, METRO MANILA
Contact Number/s : (632) 453-3662
Fax : (632) 455-2094
Contact Person: Hienrich E. Barredo - General Manager

□ Inter-Resources Brokerage & Cargo Forwarding Co.
#71 Santol Street, Galas, QUEZON CITY, METRO MANILA
Contact Number/s : (632) 714-8020 (632) 716-2010
Fax : (632) 714-2850
Email : autocraft@inter-resources.com.ph
Contact Person: Jose C. Gonzales, Jr. - General Manager; Evelyn S. Ambas - Operations Manager

□ Kingspoint Express & Logistics
Blk. 22 Lot 14 Kalayaan Avenue, Kingspoint Subdivision, Novaliches, QUEZON CITY, METRO MANILA
Contact Number/s : (632) 373-6464
Fax : (632) 411-6086
Contact Person: Mary Ann O. Co - Owner/Proprietress

□ KIS Express Cargo Services, Inc.
G/F NFP Building, 107 E. Rodriguez Sr. Avenue, QUEZON CITY, METRO MANILA
Contact Number/s : (632) 742-0826 (632) 742-0861 (632) 742-0864
Fax : (632) 731-7060
Email : kiscargo@pworld.net.ph
Contact Person: Alma P. Silla - President & General Manager

□ NSCP Delivery, Inc.
147 Mother Ignacia St., QUEZON CITY, METRO MANILA
Contact Number/s : (632) 926-3576 (632) 411-0423
Contact Person: Arion Sc. Alabado - President; Dulce C. Alabado - Treasurer

□ Peninsula Cargo Forwarders

Unit J PG Building, 63 West Avenue, Bgy. Paltoc Dist 1, QUEZON CITY, METRO MANILA
Contact Number/s : (632) 412-3376
Fax : (632) 412-3376
Email : mammoth@mail.irnet.net.ph
Contact Person: Engr. Roman S. Silvestre - Proprietor & General Manager; Victoriano B. Villanueva - Managing Supervisor

 RV Delivery Service
147-B Congressional Ave., QUEZON CITY, METRO MANILA
Contact Number/s : (632) 927-5907 (632) 927-5621
Fax : (632) 927-5621
Email : rvdelivery@skyinet.net
Contact Person: Rodolfo A. Pascua - General Manager; Ramil Magcamit - Operations Personnel

 Servlink Cargo, Inc.
2/F CUP Building, A. Roces Avenue, corner Mother Ignacia Street, QUEZON CITY, METRO MANILA
Contact Number/s : (632) 373-6640 (632) 431-9341
Fax : (632) 411-1182 (632) 410-9246
Contact Person: Alfonso R. Silvestre, Jr. - President; Conrado G. Ariola, Jr. - Vice-President; Mylene Talens - Operations Manager

 Suandiz Cargo Express
#75 Rockville Ave., Rockville Subd., San Bartolome, Novaliches, QUEZON CITY, METRO MANILA
Contact Number/s : (632) 936-3182 (632) 431-7828
Fax : (632) 937-8048
Contact Person: Vicente B. Dizon Sr. - Owner/Gen. Manager

 Synoptic Freight Int'l., Inc.
No. 39 Inaman Street, Masambong, San Francisco del Monte, QUEZON CITY, METRO MANILA
Contact Number/s : (632) 415-6797
Fax : (632) 415-6797
Contact Person: Noel M. Gabaldon - President; Greg M. Gabaldon - Operations Manager

 Valenzuela Freight Services
B-14 L-6 Goodwill Homes II, Bagbag, Novaliches, QUEZON CITY, METRO MANILA
Contact Number/s : (632) 936-8723
Fax : (632) 936-8987
Contact Person: Eduardo P. Valenzuela - President/General Manager

 Viva Pacific Star Express Freight Forwarder and Brokerage Services Co.
#802 A. Bonifacio Avenue, Balintawak, QUEZON CITY, METRO MANILA
Contact Number/s : (632) 365-2414
Fax : (632) 366-4825
Contact Person: Jefferson Jay Carub - General Manager; Norito Rondero - Customs Operations Manager

 Willex Movers, Inc.
Suite 205 Columbian Bldg., 160 West Avenue, QUEZON CITY, METRO MANILA
Contact Number/s : (632) 927-7405 (632) 924-2462
Fax : (632) 924-2462
Contact Person: Wilfredo D. Navarro - President/Willex Movers, Inc. (Philippines) ; Marina J. Navarro - President/Willex Movers, Inc. (U.S.A.)

 Northeast Freight Forwarders, Inc.
Room 402 Continental Court Building, 47 Annapolis Street, Greenhills, San Juan, SAN JUAN, METRO MANILA
Contact Number/s : (632) 722-1839
Contact Person: Dionisio O. Sudario - President; Atty. Vicky C. Fernandez - Principal Customs Broker

 Phil. Anbah Corporation
Unit #1203 Goldhill Tower, #5 Annapolis St., Greenhills, San Juan, SAN JUAN, METRO MANILA
Contact Number/s : (632) 527-6548
Fax : (632) 527-6580

Contact Person: Kyu Sam Kim - President; Mylene Dacula Nam - Administrative Officer

□ Cargo Wings and Freight Forwarder
No. 211 Valleyview Village, Mohon, TALISAY, CEBU
Contact Number/s : (632) 806-3147 (Manila, c/o Atty. Cesar Cainglet)
Fax : (6332) 272-5317
Email : j2bennett@eudoramail.com
Contact Person: Elma Galorport Bennett - Owner/Proprietress; John Jude O. Bennett - Operations Manager

□ Delfa Cargo Forwarder
Lagtang Road, Tabunak, TALISAY, CEBU
Contact Number/s : (6332) 273-3527
Contact Person: Feledelfa O. Labajo - Proprietress

□ Aloha Brokerage & Cargo Consolidator
Z3-448 Lagtang, TALISAY, CEBU
Contact Number/s : (6332) 254-5199
Fax : (6332) 254-5199
Contact Person: Feledelfa O. Labajo - Proprietress

□ Masaru Cargo Express
Phase 7B Block 3 Lot 22, Pacita Complex, San Pedro, LAGUNA
Contact Number/s : (632) 847-2930 Cell. No.: (0917) 397-2109
Fax : (632) 694-2610
Contact Person: Marisa T. Escarez - President

□ Phil. Sumitrans Logistics, Inc.
2/F Linaheim Bonded Trading Warehouse, #4 Diode Street, LISP1, Cabuyao, LAGUNA
Contact Number/s : (049) 543-0390 to 94
Fax : (049) 543-0395
Email : psli@laguna.net
Contact Person: Ryo Hirano - Managing Director; Angelito A. Alvarez - President & C.O.O.

□ Viadoy Forwarders
#66 Don P. Campos Avenue, San Agustin 2, Dasmariñas, CAVITE
Contact Number/s : (6346) 850-0965 (6346) 416-4370
Fax : (6346) 416-4370
Contact Person: Aurelia N. Viadoy - Proprietress

PRIORITY SECTORS

CONSTRUCTION MATERIALS INDUSTRY

□ Ceramic Tile Manufacturers Corp.
c/o Mariwasa Mfg., Inc. Ortigas Ave. Ext., Rosario, PASIG, METRO MANILA
Contact Number/s : 655-0281 to 88 / 628-1985
Fax : 628-1985

□ Ayala Land, Inc
30th/F Tower One & Exchange Plaza, Ayala Triangle, Ayala Ave., MAKATI, METRO MANILA
Contact Number/s : 841-5752 / 541-5751
Fax : 848-5316
Email : tumboconej@ayalaland.com.ph

□ Phil. Chamber of Commerce & Industry
14/F Multinational Bancorporation Center, Ayala Ave., MAKATI, METRO MANILA
Contact Number/s : 833-8895
Fax : 843-4102

□ Italfil Porcelain Ceramic Tiles, Inc.
Angeles Industrial Park S.E.Z., Calibutbut,, BACOLOR, PAMPANGA
Contact Number/s : 045-323-4486/045-323-4030/045-323-4489/045-887-437
Fax : 045-887-4030
Email : italfil@digitelone.com
porcelain granite tiles

MARBLE

□ Marble Association of the Phils.
c/o Marbleland Mining & Development Corp., 68 Kalayaan Ave., Diliman, QUEZON CITY, METRO MANILA
Contact Number/s : 922-5015; 922-6551; 433-4727
Fax : 921-5853

□ Ceramic Tile Manufacturing Corp.
c/o Mariwasa Mfg., Inc. Ortigas Ave.,, PASIG, METRO MANILA
Contact Number/s : 655-0281 to 88; 628-1985
Fax : 628-1985

□ Phil. Wood Producers Asso.
3/F LTA Bldg., 118 Perea Street, Legaspi Village, MAKATI, METRO MANILA
Contact Number/s : 817-6751; 817-6884 to 85; 812-1760
Fax : 817-6884
Email : philwood@epic.net

□ Filipino Galvanizers Inst.
Rm. 500 Manila Bank Bldg., Ayala Avenue, MAKATI, METRO MANILA
Contact Number/s : 810-1681; 893-7973
Fax : 812-6126
Product line: Galvanized sheets (loc)

□ Galvanized Iron Wire Manufacturers Asso., Inc.
23 Kaingin Road., Brgy. A. Samson,, QUEZON CITY, METRO MANILA
Contact Number/s : 241-1497 to 98
Fax : 241-1659; 363-9499
Product Line: galvanized iron wire

□ PVC Pipe Industries Association
c/o Emerald Vinyl, 654 Boni Ave., MANDALUYONG, METRO MANILA
Contact Number/s : 523-7963; 361-6101 to 04
Fax : 534-0554
Product Line: pvc pipes

□ Adventure Trading Corp
1011 Sitio Bumbon, Ugong, Valenzuela City; 27-31 Congressional Ave., Quezon City
Contact Number/s : 445-6102
Fax : 984-6327
Email : atcmarble@yahoo.com
Product Line: marble tiles

□ C & B Marble Corp.
Maginao, San Rafael, Bulacan
Contact Number/s : 044-677-0063
Fax : 044-677-0063
Product Line: marble tiles

□ Color My World
Marcos Hiway cor. Molave Street, Pasig City
Contact Number/s : 453-1111; 453-2222
Fax : 453-1111
Email : cmw@ngsinco.com.ph
Product Line: marble & granite

□ D. F. Sabariaga Marble
Sampaloc, San Rafael, Bulacan
Contact Number/s : 044-673-1267; 0912-3024356
Fax : 044-673-1260

□ Gillem Marble Corporation
297 Gen. Luis St., Bo. Kaybiga, Novaliches, Caloocan City
Contact Number/s : 939-5821; 418-5263
Fax : 937-3667
Product Line: marble tiles

□ Marbleland Mining & Dev't. Corp.
68 Kalayaan Ave., Diliman, Quezon City
Contact Number/s : 922-5015; 922-6551
Fax : 921-5853
Product Line: mosaic table tops

□ N.S. Salvador Marble Const. Corp
22 Oakville St., Whiteplains, Quezon City
Contact Number/s : 912-6793; 912-6794
Fax : 912-6499
Email : nsmarble@wtouch.com.ph
Product Line: marble tiles, mosaics and borders

□ Phil. Development & Industrial Corp. (PDIC)
rM. 504 State I Condo., Salcedo St., Legaspi Village, Makati City
Contact Number/s : 818-3626; 818-3627
Fax : 818-3623

□ Raphael Legacy Designs, Inc.
H. Abellana Ext., Pagsabungan, Mandaue City
Contact Number/s : 032-345-0241; 032-345-0242
Fax : 032-346-9197

□ Romblon Marble Multipurpose Coop.
41 Palo Alto Habay, Bacoor, Cavite

Contact Number/s : 046-434-8815
Fax : 046-970-0153

□ Sujo Marble Corp.
52 P. Tuazon Blvd., Cubao, Quezon City
Contact Number/s : 724-9010; 724-5221
Fax : 725-5446
Email : sujomrble@pworld.net.ph

□ Teresa Marble Corp.
117 Shaw Blvd., Pasig City
Contact Number/s : 631-9123; 631-9125
Fax : 633-5249
Email : annie@tmc.com

□ Tudor Mineral Exploration Corp.
Prince Plaza Condo.I, 106 Legaspi Street, Legaspi Village, Makati City
Contact Number/s : 892-9950
Fax : 892-9869

CERAMIC TILES

□ Filcera Mfg., Inc.
Brgy. San Vicente, SAN PEDRO, LAGUNA
Contact Number/s : 8690185, 8471730-31, 8680448, 8680471, 8690190
Fax : 8471729
Email : filcera@compass.com.ph
product line: ceramic tiles

□ Italfil Porcelain Ceramic tiles, Inc.
Angeles Industrial Park, S.E.Z., Calibutbut, BACOLOR, PAMPANGA
Contact Number/s : 045-3234486; 045-3234030; 045-3234489
Fax : 045-8874030
Email : italfil@digitelone.com
product line: porcelain granite tiles

□ Lepanto Ceramics, Inc.
Km. 54 Bo. Makiling,, CALAMBA, LAGUNA
Contact Number/s : 049-5452449; 049-5454012; 632-8450538; 8093424; 80
Fax : 049-5452413; 049-5452450
product line: vitrified homogenous & porcelain floor tiles & ceramic floor tiles

□ Mariwasa Mfg., Inc.
Ortigas Ave. Ext., Rosario,, PASIG, METRO MANILA
Contact Number/s : 6550281 to 88
Fax : 6281985
Product line: ceramic wall and wall tiles

□ Riviera Filipina
#69 South Avenue, QUEZON CITY, METRO MANILA
Contact Number/s : 9227751 to 52
Fax : 9217532
Email : sales@rivierafilipina.com.ph
product line: other dimension stones

SANITARY WARES

□ Ho Cheng
1163 Chino roces Ave., Brgy. San Antonio, MAKATI, METRO MANILA
Contact Number/s : 8955683
Fax : 8952180
product line: sanitary vitreous china, brass faucets

□ Sanitary Wares Mfg. Corp.
10/F, Feliza Bldg., 108 Herrera St., Legaspi Village, MAKATI, METRO MANILA
Contact Number/s : 8920721
Fax : 8920721; 8134810
Email : sales.ph@amstd.com
product line: water closets, flush valve, toilets, urinals, bidets, lavatories, accessories, brass fittings

□ Siam Mariwasa Toto, Inc.
Unit 903, Manila Luxury Condominium, Pearl Drive, Ortigas Center,, PASIG, METRO MANILA
Contact Number/s : 6378466 to 68; 6339065; 6378476
Fax : 6359574
product line: Sanitary ware, water closets, lavatory, bathroom fixtures, accessories

BUILDERS' WOOD-WORKS

□ Asia Wood International, Corp.
Victoria Ware Compound, Tala, Malaria,, KALOOKAN CITY, METRO MANILA
Contact Number/s : 9835020
Fax : 9835019 to 20
product line: various wooden products, door panels, windows, mouldings, frames

□ Bulacan Integrated Wood, Inc.
product line: fences, furniture

□ Consolidated Plywood Industries, Inc.
Brickwood Bldg., Km. 7, Lanang, 8000, DAVAO CITY, DAVAO DEL SUR
Contact Number/s : 082-2380049; 082-2380647
Fax : 082-2380448
product line: jambs, mouldings, furniture and drawer parts

□ Grace Park Industries
249 Rizal Ave. Ext.,, KALOOKAN CITY, METRO MANILA
Contact Number/s : 3611339; 3618881
Fax : 3618887
product line: woodworks

□ Herdex International Corporation
154 Katipunan Ave., St. Ignatius Village, Quezon City, METRO MANILA
Contact Number/s : 9116861; 9131427; 9122874; 9118185
Fax : 9127735; 9118103
Email : herdex@compass.com.ph
product line: hand-carved doors, plain panel doors, glazed type doors, door jambs, mouldings, fireplace mantels, wall brackets, architectural columns

□ Josol Home Decor Improvement Center, Inc.
E. Rodriguez Jr. Ave., Ugong Norte,, QUEZON CITY, METRO MANILA
Contact Number/s : 6311807 to 08; 6310183
Fax : 6329263
product line: doors, mouldings, fireplace mantles, parquet tiles, planks, t & g panels, ballusters, etc.

□ Makiling Technology Corp.
13 Brixton St., Bo. Kapitolyo, PASIG, METRO MANILA
Contact Number/s : 6319280; 6319279; 6359835
Fax : 6319454
product line: manufacturers of wood

□ Matimco
62 Old Samson Road, Balintawak, QUEZON CITY, METRO MANILA
Contact Number/s : 3667009
Fax : 3614805
product line: matwood, flooring, mouldings, panelling doors, finger jointed and laminated, panel boards, staircase component of wood

□ Pacific Timber Export Corp
HDC Compound, Bo. Malhacan,, MEYCAUAYAN, BULACAN
Contact Number/s : 044-8407150; 044-2283774
Fax : 044-6953800; 02-7220729
Email : pateco@pacific.net.ph
product line: finger-jointed lumber, wood components for doors and windows, moulded doors, wood mouldings

□ Scad Services Pte, Ltd.
Blk 23 Phase IV Expansion, Cavite Eco Zone,, ROSARIO, CAVITE
Contact Number/s : 046-2470822 to 25; 046-4370851
Fax : 046-437-0852
Email : scad@pacific.net.ph
product line: various wooden products, door frames, windows, window panels, walls, cabinets, shelves, etc., various housing parts assembly: window assembly, chimney assembly, sash unit assembly

□ Ying Yuan
Golden Miles Business Park,, CARMONA, CAVITE
Contact Number/s : 046-4303214 to 18
Fax : 046-4301476

□ Wu Kong Singapore Pte, Ltd
Lot 7, Blk. 9 Phase 1, Cavite Eco Zone,, ROSARIO, CAVITE
Contact Number/s : 046-4370888
Fax : 046-4370809
product line: pre assembled frames for complete house and other wooden wooden housing parts, saw mill operation, manufacture of kiln dried lumber

PVC

□ Moldex
Moldex Bldg., Ligaya St. corner west Ave.,, QUEZON CITY, METRO MANILA
Contact Number/s : 3738888
Fax : 3734009
Email : sales@moldex.com.ph
product line: sanitary and potable water pipes & fittings, telecom and electrical conduits, rigid pvc films

□ Phil. denrai
Blk. 3, Lot 5 Phase 2, PEZA-CEPZ,,
ROSARIO, CAVITE
Contact Number/s : 046-4372318; 046-4710175
Fax : 046-4371593
Email : pdenrai@pacific.com.ph
product line: PVC based garden articles/door products

□ Pacific Paint & Oil Mfg. Inc.
292 D. Tuazon St., 1115, QUEZON CITY, METRO MANILA
Contact Number/s : 3643505; 3650561 to 64; 4136560 to 65
Fax : 3617164
Email : inquiry@boysen.com.ph
architectural/house paints

ADHESIVES

□ Global Brands
Sitio Harangan, Brgy. Plaza, Aldea,, TANAY, RIZAL
Contact Number/s : 654-0881
Fax : 654-0029
product line: adhesives and glues for furniture, shoes, household, construction, coatings for automotive

GLASS

□ Asahi Glass Philippines
Bo. Pinagbuhatan, 1602, PASIG, METRO MANILA
Contact Number/s : 6416129; 6411987; 6411982
Fax : 6411988
product line: float glass, flat glass, tempered glass

MARINE PRODUCTS

□ HJR International Corporation
Rm. 407, 1000 Katigbak Bldg., Mabini St., Ermita, MANILA, METRO MANILA
Contact Number/s : 346-1086/526-7916 to 18
Fax : (32)346-0394
Contact Person : Mr. Jery Sun (Director)
Product : Frozen fishery products (octopus, shrimps and scallops)

□ Seachamp International Export Corporation
Bldg. 2 Skydragon Compound, Domestic Terminal Road, PASAY CITY, METRO MANILA
Contact Number/s : (632)854-1033 to 36/(0917)535-2469
Fax : (632)8339362
Email : chitosy@hotmail.com
Contact Person : Reyanldo R. Sy (President)
Product : Processed seafoods

□ AA Export-Import Corporation
2/F Solid House Bldg., 2285 Pasong Tamo Ext., Makati City 1200, METRO MANILA
Contact Number/s : 843-1531 to 38
Fax : 812-8270
Contact Person: Mr. Rey S. Udani, Marketing Manager Product Line: Fresh frozen shrimps

□ Philips Seafood Philippines Corporation
2nd Refrigeration Bldg., Fish Port Complex, Brgy. Tambler, Gen. Santos City,
Contact Number/s : (63 83) 302-5957
Fax : (63 83) 302-5958
Contact Person: Mr. Rock Eliseo D. Garay, Plant Manager; Product line: frozen tuna cuts (loin, fillets, steaks, saku bars)

□ AFI International Trading Corporation
Bldg., 5, Stall 502-504, FTI Complex, Taguig, Metro Manila, METRO MANILA
Contact Number/s : 838-4578; 838-4772
Fax : 838-7108
Contact Person: Mr. Jaime Martinez, Vice President Product Line: fresh frozen octopus, cuttlefish

□ Celebes Canning Corporation
Unit 606, Residencia 8888 Cond., Pearl Drive, Ortigas Center, Pasig City,
Contact Number/s : 635-5241 to 44
Fax : 635-5235
Contact Person: Ms. Marie Benitez Product Line: Canned Tuna

□ Shemberg Marketing Corporation
Parna-an, Mandaue City
Contact Number/s : 83411; 81845
Contact Person: Mary U. Dakay, President; Product Line: Processed seaweed, refined & highly refined carrageenan & jellies

□ Marcel Trading Corporation
#4 Mazaraga Street, Quezon City,

Contact Number/s : 712-2275
Contact Person: Linda Dolorato Product Line: Processed seaweeds

 King Agro-Marine International
Suite 301-302 Casa Mendoza Bldg., A. Cortes Avenue, Mandaue City,
Contact Number/s : 721-4656
Contact Person: Alberto Soriano, Liason Officer Product Line: Alkali treated and semi-refined kappa carrageenan

FOOD INDUSTRY

 Philippine Fruit Association
Institute of Plant Breeding, University of the Philippines (UP), Los Banos, Laguna
Contact Number/s : (63 49) 536-2512 loc. 242
Fax : (63 49) 536-3438
Contact Person: Dr. Rolando G. Bugayog, President

 Philippine Mango Council
c/o Diamond Star Agro Products, 5/F Enzo Bldg., 399 Sen. Gil Puyat Avenue, Makati City
Contact Number/s : (63 2) 838-4436; (63 2) 838-4921 to 22
Fax : (63 2) 838-4621
Contact Person: Mr. Reynaldo T. Mangilit, Director

 Philippine Mango Exporters Foundation, Inc.
c/o Hi-Las Marketing Corporation, KKK Processing Plant Bldg., CRB Road, FTI Complex, Taguig, Metro Manila
Contact Number/s : (63 2) 838-4941 to 42
Fax : (63 2) 838-4940
Contact Person: Mr. Roberto Amores, President

 Pilipino Banana Growers and Exporters Association (PBGEA)
145 Rizal Street, Davao City
Contact Number/s : (63 82) 277-7771; 227-9113
Fax : (63 2) 221-2024
Contact Person: Mr. Rodolfo G. del Rosario, Jr., President

 United Coconut Association of the Phils., Inc. (UCAP)
2/F PCRDF Bldg., Pearl Drive cor. Lourdes Street, Ortigas Complex, Pasig City
Contact Number/s : (63 2) 633-8029; (63 2)633-9286 to 87
Fax : (63 2) 633-8030
Contact Person: Ms. Yvonne Agustin, Executive Secretary

 Dole Philippines, Inc. (STANFILCO), Davao
Dona Socorro Drive, Belisario Hgts., Subd., Lanang, Davao City,
Contact Number/s : (63 82) 234-0241;221 6844
Fax : (63 82) 234 1834

 Dole Philippines, Inc. (Pine Division)
Kalsangi, Polomolok, South Cotabato
Contact Number/s : (63 83) 552-2516
Fax : (63 83) 553-4104

 Del Monte Philippines, Inc.
38/F Citibank Tower Building, Paseo de Roxas, Makati City
Contact Number/s : (63 2) 810-7501 to 06
Fax : (63 2) 848-0320

 Tamugan Cannery, Inc.
Tamugan, Marilog, Davao
Contact Number/s : (63 82) 227-1152 loc. 154
Fax : (63 82) 221-1141
Email : gemini@dv.weblinq..com

CONTRUCTORS

 101 READYMIX AND DEVELOPMENT CORPORATION
Maharlika Hi-way, Brgy. St. Nino, Cabanatuan City Nueva Ecija
Contact Number/s : 044-9351279
License: 22557 Amo: Alexander R. Ciruela
Org Type: Corporation Primary Classification: General Building

 11-16 CONSTRUCTION
Mac Arthur Highway, San Vicente Apalit Pampanga
Contact Number/s : 045 302-57-01

License: 29646 Amo: Criselda Dizon Tetangco Org Type: Sole Proprietorship Primary Classification: General Engineering

□ **1977 DEVELOPMENT CORPORATION**
747 Caruncho Avenue, San Nicolas Pasig City Pasig
License: 25101 Amo: William J. Maceda Org Type: Sole Proprietorship Primary Classification: General Building

□ **3RB CONSTRUCTION & sUPPLY**
Panal, Tabaco Albay
Contact Number/s : 4875913
License: 19541 Amo: Luis B. Boyon Org Type: Sole Proprietorship Primary Classification: General Engineering

□ **401 DEVELOPMENT & CONSTRUCTION**
L14-A Life St., Monte Vista Park Subd., Cainta Rizal
Contact Number/s : 656-0091
License: 26375 Amo: Jessie I. Cervatos Org Type: Sole Proprietorship Primary Classification: General Building

□ **6/42 CONSTRUCTION CORPORATION**
#16 Shorthorn cor. Aberdeen Sts., Project 8 Quezon City
Contact Number/s : none
License: 10211 Amo: Catalina B. Mabanag Org Type: Corporation Primary Classification: General Engineering

□ **A C CUNANAN CONSTRUCTION**
#3 Ignacia dela Cruz St., Culiat, Tandang Sora Quezon City
Contact Number/s : 456-7447/9520509
License: 20752 Amo: Amando C. Cunanan, Jr. Org Type: Sole Proprietorship Primary Classification: General Engineering

□ **A. C. TUMANG CONSTRUCTION**
PARIAN, Mexico Pampanga
Contact Number/s : 9660720
License: 19589 Amo: Alex C. Tumang Org Type: Sole Proprietorship Primary Classification: General Engineering

□ **A. DE GUIA CONSTRUCTION**
Antonino Alicia Isabela
Contact Number/s : 662-7099
License: 18228 Amo: Armando M. De Guia Org Type: Sole Proprietorship Primary Classification: General Engineering

□ **A. RIVERA CONSTRUCTION**
1373 Fernando Ave., Greenmeadows II, Mabiga Mabalacat Pampanga
Contact Number/s : 331-8606
License: 22051 Amo: Albert S. Rivera Org Type: Sole Proprietorship Primary Classification: General Building

□ **A.A. GARCIA CONSTRUCTION**
0108 Mercedes St., San Jose District, Pagadian City Zamboanga del Sur
Contact Number/s : 215-17-29
License: 10496 Amo: Arnulfo A. Garcia Org Type: Sole Proprietorship Primary Classification: General Building

□ **A.B. GARCIA CONSTRUCTION AND SUPPLY**
Malabago Mangaldan Pangasinan
License: 11245 Amo: Angelito B. Garcia Org Type: Sole Proprietorship Primary Classification: General Engineering

□ **A.B. NICOLAS BUILDERS & CONSTRUCTION**
San Vicente, Santa Maria Bulacan Province
License: 28119 Amo: Abelardo B. Nicolas Org Type: Sole Proprietorship Primary Classification: General Engineering

□ **A.B. SALLOMAN CONSTRUCTION & SERVICES**
14 Leon Llido St., Munda Subd., Gen. Santos City South Cotobato
Contact Number/s : 5523867
License: 22936 Amo: Almario B. Salloman Org Type: Sole Proprietorship Primary Classification: General Engineering

 A.C. BASA CONSTRUCTION AND GENERAL MERCHANDISE
Block 28 Lot 14, Diego Silang St., Commonwealth Ave., Quezon City
Contact Number/s : 428-5042
License: 11314 Amo: Anita C. Basa Org Type: Sole Proprietorship Primary Classification: General Engineering

 A.C. RIVERO DEVELOPMENT CORPORATION
2929 Burgos Extension, Bacolod City Negros Occidental
Contact Number/s : 034-4350640
License: 5122 Amo: Alfonso C. Rivero Org Type: Corporation Primary Classification: General Engineering

 A.D.P. CONST. & SUPPLY
114 Gustilo St., La Paz, Iloilo City Iloilo
Contact Number/s : 0917-6222915/033-500-1449
License: 3466 Amo: Aida Duraliza Pendon Org Type: Sole Proprietorship Primary Classification: General Engineering

 A.F.G. CONSTRUCTION AND CONSTRUCTION SUPPLY
Sterling St., Lizares Subd., Brgy. Taculing Bacolod City Negros Occidental
Contact Number/s : 4331001
License: 17161 Amo: Eva P. Fernandez Org Type: Sole Proprietorship Primary Classification: General Engineering

 A.H. CONSTRUCTION AND GENERAL SERVICES
Gov. Forbes St., San Roque Legaspi City
Contact Number/s : 7116320
License: 11892 Amo: Archie L. Huevos Org Type: Sole Proprietorship Primary Classification: General Building

 A.O. CASING CONSTRUCTION
24 Acacia Street, Matina, Davao City Davao del Sur
Contact Number/s : none
License: 3292 Amo: Arecio O. Casing Org Type: Sole Proprietorship Primary Classification: General Engineering

 A.O. TORRES COMPANY, INC.
2453 Legarda Street, Sampaloc East Manila
Contact Number/s : 734-6289
License: 2465 Amo: Arnulfo O. Torres Org Type: Corporation Primary Classification: General Engineering

 A.T. BARRAMEDA CONSTRUCTION
8 Marbella St., Intercity Homes, Muntinlupa City Muntinlupa
Contact Number/s : none
License: 25102 Amo: Amador T. Barrameda Org Type: Sole Proprietorship Primary Classification: General Engineering

 ABBE CONSTRUCTION
Camacam St., Victory Norte, Santiago Isabela
Contact Number/s : 6827060
License: 21254 Amo: Romeo T. Gonzales Org Type: Sole Proprietorship Primary Classification: General Engineering

 AC LIM CONSTRUCTION
Taupan Road, Suterville, Zamboanga City Zamboanga del Sur
Contact Number/s : 991-2810
License: 12762 Amo: Arnel E. Lim Org Type: Sole Proprietorship Primary Classification: General Building

 AC ROCKPORT CONS. & DEV. CORP.
L-4, B-59, Morgan St., Rancho, Marikina Heights Marikina
Contact Number/s : 372-21711
License: 28077 Amo: Arturo C. Arrojado Org Type: Corporation Primary Classification: General Building

 ADVANCE TECH CONSTRUCTION
Unit 832, Cityland Mega Plaza, ADB Ave., Ortigas PO Pasig City
Contact Number/s : 687-4309

License: 9717 Amo: Ramon A. Mercado Org Type: Sole Proprietorship Primary Classification: General Building

□ **ADVANCED CONCEPT BUILDERS & MGT. INC.**
210 Kingsville Comml. Arcade, Marcos Highway Antipolo Rizal
Contact Number/s : 645-9112
License: 28375 Amo: Dennis N. Villa-Ignacio Org Type: Corporation Primary Classification: General Building

□ **AGREVILLE REALTY AND DEVELOPMENT CORPORATION**
A. Morrow Street, Koronadal South Cotobato
Contact Number/s : 083-2282520
License: 20859 Amo: Adonis G. Agreda Org Type: Corporation Primary Classification: General Engineering

□ **AJN CONSTRUCTION**
#98 Rizal St., Pilar Bataan
Contact Number/s : 047-2464181
License: 10191 Amo: Pablo E. Nohay Org Type: Sole Proprietorship Primary Classification: General Engineering

□ **AL B. CONSTRUCTION**
B10, L5&7 Durian St., Trinidad Village, Calibutbut Bacolor Pampanga
Contact Number/s : 045-8873009
License: 11740 Amo: Pascual Ocampo Bognot Org Type: Sole Proprietorship Primary Classification: General Engineering

□ **AL HUSSEIN CONSTRUCTION**
MPM Bldg., Camague, Iligan City
Contact Number/s : 223-9145
License: 18438 Amo: Cosain C. Dalidig Org Type: Sole Proprietorship Primary Classification: General Engineering

□ **ALBEVA KONSTRUKT & DEVELOPMENT CORPORATION**
No. 17 Mabuhay St., cor. Chronicle St., West Triangle Quezon City
Contact Number/s : 374-1540-43

License: 25480 Amo: Alberto R. Macaraeg, Sr. Org Type: Corporation Primary Classification: General Engineering

□ **ALFIE'S CONSTRUCTION & CONSTRUCTION SUPPLY**
Rm. 305 Parklane Bldg., Tindalo Hilado Street Bacolod City Negros Occidental
Contact Number/s : 435-0367
License: 17162 Amo: Elwin S. Javelosa Org Type: Sole Proprietorship Primary Classification: General Engineering

□ **ALLIED CONSTRUCTION & DEVELOPMENT CORPORATION**
PBL Bldg. Pasig Blvd., Pasig CPO Pasig City
Contact Number/s : 641-7918
License: 1620 Amo: Henry G. Dee Org Type: Corporation Primary Classification: General Building

□ **ALRAF CONSTRUCTION & ENTERPRISES**
288B-Caburihan, Canelar St., Zamboanga City Zamboanga del Sur
Contact Number/s : 992-5126
License: 17297 Amo: Al-Hassan C. Hasiman Org Type: Sole Proprietorship Primary Classification: General Building

□ **ALRO CONSTRUCTION & DEVELOPMENT CORPORATION**
Penaranda Extension, Bonot Legaspi City Albay
Contact Number/s : 052-4808036
License: 18361 Amo: Basil Ramon C. Gutierrez Org Type: Corporation Primary Classification: General Building

□ **AMARANTH TRADING & DEVELOPMENT CORPORATION**
Lot 5 rd.9 Phase 5, Cogeo Vill., Antipolo Rizal
Contact Number/s : 9246416
License: 12407 Amo: Edilberto H. Villanueva Org Type: Corporation Primary Classification: General Building

AMERESCO COMMERCIAL & INDUSTRIAL COMPANY, INC.
4/F Gallery Frames Bldg., 2255 South Super Highway, Malate Manila
Contact Number/s : 525-5348
License: 23612 Amo: Victor T. Santos Org Type: Corporation Primary Classification: Mechanical Work

AMPERE BUILDERS CORPORATION
L11, B13, 2 Sunny Square Subd., Malanday Marikina
Contact Number/s : 9421930
License: 22940 Amo: Ibarra A. Almajose Org Type: Corporation Primary Classification: Electrical Work

APD CONSTRUCTION
Puzon Subd., San Fermin, Cauayan Isabela
Contact Number/s : 078-6345170
License: 17467 Amo: Victorino R. Dy Org Type: Sole Proprietorship Primary Classification: General Building

ARCINUE COMMERCIAL
Avenida Rizal West, Lingayen Pangasinan
Contact Number/s : none
License: 6746 Amo: Carlos LL. Arcinue Org Type: Sole Proprietorship Primary Classification: General Engineering

ARMCON CO., INC.
306 Elysium Bldg., N S Amorante St. cor. D. Tuazon Quezon City
Contact Number/s : 7432018
License: 29042 Amo: Ferdinand P. Alarilla Org Type: Corporation Primary Classification: General Engineering

ARNEL MOJICA CONSTRUCTION & GEN. SERVICES
#24 Victoria Compound Parang Marikina
Contact Number/s : 941-0899
License: 19771 Amo: Arnel E. Mojica Org Type: Sole Proprietorship Primary Classification: General Building

AROMA CONSTRUCTION
RG-17 Rizal St. Pilar Bataan
Contact Number/s : 237-2618
License: 29382 Amo: Mario Pizarro Limcumpao Org Type: Sole Proprietorship Primary Classification: Mechanical Work

ART WORKS CORPORATION
No. 7 Pulog Street Mandaluyong CPO Mandaluyong
Contact Number/s : 533-0198
License: 16140 Amo: Arthur E. Atienza Org Type: Corporation Primary Classification: General Building

ASIAPHIL MANUFACTURING INDUSTRIES, INC.
1150 Pres. Quirino Ave Extension, Paco Manila
Contact Number/s : 563-8338/42
License: 6344 Amo: Victor T. Batungbacal Org Type: Corporation Primary Classification: Electrical Work

ASSOCIATED CONSTRUCTION AND TRADING CORPORATION
2/F, CUP Bldg., Roces Ave. cor. Mother Ignacia St., Diliman Quezon City
Contact Number/s : 7914176
License: 16831 Amo: Estelito C. Gonzales Org Type: Corporation Primary Classification: General Building

ASTAN CONSTRUCTION
43-Leonarda, Tuguegarao Cagayan
Contact Number/s : 846-7091
License: 15233 Amo: Antonio S. Tan Org Type: Sole Proprietorship Primary Classification: General Engineering

ATLANTA INDUSTRIES, INC.
Goldhill Tower 5, Annapolis, Greenhills San Juan
Contact Number/s : 723-0781
License: 27076 Amo: Roberto J. Chan Org Type: Corporation Primary Classification: General Building

ATLANTIC CONSTRUCTION & REALTY

Capitol Site, Lower Lamac, Oroquieta City Misamis Occidental
Contact Number/s : 088-5311290
License: 11497 Amo: Humphrey P. Acosta Org Type: Sole Proprietorship Primary Classification: General Engineering

□ **AUTOMATION SPECIALISTS AND POWER EXPONENTS, INC.**
#55 Laura Street, Mandaluyong CPO Mandaluyong
Contact Number/s : 5325726
License: 14545 Amo: Jaime M. Briones Org Type: Corporation Primary Classification: Electrical Work

□ **AVM CONSTRUCTION AND SUPPLY**
675 Gov. Sales Street Davao City Davao del Sur
Contact Number/s : 224-4899
License: 9948 Amo: Armando V. Mesiona Org Type: Sole Proprietorship Primary Classification: General Engineering

□ **B. CAPA CONSTRUCTION, INC.**
Rm. 123-A V. Luna Ext., Sikatuna Village Quezon City
Contact Number/s : 922-0559
License: 5662 Amo: Bernardo O. Capa Org Type: Corporation Primary Classification: General Building

□ **B. VICENCIO CONSTRUCTION**
Brgy. Cagsalaosao, Maharlika Highway, Calbayog City Samar
Contact Number/s : 2091379
License: 9687 Amo: Danilo V. Roleda Org Type: Sole Proprietorship Primary Classification: General Engineering

□ **B.C. CUERPO CONSTRUCTION CORPORATION**
Garnet St., Goldriver Ville, Burgos, Rodriguez Montalban (Rodriguez) Rizal
Contact Number/s : 998-0426
License: 11898 Amo: Benilda C. Cuerpo Org Type: Corporation Primary Classification: General Building

□ **B.E. CONSTRUCTION**
c/o Asico Subd., Compania St., Molo, Iloilo City Iloilo
Contact Number/s : 033-3373167
License: 2730 Amo: Maria Elena Malaga Org Type: Sole Proprietorship Primary Classification: General Engineering

□ **B.G.T. INFRA AND DEVELOPMENT CORPORATION**
#4 Jacqueline Kennedy Project 8 Quezon City
Contact Number/s : 9206701/4565683
License: 24114 Amo: Mario R. Talatala Org Type: Corporation Primary Classification: General Engineering

□ **B.R. RAMOS CONSTRUCTION**
151 Bagbaguin Santa Maria Bulacan Province
Contact Number/s : 641-4098
License: 3304 Amo: Bartolome R. Ramos Org Type: Sole Proprietorship Primary Classification: General Engineering

□ **B.S. CHANG BUILDERS**
St. Francis Subd., National Rd., Bo. Kitang, Limay Bataan
Contact Number/s : 047-2444171/2448064
License: 22745 Amo: Bernardo S. Chang, Jr. Org Type: Sole Proprietorship Primary Classification: General Engineering

□ **B.S. VENTENILLA CONSTRUCTION & TRADING INCORPORATED**
3559-1 Mag. Villamor Street Sta. Mesa Manila
Contact Number/s : 714-5834
License: 30225 Amo: Bonifacio Sayson Ventenilla Org Type: Corporation Primary Classification: General Engineering

□ **BARMAN CONSTRUCTION CORPORATION**
6 Kennedy Drive, Pleasant View Subd., Tandang Sora Quezon City
Contact Number/s : 939-4401
License: 7974 Amo: Victorino C. Manuel Org Type: Corporation Primary Classification: General Engineering

BCT TRADING AND CONSTRUCTION
Pineda Road, Brgy. San Pedro, Puerto Princesa City Palawan
Contact Number/s : 433-4323
License: 15199 Amo: Bella C. Tiotangco Org Type: Sole Proprietorship Primary Classification: General Engineering

BDL SANTOS CONSTRUCTION AND SUPPLY
Rizal St. Legaspi City Albay
Contact Number/s : 480-5264
License: 17535 Amo: Beethoven M. Delos Santos Org Type: Sole Proprietorship Primary Classification: General Engineering

BEDUN CONSTRUCTION
Lot 6, Block 17,Magnusville Subdivision, Batangas City Batangas
Contact Number/s : 043-980-21-87
License: 15130 Amo: Berlito C. Untalan Org Type: Sole Proprietorship Primary Classification: General Engineering

BETA ELECTRIC CORPORATION
18 Bagong Calzada, Brgy. Ususan, Taguig Manila Manila
Contact Number/s : 628-4041
License: 7527 Amo: Efren M. Gancayco Org Type: Corporation Primary Classification: Electrical Work

BICON ENTERPRISES
Km. 19 Gen. Aguinaldo Hi-way, Palico 2, Imus Cavite
Contact Number/s : 046-4712210
License: 24408 Amo: Ignacio B. Zaragoza, Jr. Org Type: Sole Proprietorship Primary Classification: General Engineering

BIG BEN CONSTRUCTION
Dampol 1st, Pulilan Bulacan Province
Contact Number/s : 044-6761720
License: 15678 Amo: Ma. Asuncion M. Eusebio Org Type: Sole Proprietorship Primary Classification: General Engineering

BIG BERTHA CONSTRUCTION AND DEVELOPMENT
4300 Bernarda St., San Sebastian Vill., Tarlac Tarlac
Contact Number/s : 9823901
License: 3191 Amo: Catalino T. Urquico Org Type: Sole Proprietorship Primary Classification: General Engineering

BILLENA CONSTRUCTION
11 Fuentes St. Iloilo City Iloilo
License: 7434 Amo: Adolfo L. Billena Org Type: Sole Proprietorship Primary Classification: General Engineering

BIMBO CONSTRUCTION
Enrile Subd., Concepcion Grande Naga City Camarines Sur
Contact Number/s : 054-8112406
License: 25022 Amo: Wilfredo B. De Leon, Jr. Org Type: Sole Proprietorship Primary Classification: General Engineering

BURNET C. BLANZA CONSTRUCTION
Washington St., Brgy. Osmena Solano Nueva Vizcaya
Contact Number/s : none
License: 29600 Amo: Burnet C. Blanza Org Type: Sole Proprietorship Primary Classification: General Engineering

BUSILAC BUILDERS, INCORPORATED
Brgy. 26, 270 J.P. Rizal St., Laoag City Ilocos Norte
Contact Number/s : 771-4735
License: 7701 Amo: Romeo M. Camarillo Org Type: Corporation Primary Classification: General Engineering

C & F CONSTRUCTION & DEVELOPMENT CORPORATION
134 MacArthur Highway, Malabon Metro Manila
Contact Number/s : 3676590
License: 3509 Amo: Erasmo Gerardo S. Mendoza Org Type: Corporation Primary Classification: General Engineering

□ **C B G BUILDERS, INCORPORATED**
MUTI Bldg.,Osme?a St., Koronadal South Cotobato
Contact Number/s : 083-2283876
License: 26535 Amo: Ma. Henrietta C. Dela Pe?a Org Type: Corporation Primary Classification: General Engineering

□ **C.E.B. CONSTRUCTION**
2862 Road 3 Barretto Subd., Pandacan Manila
Contact Number/s : 562-6618
License: 20400 Amo: Eric C. Bacay Org Type: Sole Proprietorship Primary Classification: General Building

□ **C.R. DOMINGO CONSTRUCTION, INC.**
Brgy. 3, Poblacion, San Mateo Isabela
Contact Number/s : 664-2089
License: 2992 Amo: Rolando Y. Domingo Org Type: Corporation Primary Classification: General Engineering

□ **CAMECO CONSTRUCTION DEV'T CORPORATION**
J.C. Aquino Avenue Butuan City Agusan del Norte
Contact Number/s : 342-8373
License: 22381 Amo: Rosarito A. Chua Org Type: Corporation Primary Classification: General Engineering

□ **CAMIA CONSTRUCTION**
13 Gomez St., Carig, Tuguegarao Cagayan
Contact Number/s : 846-7158
License: 20506 Amo: Vito A. Loyon Org Type: Sole Proprietorship Primary Classification: General Engineering

□ **CARI CONSTRUCTION & DEVELOPMENT CORP.**
BGY. CANDADAM, Baybay Leyte
Contact Number/s : 335-2298/18
License: 1223 Amo: Felipe F. Cari Org Type: Corporation Primary Classification: General Engineering

□ **CARRASCAL INTEGRATED ENTERPRISES**
Carrascal Surigao del Sur
Contact Number/s : 032-3451253
License: 4764 Amo: Victor L. Tan Org Type: Sole Proprietorship Primary Classification: General Engineering

□ **CASMOR CONSTRUCTION CORPORATION**
306 Morato Square Bldg., T. Morato Ave. Quezon City CPO Quezon City
Contact Number/s : 426-2672
License: 26876 Amo: Alberto J. Castro Org Type: Corporation Primary Classification: General Building

□ **CASTRO BEDOY CONSTRUCTION**
Purok 4 Bulanao, Tabuk Kalinga-Apayao
License: 25999 Amo: Castro B. Bedoy Org Type: Sole Proprietorship Primary Classification: General Engineering

□ **C-E DIMACALI CONSTRUCTION**
22 BAC 1-11 Don Carlos Vill., Pasay City
License: 27900 Amo: Eulogio L. Dimacali Org Type: Sole Proprietorship Primary Classification: General Engineering

□ **CEAM TECHNICAL SERVICES CORPORATION**
Lot 6 Blk.11 Phase 1, Jasmin St.,Elvinda Vill. San Pedro Laguna
Contact Number/s : 868-8741/4262
License: 29357 Amo: Chito C. Amora Org Type: Corporation Primary Classification: Electrical Work

□ **CEBU YOUNG CONSTRUCTION**
61 Sindulan St., Cebu City Cebu
Contact Number/s : 2314079
License: 3195 Amo: Domingo A. Royeca Org Type: Sole Proprietorship Primary Classification: General Building

□ **CHARLZ CONSTRUCTION**
1417 Vasquez Street Surigao City Surigao City

Contact Number/s : none
License: 8709 Amo: Charles L. Gosingco Org Type: Sole Proprietorship Primary Classification: General Building

 CHIEF CONSTRUCT INC.
2 Turo Bocaue Bulacan Province
License: 30094 Amo: Christian D.L. Mendoza Org Type: Corporation Primary Classification: General Engineering

 CLANE CONSTRUCTION
074 Sta. Filomena, Dipolog City Zamboanga del Norte
Contact Number/s : 212-5639
License: 6933 Amo: Abundio D. Marapao, Jr. Org Type: Sole Proprietorship Primary Classification: General Engineering

 COLLERA'S CONSTRUCTION
346 Brgy. 62-A, Sgkahan Tacloban City Leyte
Contact Number/s : 053-3255576
License: 13246 Amo: Agustin R. Collera, Jr. Org Type: Sole Proprietorship Primary Classification: General Building

 CONMECH CONSTRUCTION AND DEVELOPMENT CORPORATION
FSA Corporate Plaza #132 San Francisco St., Mandaluyong City Mandaluyong
Contact Number/s : 534-6823
License: 29325 Amo: Jose Ramon A. Gonzalez Org Type: Corporation Primary Classification: General Building

 CONSUNJI CONSTRUCTION
Lalawigan, Samal, Samal Bataan
Contact Number/s : 047-4512177
License: 26080 Amo: Jorge M. Consunji Org Type: Sole Proprietorship Primary Classification: General Building

 COVENANT CONSTRUCTION GROUP, INC.
B-7, L-9 Road #2, GSIS Hills, Talipapa Novaliches Proper Quezon City
Contact Number/s : 983-0090
License: 22278 Amo: Manuel C. Ortiz III Org Type: Corporation Primary Classification: General Building

 CTC BUILDER
Rizal Street, Punta, Donsol Sorsogon
Contact Number/s : (052)4833226/8240208
License: 12088 Amo: Charles T. Clemente, Sr. Org Type: Sole Proprietorship Primary Classification: General Building

 D. ISAAC BUILDERS, INC.
#54 Detroit Street Cubao Quezon City
Contact Number/s : 414-2969
License: 24820 Amo: Ricardo M. Isaac Org Type: Corporation Primary Classification: General Building

 D.M. BRIONES CONSTRUCTION ENTERPRISES, INC.
Diamond St., RGA Village, Cabaguio Ave., Davao City Davao del Sur
Contact Number/s : 221-6490
License: 28332 Amo: Daniel M. Briones Org Type: Corporation Primary Classification: General Building

 DAHL CONSTRUCTION
98-C Cenacle Drive Sunville St., Project 6 Quezon City
Contact Number/s : none
License: 8931 Amo: Arthur Z. Lava Org Type: Sole Proprietorship Primary Classification: General Engineering

 DARUMA CORPORATION
1402 14F Marbella I Condo, 2223 Roxas Blvd Pasay City Pasay City
Contact Number/s : 5511912
License: 29041 Amo: Fred N. Mendoza Org Type: Corporation Primary Classification: General Building

 DASTA BUILDERS
45 Naval St., Cupang North Balanga Bataan
Contact Number/s : 047-2371089

License: 26960 Amo: Edmundo C. Dasig III Org Type: Sole Proprietorship Primary Classification: General Building

□ **DAVAO CONCRETE PRODUCTS**
0966 Osmena Street, Tagum Davao del Norte
Contact Number/s : 084-2173345
License: 12090 Amo: Llewellyn M. Mangilet, Sr. Org Type: Sole Proprietorship Primary Classification: General Engineering

□ **DCT CONSTRUCTION**
#7 Paddad, Alicia Isabela
Contact Number/s : 078-6627104
License: 14414 Amo: Dominador C. Torio Org Type: Sole Proprietorship Primary Classification: General Building

□ **DELTON CONSTRUCTION & ELECTRICAL SERVICES**
46 Sct. Chuatoco St., Roxas District Quezon City
License: 24101 Amo: Antonio Delfin Singson Sumabat III Org Type: Sole Proprietorship Primary Classification: General Building

□ **DETY CONSTRUCTION & DEVELOPMENT CORPORATION**
12 A.Marquez St.,Union Village Tandang Sora Quezon City
Contact Number/s : 931-4671
License: 6126 Amo: Romulo M. Austria Org Type: Corporation Primary Classification: General Building

□ **DIGITAL NETWORK COMMUNICATIONS & COMPUTERS, INC.**
30F Antel Global Corp. center, Dona Julia Vargas Ave. Ortigas PO Pasig City
Contact Number/s : 636-2888/638-3630
License: 30194 Amo: Manuel Gaerlan Ong, Jr. Org Type: Corporation Primary Classification: Communication Facilities

□ **DIPOLOG TOP CONSTRUCTION AND DEVELOPMENT CORPORATION**
Sta. Filomena, Dipolog City Zamboanga del Norte
Contact Number/s : 2122740
License: 6678 Amo: Olegario Y. Uy Org Type: Corporation Primary Classification: General Engineering

□ **DJ BUILDERS CORPORATION**
BLK.10,LOT 1,LAGUNA INTERNATIONAL INDUSTRIAL PARK,MAMPLASAN, Bi?an Laguna
Contact Number/s : 9123158520
License: 9688 Amo: Chun Bae Kim Org Type: Corporation Primary Classification: General Engineering

□ **DQT BUILDERS**
2/F DQT Bldg., Enverga cor Merchan Sts., Lucena City Quezon Province
Contact Number/s : 042-7103753/6783
License: 7950 Amo: Domingo Q. Tan Org Type: Sole Proprietorship Primary Classification: General Engineering

□ **DS B CONSTRUCTION & SUPPLY**
Barangay 1, Magsaysay Ave., Bacacay Albay
Contact Number/s : 052-4803970
License: 16126 Amo: Dante S. Bombales Org Type: Sole Proprietorship Primary Classification: General Engineering

□ **DSM CONSTRUCTION AND DEVELOPMENT CORPORATION**
41 Victoria Ave., cor. 10th St., New Manila Quezon City
Contact Number/s : 722-5013
License: 19380 Amo: Dennis S. Masigan Org Type: Corporation Primary Classification: General Building

□ **DURIAN CONSTRUCTION AND SUPPLY**
76 Agton St., Toril, Davao City Davao del Sur
Contact Number/s : 291-0036
License: 6337 Amo: Bienvenido A. Dulla Org Type: Sole Proprietorship Primary Classification: General Engineering

□ **E F T BUILDERS**
Nonoc, Larena Siquijor
Contact Number/s : 035-3772089

License: 15687 Amo: Earl Francis R. Tan Org Type: Sole Proprietorship Primary Classification: General Engineering

E N J CONSTRUCTION & DEVELOPMENT CORP.
#4951 Guerrero St., Brgy. Poblacion, Makati
Contact Number/s : 895-4111
License: 28015 Amo: Jessie M. Tolentino Org Type: Corporation Primary Classification: General Building

E. GARCIA CONSTRUCTION & E. GARCIA GRAVEL & SAND
Cotabato City St., Gimenez Subd., Naga City Camarines Sur
Contact Number/s : 054-4752798
License: 7243 Amo: Elizabeth S. Garcia Org Type: Sole Proprietorship Primary Classification: General Engineering

E. GARDIOLA CONSTRUCTION
Rm.303 Pasda Mansion Bldg., Timog cor. Panay Ave., Quezon City CPO Quezon City
Contact Number/s : 931-4046
License: 17542 Amo: Elaine B. Gardiola Org Type: Sole Proprietorship Primary Classification: General Engineering

E. LAPUS ENTERPRISES
15 Liverpool St., Merville, Para?aque CPO Para?aque
License: 10813 Amo: Evangeline Y. Lapus Org Type: Sole Proprietorship Primary Classification: General Engineering

E.A. RAMIREZ CONSTRUCTION, INC.
7 Pascual St., Remarville Subd., Bagbag, Novaliches Proper Quezon City
Contact Number/s : 9379495
License: 11631 Amo: Eduardo A. Ramirez Org Type: Corporation Primary Classification: General Building

E.A. YGONA CONSTRUCTION
15 Mahabagin St., Teacher's Village West Diliman Quezon City
Contact Number/s : 9326206
License: 23229 Amo: Edgar Allan G. Ygona Org Type: Sole Proprietorship Primary Classification: General Engineering

E.C. TIMBANCAYA ENTERPRISES
Fernandez Extn. Puerto Princesa City Palawan
License: 15244 Amo: Edgar A. Timbancaya Org Type: Sole Proprietorship Primary Classification: General Engineering

E.I. TEMPLONUEVO AND ASSOCIATES, INCORPORATED
Bulmang Numancia Aklan
Contact Number/s : 036-2624702
License: 1090 Amo: Jeserel T. Templonuevo Org Type: Corporation Primary Classification: General Engineering

E.M. LAPUZ CONSTRUCTION
Rizal Nueva Ecija
Contact Number/s : 925-4977
License: 22943 Amo: Eladio M. Lapuz Org Type: Sole Proprietorship Primary Classification: General Engineering

E.P. CORNEJO CONSTRUCTION
L8, B7, Aphrodite St., Crestview Subd., Mayamot, Antipolo Rizal
Contact Number/s : 646-8790
License: 11633 Amo: Edmundo P. Cornejo Org Type: Sole Proprietorship Primary Classification: General Building

E.P. MANANTAN CONSTRUCTION AND DEVELOPMENT CORPORATION
National Highway, Visayan Village, Tagum Davao del Norte
Contact Number/s : 084-4002380
License: 6457 Amo: Emilio P. Manantan Org Type: Corporation Primary Classification: General Engineering

E.R. VENZON CONSTRUCTION
Sunflower St., Dona Francisca Subd., Balanga Bataan
Contact Number/s : 047-7912795

License: 19013 Amo: Noli A. Venzon Org Type: Sole Proprietorship Primary Classification: General Engineering

□ **E.T.V.R. TRADING AND CONSTRUCTION**
Rosal St., Lumang Bayan, Calapan Mindoro Oriental
Contact Number/s : 043-2867312
License: 14581 Amo: Emelyn Vanguardia Rivera Org Type: Sole Proprietorship Primary Classification: General Building

□ **EARL CONSTRUCTION**
36 Lantana Street, Cubao Quezon City
Contact Number/s : none
License: 8461 Amo: Mario L. Mangsal Org Type: Sole Proprietorship Primary Classification: General Building

□ **EASTERN MINDANAO CONSTRUCTION AND DEVELOPMENT**
Cor. Tutu & Gomez Sts. cor. Tutu Sts., Ginogoog City Misamis Oriental
Contact Number/s : 861-1452
License: 11491 Amo: Rosauro Nivera Kionisala Org Type: Sole Proprietorship Primary Classification: General Engineering

□ **EDGAR C. ADLAWAN CONSTRUCTION**
LIPATA, MINGLANILLA Cebu
Contact Number/s : 346-0313
License: 2978 Amo: Edgar C. Adlawan Org Type: Sole Proprietorship Primary Classification: General Engineering

□ **EGB CONSTRUCTION**
Alibagu Ilagan Isabela
Contact Number/s : 078-6222775
License: 13722 Amo: Erni G. Baggao Org Type: Sole Proprietorship Primary Classification: General Building

□ **ELECTROBUS CONSOLIDATED, INC.**
102 Panay Ave. Quezon City
Contact Number/s : 372-3935
License: 7363 Amo: Antonio S. Herrera, Jr. Org Type: Corporation Primary Classification: Electrical Work

□ **EM PAULE CONSTRUCTION AND TRADING**
#40 Payna Street, Veterans Village Project 7 Quezon City
Contact Number/s : 415-82-82
License: 19006 Amo: Eduardo M. Paule Org Type: Sole Proprietorship Primary Classification: General Building

□ **EMCY CONSTRUCTION, INC.**
3915 Marigold St. Sunvalley Subd., Para?aque CPO Para?aque
Contact Number/s : 8231377/80
License: 13254 Amo: Mario T. Cortez Org Type: Corporation Primary Classification: General Engineering

□ **ERA AGGREGATES CONSTRUCTION**
Lagman Bldg. V. Tiomico St. San Fernando Pampanga
Contact Number/s : 961-26-04
License: 13663 Amo: Erlinda A. Hipolito Org Type: Sole Proprietorship Primary Classification: General Engineering

□ **ESPERAS CONSTRUCTION AND DEVELOPMENT CORPORATION**
Greenville, Marasbaras, Tacloban City Leyte
License: 5368 Amo: Victorio L. Esperas Org Type: Corporation Primary Classification: General Engineering

□ **EVERLAST CONSTRUCTION**
Ever Theater Bldg. T. Claudio Street, Zamboanga City Zamboanga del Sur
Contact Number/s : 991-7391
License: 2364 Amo: Benito L. Ong Org Type: Sole Proprietorship Primary Classification: General Engineering

□ **F. ALARCON CONSTRUCTION CORPORATION**
Jacinto St., Poblacion, San Jose Mindoro Occidental
Contact Number/s : none

License: 17612 Amo: Feliciano S. Alarcon, Sr. Org Type: Corporation Primary Classification: General Engineering

F.B.G. CONSTRUCTION AND SUPPLIES
No. 2 Green St., Sunrise Subd., Washington Drive, Legaspi City Albay
Contact Number/s : 052-4814622/362-4363
License: 15565 Amo: Francisco B. Gomez Org Type: Sole Proprietorship Primary Classification: General Engineering

F.C.S. CONSTRUCTION
San Vicente Tarlac Tarlac
Contact Number/s : 982-1365
License: 4069 Amo: Felicitas C. Sumera Org Type: Sole Proprietorship Primary Classification: General Engineering

F.P. DE GUZMAN CONSTRUCTION, INC.
4 Bagbaguin, Santa Maria Bulacan Province
Contact Number/s : 044-6413520
License: 10296 Amo: Daniel C. De Guzman Org Type: Corporation Primary Classification: General Engineering

FABCON PHILIPPINES, INC.
12/F Jollibee Center, San Miguel Ave. Pasig CPO Pasig City
Contact Number/s : 633-4234/39
License: 16836 Amo: Reynaldo O. Navarro Org Type: Corporation Primary Classification: General Building

FASCON (MANILA), INC.
256 Roosevelt Avenue, Quezon City CPO Quezon City
Contact Number/s : 374-2715/374-3638/412-8145
License: 274 Amo: Federico A. Santander Org Type: Corporation Primary Classification: General Engineering

FER-AN CONSTRUCTION
Parada, Santa Maria Bulacan Province
License: 14502 Amo: Carlito G. Fernando Org Type: Sole Proprietorship Primary Classification: General Engineering

FERDSTAR BUILDERS CONTRACTORS
San Antonio, Lubao Pampanga
Contact Number/s : 910-774
License: 4965 Amo: Ferdinand L. Beltran Org Type: Sole Proprietorship Primary Classification: General Engineering

FERMAEL INDUSTRIAL SALES & GENERAL CONTRACTOR
Sta. Clara, Batangas City Batangas
Contact Number/s : 4021420/7231598
License: 9207 Amo: Fernando C. Serrano Org Type: Sole Proprietorship Primary Classification: General Building

FIL-ASIAN BUILDERS INCORPORATED
2496 F, Bayview Drive, Tambo Para?aque
Contact Number/s : 853-5551
License: 24689 Amo: Pablo R. Rostata Org Type: Corporation Primary Classification: General Engineering

FILCOR CONSTRUCTION AND DEVELOPMENT CORPORATION
No. 20-18th Ave., Murphy, Cubao Quezon City
Contact Number/s : 9119446
License: 4150 Amo: Pastor M. Sta. Maria Org Type: Corporation Primary Classification: General Building

FIRST INTERISLAND BUILDERS CORPORATION
152-154 ARELLANO ST., San Juan
License: 23247 Amo: Danilo B. Aquino Org Type: Corporation Primary Classification: General Building

FIT & SONS INDUSTRIES, INC.
Sulpicio St., Luz Vill. Butuan City Agusan del Norte
Contact Number/s : 085-3425179
License: 5555 Amo: Sulpicio M. Tolentino Org Type: Corporation Primary Classification: General Engineering

□ **FLOBAR CONSTRUCTION AND SUPPLIES**
c/o Autofill Petron Service Station, Brgy. Gredu Panabo Davao del Norte
Contact Number/s : 084-6284013
License: 13783 Amo: Flor L. Barrios-Hayag
Org Type: Sole Proprietorship Primary
Classification: General Engineering

□ **G. UYMATIAO JR. CONSTRUCTION**
#49 Sta. Catalina Street, Dumaguete City Negros Oriental
Contact Number/s : 2254717
License: 6663 Amo: Gregorio L. Uymatiao, Jr.
Org Type: Sole Proprietorship Primary
Classification: General Engineering

□ **G. V. GANDIA CONSTRUCTION**
2F Penalosa Bldg., Sgt. Legaspi St., Binakayan Kawit Cavite
Contact Number/s : 434-19-50
License: 21700 Amo: Gilbert V. Gandia Org
Type: Sole Proprietorship Primary
Classification: General Engineering

□ **G.A. FLORES CONSTRUCTION, INC.**
12 Maya St., Dizon Subd., Baguio City Benguet
Contact Number/s : 4422880
License: 611 Amo: Gamaliel A. Flores Org
Type: Corporation Primary Classification:
General Engineering

□ **G.E.A. CONSTRUCTION CORPORATION**
1209 Sampaloc st., San Jose Mindoro Occidental
Contact Number/s : 434911730
License: 10163 Amo: Edgardo V. Alarcon Org
Type: Corporation Primary Classification:
General Engineering

□ **GACUTAN CONSTRUCTION**
Tanguile Street, Minante I Cauayan City Isabela
Contact Number/s : 078-6522335
License: 10789 Amo: Bethilda G. Wisco Org
Type: Sole Proprietorship Primary
Classification: General Engineering

□ **GEM CONSTRUCTION & SUPPLY**
126 Malainin, Ibaan Batangas
Contact Number/s : 043-3112274
License: 29732 Amo: Miguela Zarraga Micosa
Org Type: Sole Proprietorship Primary
Classification: General Engineering

□ **GEMMA CONSTRUCTION SUPPLY**
Cor. Aquino St., Gen. Santos Drive, Koronadal South Cotobato
Contact Number/s : 2282366
License: 5044 Amo: Arturo A. Uy, Sr. Org
Type: Sole Proprietorship Primary
Classification: General Engineering

□ **GEOMETRIC CONSTRUCTION & SUPPLIES**
22 Palangingan, Iba Zambales
Contact Number/s : 047-8111362
License: 6996 Amo: Rolando R. Huang Org
Type: Sole Proprietorship Primary
Classification: General Building

□ **GEONOR 2000 TRADING & CONSTRUCTION**
72 4th St., Damayan Lagi, New Manila Quezon City CPO Quezon City
Contact Number/s : 700-4214
License: 29991 Amo: Georgia Nacianceno Shirar Org Type: Sole Proprietorship Primary
Classification: General Building

□ **GICAR CONSTRUCTION**
232 San Nicolas Street Surigao City Surigao del Norte
Contact Number/s : 231-7255
License: 12624 Amo: Ernesto G. Chua Org
Type: Sole Proprietorship Primary
Classification: General Engineering

□ **GLODA BUILDERS & DEV.**
Rm. 402 Park Avenue Mansion, Park Avenue, Pasay City
Contact Number/s : 83212223
License: 22081 Amo: Gloria A. Chico Org
Type: Sole Proprietorship Primary
Classification: General Engineering

□ **GOLD DUST CONSTRUCTION**
Sto. Nino Street, Dagami Leyte
Contact Number/s : 321-4269
License: 12101 Amo: Juan Gilbert E. Vertulfo Org Type: Sole Proprietorship Primary Classification: General Engineering

□ **GOLDCOAST CONSTRUCTION**
Yati, Liloan Cebu
Contact Number/s : 564-3580
License: 28837 Amo: Joselito H. Mantuhac Org Type: Sole Proprietorship Primary Classification: General Building

□ **GOOD FORTUNE INTERNATIONAL, INCORPORATED**
Newtown Bldg., Quezon Street, Iloilo City Iloilo
Contact Number/s : 3351252
License: 9246 Amo: Ailyn Haro Galaraga Org Type: Corporation Primary Classification: General Building

□ **GPE BUILDERS, INC.**
32 Cristine St., Parkway Village, San Frnacisco Del Monte, Q.C. Quezon City
Contact Number/s : 412-9970/71
License: 13470 Amo: Engracio P. De Gracia Org Type: Corporation Primary Classification: General Building

□ **GRANBY TRADING & CONSTRUCTION**
Unit 14-E, One Burgundy Plaza, 307 Katipunan Ave., Loyola Heights Quezon City
Contact Number/s : 4353434
License: 27554 Amo: Ma. Leuvina Sofia G. Llana Org Type: Sole Proprietorship Primary Classification: General Building

□ **GREYROCK CONSTRUCTION**
Ruste Drive, San Jose St., Zamboanga City Zamboanga del Sur
Contact Number/s : 9932257
License: 9296 Amo: Reynaldo R. Lim Org Type: Sole Proprietorship Primary Classification: General Engineering

□ **GRO RAD CONSTRUCTION & DEVELOPMENT CORP.**
Rm. 202 Ferros Ave., 176 Salcedo Village Makati City
Contact Number/s : 8133581
License: 29482 Amo: Antonio H.K.S. Co Org Type: Corporation Primary Classification: General Engineering

□ **H C M CONSTRUCTION CORPORATION**
HCM Building, 1467 B Champaca St., Castillo Park Subd., Almanza Las Pi?
Contact Number/s : 5604142
License: 19382 Amo: Henry C. Medina Org Type: Corporation Primary Classification: General Engineering

□ **H.B. LOTILLA CONSTRUCTION COMPANY, INC.**
650 CRM Avenue cor. St. Joseph St. BF Almanza Las Pi?
Contact Number/s : 8922758
License: 1855 Amo: Humberto B. Lotilla Org Type: Corporation Primary Classification: General Building

□ **H.I.S. CONSTRUCTION**
Blk.#1 Unit #7,Romarosa Townhomes, Luzon Avenue Quezon City CPO Quezon City
Contact Number/s : 932-7340/932-7361
License: 12665 Amo: Hermenigildo I. Sanceja Org Type: Sole Proprietorship Primary Classification: General Building

□ **H.L.J. CONSTRUCTION & ENTERPRISES**
Lirasan St., Kabangkalan Negros Occidental
Contact Number/s : 4712897
License: 18080 Amo: Henry L. Jordan Org Type: Sole Proprietorship Primary Classification: General Building

□ **H.T.L. CONSTRUCTION**
Calao West Santiago Isabela
Contact Number/s : (078) 6828384
License: 3962 Amo: Henry T. Lim Org Type: Sole Proprietorship Primary Classification: General Engineering

□ **HALREY CONSTRUCTION, INC.**
282 Gov. F.F. Halili Ave., Santa Maria Bulacan Province
Contact Number/s : 044-6412496
License: 2267 Amo: Ma. Josefa A. Halili Org Type: Corporation Primary Classification: General Engineering

□ **HANIN CORPORATION**
Unit 108 Chateau Verde Condo. Valle Verde I Pasig CPO Pasig City
Contact Number/s : 671-0579
License: 28872 Amo: Catherine G. Morano Org Type: Corporation Primary Classification: General Building

□ **HDC CORPORATION**
U102 Alpine Gardens Condo. 100 F. Manalo St., Cubao Quezon City
Contact Number/s : 4103712
License: 24832 Amo: Hermando A. Dela Cruz Org Type: Corporation Primary Classification: General Engineering

□ **HERBERT MALMIS GENERAL MERCHANDISE & CONTRACTOR, INC.**
M.H. Del Pilar Street, Tagbilaran City Bohol
Contact Number/s : 411-3190
License: 4593 Amo: Herbert Malmis Org Type: Corporation Primary Classification: General Engineering

□ **HI ELES INDUSTRIAL CORPORATION**
1351 Angono Street, Makati CPO (inc. Buendia up to Edsa) Makati
Contact Number/s : 899-0530
License: 27749 Amo: Carlos V. Co Org Type: Corporation Primary Classification: Elevator and Escalator Work

□ **HOMEWORLD ENGINEERING**
Room 202 TG I Building, Gatuslao St. Bacolod City Negros Occidental
Contact Number/s : 034-4348706
License: 14725 Amo: Crisanto H. Lim Org Type: Sole Proprietorship Primary Classification: General Building

□ **HONG EQUIPMENT AND DEVELOPMENT CORPORATION**
629 Bulacao Pardo, Cebu City Cebu
Contact Number/s : 032255-5304
License: 7551 Amo: George B. Hong Org Type: Corporation Primary Classification: General Engineering

□ **HYDROCK WELLS, INC.**
Bolcan St., Agdao, Davao City Davao del Sur
Contact Number/s : 227-2766
License: 2690 Amo: Roberto G. Puentespina Org Type: Corporation Primary Classification: General Engineering

□ **I&E CONSTRUCTION**
MTC Zapote Alabang Rd. cor. Admiral Subd Las Pi?as CPO Las Pi?
License: 10410 Amo: Manuel A. Ilagan Org Type: Sole Proprietorship Primary Classification: General Engineering

□ **I.F. BLANCO'S CONSTRUCTION**
M.H. Del Pilar St., Pinamalayan Mindoro Oriental
Contact Number/s : 043-4431103
License: 25350 Amo: Isagani F. Blanco Org Type: Sole Proprietorship Primary Classification: General Engineering

□ **INCO (GENERAL CONTRACTOR) PHILIPPINES CORPORATION**
307 Pamana Languages Int"l. Bldg., 926 Pasay Rd., Makati City
Contact Number/s : 840-4170
License: 14919 Amo: Renel A. Lobo Org Type: Corporation Primary Classification: General Engineering

□ **INDUSTRIAL AND TECHNOLOGICAL PROPONENTS, INCORPORATED**
Grd. FLr., Lili Bldg. 101 Malakas St., Pinyahan, Diliman Quezon City
Contact Number/s : 433-0784
License: 14822 Amo: Eugenio S. Ozarraga Org Type: Corporation Primary Classification: General Building

□ **INTER CONGLOMERATES, INCORPORATED**
14F, Belvedere Tower, 15 San Miguel Ave. Ortigas Ctr., Pasig CPO Pasig City
Contact Number/s : 637-8577/80
License: 20547 Amo: Emmanuel S. Dizon Org Type: Corporation Primary Classification: Electrical Work

□ **INTERDEC GROUP CO. INC.**
Rm.301 West City Plaza, 66 West Ave., Quezon City CPO Quezon City
Contact Number/s : 410-3501
License: 29188 Amo: Arturo R. Bandong Org Type: Corporation Primary Classification: Electrical Work

□ **ISOMETRIC ENTERPRISES**
8/F Fil Garcia Tower, Kallayaan Avenue, Diliman Quezon City
Contact Number/s : 433-0181/84
License: 19421 Amo: Bernardino M. Landicho Org Type: Sole Proprietorship Primary Classification: General Engineering

□ **J. LEE CONSTRUCTION**
Gate 2 Lee Bldg., Libertad ext., Bacolod City Negros Occidental
License: 9876 Amo: Juan L. Lee Org Type: Sole Proprietorship Primary Classification: General Building

□ **J.C. CRUZ CONSTRUCTION**
3 Sta. Ana St., Sto. Rosario Village, Malabon Malabon
Contact Number/s : 361-2319/3634952
License: 581 Amo: Jose C. Cruz, Sr. Org Type: Sole Proprietorship Primary Classification: General Engineering

□ **J.D. MANAID CONSTRUCTION**
418 Old Farm Rd., Greenfield, Sindalan San Fernando Pampanga
License: 26371 Amo: Jaime D. Manaid Org Type: Sole Proprietorship Primary Classification: General Engineering

□ **J.I.L. TRADING AND CONSTRUCTION CO.**
Rm. 407 Park Avenue Mansion, Park Ave., Pasay City CPO - Malibay Pasay City
Contact Number/s : 2517295
License: 14634 Amo: Timoteo V. Rabano Org Type: Partnership Primary Classification: General Building

□ **J.V. CABALQUINTO CONSTRUCTION, INC.**
3 Del Carmen St., Sta. Teresita Vill., Lamuan, Marikina Heights Marikina
Contact Number/s : 942-0959/9416079
License: 6582 Amo: Javier V. Cabalquinto Org Type: Corporation Primary Classification: General Engineering

□ **JADE EAST TRADING AND CONSTRUCTION**
55-A Sto. Tomas St., Quezon City CPO Quezon City
Contact Number/s : 732-0480
License: 6960 Amo: Robert Y. Ong Uy Org Type: Sole Proprietorship Primary Classification: General Engineering

□ **JBGM CONSTRUCTION**
San Fermin, Cauayan Isabela
Contact Number/s : 078-6522069
License: 19897 Amo: Jose Bernardo G. Mallillin Org Type: Sole Proprietorship Primary Classification: General Engineering

□ **J-BROS CONSTRUCTION**
98 Amity Ext., Annex 7 BLS Para?aque CPO Para?aque
License: 27587 Amo: Abelardo S. Balota Org Type: Sole Proprietorship Primary Classification: General Engineering

□ **JDK BUILDER**
Km. 142 Aningway, Subic Subic Zambales
Contact Number/s : 2322426
License: 8308 Amo: Necita S. Domingo Org Type: Sole Proprietorship Primary Classification: General Engineering

□ **JEFF CONSTRUCTION**
Magang, Daet Camarines Norte
Contact Number/s : 440-1798
License: 14774 Amo: Florendo P. Bernal Org Type: Sole Proprietorship Primary Classification: General Engineering

□ **JEGMA CONSTRUCTION AND DEVELOPMENT CORPORATION**
NS-1A Abella Cmpd., Ma. Gochan St., Manbaling, Cebu City Cebu
Contact Number/s : 261-5444
License: 14775 Amo: Gabriel Uy Alonzo Org Type: Corporation Primary Classification: General Building

□ **JEJOR'S CONSTRUCTION CORPORATION**
Pres. Quirino St., Cogon Cagayan De Oro City Misamis Oriental
Contact Number/s : 08822-723736
License: 5143 Amo: Antonio H. Tiu Org Type: Corporation Primary Classification: General Engineering

□ **JEM CONSTRUCTION, INCORPORATED**
55 Katipunan St., Concepcion, Marikina City
Contact Number/s : 9481769
License: 3560 Amo: Eduardo Macapugay Manuel Org Type: Sole Proprietorship Primary Classification: General Building

□ **JHJ CONSTRUCTION**
23 Huervana Street, La Paz, Iloilo City Iloilo
License: 3781 Amo: Jorge H. Jaruda Org Type: Sole Proprietorship Primary Classification: General Engineering

□ **JJEFWA BUILDERS**
Bunsuran 1st., Pandi Bulacan Province
Contact Number/s : 661-0010
License: 20868 Amo: Ceferino J. Capalad Org Type: Sole Proprietorship Primary Classification: General Engineering

□ **JK MORENO CONSTRUCTION**
Cuta Poblacion West Lagawe Ifugao
Contact Number/s : 658-8419
License: 26713 Amo: John Kenneth T. Moreno Org Type: Sole Proprietorship Primary Classification: General Building

□ **JM NAPAY CONSTRUCTION, INCORPORATED**
#37 Amalingan Ave., Greenheights Village, Sucat Para?aque CPO Para?aque
Contact Number/s : none
License: 18158 Amo: Juanito M. Napay II Org Type: Corporation Primary Classification: General Engineering

□ **JMARP TRADING AND CONSTRUCTION**
No. 56 or 60 Luarca St., Vista Verde Exec. Village, Cainta Rizal
Contact Number/s : 646-0268
License: 26309 Amo: Antonio M. Pulido Org Type: Sole Proprietorship Primary Classification: General Engineering

□ **JMT CONSTRUCTION**
Km. 4, Brgy. Luna, Surigao City Surigao del Norte
Contact Number/s : 2326202
License: 14186 Amo: Joey M. Tan Org Type: Sole Proprietorship Primary Classification: General Engineering

□ **JORVIVS CONSTRUCTION**
Cor C.M. Recto & Gov. Rubin Sts., Malaybalay Bukidnon
Contact Number/s : 088-2212401
License: 6527 Amo: Jorge C. Lagumbay Org Type: Sole Proprietorship Primary Classification: General Engineering

□ **JS & V ENTERPRISES GENERAL CONTRACTOR, INC.**
31 St. simon St., St. Charbel Exec. Vill., Phase 2, Mindanao Avenue Quezon City
Contact Number/s : 983-4047
License: 10420 Amo: Francis A. Paderna Org Type: Corporation Primary Classification: General Building

□ **JTA BUILDERS**

UNDAC Bldg., Osmena St. Cor., Cabili St. Banggolo Marawi City
Contact Number/s : 63520150
License: 18401 Amo: Jaylani T. Alonto Org Type: Sole Proprietorship Primary Classification: General Building

JTA CONSTRUCTION
2/F JTA Bldg., 254 Hayes St., Pinikitan, Camaman-an Cagayan de Oro City Misamis Oriental
Contact Number/s : 08822-726402
License: 4371 Amo: Jauhali T. Abu Org Type: Sole Proprietorship Primary Classification: General Engineering

JUAN BUILDERS
#75-B M. Salamat St., Project 4 Quezon City
Contact Number/s : 927-4742
License: 21840 Amo: Manuel L. Paguirigan, Jr. Org Type: Sole Proprietorship Primary Classification: General Engineering

JULIUS CADAVA CONSTRUCTION & SUPPLIES
Sandaan, Midsayap North Cotobato
Contact Number/s : 064-2297207
License: 11814 Amo: Julius T. Cadava Org Type: Sole Proprietorship Primary Classification: General Building

KALANTAS CONSTRUCTION & DEVELOPMENT CORPORATION
175 Montilla Blvd., Butuan City Agusan del Norte
Contact Number/s : 085-3423436
License: 23915 Amo: Luis C. Reyes Org Type: Corporation Primary Classification: General Engineering

KALAYAAN ENGINEERING COMPANY, INCORPORATED
4253 Emilia St., Palanan, Makati City Makati
Contact Number/s : 844-0158
License: 247 Amo: Victorino V. Lahoz Org Type: Corporation Primary Classification: Air-conditioning and Refrigeration Work

KC WATER SYSTEM CONSTRUCTION CORPORATION
#29 Banawe St., Quezon City CPO Quezon City
Contact Number/s : 721-0747
License: 6768 Amo: Kwok Cheung Org Type: Corporation Primary Classification: General Engineering

KCJ CONSTRUCTION DEVELOPMENT CORPORATION
#75 Kalayaan Ave., Diliman Quezon City
Contact Number/s : 928-0261
License: 14976 Amo: Angel A. Alarilla Org Type: Corporation Primary Classification: General Building

KIDAPAWAN WJM BUILDERS & CONSTRUCTION SUPPLIES
Corner Aglipay Zamora St., Kabacan Cotabato City
Contact Number/s : 248-2068
License: 23665 Amo: William L. Matalam Org Type: Sole Proprietorship Primary Classification: General Engineering

KONSTANZA CONSTRUCTION ENTERPRISE INCORPORATED
No. 16-20 JL Bldg., Dona Soledad Ave., Ext. Chatteeaville, Better Living Subd. Para?aque
License: 30281 Amo: Lourdes Jaba Loser Org Type: Corporation Primary Classification: General Engineering

KONTECH SYSTEMS, INC.
Romm 404 Topaz Bldg., No. 99-101 Kamias Road Quezon City CPO Quezon City
Contact Number/s : 928-3686/920-1988
License: 27467 Amo: Ermie R. Lanas Org Type: Corporation Primary Classification: General Building

KP ECO CONSTRUCTION & DEVELOPMENT CORPORATION
Suite 412 Delta Bldg., Quezon Ave., Quezon City CPO Quezon City
Contact Number/s : 3733221

License: 9619 Amo: Efren O. Capa Org Type: Corporation Primary Classification: General Engineering

□ **KRAMNEJ CONSTRUCTION**
103-F.E. Rodriguez Avenue, Quezon City
Contact Number/s : 742-1886/84
License: 10307 Amo: Miguel A. Yap, Jr. Org Type: Sole Proprietorship Primary Classification: General Building

□ **KRIZKA CONSTRUCTION AND DEVELOPMENT CORPORATION (Formerly: New Krizka Construction and Supply)**
Aningway, Subic Zambales
Contact Number/s : 047-2322372
License: 13400 Amo: Jocelyn K. Fernandez Org Type: Corporation Primary Classification: General Building

□ **KUATAKO CONSTRUCTION BUILDING AND GENERAL CONTRACTOR**
99 F. Mayo Ext., Ambiong Rd., Baguio City Benguet
Contact Number/s : 074-4434903
License: 11224 Amo: Harry L. Ciriaco Org Type: Sole Proprietorship Primary Classification: General Building

□ **L. BALTONADO CONSTRUCTION & DEVELOPMENT CORPORATION**
San Isidro Ormoc City Leyte
Contact Number/s : 225-4171
License: 25250 Amo: Lorenzo C. Baltonado Org Type: Corporation Primary Classification: General Engineering

□ **L. C. TING CONSTRUCTION**
Baan, Buhangin Butuan city Agusan del Norte
License: 23666 Amo: Laurence C. Ting Org Type: Sole Proprietorship Primary Classification: General Engineering

□ **L. EUSEBIO ACE DEVELOPMENT CORPORATION**
Armal Bldg., Pasig Blvd., Ext. Maybunga Pasig CPO Pasig City
Contact Number/s : 641-1500

License: 13522 Amo: Clemente T. Manlapit Org Type: Corporation Primary Classification: General Engineering

□ **L.A. DIONISIO TRADING & CONSTRUCTION**
2384 F.B. Harrison St., Pasay City Pasay
Contact Number/s : 8340141
License: 11056 Amo: Luz A. Dionisio Org Type: Sole Proprietorship Primary Classification: General Building

□ **L.A. TAN CONSTRUCTION AND SUPPLY**
277 Gabriel Village, Libertad Butuan City Agusan del Norte
Contact Number/s : 085-2254504
License: 8832 Amo: Luis A. Tan Org Type: Sole Proprietorship Primary Classification: General Engineering

□ **L.M. POWER ENGINEERING CORPORATION**
106 E. Rodriguez Jr. Ave., Libis Quezon City
Contact Number/s : 633-1441/44
License: 1787 Amo: Luis L. Mendoza Org Type: Corporation Primary Classification: Electrical Work

□ **L.N.R. CONSTRUCTION**
D-3 Mansahing Bldg., Arboleda St., Ilawod I, Daraga (Locsin) Albay
Contact Number/s : 052-8241447
License: 14148 Amo: Lester N. Rey Org Type: Sole Proprietorship Primary Classification: General Engineering

□ **LANAO BUILDER AND ENTERPRISES**
0325 Raymund Jeffrey Rd. Ext. Mahayahay, Iligan City Lanao del Norte
Contact Number/s : 2212731
License: 15982 Amo: Rosemia Bacarat Noor Org Type: Sole Proprietorship Primary Classification: General Engineering

□ **LANDMARK BUILDERS**
Sobrecarey Cor. Alzate St., Bo. Obrero Davao City Davao del Sur
Contact Number/s : 222-4506

License: 7400 Amo: Henry L. Bernales Org Type: Sole Proprietorship Primary Classification: General Engineering

LBS CONSTRUCTION AND DEVELOPMENT CORPORATION
194 Wayan St., Masambong, SFDM Quezon City
Contact Number/s : 4141198
License: 24464 Amo: Virgilio C. Yu Org Type: Corporation Primary Classification: General Engineering

LEDA CONSTRUCTION INCORPORATED
L17, B3, Phase 5, V & G Subd., Tacloban City Leyte
Contact Number/s : 053-3271302
License: 12229 Amo: Anacleto M. Berenguer Org Type: Corporation Primary Classification: General Engineering

LEGAZPI PREMIUM DEVELOPMENT CORPORATION
2nd Flr. Legaspi Premium Mktg. Bldg., Rizal St., Cabangan Legaspi City Albay
Contact Number/s : 243459
License: 20701 Amo: Danilo Y. Nieva Org Type: Corporation Primary Classification: General Engineering

LEO-RAM BUILDERS
118-B Sct. Rallos St., Brgy. Sacred Heart, Quezon City CPO Quezon City
Contact Number/s : 9284007
License: 21522 Amo: Josefino D. Ramos Org Type: Sole Proprietorship Primary Classification: General Engineering

LEPANTO BUILDERS, INC.
904 San Diego St., Sampaloc East Manila
Contact Number/s : 7322754
License: 2197 Amo: Helena C. Tobia Org Type: Corporation Primary Classification: General Engineering

LO-TONE CONSTRUCTION & SUPPLY
D-17 & 18 J&M Bldg. Rizal Street Legaspi City Albay

License: 23385 Amo: Christopher S. Co Org Type: Sole Proprietorship Primary Classification: General Engineering

LOTRIM CONSTRUCTION, INCORPORATED
31 Quimpo Blvd., Ecoland Subd., Matina, Davao City Davao del Sur
Contact Number/s : 297-1926
License: 12273 Amo: Odilon Marlon L. Gaviola Org Type: Corporation Primary Classification: General Building

LOXON PHILIPPINES, INC.
3/F Dolmar Bldg.,#56 EDSA Mandaluyong CPO Mandaluyong
Contact Number/s : 7230521/26
License: 7553 Amo: Edilberto C. Esmerio Org Type: Corporation Primary Classification: Mechanical Work

LUCAS WELL-DRILLING AND WATER SUPPPLY CO., INC.
62 Int. Comercio St., Tugatog Malabon
Contact Number/s : 288-7908
License: 8310 Amo: Ernesto T. Lucas Org Type: Corporation Primary Classification: Well Drilling Work

LUCK-WELL CONSTRUCTION
398 General Capinpin St., San Jose, Balanga Bataan
Contact Number/s : (047) 237-1585
License: 17510 Amo: Ronald V. Del Rosario Org Type: Sole Proprietorship Primary Classification: General Engineering

LUDOLFO P. MUNOZ, JR. CONSTRUCTION
Fernando Avenue, Dona Maria Subd., Daraga (Locsin) Albay
Contact Number/s : 4832131
License: 13547 Amo: Ludolfo P. Munoz, Jr. Org Type: Sole Proprietorship Primary Classification: General Engineering

LUYM CONSTRUCTION AND DEVELOPMENT CORPORATION

Km. 3 Songculan Dauis Bohol
Contact Number/s : 038-4114833
License: 24098 Amo: Nelson N. Yu Org Type: Corporation Primary Classification: General Engineering

LVRO CONSTRUCTION AND SUPPLY
Barangay Rizal, Surigao City Surigao del Norte
Contact Number/s : 232-7040
License: 18116 Amo: Von Ronald M. Ocenar Org Type: Sole Proprietorship Primary Classification: General Engineering

M. BERNARDO CONSTRUCTION
#34 Harvard St., Cubao Quezon City
Contact Number/s : 9110632
License: 6363 Amo: Manuel A.S. Bernardo Org Type: Sole Proprietorship Primary Classification: General Building

M.P. VILLEGAS CONSTRUCTION
No. 11 Omicron St., San Bartolome, Novaliches Proper Quezon City
Contact Number/s : 937-3494
License: 16683 Amo: Modesto P. Villegas Org Type: Sole Proprietorship Primary Classification: General Engineering

M.S.C. CONSTRUCTION
San Roque, San Rafael Bulacan Province
Contact Number/s : 0912-3877979/0912-3048902
License: 3340 Amo: Manuel S. Cruz, Jr. Org Type: Sole Proprietorship Primary Classification: General Engineering

MAER SUMMIT KONSTRUKT CO.
210 Quibod Bldg., JP Laurel Ave., cor. Davao City Davao del Sur
Contact Number/s : 222-8768
License: 25262 Amo: Dino Mae D. Suelto Org Type: Partnership Primary Classification: General Engineering

MAGSAYSAY DIZON BERNARDO CONSTRUCTION CORP.
18 Don A Roces Ave., Diliman Quezon City
License: 29749 Amo: Osmundo Christopher Reyes Dizon Org Type: Corporation Primary Classification: General Building

MANILA KYOWA, INC.
4153 Sampaguita St., Sun Valley Subd., Para?aque CPO Para?aque
Contact Number/s : 8214040/43
License: 25911 Amo: Crisanto R. Ramos Org Type: Corporation Primary Classification: General Building

MANN BUILDERS & DEVELOPERS, INC.
Valbuena, Pinili Ilocos Norte
Contact Number/s : 655-0271
License: 22260 Amo: Antonio C. Sabater Org Type: Corporation Primary Classification: General Building

MARCONS BUILDER
#90 Naguilian Road, Baguio City Benguet
Contact Number/s : 443-4946
License: 8044 Amo: Marciano L. Garcia Org Type: Sole Proprietorship Primary Classification: General Engineering

MARCUS CONSTRUCTION
198 Panares Subd., Poblacion 7, Midsayap North Cotobato
Contact Number/s : (064)-2297401
License: 12601 Amo: Marlyn Custodio Damay Org Type: Sole Proprietorship Primary Classification: General Engineering

MARS INDUSTRIAL SERVICES, INC.
407 Katwiran St., Bacood, Sta. Mesa Manila
Contact Number/s : 812-8091/93
License: 25083 Amo: Noriel C. Fule Org Type: Corporation Primary Classification: Electrical Work

MDL RESORT CONSTRUCTORS, INC.
#178 A. Aquirre Ave., BF Homes, Para?aque CPO Para?aque
Contact Number/s : 809-0501/03
License: 5726 Amo: Mario D. De Leon Org Type: Corporation Primary Classification: General Engineering

 MECA BUILDERS AND TRADERS
#26 Pagatpat St., Project 7 Quezon City
Contact Number/s : 365-1059
License: 10952 Amo: Mary Ann C. Mendoza Org Type: Sole Proprietorship Primary Classification: General Engineering

 MECHATRENDS CONTRACTOR'S CORPORATION
Manggahan St., Binakayan, Kawit Cavite
License: 25912 Amo: Abelardo C. Papa Org Type: Corporation Primary Classification: General Engineering

 MELCOM CORPORATION
189 Unit J, Katipunan Ave., Project 4 Quezon City
Contact Number/s : 438-6785/86
License: 26716 Amo: Armando D. De Guzman Org Type: Corporation Primary Classification: General Engineering

 MELTECH CONSTRUCTION
16 Basilan Rd., Philam Homes West Avenue Quezon City CPO Quezon City
Contact Number/s : 9251575
License: 14551 Amo: Carmela G. Balagtas Org Type: Sole Proprietorship Primary Classification: General Building

 MICHAEL MARTIN CONSTRUCTION & TRADING CORPORATION
2317 Tejeron St., Sta. Ana Sta. Ana Manila
Contact Number/s : 2521366
License: 27081 Amo: Bernardo L. Merchan Org Type: Corporation Primary Classification: General Engineering

 MIG-WELLS CONSTRUCTION CORPORATION
2/F, 29-13th Avenue, Murphy, Cubao Quezon City
Contact Number/s : 911-7683
License: 11365 Amo: Miguel V. Piso Org Type: Corporation Primary Classification: General Engineering

 MILESTONE INFRA BUILDERS
Brgy., Buhang, Jaro Iloilo City Iloilo
Contact Number/s : 329-5346
License: 4193 Amo: Gertrudes M. Lim Org Type: Sole Proprietorship Primary Classification: General Engineering

 MJMI CONSTRUCTION & TRADING
Metro Bank Bldg. Gen. Aguinaldo Highway, Anabu II Imus Cavite
Contact Number/s : 046-4721411
License: 25252 Amo: Editha S. Maliksi Org Type: Sole Proprietorship Primary Classification: General Engineering

 MOLTE ARIES CONSTRUCTION & INDUSTRIES
Lingsat, San Fernando La Union
Contact Number/s : 700-3346
License: 3684 Amo: Rodolfo M. Abat Org Type: Sole Proprietorship Primary Classification: General Engineering

 MONARK CONSTRUCTORS CORPORATION
Level 10 Galleria Corporate Center, EDSA Ortigas Avenue Quezon City
Contact Number/s : 633-1541/50
License: 8696 Amo: Luis Manuel T. Banson Org Type: Corporation Primary Classification: General Engineering

 MONTA?O CONSTRUCTION & DEVELOPMENT CORPORATION
Turno, Dipolog City Zamboanga del Norte
Contact Number/s : 065-2127272
License: 19473 Amo: Francisco A. Monta?o Org Type: Corporation Primary Classification: General Engineering

 MORANTE BUILDERS & SUPPLY
Brgy. 24, Rizal St., Legaspi City Albay
Contact Number/s : 243370
License: 23396 Amo: Alan M. Morante Org Type: Sole Proprietorship Primary Classification: General Engineering

□ **MUA?A CONSTRUCTION**
Cor. Tupaz-Flores Sts., Cebu City Cebu
Contact Number/s : 261-4184
License: 9354 Amo: Ricardo G. Mua?a Org Type: Sole Proprietorship Primary Classification: General Building

□ **MULTI-GLOBAL CONSTRUCTION CORPORATION**
6/F Tower Renaissance Crt. Meralco Ave. Pasig CPO Pasig City
Contact Number/s : 6375237
License: 26885 Amo: Randolph L. Ang Org Type: Corporation Primary Classification: General Engineering

□ **N.B. SALBO CONSTRUCTION**
05 Perez Street Marawi City Lanao del Sur
Contact Number/s : 9184911739
License: 6091 Amo: Nasser B. Salbo Org Type: Sole Proprietorship Primary Classification: General Engineering

□ **N.B.S. CONSTRUCTION & SAND & GRAVEL SUPPLIER**
Door 6, Chuanseng Apt., Carangan Ozamis City Zamboanga del Sur
Contact Number/s : 521-3054
License: 16549 Amo: Nicanor B. Salomon Org Type: Sole Proprietorship Primary Classification: General Engineering

□ **N.C. TAVU & ASSO. CORP.**
656 Cupang, Muntinglupa City Muntinlupa
Contact Number/s : 8502679/7223917
License: 25659 Amo: Neil C. Tavu Org Type: Corporation Primary Classification: General Building

□ **N.P. UY BUILDERS**
2845 A. Beata Street, Pandacan Manila
Contact Number/s : 564-2515
License: 16551 Amo: Nilo P. Uy Org Type: Sole Proprietorship Primary Classification: General Engineering

□ **NAGA E.S. CONSTRUCTION AND SUPPLY**
#22 Concepcion Grande, Naga City Camarines Sur
Contact Number/s : 472-3599
License: 6593 Amo: Ernesto C. Cayetano, Jr. Org Type: Sole Proprietorship Primary Classification: General Engineering

□ **NESGIN BUILDERS & SUPPLIES**
No. 404 MacArthur Hi-way, del Pilar, San Fernando Pampanga
Contact Number/s : 045-9615627
License: 26167 Amo: Ernesto M. Cunanan Org Type: Sole Proprietorship Primary Classification: General Engineering

□ **NEW ARCOND BUILDERS INCORPORATED**
107 Mabilis Street, Brgy. Pinyahan, Diliman Quezon City
Contact Number/s : 9225736
License: 9614 Amo: Arturo C. Dimaguila Org Type: Corporation Primary Classification: General Engineering

□ **NEW TBP CONSTRUCTION & DEVELOPMENT CORPORATION**
Noble St., Dagupan City Pangasinan
Contact Number/s : 522-0907
License: 29155 Amo: Jose S. Tan Org Type: Corporation Primary Classification: General Engineering

□ **NEWCO BUILDERS AND DEVELOPMENT CORPORATION**
926 A. Bonifacio Avenue, Balintawak Quezon City
Contact Number/s : 367-5106
License: 8995 Amo: Warlito S. Kho Org Type: Corporation Primary Classification: General Building

□ **NGP CONSTRUCTION**
No.01 Dona Rosa Adou St., Toril Davao City Davao del Sur
Contact Number/s : 291-2320
License: 11369 Amo: Noel G. Punu Org Type: Sole Proprietorship Primary Classification: General Building

NGY CONSTRUCTION
220 B Ilocos St., Brgy. Sto. Cristo, Bago Bantay Quezon City
Contact Number/s : 453-2570
License: 25401 Amo: Nestor G. Yanquiling Org Type: Sole Proprietorship Primary Classification: General Building

NINE-CHAR CONSTRUCTION AND DEVELOPMENT CORPORATION
11 President Ave., B.F. Homes, Para?aque CPO Para?aque
License: 6437 Amo: Dave G. Fabon Org Type: Corporation Primary Classification: General Engineering

NIRVANA CONSTRUCTION AND SUPPLIES
59 A. Morrow St., Zone I Koronadal South Cotobato
Contact Number/s : 2282264
License: 18691 Amo: Moises Rhonell Tan Hollite II Org Type: Sole Proprietorship Primary Classification: General Engineering

NORTHERN COTABATO CONSTRUCTION AND SUPPLY
Poblacion Carmen, Cotobato City Maguidanao
Contact Number/s : 0917-3643944
License: 15515 Amo: Noemi J. Talino Org Type: Sole Proprietorship Primary Classification: General Building

NORTHLINE SUBIC DEVELOPERS
S-307 Whitehouse Bldg., 420 Araneta Ave. Quezon City CPO Quezon City
Contact Number/s : 723-1555
License: 21530 Amo: Jeannette D. Khonghun Org Type: Sole Proprietorship Primary Classification: General Engineering

NOVA STRUCTURA DEVELOPMENT AND MANAGEMENT CORPORATION
14F One Magnificient Mile Bldg., San Miguel Ave., Ortiga Ctr., Ortigas PO Pasig City
Contact Number/s : none
License: 24717 Amo: Ricardo P. Cuerva Org Type: Corporation Primary Classification: General Building

O.G. SANTOS CONSTRUCTION
#3 Pioneer Village, Buhangin, Davao City Davao del Sur
Contact Number/s : 082-2412179
License: 2050 Amo: Oliver G. Santos Org Type: Sole Proprietorship Primary Classification: General Building

O.M. AGUILAR CONSTRUCTION
88-1C Don Manuel, Sta. Mesa Heights Quezon City CPO Quezon City
Contact Number/s : 415-8711/7323724
License: 23620 Amo: Oliver M. Aguilar Org Type: Sole Proprietorship Primary Classification: Electrical Work

ONAN CONSTRUCTION
Drs.19 & 20 SMRAA Sports Complex, Alunan Ave. Koronadal South Cotobato
Contact Number/s : 083-2282335/3061
License: 29462 Amo: Mariano R. Ong Ante, Jr. Org Type: Sole Proprietorship Primary Classification: General Engineering

OQC CONSTRUCTION
Malvar, Santiago Isabela
Contact Number/s : 078-6828618
License: 22690 Amo: Oscar Q. Chua Org Type: Sole Proprietorship Primary Classification: General Engineering

ORIENTECH CONSTRUCTION & DEVELOPMENT CORPORATION
Regalado Ave., Ipil St., North Fairview, Fairview North Quezon City
Contact Number/s : 937-6730/45
License: 8874 Amo: Antonio V. Madrid Org Type: Corporation Primary Classification: General Engineering

P.R. DE DIOS CONSTRUCTION
#45 Gapan-Olongapo Rd., Masangsang Mexico Pampanga
Contact Number/s : 459660214

License: 2051 Amo: Pepito R. De Dios Org Type: Sole Proprietorship Primary Classification: General Engineering

□ **PACER CONSTRUCTION & DEVELOPMENT CORPORATION**
83 Paraiso, Brgy. San Jose Tacloban City leyte
Contact Number/s : 323-3128
License: 4839 Amo: Jose M. Asturias Org Type: Corporation Primary Classification: General Engineering

□ **PACIFIC TECHNO-RESOURCES**
#22 Pres. Roxas St., South Admiral Vill. Para?aque CPO Para?aque
Contact Number/s : 536-28-77
License: 7394 Amo: Gilberto G. Tongco Org Type: Sole Proprietorship Primary Classification: General Building

□ **PARABOLIC BUILDERS, INC.**
G-61 South Star Plaza, 932 Pres. Osmena Highway, Makati City
Contact Number/s : 8941459
License: 4841 Amo: Danilo L. Perez Org Type: Corporation Primary Classification: General Building

□ **PEARLY CONSTRUCTION**
#50 Jupiter St., Puentebella Subd., Brgy. Taculing Bacolod City Negros Occidental
Contact Number/s : 446-1838
License: 5953 Amo: Lily D. Lim Org Type: Sole Proprietorship Primary Classification: General Building

□ **PEER MANAGEMENT-CONSTRUCT, INC.**
30 Don Diosdado St., Don Enrique Heights, Brgy. Holy Spirit Quezon City CPO Quezon City
Contact Number/s : 931-4841
License: 19265 Amo: Pedrito M. Condeno Org Type: Corporation Primary Classification: General Building

□ **PGO CONSTRUCTION**
Juan Luna Street Cadiz City Negros Occidental
Contact Number/s : 493-1614
License: 15153 Amo: Wilson C. Ong Org Type: Sole Proprietorship Primary Classification: General Engineering

□ **PHILCOX (PHIL.), INC.**
8/F Philcox Bldg., Salcedo St., 172 Salcedo St.., Legaspi Vill. Makati City
Contact Number/s : 816-1191
License: 836 Amo: Antonio Tioco Org Type: Corporation Primary Classification: General Building

□ **PIRRA CONSTRUCTION ENTERPRISES**
61 Bunlo, Bocaue Bulacan Province
Contact Number/s : 044-6921648
License: 10545 Amo: Artemio R. Perez Org Type: Sole Proprietorship Primary Classification: General Engineering

□ **PLD CONSTRUCTION**
Tabok, Mandaue City Cebu
Contact Number/s : 3451452
License: 1859 Amo: Peter L. Dy Org Type: Sole Proprietorship Primary Classification: General Building

□ **PLERM CONSTRUCTION AND DEVELOPMENT CORPORATION**
Tindalo St., Sta. Clara Santa Maria Bulacan Province
Contact Number/s : 044-6410965-69/044-6412363
License: 8904 Amo: Efren M. Martinez Org Type: Corporation Primary Classification: General Engineering

□ **POLYGON VENTURES AND LAND DEVELOPMENT CORP.**
Unit A Bricklane Condo., No. 28 N.Domingo Street, New Mla. Quezon City CPO Quezon City
Contact Number/s : 725-5296/726-6954
License: 8435 Amo: Ezra Singson Castillo Org Type: Corporation Primary Classification: General Building

□ **POWER - AIDED ENTERPRISES**
Market Site, San Ramon Dinalupihan Bataan
Contact Number/s : 047-4811384
License: 26530 Amo: Arcadio A. Navale, Jr. Org Type: Sole Proprietorship Primary Classification: Electrical Work

□ **PRESTIGE CONSTRUCTION**
2nd Flr. Recar Bldg., Balanga Bataan
Contact Number/s : 237-1552
License: 8526 Amo: Manuel N. Beltran Org Type: Sole Proprietorship Primary Classification: General Engineering

□ **PROJECT MANAGEMENT & TECHNICAL RESOURCES CORPORATION**
56 Madison St., Mandaluyong CPO Mandaluyong
Contact Number/s : 637-9246-47
License: 29669 Amo: Alexander O. Tan Org Type: Corporation Primary Classification: General Building

□ **R. CALINGASAN CONSTRUCTION**
San Isidro, Batangas City Batangas
Contact Number/s : 980-7967
License: 8173 Amo: Romeo R. Calingasan Org Type: Sole Proprietorship Primary Classification: General Engineering

□ **R. N. H. BENTULAN CONSTRUCTION**
Purok-12 Poblacion Prosperidad Agusan del Sur
Contact Number/s : 241-3098
License: 19484 Amo: Reynaldo V. Bentulan Org Type: Sole Proprietorship Primary Classification: General Engineering

□ **R. S. JARDIN CONSTRUCTION**
No. 17 Production St., GSIS Village Project 8 Quezon City
Contact Number/s : 4554563-64
License: 29190 Amo: Redentor S. Jardin Org Type: Sole Proprietorship Primary Classification: General Engineering

□ **R.A.M. BUILDERS**
Exec. Vill. Subd., Brgy. Kanluran, Mayao Lucena City Quezon Province
Contact Number/s : 7104631
License: 10549 Amo: Miguelin M. Arquiza Org Type: Sole Proprietorship Primary Classification: General Engineering

□ **R.B. OMBAO CONSTRUCTION**
2nd Flr. Post Office Bldg., BEZ Mariveles Bataan
Contact Number/s : 5623702
License: 17042 Amo: Raul B. Ombao Org Type: Sole Proprietorship Primary Classification: General Building

□ **R.B. URIARTE CONSTRUCTION**
RM. 10 J.S. BLDG., Lacson-Galo st., Bacolod City Negros Occidental
Contact Number/s : 707-3226
License: 7518 Amo: Rogelio B. Uriarte Org Type: Sole Proprietorship Primary Classification: General Engineering

□ **R.D. SADSAD CONSTRUCTION AND TRADING**
Jupiter Street, Sto. Nino San Fernando Pampanga
Contact Number/s : 961-3001
License: 19240 Amo: Roman D. Sadsad Org Type: Sole Proprietorship Primary Classification: General Engineering

□ **R.G. YNIGUEZ CONSTRUCTION**
Yniguez Bldg., R. Castillo St., Agdao, Davao City Davao del Sur
Contact Number/s : 235-2026
License: 8616 Amo: Raul G. Yniguez Org Type: Sole Proprietorship Primary Classification: General Engineering

□ **R.J. FLORES CONSTRUCTION**
Natividad Naguillan La Union
Contact Number/s : 072-6091048
License: 4905 Amo: Romulo J. Flores Org Type: Sole Proprietorship Primary Classification: General Engineering

□ **R.L. QUIAMBAO CONSTRUCTION**

Brgy. San Pedro Tumauini Isabela
Contact Number/s : 078-6324104/722-7274
License: 26168 Amo: Raymundo L. Quiambao
Org Type: Sole Proprietorship Primary
Classification: General Engineering

□ **R.M. VITUG CONSTRUCTION**
San Pablo 2nd, Lubao Pampanga
Contact Number/s : none
License: 9227 Amo: Rommel M. Vitug Org Type: Sole Proprietorship Primary Classification: General Building

□ **R.O. BUILDERS & DEV. CORP.**
Centro, Bayombong Nueva Vizcaya
Contact Number/s : 3213846
License: 22393 Amo: Renato O. Ongtao Org Type: Corporation Primary Classification: General Engineering

□ **R.R. SEISMUNDO CONSTRUCTION & SUPPLY**
National Highway, Visayan Village, Tagum City Davao del Norte
Contact Number/s : 2173607
License: 10961 Amo: Ruplino R. Seismundo
Org Type: Sole Proprietorship Primary
Classification: General Building

□ **R.S. GATBONTON CONSTRUCTION**
No. 32 Carnation St., St. Dominic 5, Quezon City Manila
Contact Number/s : 920-4014
License: 8950 Amo: Rene S. Gatbonton Org Type: Sole Proprietorship Primary Classification: General Engineering

□ **R.V. GARCIA GENERAL CONTRACTOR**
38 M. Ponce Bagong Barrio Caloocan City
License: 22950 Amo: Romeo V. Garcia Org Type: Sole Proprietorship Primary Classification: General Building

□ **R.V. LABORTE BUILDERS**
34 Habito St., Brgy., Iyam Lucena City Quezon Province
Contact Number/s : 042-7104781/373-1002
License: 20459 Amo: Reynaldo V. Laborte, Jr.
Org Type: Sole Proprietorship Primary
Classification: General Engineering

□ **R.V. RABAJA CONSTRUCTION, INC.**
375 J. Rizal St., 25 Merryland Village Mandaluyong CPO Mandaluyong
Contact Number/s : none
License: 14435 Amo: Rogelio V. Rabaja Org Type: Corporation Primary Classification: General Building

□ **RBI ENGINEERING & CONSTRUCTION**
124 Sct. Lozano, Sacred Heart Quezon City
Contact Number/s : 928-3191
License: 25310 Amo: Roberto B. Inumerable
Org Type: Sole Proprietorship Primary
Classification: General Building

□ **R'CEL GEN. CONTRACTOR & GEN. MERCHANDISE**
1736 Cardel Bldg., A. Bonifacio St., Santa Cruz Laguna
Contact Number/s : 049-8082985
License: 13385 Amo: Rolando T. Ang Org Type: Sole Proprietorship Primary Classification: General Engineering

□ **RD SQUARE CONSTRUCTION**
#10-D New York St., Cor. Manalo St., Cubao Quezon City
Contact Number/s : 723-9969
License: 7346 Amo: Ricardo C. Dizon, Jr. Org Type: Sole Proprietorship Primary Classification: General Building

□ **RED MOLE CONSTRUCTION**
Iron Wood St., Richview Square Subd., Bakakeng Road Baguio City Benguet
Contact Number/s : 919-5727999
License: 15710 Amo: Edgardo N. Sanchez
Org Type: Sole Proprietorship Primary
Classification: General Engineering

□ **REGORON PROJECT SUPPORT SERVICES**
26 Tennis Street, NSFV Cainta Rizal
Contact Number/s : 655-4210

License: 30269 Amo: Rene Andres Gonzales Ronquillo Org Type: Sole Proprietorship Primary Classification: General Building

REYDAN BUILDERS
782 A. Morrow Street, Koronadal South Cotobato
Contact Number/s : 083-2286073
License: 13059 Amo: Danilo F. Aranez Org Type: Sole Proprietorship Primary Classification: General Engineering

RG BASIT CONSTRUCTION CORPORATION
U-26PC, Eisenhower Cond., #7, Eisenhower St. Greenhills PO San Juan
Contact Number/s : 721-3617
License: 6870 Amo: Reynaldo S. Medrano Org Type: Corporation Primary Classification: General Engineering

RGS CONSTRUCTION
WTO Bldg., Gen. Luna st., Dipolog City Zamboanga del Norte
Contact Number/s : 2122751
License: 14095 Amo: Rey C. Samonte Org Type: Sole Proprietorship Primary Classification: General Engineering

RHH CONSTRUCTION
Maharlika Road, Villasis Santiago Isabela
Contact Number/s : 682-8195
License: 11467 Amo: Rosita Darisan Chua Org Type: Sole Proprietorship Primary Classification: General Engineering

RICHBELLE CONSTRUCTION CORPORATION
No. 15 Mines St., Vasra Village Project 6 Quezon City
Contact Number/s : 927-8964
License: 4641 Amo: Floresto M. Villanueva Org Type: Corporation Primary Classification: General Engineering

RICSONS CORPORATION
16 Atherton St., North Fairview Quezon City
Contact Number/s : 9368167

License: 29699 Amo: Frederico L. Bulseco, Jr. Org Type: Corporation Primary Classification: General Building

RIGHT TEAM BUILDERS CORPORATION
10F, Telecoms Plaza Bldg., Sen Gil Puyat Ave. Makati City Makati
Contact Number/s : 810-9009
License: 28376 Amo: Chito P. Africa Org Type: Corporation Primary Classification: General Building

RIM CONSTRUCTION
Poblacion, Tabuk Kalinga-Apayao
Contact Number/s : 872-2021
License: 15938 Amo: Rolando M. Mayangao Org Type: Sole Proprietorship Primary Classification: General Engineering

RITVIT CONSTRUCTION AND DEVELOPMENT CORPORATION
2/F URCI Bldg., Real St., Pamplona, Las Pi?as City
Contact Number/s : 873-9285
License: 9426 Amo: Alexander C. Roque Org Type: Corporation Primary Classification: General Building

ROADTECH CONSTRUCTION
Petron Station, McArthur Highway, San Miguel Calasiao Pangasinan
License: 17580 Amo: Kenneth C. Tan Org Type: Sole Proprietorship Primary Classification: General Engineering

RODOLFO R. SANTIAGO CONSTRUCTION
Salacot San Miguel Bulacan Province
Contact Number/s : 044-6780117/6780922/241-4563
License: 4492 Amo: Rodolfo R. Santiago Org Type: Sole Proprietorship Primary Classification: General Engineering

RR & B FINEST CONSTRUCTION & DEVELOPMENT CORPORATION
18 Daanghari St., Navotas Navotas
Contact Number/s : 283-0113

License: 14849 Amo: Joselito R. Ramos Org Type: Corporation Primary Classification: General Engineering

□ **RSP LIM CONSTRUCTION COMPANY, INC.**
Blk 7 Lot 11 Ph. 2B1 Katiyagaan Rd., Karangalan Vill., Pasig CPO Pasig City
Contact Number/s : 646-4224
License: 17664 Amo: Rogelio SP. Lim Org Type: Corporation Primary Classification: General Building

□ **S.D. MERCHANDISING & CONSTRUCTION**
Borres Subd., Tabucan, Mandurriao Iloilo City Iloilo
Contact Number/s : 3211825
License: 11186 Amo: Sanny B. Delfin Org Type: Sole Proprietorship Primary Classification: General Engineering

□ **S.R. SANTIAGO CONSTRUCTION, INC.**
30 Mercedez Ave., San Miguel, Pasig City Pasig City
Contact Number/s : 6410179
License: 5241 Amo: Serafin R. Santiago, Jr. Org Type: Corporation Primary Classification: General Engineering

□ **SABUTAN CONSTRUCTION**
340 Batangas South, Ayala Alabang Vill. Muntinlupa CPO Muntinlupa
Contact Number/s : 850-6009
License: 5520 Amo: Josephine C. Villasenor Org Type: Sole Proprietorship Primary Classification: General Engineering

□ **SAFEKONSTRUCT BUILDERS GROUP INC.**
Villanueva Comp., J. Aguilar Ave., Pamplona Las Pi?as CPO Las Pi?
Contact Number/s : 8712525
License: 28610 Amo: Antonio P. Suiza Org Type: Corporation Primary Classification: General Engineering

□ **SAGUN CONSTRUCTION, INCORPORATED**
107 Mabilis Street Diliman Quezon City
Contact Number/s : 9225736
License: 9582 Amo: Ceferino G. Sagun, Jr. Org Type: Corporation Primary Classification: General Engineering

□ **SAN JACINTO CONSTRUCTION SERVICES & GENERAL MERCHANDISING**
No. 4 Mabini Street, Brgy. Centro, Tuguegarao Cagayan
Contact Number/s : 844-5373
License: 17242 Amo: Marlo Z. Liban Org Type: Sole Proprietorship Primary Classification: General Engineering

□ **SANTOS LAND DEVELOPMENT CORPORATION**
Santos Bldg., Malvar Ext., Davao City Davao del Sur
Contact Number/s : 2210318
License: 2261 Amo: Antonio S. Domingo Org Type: Corporation Primary Classification: General Engineering

□ **SANVAR DEVELOPMENT CORPORATION**
No.08 Ugu Street, Araneta Subd., Quezon City CPO Quezon City
Contact Number/s : 714-08-35
License: 2342 Amo: Romeo O. Fajardo, Jr. Org Type: Corporation Primary Classification: General Engineering

□ **SARCA ESTATE DEVELOPMENT CORPORATION**
Km. 133 Diversion Rd., Kanlurang Mayao, Lucena City Quezon Province
Contact Number/s : 0427102216/3736210
License: 20520 Amo: Recaredo L. Sarmiento IV Org Type: Corporation Primary Classification: General Engineering

□ **SARIGUMBA CONSTRUCTION**
Booy District, Tagbilaran City Bohol
Contact Number/s : 4112041

License: 14325 Amo: Petronilo S. Sarigumba Org Type: Sole Proprietorship Primary Classification: General Engineering

SEGNOR CONSTRUCTION & DEVELOPMENT CORPORATION
Unit 302 EHS Bldg., 4429 Calatagan Street Palanan Makati
Contact Number/s : 757-0916/757-0917
License: 30237 Amo: Segundo Tayag David Org Type: Corporation Primary Classification: General Building

SHINEFORD CONSTRUCTION
Purok 2. Dao Tagbilaran City
Contact Number/s : 434-4487
License: 20746 Amo: Sinforiano J. Lavastida Org Type: Sole Proprietorship Primary Classification: General Engineering

SIG CONSTRUCTION AND INDUSTRIAL CORPORATION
Unit 208, Eagle Court Condo., 26 Matalino St., Diliman Quezon City
Contact Number/s : 922-7876
License: 14335 Amo: Enrique R. Pastor Org Type: Corporation Primary Classification: General Engineering

SOCOR CONSTRUCTION CORPORATION
Pier 4, Reclamation Area, Subangdaku, Cebu City Cebu
Contact Number/s : 232-7881
License: 8020 Amo: Sofia O. Sanchez Org Type: Corporation Primary Classification: General Engineering

SOLID BUILDERS ENGINEERING CONTRACTOR
10 Banner St., Green Valley Subd., Pasig City
Contact Number/s : 6715661/7286
License: 1255 Amo: Eduardo S. Conde Org Type: Sole Proprietorship Primary Classification: General Engineering

SPAM ENGINEERING ENTERPRISE
946 Pareja Subd., J.C. Aquino Avenue Butuan City Agusan del Norte
Contact Number/s : 341-3335
License: 14205 Amo: Pedro T. Mones, Jr. Org Type: Sole Proprietorship Primary Classification: General Building

SPECTRUM BUILDERS
45 Dona Juana, Palao Iligan City Lanao del Norte
Contact Number/s : 925-2978
License: 8124 Amo: Casan M. Maquiling Org Type: Sole Proprietorship Primary Classification: General Building

SPECTRUM CONSTRUCTION AND DEVELOPMENT CORP.
Rm. 4, 3-F Rodel Bldg., Carantes St., Baguio City Benguet
Contact Number/s : 443-77-28
License: 670 Amo: Arnulfo S. Pilando Org Type: Corporation Primary Classification: General Engineering

SSJ CONSTRUCTION
B14 L2 Kasanyangan Village, Jolo Sulu
License: 13277 Amo: Sahibul S. Jadjuli Org Type: Sole Proprietorship Primary Classification: General Engineering

ST. RAYMUND CONSTRUCTION, INC.
Mabini St., Brgy. Talaban, Himamaylan Negros Occidental
Contact Number/s : 744-6110
License: 19242 Amo: Jose P. Egalin Org Type: Corporation Primary Classification: General Engineering

STO. CRISTO CONSTRUCTION
Sto. Cristo, Hermosa Bataan
Contact Number/s : 4912564
License: 26096 Amo: Noel J. Cruz Org Type: Sole Proprietorship Primary Classification: General Building

STO. NINO CONSTRUCTION
199 Rizal Avenue, Pagadian City Zamboanga del Sur

Contact Number/s : 215-1512
License: 4867 Amo: Rosa C. Sayson-Chan
Org Type: Sole Proprietorship Primary
Classification: General Engineering

□ **STRUCTURAL ENGINEERING AND CONSTRUCTION**
Suite 825 City & Land Cond., Mega Plaza, ADB Ave., Pasig City
Contact Number/s : 635-9214
License: 14207 Amo: Samuel F. Santiago Org Type: Sole Proprietorship Primary Classification: General Engineering

□ **STRUKTURA TEKNIKA SERVICES COMPANY**
#8 Skylark St., Vista Verde Country Homes Cainta Rizal
Contact Number/s : 656-1013
License: 16646 Amo: Juanito V. Pasia Org Type: Partnership Primary Classification: General Building

□ **SUN & RAIN GENERAL CONSTRUCTION**
Z-5 Panal, Tabaco Albay
Contact Number/s : 052-8301260
License: 18431 Amo: Henry C. Goyena Org Type: Sole Proprietorship Primary Classification: General Engineering

□ **SUPREME COMMERCIAL ENTERPRISES**
7 Artacho St., Lingayen, Lingayen Pangasinan
Contact Number/s : 542-6042
License: 21468 Amo: Eladio S. Sison Org Type: Sole Proprietorship Primary Classification: General Building

□ **SYNERGY CONSTRUCTION & DEVELOPMENT CORP.**
Rm. 705 Tytana Plaza, Plaza Lorenzo Ruiz, Binondo Manila
Contact Number/s : 241-0053
License: 24562 Amo: Francis T. Sy Org Type: Corporation Primary Classification: General Building

□ **T. TAN PAREDES CONSTRUCTION**
Pamacan Narra (Panacaan) Palawan
Contact Number/s : 7262493
License: 10439 Amo: Tomas Tan Paredes
Org Type: Sole Proprietorship Primary
Classification: General Engineering

□ **TAHANAN BUILDERS, INCORPORATED**
365 A. Mabini St., Kalookan City
Contact Number/s : 2886454
License: 5931 Amo: Enrique G. Santos Org Type: Corporation Primary Classification: General Engineering

□ **TAISEI PHILIPPINE CONSTRUCTION INCORPORATED**
23/F, Equitable Bank Tower, Paseo de Roxas Salcedo Vill. Makati City
Contact Number/s : 886-0670/8860663
License: 7915 Amo: Edgardo H. Angeles Org Type: Corporation Primary Classification: General Building

□ **TANDEM POWER SYSTEMS, INC.**
210 Zodiac St., Simuangco Bldg., Palm Vill., Makati City Makati
Contact Number/s : 8900992
License: 21819 Amo: Dennis S. Jumangit Org Type: Corporation Primary Classification: Electrical Work

□ **TANTUCO CONSTRUCTION & TRADING CORPORATION (Formerly: Tantuco Lumber & Construction Supply)**
Bo. Balubal, Sariaya Quezon Province
Contact Number/s : 042-5258188/651-1188
License: 7255 Amo: Rafael N. Tantuco, Sr. Org Type: Corporation Primary Classification: General Engineering

□ **TETSON CONSTRUCTION**
65 Rosenda St., Dau Mabalacat Pampanga
Contact Number/s : 3321015
License: 29856 Amo: Jaime Maglalang Tetangco Org Type: Sole Proprietorship Primary Classification: General Engineering

□ **THE C O B DESIGN GROUP, INC.**
166 Shaw Blvd., Pasig City Pasig City Pasig
Contact Number/s : 671-6756

License: 29442 Amo: Baron H. Amuan Org Type: Corporation Primary Classification: General Building

□ **THE STEADFAST BUILDERS**
Lot 3B, B5 Villacorrina Subd., Pasong Tamo Tandang Sora Quezon City
Contact Number/s : 454-9137
License: 8176 Amo: Felix M. Galvez Org Type: Sole Proprietorship Primary Classification: General Engineering

□ **TIMBOL TRADING CORPORATION**
Timbol Hardware Bldg., Henson St., Angeles City Pampanga
Contact Number/s : 458881641
License: 9258 Amo: Nelson D. Timbol Org Type: Corporation Primary Classification: General Engineering

□ **TLI CONSTRUCTION**
232 A.B. Fernandez Avenue Dagupan City Pangasinan
Contact Number/s : 522-0158
License: 19209 Amo: Felipe L. Chua Org Type: Sole Proprietorship Primary Classification: General Building

□ **TRACSOM BUILDERS INCORPORATED**
Rm.203 M.S. Bldg.,#146 Shaw Blvd., cor. San Roque st., Pasig City Pasig
Contact Number/s : 632-1022
License: 5935 Amo: Salud B. Maliuanag Org Type: Corporation Primary Classification: General Building

□ **TRI-CAR BUILDERS, INC.**
14 Quimpo Blvd., Ecoland, Davao City Davao del Sur
License: 27945 Amo: Ernesto R. Avila Org Type: Corporation Primary Classification: General Engineering

□ **TRIUMPH BUILDERS & STEEL, INC.**
3/F Victoria Bldg., 142 Mindanao Ave., Quezon City CPO Quezon City
Contact Number/s : 9245091

License: 2272 Amo: Liwanag R. Victoria Org Type: Corporation Primary Classification: General Engineering

□ **TRI-WEB CONSTRUCTION**
61 Stanford Street Cubao Quezon City
Contact Number/s : 9113047
License: 24720 Amo: Roberto Q. Pascua Org Type: Sole Proprietorship Primary Classification: General Building

□ **TRJ CONSTRUCTION**
255 Riverside Drive, Provident Village Marikina City Marikina
Contact Number/s : 941-7279
License: 10777 Amo: Tito T. Rosario, Jr. Org Type: Sole Proprietorship Primary Classification: General Engineering

□ **TRPL CONSTRUCTION**
2 Lopez Jaena St., Lapaz, I lloilo City Iloilo
Contact Number/s : 3207926
License: 14236 Amo: Tomas J. Hautea Org Type: Sole Proprietorship Primary Classification: General Engineering

□ **TSD BUILDERS CONSTRUCTION AND SUPPLY**
L9, B9, Ramylu Vill., Tangub, Bacolod City Negros Occidental
Contact Number/s : 444-2025
License: 22129 Amo: Ma. Jesusa D. Deloso Org Type: Sole Proprietorship Primary Classification: General Building

□ **TWO ACES CONSTRUCTION AND SUPPLY**
216 Nangka Road, Butuan City Agusan del Norte
Contact Number/s : 342-36-17
License: 15413 Amo: Milagros A. Azote Org Type: Sole Proprietorship Primary Classification: General Engineering

□ **ULTRABILT CONSTRUCTION INCORPORATED**
2/F Facilities Center, Shaw Blvd. Mandaluyong CPO Mandaluyong

Contact Number/s : 724-4361
License: 20117 Amo: Johnny K. Ting Org Type: Corporation Primary Classification: General Building

□ **ULTRALITE ELECTRICAL COMPANY, INC.**
567 G. Araneta Blvd., Quezon City CPO Quezon City
Contact Number/s : 712-0153
License: 394 Amo: Charles L. Yang Org Type: Corporation Primary Classification: Electrical Work

□ **UNI-FIL TECHNICAL SERVICES CORPORATION**
RM. 408B SMS Bldg., 213 G. Puyat Ave., Makati CPO (inc. Buendia up to Edsa) Makati
Contact Number/s : 8446383
License: 10379 Amo: Mauro M. Cocjin Org Type: Corporation Primary Classification: General Building

□ **UNITED ENGINEERS CORPORATION**
63 Congressional Avenue Project 8 Quezon City
Contact Number/s : 926-3379
License: 321 Amo: Jose N. Mercado Org Type: Corporation Primary Classification: Mechanical Work

□ **UY CONSTRUCTION AND DEVELOPMENT**
89 Airport Road, Piapil Dumaguete City Negros Oriental
Contact Number/s : 2250341
License: 12336 Amo: Sylvia V. Uy Org Type: Sole Proprietorship Primary Classification: General Engineering

□ **V.C.P. CONCRETE PRODUCTS**
1026 Jacinto Extension, Davao City Davao del Sur
Contact Number/s : 082-2272911
License: 7713 Amo: Valentino C. Piatos Org Type: Sole Proprietorship Primary Classification: General Engineering

□ **V.R. PATRON BUILDERS & DEVELOPERS**
Bo. Bihis, Tawilisan, Taal Batangas
Contact Number/s : 043-4080191
License: 13487 Amo: Valentino R. Patron Org Type: Sole Proprietorship Primary Classification: General Building

□ **VICTORIANO C. LIM CONSTRUCTION**
Don Anselmo Bernad Avenue Ozamis City Misamis Occidental
Contact Number/s : 521-0103
License: 25318 Amo: Victoriano C. Lim Org Type: Sole Proprietorship Primary Classification: General Engineering

□ **VIGUZ CONSTRUCTION CORPORATION**
Banezville I, Apitong, Tacloban City Leyte
Contact Number/s : 053321-5813
License: 8178 Amo: Julio V. De Guzman Org Type: Corporation Primary Classification: General Engineering

□ **VINNELL-BELVOIR CORPORATION**
6/F DPC Place Bldg., Don Chino Roces Ave. Extension, Makati CPO (inc. Buendia up to Edsa) Makati
Contact Number/s : 889-8654/56
License: 149 Amo: Narciso G. Ballesca Org Type: Corporation Primary Classification: General Engineering

□ **VIRTUOSO CONSTRUCTION & DEVELOPMENT**
17-18 Grand View Subd., Mabiga, Mabalacat Pampanga
Contact Number/s : 3315976
License: 27469 Amo: Jose T. Yulo Org Type: Sole Proprietorship Primary Classification: General Engineering

□ **VRF CONSTRUCTION**
Narra Mampulog, Bitas Cabanatuan City Nueva Ecija
Contact Number/s : 364-3526
License: 15301 Amo: Vic Roel C. Ferrer Org Type: Sole Proprietorship Primary Classification: General Engineering

□ **VSL SPECIALISTS, INC.**
G/F Realty Investment Bldg., 195 EDSA, East Edsa Mandaluyong
Contact Number/s : 725-9978
License: 23268 Amo: Benjamin R. Wamelda Org Type: Corporation Primary Classification: Concrete Pre-casting and Pre-stressing Work

□ **W. M. MENDOZA CONSTRUCTION COMPANY**
Rm.309 3/F Osmena Bldg., Osmena Blvd., cor. Jakosalem St. Cebu City Cebu
Contact Number/s : 254-2274
License: 26295 Amo: Wenceslao M. Mendoza Org Type: Partnership Primary Classification: General Building

□ **W.A. OUTPUT CONSTRUCTION, INC.**
912 J. Delgado Ave. Barugo Leyte
Contact Number/s : 331-4003
License: 7622 Amo: Eli P. Avestruz Org Type: Corporation Primary Classification: General Engineering

□ **W.C.T. ENTERPRISES & CONSTRUCTION DEVELOPMENT**
#868 Tayuman Street Tondo North Manila
Contact Number/s : 254-36-96
License: 8319 Amo: Julie T. Tecson Org Type: Sole Proprietorship Primary Classification: General Engineering

□ **W.D. NAVARRO CONSTRUCTION CO.**
#13 Ruby St., Fairview Quezon City
Contact Number/s : 937-1875
License: 14327 Amo: Wilfredo D. Navarro Org Type: Partnership Primary Classification: General Building

□ **WEE BUILDERS**
Baliwasan Grande Zamboanga City Zamboanga del Sur
Contact Number/s : 9910309
License: 16375 Amo: Wee Han Biog Org Type: Sole Proprietorship Primary Classification: General Building

□ **WILCOR CONSTRUCTION**
260 Cutcot Pulilan Bulacan Province
Contact Number/s : 442156384
License: 2866 Amo: Guillermo L. Leonardo Org Type: Sole Proprietorship Primary Classification: General Engineering

□ **WILCU CONSTRUCTION**
Cerville Subd., Sto. Nino, Guagua Pampanga
Contact Number/s : 045-9715377
License: 23650 Amo: Wilfrido C. Cubacub, Jr. Org Type: Sole Proprietorship Primary Classification: General Building

□ **WILKINSON CONSTRUCTION**
Door 4, Asian Dragon Bldg., Lacson St. Bacolod City Negros Occidental
Contact Number/s : 433-1268
License: 21422 Amo: Wilkinson Y. Ong Org Type: Sole Proprietorship Primary Classification: General Engineering

□ **WMLC TRADING & CONSTRUCTION SUPPLY**
San. Agustin, Santo Tomas Batangas
License: 24535 Amo: Wilfredo E. Carpio Org Type: Sole Proprietorship Primary Classification: General Building

□ **YAP MABUHAY ENTERPRISES, INCORPORATED**
Cor. Cagampang & Mansanitas Streets Gen. Santos City South Cotobato
Contact Number/s : 552-5205
License: 15540 Amo: Allan Du Yaphochun Org Type: Corporation Primary Classification: General Engineering

□ **YSL BUILDER**
General Luna St., Dipolog City Zamboanga del Norte
Contact Number/s : 065-2122259
License: 19516 Amo: Joseph Y. Lim Org Type: Sole Proprietorship Primary Classification: General Building

□ **Z.A.S. CONSTRUCTION**

Brgy. 95-A Caibaan, Maharlika Highway, Tacloban City Leyte
Contact Number/s : 327-1713
License: 8971 Amo: Zaldy S. Adriano Org
Type: Sole Proprietorship Primary Classification: General Building

Z.B. DEVORA CONSTRUCTION
127 El Salvador, Brgy. 109-A Tacloban City Leyte
Contact Number/s : 327-1765
License: 26441 Amo: Zaldy B. Devora Org
Type: Sole Proprietorship Primary Classification: General Engineering

A N D CONSTRUCTION
1221 Safiro St., Blk. I, San Nicolas, Tarlac City
Contact Number/s : 982-9327
License: 3399 Amo: Alfredo N. Dizon Org
Type: Sole Proprietorship Primary Classification: General Building

A T Y INTERNATIONAL CO., INC.
1521 V. Fugoso St., Sta. Cruz North Manila
Contact Number/s : 711-42-71
License: 29927 Amo: Alberto Tao Yu Org
Type: Corporation Primary Classification: General Building

A V T CONSTRUCTION
#3 Romeo St., San Sebastian Vill. Tarlac Tarlac
Contact Number/s : 9824588
License: 1578 Amo: Avelino V. Tanjuakio Org
Type: Sole Proprietorship Primary Classification: General Engineering

A.B. AGUINALDO CONST. CO., INC.
Binakayan Kawit Cavite
Contact Number/s : 817-4590
License: 588 Amo: Achilles B. Aguinaldo Org
Type: Corporation Primary Classification: General Engineering

A.C. ELECTRICAL CORPORATION
Unit 3-D Rubille Bldg., 748 EDSA, West Kamias Quezon City
Contact Number/s : 921-3522
License: 18587 Amo: Amador L. Cruz Org
Type: Corporation Primary Classification: General Building

A.D. GOSECO CORPORATION
5 Campanilla St., New Manila Quezon City
Contact Number/s : 722-8962
License: 26704 Amo: Alfonso D. Goseco Org
Type: Corporation Primary Classification: General Engineering

A.G. HERRERA CONSTRUCTION CORP.
Sapang Palay Proper, San Jose Del Monte Bulacan Province
Contact Number/s : none
License: 26307 Amo: Apolonio G. Herrera Org
Type: Corporation Primary Classification: General Building

A.M. MODULAR BUILDERS & DEVELOPERS CORPORATION
#26 Dona Luz St., Ireneville Subd., Sucat Para?aque CPO Para?aque
Contact Number/s : 820-3106/9615
License: 17152 Amo: Mauro L. Del Rosario, Sr. Org Type: Corporation Primary Classification: General Building

A.P. CANLAS CONSTRUCTION
#18 San Miguel St.Bo., Kapitolyo Pasig City
Contact Number/s : 631-4981/6327666
License: 1575 Amo: Ananias P. Canlas Org
Type: Sole Proprietorship Primary Classification: General Engineering

A.S. TOPACIO CONSTRUCTION CORPORATION
189 Bayan Luma I, Imus Cavite
Contact Number/s : 046-4710387
License: 2828 Amo: Augusto S. Topacio Org
Type: Corporation Primary Classification: General Engineering

A.V.I. CONSTRUCTION
16 Santan St., Almar Subd., Camarin Kalookan City
Contact Number/s : 9610002

License: 19025 Amo: Amor V. Inay Org Type: Sole Proprietorship Primary Classification: General Building

□ **ABM CONSTRUCTION**
2/F Pundaoda Bldg., 0177 National Hi-way Cianuri Subd, Camague, Iligan Iligan City
Contact Number/s : 2216872
License: 20332 Amo: Alexander B. Menor Org Type: Sole Proprietorship Primary Classification: General Engineering

□ **ACME BUILDERS CORPORATION**
176-184 P. Gomez Street Tacloban City Leyte
Contact Number/s : 325-5046
License: 6442 Amo: Virgilio Junie C. Andrade Org Type: Corporation Primary Classification: General Engineering

□ **ADAMAS CONSTRUCTION CORPORATION**
Poblacion Norte, Sta. Maria Santa Maria Ilocos Sur
Contact Number/s : none
License: 29525 Amo: Frederick Raymond D. De Castro Org Type: Corporation Primary Classification: General Engineering

□ **ADELFA & CHARLIE ENTERPRISES**
INOCENTES, SANTISIMO ROSARIO NAVAL Biliran Sub-province
Contact Number/s : 5009048-49
License: 11569 Amo: Adelfa A. Chong Org Type: Sole Proprietorship Primary Classification: General Building

□ **ADNYL CONSTRUCTION AND DEVELOPMENT CORPORATION**
No. 20 E.S. Cruz St., Cruzville Subd., Novaliches Proper Quezon City
Contact Number/s : 939-76-88
License: 17153 Amo: Hector G. Nuguit Org Type: Corporation Primary Classification: General Building

□ **ADVANCE ENGINEERING CORPORATION**
2208 Singalong St., Malate, Manila Manila
Contact Number/s : 5238711-16
License: 1619 Amo: Moises S. Manego Org Type: Corporation Primary Classification: General Engineering

□ **AGCHEM CONSTRUCTION & DEVELOPMENT CORPORATION**
195 Dona Soledad Ave, Better Living Subd Paranaque Para?aque
Contact Number/s : 8245943
License: 4913 Amo: Danilo J. Teodosio Org Type: Corporation Primary Classification: General Engineering

□ **AJYSC MARKETING**
Poblacion Tacurong, Sultan Kudarat Maguidanao
Contact Number/s : 064-2003529
License: 26924 Amo: Aleth Joy S. Caderao Org Type: Sole Proprietorship Primary Classification: General Engineering

□ **AL MOHANDIS CONSTRUCTION COMPANY**
KF Homes Capiton Datu Odin Sinsuat Maguindanao
Contact Number/s : 431-0271
License: 6192 Amo: Musib K. Kamensa Org Type: Partnership Primary Classification: General Engineering

□ **AL SHIDDIQ DEVELOPMENT AND CONSTRUCTION SERVICES**
Lilod-Saduc Ext. Marawi City Marawi
License: 26368 Amo: Hadji Mohamad Shiddiq Org Type: Sole Proprietorship Primary Classification: General Engineering

□ **AL-BADR CONSTRUCTION**
Ting-ting'''s Bakeshop, Bo. Naga Marawi City Lanao del Sur
Contact Number/s : 520040/010
License: 11387 Amo: Badar A. Abdulhalim Org Type: Sole Proprietorship Primary Classification: General Engineering

□ **ALCCO LUMBER CORPORATION**

National Highway, Catbangen, San Fernando La Union
Contact Number/s : 888-2308/09
License: 388 Amo: Benito Gapuz Te Org Type: Corporation Primary Classification: General Building

ALFONSO V. ADLAWAN CONSTRUCTION
Lipata, Minglanilla Cebu
Contact Number/s : 2723237
License: 1837 Amo: Alfonso V. Adlawan Org Type: Sole Proprietorship Primary Classification: General Engineering

ALFREDO D. SABARILLO, JR. ENGINEER-CONTRACTOR
Unit 4, 2/F Susana Arcade, 476 Real St., Almanza, Las Pinas City Las Pi?
Contact Number/s : 800-3832
License: 15231 Amo: Alfredo D. Sabarillo, Jr. Org Type: Sole Proprietorship Primary Classification: General Building

ALNOR CONSTRUCTION AND CONSTRUCTION SUPPLIES
P-1, Mabua, Surigao City Surigao City Surigao del Norte
License: 26705 Amo: Norberto C. Perez Org Type: Sole Proprietorship Primary Classification: Mechanical Work

ALPA-PCM, INCORPORATED
3-M Puso ng Baguio Bldg., Session Road Baguio City Benguet
Contact Number/s : 442-2338
License: 8849 Amo: Mario R. Alzona, Jr. Org Type: Corporation Primary Classification: General Engineering

ALPHA RYDER CONSTRUCTION AND SUPPLIES
2733 Monreal Street , Polvorista Sorsogon
Contact Number/s : 056-2111843
License: 12197 Amo: Albert B. Tison Org Type: Sole Proprietorship Primary Classification: General Engineering

ALTA CONSTRUCTION
198 J.C. Aquino Ave., Butuan City Agusan del Norte
Contact Number/s : (085) 2252-456/(02) 931-7138
License: 587 Amo: Alfredo O. Taruc Org Type: Sole Proprietorship Primary Classification: General Engineering

AM & M CONSTRUCTION
San Pedro Bacacay Albay
Contact Number/s : 052-4807800
License: 18818 Amo: Annalyn M. Matsuoka Org Type: Sole Proprietorship Primary Classification: General Engineering

AMIGO STEEL INDUSTRIES, INC.
94 J.P. Ramoy St., Talipapa Caloocan City Kaloocan City
Contact Number/s : 983-1256
License: 29319 Amo: Albino A. Kaw Org Type: Corporation Primary Classification: Structural Steel Work

AMMAP BUILDERS & EQUIPMENT LESSOR
1st Crub St., Digos Davao del Sur
Contact Number/s : 082-5522869
License: 24711 Amo: Alfredo M. Angeles Org Type: Sole Proprietorship Primary Classification: General Engineering

AMOR RAMOS CONSTRUCTION
Shortcut, Valdefuente, Cabanatuan City Nueva Ecija
Contact Number/s : 600-4964
License: 4520 Amo: Amor D. Ramos Org Type: Sole Proprietorship Primary Classification: General Engineering

AMYES BUILDERS
L.A. Samson Bldg., Ortigas Ave. Ext., Cainta Rizal
Contact Number/s : 9157929
License: 28998 Amo: Amelito Y. Estacio Org Type: Sole Proprietorship Primary Classification: General Engineering

□ **ANAM CONSTRUCTION AND DEVELOPMENT PHILS., INC.**
NSC Compound, East Service Road, Km. 22 Muntinlupa City Muntinlupa
Contact Number/s : 844-2733-35
License: 20292 Amo: Leonardo P. Loreto, Jr. Org Type: Corporation Primary Classification: General Building

□ **ARDI DEVELOPMENT & CONSTRUCTION, INC.**
3/f Samuel One Bldg., 3482 Honda St,., Cor. EDSA Guadalupe Makati CPO (inc. Buendia up to Edsa) Makati
Contact Number/s : 883-3853 - 54
License: 30093 Amo: Mac Rino Martinez Magsombol Org Type: Corporation Primary Classification: General Building

□ **ARGUS DEVELOPMENT CORPORATION**
203 Ferros Bldg., 176 Salcedo St.,Legaspi Vill., Makati City
Contact Number/s : none
License: 11896 Amo: Melchor D. Elegado Org Type: Corporation Primary Classification: General Building

□ **ARJER CONSTRUCTION**
SAN NICOLAS ST. Surigao City Surigao del Norte
License: 10110 Amo: Jaime Tan Org Type: Sole Proprietorship Primary Classification: General Building

□ **ARMANDO U. KHONG HUN GENERAL CONTRACTOR**
Calamagui 2nd, Ilagan Isabela
License: 16163 Amo: Armando U. Khong Hun Org Type: Sole Proprietorship Primary Classification: General Engineering

□ **ARQUITECTONICA BUILDERS & CONSTRUCTION SUPPLIES**
Expressway, San Miguel, Calasiao Pangasinan
Contact Number/s : 075-5225575
License: 13241 Amo: Paul Francis T. Co Org Type: Sole Proprietorship Primary Classification: General Engineering

□ **ARQUIZA CONSTRUCTION**
Socorro St., RGR Subd., Bo. Kaunlarang Mayao Lucena City Quezon Province
Contact Number/s : 7104403/7420812
License: 10256 Amo: Mylvin M. Arquiza Org Type: Sole Proprietorship Primary Classification: General Engineering

□ **ARROWHEAD CONSTRUCTION**
#63-02 Ilang-Ilang St., Timog Park, Angeles City Pampanga
Contact Number/s : 045-9634306
License: 22597 Amo: Antonio P. De Jesus Org Type: Sole Proprietorship Primary Classification: General Engineering

□ **ARSANT ENGINEERING**
Unit 8 Ivory Crest Mansion, 11th St., New Manila Quezon City
Contact Number/s : 7221498
License: 12028 Amo: Nazario M. Santos Org Type: Sole Proprietorship Primary Classification: General Building

□ **AS AGUILANA CONSTRUCTION AND SUPPLY**
Blk. 13, Lot 1, University Homes Catarman Northern Samar
Contact Number/s : 0917-4813630
License: 20766 Amo: Alex S. Aguilana Org Type: Sole Proprietorship Primary Classification: General Engineering

□ **ASIAN ELECTROSYSTEMS CORPORATION**
AEC Bldg., 13th St., United Paranaque Subd., V, Sucat Para?aque CPO Para?aque
Contact Number/s : 829-3952/56/59
License: 14698 Amo: Cipriano P. Abdon Org Type: Corporation Primary Classification: Electrical Work

□ **ATARI CONSTRUCTION DEVELOPMENT CORPORATION**
1067 J. Felipe Blvd., Sta. Cruz, Cavite City Cavite City
Contact Number/s : 8017218

License: 8646 Amo: Lamberto L. Lee, Jr. Org Type: Corporation Primary Classification: General Engineering

□ **ATLANTIC PACIFIC EMPIRE CONSTRUCTION CORPORATION**
1145 G. Masangkay St., Sta. Cruz, Manila Manila
Contact Number/s : 253-0044
License: 26175 Amo: Victor T. Dionisio Org Type: Corporation Primary Classification: General Engineering

□ **ATLAS ENTERPRISES**
Necosip Compound Daan Sarile, Cabanatuan City Nueva Ecija
Contact Number/s : 044-4633273
License: 4953 Amo: Tomas N. Joson III Org Type: Sole Proprietorship Primary Classification: General Engineering

□ **AVECS CORPORATION**
21 Don Gregorio St., Don Antonio Heights Diliman Quezon City
Contact Number/s : 931-0574
License: 23228 Amo: Celestino D. Baldonado Org Type: Corporation Primary Classification: General Engineering

□ **AVP INDUSTRIES, INCORPORATED**
888 Amang rodriguez Ave., Santolan Pasig City
Contact Number/s : 645-0389/915-2857
License: 25398 Amo: Arnold V. Pulhin Org Type: Corporation Primary Classification: Mechanical Work

□ **AYLAN CONSTRUCTION AND TRADING**
16 St. Anthony St., Gulod, Novaliches Proper Quezon City
License: 11884 Amo: Rene M. Leano Org Type: Sole Proprietorship Primary Classification: General Building

□ **AZUL BUILDERS**
Maysan Road, Maysan Valenzuela Metro Manila
Contact Number/s : 2928250

License: 21870 Amo: Nicomedes A. Fernando Org Type: Sole Proprietorship Primary Classification: General Building

□ **B C A CONSTRUCTION SUPPLY**
C-257 J.P. Rizal St. Cabuyao Laguna
Contact Number/s : 5312492/706364/709036
License: 14278 Amo: Barbara C. Arenas Org Type: Sole Proprietorship Primary Classification: General Building

□ **B.A. TONGOL CONSTRUCTION**
11th Avenue, Unisite Subd., San Fernando Pampanga
Contact Number/s : 961-5348
License: 16166 Amo: Bienvenido A. Tongol Org Type: Sole Proprietorship Primary Classification: General Engineering

□ **B.F.T. CONSTRUCTION**
Del Corro Street, San Lorenzo Gapan Nueva Ecija
Contact Number/s : 4860564
License: 14424 Amo: Benjamin F. Tan Org Type: Sole Proprietorship Primary Classification: General Engineering

□ **B.S. CANSANA CONSTRUCTION**
No. 8 Market Ave., Palatiw, Pasig CPO Pasig City
Contact Number/s : 6412087
License: 3501 Amo: Benedicto S. Cansana Org Type: Sole Proprietorship Primary Classification: General Engineering

□ **BAR CONSTRUCTION DEVELOPMENT CORPORATION**
Barcenaga, Naujan Mindoro Oriental
Contact Number/s : 9182320120
License: 22255 Amo: Lucrecia M. Angeles Org Type: Corporation Primary Classification: General Engineering

□ **BARACON, INCORPORATED**
16 Kisad Road cor. Chanum St., Baguio City Benguet
Contact Number/s : 074-3042028

License: 27123 Amo: Francisco P. Baraquel, Sr. Org Type: Corporation Primary Classification: General Engineering

□ **BENNELL TRADING & CONSTRUCTION**
358 AREA 6 SIKATUNA BLISS, Quezon City CPO Quezon City
Contact Number/s : 434-83-27 / 9515590
License: 24640 Amo: Ledenilla S. Ragos Org Type: Sole Proprietorship Primary Classification: General Engineering

□ **BIP DESIGN, CON ARCHITECTS, ENGINEERS, GENERAL CONTRACTORS**
1 Purok 7, `Bakakeng Norte, Baguio City Benguet
Contact Number/s : 444-4830
License: 29558 Amo: Bonifacio Ilao Dela Pena Org Type: Sole Proprietorship Primary Classification: General Building

□ **BISLIG VENTURE CONSTRUCTION & DEV'T. INC.**
#5 Hart St., Filinvest Vill., Quezon City
License: 28331 Amo: Peter Paul Jed C. Falcon Org Type: Corporation Primary Classification: General Engineering

□ **BLG CONSTRUCTION**
Rizal Ave. Extension, Estaka Dipolog City Dipolog City
Contact Number/s : 2122480
License: 2277 Amo: Benjamin L. Gawchua Org Type: Sole Proprietorship Primary Classification: General Building

□ **BODIONGAN CONSTRUCTION**
1617 Upper Bontong Camaman-an, Cagayan de Oro City Cagayan de Oro City
Contact Number/s : 857-4923
License: 2076 Amo: Estanislao B. Bodiongan Org Type: Sole Proprietorship Primary Classification: General Building

□ **BONA FIDES BUILDERS COMPANY, INC.**
10 RECORD STREET, GSIS VILLAGE, PROJECT 8 QUEZON CITY
Contact Number/s : 925-2882
License: 19001 Amo: Domingo O. Bautista Org Type: Corporation Primary Classification: General Building

□ **BONYLL CONSTRUCTION & SUPPLY**
Switch, Magsaysay Zamboanga del Sur
Contact Number/s : 062-2251765
License: 19363 Amo: Bonifacio B. Lagura Org Type: Sole Proprietorship Primary Classification: General Building

□ **BPL PHILIPPINES, INC.**
Suite 3B, ILO Bldg., 195 G. Araneta Ave. Quezon City CPO Quezon City
Contact Number/s : 7166427-28
License: 24819 Amo: Edwin F. Ong Org Type: Corporation Primary Classification: Foundation Work

□ **BRAINS AND BRAWN CONSTRUCTION AND DEVELOPMENT CORPORATION**
1355 Candelaria St., Makati, Metro Manila Makati
Contact Number/s : 890-2758
License: 15649 Amo: Willen A. Kho Org Type: Corporation Primary Classification: General Building

□ **BRITT ENTERPRISES**
131 Delgado St. Iloilo City Iloilo
Contact Number/s : 3378544
License: 10506 Amo: Filemon T. Tubola Org Type: Sole Proprietorship Primary Classification: General Engineering

□ **BUILDERS ZONE AND SALES CORPORATION**
143 Yakal St., Brgy. San Vicente Angono Rizal
Contact Number/s : 6510697
License: 26957 Amo: Jose L. Brizuela Org Type: Corporation Primary Classification: General Engineering

□ **C.B. LOTILLA ENGINEERING**
305 Do?a Margarita Bldg. J.P. Rizal St., Makati City Makati

Contact Number/s : 861-9321
License: 3142 Amo: Crisostomo B. Lotilla Org Type: Sole Proprietorship Primary Classification: General Engineering

C.C.M. CONSTRUCTION
C.P.G. North Avenue, Booy Dist., Tagbilaran City Bohol
Contact Number/s : 411-2868
License: 11043 Amo: Cesar C. Maluenda Org Type: Sole Proprietorship Primary Classification: General Engineering

C.S. TRINIDAD FURNITURE AND GENERAL CONTRACTOR
366 MacArthur Highway, Wawa, Balagtas, Bulacan Bulacan
Contact Number/s : none
License: 25449 Amo: Warlito G. Trinidad Org Type: Sole Proprietorship Primary Classification: General Engineering

CANSCOR CONSTRUCTION AND DEVELOPMENT INCORPORATED
29 Evangelista St. Santolan Pasig City
Contact Number/s : 646-4451/9158618
License: 20144 Amo: Armando A. Baler Org Type: Corporation Primary Classification: General Engineering

CAPITOL INDUSTRIAL CONSTRUCTION GROUPS, INC.
Km. 18 Ortigas Ave. Ext. Cainta Rizal
Contact Number/s : 6551751-53
License: 1658 Amo: Ramon C. Arroyo Org Type: Corporation Primary Classification: General Engineering

CAPUYAN CONSTRUCTION
168 Balili, km.5, Balili, La Trinidad, Benguet Benguet
Contact Number/s : 422-2314
License: 7180 Amo: Wilson G. Capuyan Org Type: Sole Proprietorship Primary Classification: General Engineering

CARAG BUILDERS INCORPORATED
2/F R&F Bldg., Aurora Blvd. Cor. Harvard Sts., Cubao Quezon City
Contact Number/s : 9125159
License: 11200 Amo: Inocencio P. Carag Org Type: Corporation Primary Classification: General Building

CARMEL CONSTRUCTION
Rizal St., Gen. Tinio Nueva Ecija
Contact Number/s : 9281757
License: 11557 Amo: Morfino B. Bote Org Type: Sole Proprietorship Primary Classification: General Engineering

C-CONSTRUCTION & SUPPLY
#170 Araneta St., Singcang, Bacolod City Negros Occidental
Contact Number/s : 034-4344176
License: 27986 Amo: Eduardo Francis Q. Conde, Jr. Org Type: Sole Proprietorship Primary Classification: General Engineering

CENTURY IRON WORKS, INCORPORATED
289 cor. 4th Street, 8th Avenue Kalookan City CPO Kalookan City (South)
Contact Number/s : 363-8603
License: 7688 Amo: George L. Chua Org Type: Corporation Primary Classification: General Building

CESMA ENGINEERING & DEVELOPMENT CORPORATION
Don Juan St., Villa Cecilia Subd., Bo. Mambugan, Antipolo Rizal
Contact Number/s : 646-1236
License: 318 Amo: Cesar J. Mata Org Type: Corporation Primary Classification: General Engineering

CHI CONSTRUCTION & SUPPLIES
Maharlika Road, Ramar Village San Jose City Nueva Ecija
Contact Number/s : 511-4191
License: 15661 Amo: Ronaldo L. Ty Org Type: Sole Proprietorship Primary Classification: General Building

CHM CONSTRUCTION, INC.
42 E. Abada St., Loyola Heights Quezon City
Contact Number/s : 929-9151
License: 14491 Amo: Arthur S. Ignacio Org Type: Corporation Primary Classification: General Engineering

CHU CONSTRUCTION
Brgy. 85, San Jose, Tacloban City Leyte
Contact Number/s : 523-2875
License: 10787 Amo: Sixto N. Chu Org Type: Sole Proprietorship Primary Classification: General Building

CNG CONSTRUCTION AND DEVELOPMENT CORP.
16 (G) delos Santos Street, Ampid I San Mateo Rizal
Contact Number/s : 998-2806
License: 28757 Amo: Crispino C. Santiago Org Type: Corporation Primary Classification: General Engineering

COASTLAND CONSTRUCTION AND DEVELOPMENT CORPORATION
12 A. Mabini Ext. Dona Vicenta Village, Davao City Davao City
Contact Number/s : none
License: 11487 Amo: Manuel S. Gonzales Org Type: Corporation Primary Classification: General Building

COLOSSUS CONSTRUCTION AND SUPPLY
49 Morales Ave., General Paulino Santos, Koronadal South Cotobato
Contact Number/s : (083) 228-2398
License: 28035 Amo: Joel Y. Salanga Org Type: Sole Proprietorship Primary Classification: General Engineering

COMM TECHNOLOGY PHILS., INC.
755 Maria Clara St., Mandaluyong CPO Mandaluyong
License: 25937 Amo: Proceso U. Cobarde Org Type: Corporation Primary Classification: General Building

COMMERCIAL CONSTRUCTION CORPORATION
9321 Dungon St., San Antonio Village Makati City
Contact Number/s : 8966643
License: 18513 Amo: Ricardo M. Alindayu Org Type: Corporation Primary Classification: General Engineering

COMPACT BUILDERS, INCORPORATED
949 Rosario St., Sampaloc, Sampaloc East Manila
Contact Number/s : 714-1158
License: 14492 Amo: Mylene E. Hizon Org Type: Corporation Primary Classification: General Engineering

CONSTRUCTION & DRILLING SPECIALIST, INC.
Suite 401, ALCCO Bldg. Ortigas Ave., Greenhills San Juan M.M. San Juan
Contact Number/s : 726-0649
License: 8572 Amo: Esmeraldo O. Salvana Org Type: Corporation Primary Classification: General Engineering

CRUZ-ESGUERRA CONSTRUCTION
#221 Roadside View Subd., Norsagaray Bulacan Province
Contact Number/s : 044-6940027
License: 17007 Amo: Arturo S. Cruz Org Type: Sole Proprietorship Primary Classification: General Building

CSPL PHILIPPINES, INC.
R604,Do?a Felisa Syjuco Bldg., Remedios St. cor. Taft Malate Manila
Contact Number/s : 523-0989/20
License: 26668 Amo: Miguel C. Cerdeno Org Type: Corporation Primary Classification: General Engineering

CTC CONSTRUCTION CORPORATION
124 G. Araneta Ave., Quezon City Quezon City
Contact Number/s : none
License: 20259 Amo: Alex L. Coseto Org Type: Corporation Primary Classification: General Building

□ **CTM CONSTRUCTION & DEVELOPMENT CORPORATION**
Pajo, Lapu-lapu City Cebu
License: 29043 Amo: James G. Ang Org Type: Corporation Primary Classification: General Engineering

□ **CURRIMAO INTEGRATED BUILDERS CORPORATION**
48-C Kabignayan St., Quezon City CPO Quezon City
Contact Number/s : 712-3130/42
License: 8738 Amo: Onofre T. Menor Org Type: Corporation Primary Classification: General Engineering

□ **CYGNET CONSTRUCTION**
270 San Isidro 1 Paombong Bulacan Province
Contact Number/s : 044-7910553
License: 16517 Amo: Gerardo L. Magsakay Org Type: Sole Proprietorship Primary Classification: General Engineering

□ **CYO CONSTRUCTION**
109-A, Km. 7 Bancasi, Butuan City Agusan del Norte
Contact Number/s : 085-3423175/085-3420167
License: 12493 Amo: Cleto Y. Ongluico Org Type: Sole Proprietorship Primary Classification: General Building

□ **D & D CONSTRUCTION**
68 Magallanes St., Zone V Bangued Abra
Contact Number/s : 752-8450
License: 7837 Amo: Dominic B. Valera Org Type: Sole Proprietorship Primary Classification: General Engineering

□ **D.A. ATIENZA CONSTRUCTION**
23 Chelsea St., East Fairview Subd. Fairview Quezon City
Contact Number/s : 0919-8458598
License: 20412 Amo: Dante A. Atienza Org Type: Sole Proprietorship Primary Classification: General Building

□ **D.A.P. CONSTRUCTION**
#38 Camella St., Greenpark Village Cainta Rizal
License: 8766 Amo: David A. Pau Org Type: Sole Proprietorship Primary Classification: General Building

□ **D.K. JOCSON CONSTRUCTION**
Mabini St., Talisay Negros OccidentaL Negros Occidental
Contact Number/s : 495-2844
License: 6896 Amo: Danilo K. Jocson Org Type: Sole Proprietorship Primary Classification: General Engineering

□ **D.M.L. CONSTRUCTION & SUPPLY**
Villa Matilde Subd., Jalandoni St., Jaro Iloilo City Iloilo
Contact Number/s : 329/8048
License: 7360 Amo: Danilo M. Lamparero Org Type: Sole Proprietorship Primary Classification: General Engineering

□ **DAIRUB CONST. CONTRACTOR INC.**
Blk. 10, Lot 11, Sison Subd., Tagum Davao del Norte
Contact Number/s : 2172167
License: 24172 Amo: Annie L. Romera Org Type: Corporation Primary Classification: General Engineering

□ **DAN-BEL CONSTRUCTION & SUPPLY**
Purok Mercury, Poblacion 8, Green Valley Midsayap North Cotobato
Contact Number/s : 064-4510210
License: 17375 Amo: Bella B. Beray Org Type: Sole Proprietorship Primary Classification: General Building

□ **DANITECH POWER SYSTEM**
Unit 5 R. Syjuco Bldg., 299 Tandang Sora Ave., Quezon City
Contact Number/s : 932-0139
License: 23226 Amo: Imelda C. Ulnagan Org Type: Sole Proprietorship Primary Classification: Electrical Work

 DAVAO RJB CONSTRUCTION CORPORATION
#25 Sierra Madre cor. Apo St., Rolling Hills Subd., Bacaca, Bajada Davao City Davao del Sur
Contact Number/s : 222-9288
License: 6856 Amo: Cesnero A. Borras Org Type: Corporation Primary Classification: General Engineering

 DAVAWENO ENTERPRISES
Km. 56 National Highway, Tagum, Davao
Contact Number/s : 217-3541
License: 6672 Amo: Cresencio S. Bano Org Type: Sole Proprietorship Primary Classification: General Engineering

 DE CONSTRUCTION & DEVELOPMENT CORPORATION
No. 1, Pulsar St., Village East Subd., Cainta Rizal
Contact Number/s : 656-3681
License: 21473 Amo: Danilo A. Escares Org Type: Corporation Primary Classification: General Engineering

 DECOR CONSTRUCTION AND DEVELOPMENT CORPORATION
8115 Santol St., Phase IV, Marcelo Green Village, Para?aque CPO Para?aque
Contact Number/s : 8241785
License: 22030 Amo: Marilyn T. Ginete Org Type: Corporation Primary Classification: General Building

 DEL-ART INCORPORATED
Blk. 146 Lot 2 Sitio Central Bicutan Taguig
License: 29596 Amo: Delia V. Alit Org Type: Corporation Primary Classification: General Building

 DELL EQUIPMENT AND CONSTRUCTION CORPORATION
3F Cainta Town Center, Felix Avenue Cainta Rizal
Contact Number/s : 6559292
License: 29698 Amo: Paterno C Pajares Org Type: Corporation Primary Classification: General Engineering

 DESCONS CONSTRUCTION & DEVELOPMENT CORPORATION
#42 Tomas Morato Avenue Quezon City CPO Quezon City
Contact Number/s : 411-5897
License: 19103 Amo: Marcial L. Edillon Org Type: Corporation Primary Classification: General Building

 DIGOS TESSTON CONSTRUCTION & SUPPLIES
036 Quezon Avenue, Digos Davao del Sur
Contact Number/s : 082-5532351
License: 8921 Amo: Antonio C. Te Org Type: Sole Proprietorship Primary Classification: General Engineering

 DMI CONSTRUCTION
No. 384 Far East Asia Comm"l. Center Visayas Avenue Quezon City CPO Quezon City
Contact Number/s : 927-8820
License: 14127 Amo: Dionisio M. Ines Org Type: Sole Proprietorship Primary Classification: General Engineering

 DTS DIGITAL TELECOM SYSTEMS, INC.
90 Anonas St., East Kamias Quezon City Quezon City
Contact Number/s : 922-1190
License: 25206 Amo: George M. Sales Org Type: Corporation Primary Classification: Communication Facilities

 DYNA V ENGINEERING SERVICES
260 J.P. Rizal St., Cabugao Laguna
Contact Number/s : 049-531-4796
License: 30072 Amo: Mario Callao Vargas Org Type: Sole Proprietorship Primary Classification: Electrical Work

 DYNAMIC BUILDERS & CONSTRUCTION CO. (PHIL.), INC.
Ceres Compound, Mansilingan, Bacolod City Negros Occidental
Contact Number/s : (034) 446-1558 / 446-0107

License: 24712 Amo: Ricardo V. Yanson, Jr. Org Type: Corporation Primary Classification: General Engineering

□ **E. C. CALDEJON CONSTRUCTION**
292 Little Baguio Street, Wawa 3 Rosario Cavite
Contact Number/s : 046-4382231
License: 23866 Amo: Edmundo C. Caldejon Org Type: Sole Proprietorship Primary Classification: General Building

□ **E. C. MALLARI CONSTRUCTION**
#372 Visayas Ave., Tandang Sora, Quezon City Quezon City
Contact Number/s : none
License: 13889 Amo: Edgardo C. Mallari Org Type: Sole Proprietorship Primary Classification: General Engineering

□ **E. MALAYA CONSTRUCTION AND GENERAL MERCHANDISE**
42 New Orleans St., Pingakaisahan, Cubao Quezon City Quezon City
Contact Number/s : 715-5542
License: 15339 Amo: Erwin M. Malaya Org Type: Sole Proprietorship Primary Classification: General Building

□ **E.B.A. CONSTRUCTION**
Roman Superhighway, Balanga Bataan
Contact Number/s : 472371697
License: 6210 Amo: Eusebio B. Aquino Org Type: Sole Proprietorship Primary Classification: General Engineering

□ **E.C. COLIAMCO BUILDERS**
Estacion Paniqui Tarlac
Contact Number/s : 931-0652
License: 11339 Amo: Eleanor C. Coliamco Org Type: Sole Proprietorship Primary Classification: General Engineering

□ **E.E. BLACK, LTD.**
53 Paseo de Roxas, Urdaneta Village Makati CPO Makati
Contact Number/s : 812-8166
License: 121 Amo: Antonio I. Habana Org Type: Corporation Primary Classification: General Engineering

□ **E.G. BAHANI CONSTRUCTION FOUNDATION SPECIALIST**
30 M. Calixto Street, Zamboanga City Zamboanga del Sur
Contact Number/s : 991-26-58
License: 21461 Amo: Eduardo G. Bahani Org Type: Sole Proprietorship Primary Classification: General Engineering

□ **E.K.C. CONSTRUCTION AND AGREGGATES**
O B 170 Tawang, La Trinidad Benguet
Contact Number/s : 422-5157
License: 14833 Amo: Eusebio K. Cupido Org Type: Sole Proprietorship Primary Classification: General Engineering

□ **E.P.G. CONSTRUCTION, INC.**
#13 Central Avenue, Brgy. Culiat, Quezon City CPO Quezon City
Contact Number/s : 924-0769/9216477
License: 3748 Amo: Emmanuel P. De Guzman Org Type: Corporation Primary Classification: General Engineering

□ **EASTERN CONSTRUCTION COMPANY, INC.**
497 E. Rodriguez Sr. Ave. Quezon City Quezon City
Contact Number/s : 743-7391/98
License: 2225 Amo: Reginaldo S. San Juan Org Type: Corporation Primary Classification: General Engineering

□ **EDROX CONSTRUCTION INC.**
Concepcion Grande, Naga City Camarines Sur
Contact Number/s : 756279
License: 10926 Amo: Rosario C. Roxas Org Type: Corporation Primary Classification: General Engineering

□ **EDWIN F. SALAZAR CONSTRUCTION EQUIPMENT RESOURCES**

Level 2, Salazar Construction Building, 211 N. Bacalso Ave., 211 Cebu City Cebu City
Contact Number/s : 261-9548
License: 18278 Amo: Edwin F. Salazar Org Type: Sole Proprietorship Primary Classification: General Building

ELG CONSTRUCTION
DIimayuga St., Mataas na Kahoy Batangas
Contact Number/s : 043-7560887
License: 17009 Amo: Edwin L. Gardiola Org Type: Sole Proprietorship Primary Classification: General Building

EMECO INTERNATIONAL TRADING & CONSTRUCTION
14 St., Thomas St., Don Bosco Village Paranaque, M.M. Para?aque
Contact Number/s : 776-6283
License: 24591 Amo: Eliza M. Concepcion Org Type: Sole Proprietorship Primary Classification: General Building

EMPIRE STATE CONSTRUCTION
#4 Bentley St., St. Dominic Villa, San Juan Agustin San Fernando Pampanga
Contact Number/s : 725-4096
License: 28456 Amo: Rene Paulo M. Legaspi Org Type: Sole Proprietorship Primary Classification: General Engineering

EMS SARMIENTO CONSTRUCTION
#3 Paseo Lucy St., Ma. Luisa Park, Banilad, Cebu City Cebu
Contact Number/s : 3467416
License: 29097 Amo: Edgar Mary S. Sarmiento Org Type: Sole Proprietorship Primary Classification: General Engineering

ENERGY FACTORS, INC.
EFI Corporate Center, 74 P. Cruz St., Brgy. New Zaniga Mandaluyong City
Contact Number/s : 533-5571/5357660
License: 18675 Amo: Nicanor A. Fabian Org Type: Corporation Primary Classification: General Engineering

ENRIQUE CHUA GENERAL CONTRACTORS
#14 Bayanihan Drive, RD. 20, Project 8 Quezon City
Contact Number/s : 455-6427
License: 7789 Amo: Enrique S. Chua Org Type: Sole Proprietorship Primary Classification: General Engineering

EQUIS CONSTRUCTION CORP.
Unit 5 G/F Corporate House, No. 239 Boni Serrano Quezon City CPO Quezon City
Contact Number/s : 726-01-62
License: 29855 Amo: Jesus Lazo Caacbay Org Type: Corporation Primary Classification: General Engineering

ERSAN CONSTRUCTION
DEL PILAR STREET, Cabanatuan City Nueva Ecija
Contact Number/s : 044-9650085
License: 6565 Amo: Emiliano R. Santiago, Jr. Org Type: Sole Proprietorship Primary Classification: General Engineering

EXCELLENT TECHNOLOGY CONSTRUCTION CORP.
95-A 12th Avenue, Cubao Cubao Quezon City
License: 16708 Amo: Editha D. Pastorfide Org Type: Corporation Primary Classification: General Building

F. GUTIERREZ CONSTRUCTION CORPORATION
18 Fl., Unit 4, Antel Global Corporate Center Julia Vargas Ave. Ortigas PO Pasig City
Contact Number/s : 6372155/57
License: 25734 Amo: Evangeline C. Descallar Org Type: Corporation Primary Classification: General Engineering

F.L. ALDANA CONSTRUCTION
294 Real St., Pulang Lupa, Las Pi?as Manila
Contact Number/s : 543-5972
License: 4350 Amo: Florencio L. Aldana Org Type: Sole Proprietorship Primary Classification: General Engineering

□ **F.L. BONDOC & ASSOCIATES, INC.**
30 Barcelona Cmpd., Bahay Toro Quezon City CPO Quezon City
Contact Number/s : 455-0679/6438
License: 25910 Amo: Fred L. Bondoc Org Type: Corporation Primary Classification: Electrical Work

□ **F.M. HAIM CONSTRUCTION**
Rm. 208, 2nd/F, Diocesan Centrum Bldg., Iligan City Lanao del Norte
Contact Number/s : 2212998/492-1061
License: 17978 Amo: Felito M. Haim Org Type: Sole Proprietorship Primary Classification: General Building

□ **F.M.C. ENGINEERING & CONSTRUCTION**
151 Sisa St., Cor. Gov. Pascual Ave. Acacia Malabon
Contact Number/s : 2885381
License: 4575 Amo: Fernando M. De Castro, Jr. Org Type: Sole Proprietorship Primary Classification: General Engineering

□ **F.P. CARREON CONSTRUCTION**
402 M. Fortich St., Poblacion Valencia Bukidnon
Contact Number/s : 088-8282077
License: 10277 Amo: Felipe P. Carreon Org Type: Sole Proprietorship Primary Classification: General Building

□ **F.P.N. CONSTRUCTORS INC.**
31-B Road 7, Bagong Pag-asa Quezon City
License: 28579 Amo: Fernando P. Tolentino Org Type: Corporation Primary Classification: General Building

□ **FABMIK CONSTRUCTION AND EQUIPMENT CO., INC.**
Unit 1614 Cityland Condo 10 T2, H. V. dela Costa Makati Commercial Ctr. Makati
Contact Number/s : 867-4489
License: 24966 Amo: Isabelo A. Braza Org Type: Corporation Primary Classification: Electrical Work

□ **FANTA CONS. & DEV. CORPORATION**
569 Juna Luna Street Tondo North Manila
License: 29647 Amo: Albert Aquino Dy Org Type: Corporation Primary Classification: General Building

□ **FASTDUCS BUILDERS**
#13 Mabini Street, Vigan Ilocos Sur
Contact Number/s : 722-2615
License: 17450 Amo: Rebecca N. Sangco Org Type: Sole Proprietorship Primary Classification: General Engineering

□ **FEL-GENE CONSTRUCTION**
63 Paso de Blas, Valenzuela Metro Manila Valenzuela
Contact Number/s : 292-8426
License: 22920 Amo: Felino P. Eugenio Org Type: Sole Proprietorship Primary Classification: General Engineering

□ **FEMSCO INDUSTRIES, INC.**
Unit 14 Facilities Center,548 Shaw Blvd. Mandaluyong City Mandaluyong
Contact Number/s : 531-4871/76
License: 8305 Amo: Alfonso Lim Po Org Type: Corporation Primary Classification: Electrical Work

□ **FIERASEC BUILDERS**
#26 Maria Manguiat St., Tierra Pura Subd Tandang Sora Quezon City
Contact Number/s : 931-3880
License: 28212 Amo: Roseadel G. Del Fierro Org Type: Sole Proprietorship Primary Classification: General Engineering

□ **FIL GARCIA CONSTRUCTION, INC.**
140 Kalayaan Avenue, Cor. Mayaman St. Diliman Quezon City
Contact Number/s : 924-2385
License: 3536 Amo: Filomeno T. Garcia Org Type: Corporation Primary Classification: General Building

□ **FILNET CONSTRUCTION & TRADING**
Km. 75 Gapan Olongapo Road, Cabetican, Bacolor Pampanga

Contact Number/s : 045-912364
License: 16337 Amo: Filipinas F. Manalastas Org Type: Sole Proprietorship Primary Classification: General Building

FIRST AGRICULTURAL RESOURCE MANAGEMENT, INC.
70 Sct. Madrinan cor. Sgt. Esguerra Ave., South Triangle Quezon City CPO Quezon City
Contact Number/s : 4108484
License: 27297 Amo: Obdulia S. Gamboa Org Type: Corporation Primary Classification: General Building

FIRST PHILIPPINE ENERGY CORPORATION
3rd Flr. Benpres Bldg., Exchange Rd. cor. Meralco Ave. Ortigas PO Pasig City
Contact Number/s : 631-4091
License: 29608 Amo: Ernesto T. Fadullon Org Type: Corporation Primary Classification: Electrical Work

FLORES, SAGAD & SONS, INC.
Units 807-809, Future Point Plaza 1, 112 Panay Ave., Quezon City Quezon City
Contact Number/s : 4162044/86
License: 8852 Amo: Juanito S. Flores Org Type: Corporation Primary Classification: General Engineering

FLORIANE CONSTRUCTION AND SUPPLY
993 2nd St., Guingona Subd. Butuan City Agusan del Norte
Contact Number/s : 225-4873
License: 12261 Amo: Florencio D. Agot Org Type: Sole Proprietorship Primary Classification: General Engineering

FM BUILDERS
Tatlong Hari St., Sta. Rosa Laguna
Contact Number/s : 049-2479044
License: 15497 Amo: Fernando G. Puzon Org Type: Sole Proprietorship Primary Classification: General Building

FNSP (PHILIPPINES), INC.
MMC House M. Ocampo cor. S. Jacinto Sts. Pio Del Pilar, Makati City Makati
Contact Number/s : 8672669
License: 28414 Amo: Jerome A. Santos Org Type: Corporation Primary Classification: General Engineering

FRACIA DEVELOPMENT CORPORATION
M.H. Del Pilar St., Cupang Balanga, Bataan Bataan
Contact Number/s : 477913132
License: 2411 Amo: Jose G. Zabala Org Type: Corporation Primary Classification: General Engineering

FUCHIGAMI CONSTRUCTION & BORING PROPRIETARY
373 Cruz La Trinidad, Benguet Benguet
Contact Number/s : 074-4222613
License: 14063 Amo: Walter T. Fuchigami Org Type: Sole Proprietorship Primary Classification: General Building

G M J CONSTRUCTION
31 San Joaquin cor. Sto. Nino Sts., Mandaluyong City Mandaluyong
Contact Number/s : 532-0456
License: 14126 Amo: George R. Joson Org Type: Sole Proprietorship Primary Classification: General Building

G.M. MANINGAS CONSTRUCTION, INCORPORATED
#33 Kayumangi St., Mandaluyong City Mandaluyong
Contact Number/s : none
License: 16338 Amo: German M. Maningas Org Type: Corporation Primary Classification: General Engineering

G.M. SALES CONSTRUCTION CORPORATION
90-B Anonas St., Kamias Quezon City CPO Quezon City
Contact Number/s : 922-1190/9221464
License: 18646 Amo: George M. Sales Org Type: Corporation Primary Classification: General Engineering

□ **G.O. EASTERN CONSTRUCTION CORP.**
Rm.403 Jafer Place, #19 Eisenhower St., Greenhills Greenhills North San Juan
Contact Number/s : 727-6129
License: 28860 Amo: Victor D. Oreta Org Type: Corporation Primary Classification: General Engineering

□ **GAMMATECH CONSTRUCTION CORPORATION**
Gammatech Compound, Tibasak, Macasandig, Cagayan dE Oro City Cagayan de Oro City
Contact Number/s : 8573284
License: 16086 Amo: Rolando U. Gironella, Jr. Org Type: Corporation Primary Classification: General Building

□ **GAMPIK CONSTRUCTION & DEVELOPMENT, INC.**
#3 Guatamela St., Loyola Grand Villas Quezon City
Contact Number/s : 9220334
License: 8019 Amo: Zenaida E. Balmaceda Org Type: Corporation Primary Classification: General Building

□ **GELO CONSTRUCTION ENTERPRISES**
Juliana Subdivision, Brgy. VII Calamba Laguna
Contact Number/s : 545-2073
License: 20173 Amo: Rownel G. Sipriaso Org Type: Sole Proprietorship Primary Classification: General Engineering

□ **GEMINI ELECTRICAL AND COMMUNICATION CONTRACTOR**
Rm. 1001 BPI Bldg., 560 Quintin Paredes St., Binondo Manila
Contact Number/s : 241-0864/48
License: 8555 Amo: Robert C. Uy Org Type: Sole Proprietorship Primary Classification: Electrical Work

□ **GENIALS TRADING AND CONTRACTING COMPANY, INC.**
G/F Suite C-1 Oyster Plaza Bldg., Naia Road Para?aque CPO Para?aque
Contact Number/s : 02-8291923/8291925
License: 29592 Amo: Antonio M. Obien Org Type: Corporation Primary Classification: General Engineering

□ **GEOSTAR PHILIPPINES, INC.**
Su.307 BPI Bldg., 150 Plaza Cervantes, Binondo Manila
Contact Number/s : 2420887/55
License: 12883 Amo: Edwin A. Llamas Org Type: Corporation Primary Classification: Electrical Work

□ **GIOVANNI CONSTRUCTION**
863 Imadejas Subd. Along Capitol Bonbon Rd., Butuan City Agusan del Norte
Contact Number/s : 815-3334
License: 12168 Amo: Ostric R. Rivera, Jr. Org Type: Sole Proprietorship Primary Classification: General Engineering

□ **GLOBAL TECHNOLOGY SYSTEMS PHILIPPINES, INC.**
No. 65 - B Shaw Blvd., cor. Marielane St., Brgy. Kapitolyo, Pasig CPO Pasig City
Contact Number/s : 637-9489/90
License: 24804 Amo: Fedencio L. Merza, Jr. Org Type: Corporation Primary Classification: Electrical Work

□ **GNQ INDUSTRIAL AND CONTRACTING CORPORATION**
#80 Baler St., Brgy. Paltok, San Francisco Del Monte Quezon City
Contact Number/s : 416-8128
License: 24356 Amo: Francisco C. Gotauco Org Type: Corporation Primary Classification: Mechanical Work

□ **GOLD BAND CONSTRUCTION ENTERPRISE**
Gold Band Bldg., Km 25 Gen. Aguinaldo Hi-way,Anabu II, Imus Cavite
Contact Number/s : 046-4710007
License: 7691 Amo: Teresita M. Diato Org Type: Sole Proprietorship Primary Classification: General Engineering

□ **GOLDEN BELL CONSTRUCTION & GENERAL SERVICES**
117 Osmena St., Cabuyao Laguna
License: 28554 Amo: Alejandro P. Trinos Org Type: Sole Proprietorship Primary Classification: General Building

□ **GONZALO CONSTRUCTION**
MA-25, Puguis, La Trinidad, La Trinidad Benguet
Contact Number/s : 422-2341
License: 1826 Amo: Domingo N. Gonzalo Org Type: Sole Proprietorship Primary Classification: General Building

□ **GOSSET BUILDERS INC.**
#277 Sto. Rosario St., Plainview Mandaluyong CPO Mandaluyong
Contact Number/s : 534-9436
License: 25248 Amo: Edgar Daniel O. Dycoco Org Type: Corporation Primary Classification: General Building

□ **GOTESCO CONSTRUCTION & DEVELOPMENT CORP.**
5/f Ever-Gotesco Corporate Center Bilibid Viejo St., Gil Puyat Quiapo Manila
License: 29978 Amo: Michael L. Go Org Type: Corporation Primary Classification: General Building

□ **GRAS BUILDERS, INC.**
Unit 1 & 2, 2nd-F, Kenwood Bldg., 8272 Dasa, Paranaque City Para?aque
Contact Number/s : 826-2622/17
License: 23232 Amo: Rolando C. De Guzman Org Type: Corporation Primary Classification: General Building

□ **GREAT WALL CONSTRUCTION SUPPLY**
Gomez Extension, Red-V., Lucena City Quezon Province
Contact Number/s : 710-2458
License: 7600 Amo: Ignacio T. Tan, Jr. Org Type: Sole Proprietorship Primary Classification: General Building

□ **GREMA CONSTRUCTION & DEVELOPMENT CORPORATION**
#9 Gen. Luna St., G.B.1, San Mateo Rizal
Contact Number/s : 913-6247
License: 2940 Amo: Gregorio F. Manahan Org Type: Corporation Primary Classification: General Engineering

□ **GRL ELECTRIC CORPORATION**
Rm. 6 & 7 Framel Bldg., 676 EDSA, Cubao Quezon City
Contact Number/s : 9123464
License: 24375 Amo: Pablito R. Freo Org Type: Corporation Primary Classification: Electrical Work

□ **H.S. LOPEZ CONSTRUCTION & DEVELOPMENT**
#14 Walnut, Fairview Quezon City
Contact Number/s : none
License: 23781 Amo: Hiram S. Lopez, Jr. Org Type: Sole Proprietorship Primary Classification: General Building

□ **HANPHIL STEEL TOWER & STRUCTURE SPECIALIST CORP.**
2F CBC Bldg., Brgy. P. Tamo, Visayas Avenue Quezon City CPO Quezon City
Contact Number/s : 426-4494
License: 24366 Amo: Chu Poong Lee Org Type: Corporation Primary Classification: General Engineering

□ **HEAVEN'S GATE CONSTRUCTION & EQUIPMENT RENTALS, INC.**
#202 Banlat Road, Tandang Sora Quezon City
Contact Number/s : 456-8900
License: 16980 Amo: Luis Uy Lim Org Type: Corporation Primary Classification: General Building

□ **HI-SPEED CONSTRUCTION CORPORATION**
800 A.S. Fortuna Street Mandaue City Cebu
Contact Number/s : 3460113
License: 5393 Amo: John P. Young Org Type: Corporation Primary Classification: General Building

□ **HITEK GROUP, INC.**
3/F, Christine's Bldg., #9 Sampaguita St., Pembo, Fort Bonifacio (Camp) Makati
Contact Number/s : 728-7626
License: 28078 Amo: Florencio S. Atanacio Org Type: Corporation Primary Classification: General Engineering

□ **HONEYVILLE CONSTRUCTION**
San Isidro Magarao Camarines Sur
Contact Number/s : 4735170
License: 14290 Amo: Eden A. Lee Org Type: Sole Proprietorship Primary Classification: General Engineering

□ **HORAMABI BUILDERS**
Emerald cor. Jade Sts., Taglesville Subd., San Jose, Balanga Bataan
Contact Number/s : 237-2887
License: 24129 Amo: Renedel R. Mendoza Org Type: Sole Proprietorship Primary Classification: General Building

□ **HPL CONSTRUCTION AND GENERAL SERVICES, INC.**
97, 4th St., 6th Avenue, Grace Park, Kalookan City CPO Kalookan City (South)
Contact Number/s : 3654296/97
License: 28632 Amo: Romeo C. Cheng Org Type: Corporation Primary Classification: General Building

□ **HR CONSTRUCTION CORPORATION**
Unit A-8, Plaza de Luisa, Ramon Magsaysay Ave., Davao C. Davao City
Contact Number/s : 224-2339
License: 18897 Amo: Willy T. Ho Org Type: Corporation Primary Classification: General Engineering

□ **HUANG CONSTRUCTION CORPORATION**
22 Rizal Street, Palanginan Iba Zambales
Contact Number/s : 047-8111362
License: 14248 Amo: Ofelia I. Huang Org Type: Corporation Primary Classification: General Engineering

□ **HVC SAGITTARIUS COMMERCIAL AND CONSTRUCTION**
Morales Ave., Gen. Paulino Santos Koronadal South Cotobato
Contact Number/s : 2282720
License: 12954 Amo: Violeta L. Cumbe Org Type: Sole Proprietorship Primary Classification: General Engineering

□ **I.A. BOSQUE CONSTRUCTION CORP.**
Camia St., Capistrano Subd., Lucena City Quezon Province
Contact Number/s : 373-4008
License: 12597 Amo: Edgardo G. Alcayde Org Type: Corporation Primary Classification: General Engineering

□ **ILIGAN ROD AND BAR MILL CORPORATION**
Suarez, Iligan City Iligan City
Contact Number/s : 221-1762
License: 13316 Amo: Licerio E. Gedalanga Org Type: Corporation Primary Classification: Electrical Work

□ **IMMACON CONSTRUCTION AND DEVELOPMENT CORPORATION**
No. 12 West Drive, Marikina Heights, Marikina, Metro Manila Marikina
Contact Number/s : 948-5358/59
License: 20866 Amo: Mario Z. Bagunu Org Type: Corporation Primary Classification: General Building

□ **INPHASE INDUSTRIAL - CONSTRUCT, INC.**
#215 & 217 Mayfair St., Montevista Park Subd., Ortigas Avenue Ext. Cainta Rizal
Contact Number/s : 656-7642/240-2068/655-3732
License: 19747 Amo: Ruperto B. Rejas, Jr. Org Type: Corporation Primary Classification: Electrical Work

□ **INTEGRITY BUILDERS, INC.**
74 15th Ave., Cor. Main Ave., Murphy, Quezon City Quezon City

Contact Number/s : 912-1102/03
License: 7310 Amo: Francisco H. Lim Org Type: Corporation Primary Classification: General Engineering

INTERFACE INDUSTRIAL CORPORATION
1679 Dian St., Makati City Makati
Contact Number/s : 843-6621
License: 11454 Amo: Edward L. Mendoza Org Type: Corporation Primary Classification: Electrical Work

ISH CONSTRUCTION
38 Carmina Drive, South Green Park Subd., Project 6 Quezon City
Contact Number/s : 9277981
License: 15757 Amo: Imelberto S. Hollero Org Type: Sole Proprietorship Primary Classification: General Building

J & A PIMENTEL CONSTRUCTION
Tello St. Bongtod Tandag Surigao del Sur
License: 7953 Amo: Johnny T. Pimentel Org Type: Sole Proprietorship Primary Classification: General Engineering

J. C. BOLOS CONSTRUCTION CORPORATION
#12 Saint John Street, Perpetual Village Taguig
Contact Number/s : 837-9901 - 04
License: 29750 Amo: Jose C. Bolos, Jr. Org Type: Corporation Primary Classification: General Building

J. TY CONSTRUCTION AND DEVELOPMENT CORPORATION
1596 Maharlika Road, San Jose City Nueva Ecija
Contact Number/s : (044) 511-4135
License: 14250 Amo: Juanito L. Ty Org Type: Corporation Primary Classification: General Engineering

J.B.S. CONSTRUCTION, INCORPORATED
No. 86, Dr. Alejos St., Sta. Mesa Hts., Quezon City Quezon City
Contact Number/s : 731-1032
License: 679 Amo: Jose B. Sahagun Org Type: Corporation Primary Classification: General Engineering

J.D. MACAPAGAL CONSTRUCTION, INC.
#52 Kalayaan Ave. Quezon City Quezon City
Contact Number/s : 9224395/96
License: 1093 Amo: Julito D. Macapagal Org Type: Corporation Primary Classification: General Building

J.E. CAINA CONSTRUCTION
21st -27th Sts., Nazareth Subdivision, Cagayan De Oro City
Contact Number/s : 728380
License: 21055 Amo: Jimmy E. Caina Org Type: Sole Proprietorship Primary Classification: General Building

J.O. CONSTRUCTION, INCORPORATED
19 Don Julio Florente St., Capitol Site Cebu City Cebu
Contact Number/s : 253-5651/255-4793
License: 10230 Amo: Jose Y. Ong Org Type: Corporation Primary Classification: General Engineering

J.Q.G. CONSTRUCTION
Jaral Building, Sto. Cristo, Tarlac Tarlac
Contact Number/s : 982-0311
License: 10530 Amo: Jose Q. De Guzman, Jr. Org Type: Sole Proprietorship Primary Classification: General Engineering

J.R. BATARA VENTURE
077 Amai-Manabilang St., Marawi City Lanao del Sur
Contact Number/s : 63520484
License: 27078 Amo: Abdul Hamed Batara, Jr. Org Type: Sole Proprietorship Primary Classification: General Engineering

J.W.D. CONSTRUCTION
Brgy. Tigbakin, Atimonan Quezon Province

Contact Number/s : 316-5205
License: 22291 Amo: Wilson S. Dasig Org Type: Sole Proprietorship Primary Classification: General Engineering

□ **JAIME M. STA. MARIA CONSTRUCTION**
No.24 Pangilinan St., Friendly Village Concepcion Marikina
Contact Number/s : 941-8478
License: 2845 Amo: Jaime M. Sta. Maria Org Type: Sole Proprietorship Primary Classification: General Engineering

□ **JALSE CONSTRUCTION**
Corrales - Fernandez St., Cagayan de Oro City Misamis Oriental
Contact Number/s : 72-40-87
License: 13839 Amo: Antonio E. Dela Cruz Org Type: Sole Proprietorship Primary Classification: General Engineering

□ **JAMIKAR CONSTRUCTION**
Rm. 207 GJ Building, 385 Quezon Ave., Quezon City Quezon City
Contact Number/s : 3717805
License: 20512 Amo: Alfredo L. Salazar, Jr. Org Type: Sole Proprietorship Primary Classification: General Engineering

□ **JAYA BUILDERS**
Datu Halun St., Bongao Tawi-tawi
Contact Number/s : 0918-9127200
License: 18452 Amo: Ellen N. Ho Org Type: Sole Proprietorship Primary Classification: General Building

□ **JC LEE CONSTRUCTION**
39-21ST St., West Bajac-Bajac, Olongapo City Zambales
Contact Number/s : 223-4669
License: 14550 Amo: Jose Co Lee Org Type: Sole Proprietorship Primary Classification: General Building

□ **JCL BUILDERS**
239 EJ BLANCO EXT., DARO DUMAGUETE CITY Negros Oriental
Contact Number/s : 225-5844
License: 11538 Amo: Jesus C. Lacson Org Type: Sole Proprietorship Primary Classification: General Engineering

□ **JEFRECO REALTY AND CONSTRUCTION COMPANY, LTD.**
14 Engineer""s Hill, Baguio City Benguet
Contact Number/s : 442-3209
License: 17473 Amo: Jefferson B. Cosalan Org Type: Partnership Primary Classification: General Engineering

□ **JEPA CONST. & DEV. CORP.**
20-A Maginhawa St., UP Vill., Quezon City Quezon City
Contact Number/s : 435-9186
License: 28730 Amo: Rey C. Tibayan Org Type: Corporation Primary Classification: General Engineering

□ **JESI CONSTRUCTION**
#8 Alicia Road, Brgy. 1, Poblacion, San Mateo Isabela
Contact Number/s : 078-6642577
License: 25137 Amo: Bartolome R. Valderama Org Type: Sole Proprietorship Primary Classification: General Engineering

□ **JM FELICIANO CONSTRUCTION**
Mac-arthur Highway, Ninabel Subd., Dau Mabalacat Pampanga
Contact Number/s : 045-3314527
License: 24936 Amo: Jose M. Feliciano, Jr. Org Type: Sole Proprietorship Primary Classification: General Building

□ **JMBOZA BUILDERS & CONSTRUCTION SUPPLY**
Badelles St., Iligan City Iligan City
Contact Number/s : none
License: 26883 Amo: Jose Ma. L. Boza Org Type: Sole Proprietorship Primary Classification: General Engineering

□ **JMG CONSTRUCTION & SUPPLY**
#21 Ancheta Street, San Fernando La Union
Contact Number/s : none

License: 11586 Amo: Edgardo A. Ganaden Org Type: Sole Proprietorship Primary Classification: General Building

JOAN CONSTRUCTION
088-B Surdilla Compound, Camino Nuevo Zamboanga City Zamboanga del Sur
Contact Number/s : 085-3411551/288-9489
License: 13840 Amo: Cornelio I. Macoto Org Type: Sole Proprietorship Primary Classification: General Engineering

JOHNDORF VENTURES CORPORATION
Two Corner Benito Ong. St., Pala-o, Iligan City Lanao del Norte
Contact Number/s : 063-2213365
License: 26677 Amo: Richard Dy Lim Org Type: Corporation Primary Classification: General Engineering

JOUBERT CONSTRUCTION, INC.
Rm. 406 Chateau Verde Condo., Pasig CPO Pasig City
Contact Number/s : 8189066
License: 12643 Amo: Roberto Y. Ponciano, Jr. Org Type: Corporation Primary Classification: General Building

JPM CAVAT CONSTRUCTION
#515 Gov. Forbes St., cor. Alcantara St. Sampaloc Manila
Contact Number/s : 732-0742
License: 24096 Amo: Jose T. Macadaeg, Jr. Org Type: Sole Proprietorship Primary Classification: General Engineering

JSG CONSTRUCTION COMPANY, INC.
Mataas Na Kahoy, Batangas City Batangas
Contact Number/s : 043-7560887
License: 9350 Amo: Judy S. Gardiola Org Type: Corporation Primary Classification: General Engineering

JSU CONSTRUCTION AND DEVELOPMENT
V. Gustillo Street, San Carlos City Negros Occidental
Contact Number/s : 343125133

License: 20726 Amo: Johnson S. Uy Org Type: Sole Proprietorship Primary Classification: General Engineering

JUTLAND CONSTRUCTION & TRADING
16 Anonas St., Greenpark, Cainta Rizal
Contact Number/s : 851-0339
License: 28018 Amo: Rolando P. Juta Org Type: Sole Proprietorship Primary Classification: General Building

JV LAGON CONSTRUCTION CORPORATION
Lagon Compound, National Highway Tacurong City South Cotobato
Contact Number/s : 083-5535501/805-4310
License: 11561 Amo: Jose V. Lagon, Sr. Org Type: Corporation Primary Classification: General Engineering

KAWATETSU ELECTRICAL & MECHANICAL TECHNOLOGIES CORPORATION
Rm. 308 Hanston Bldg. Emerald Ave., Ortigas, Pasig CPO Pasig City
Contact Number/s : 914-3163/64
License: 23461 Amo: Gabriel B. Evangelista Org Type: Corporation Primary Classification: Mechanical Work

KISAN LU REALTY, INCORPORATED
KLR Group Bldg., San Pablo St., Davao City Davao City
Contact Number/s : 2213600
License: 22568 Amo: Kisan D. Lu Org Type: Corporation Primary Classification: General Engineering

KNC CONSTRUCTION AND DEVELOPMENT CORP.
Su 1110, Jolibee Plaza, Emerald Ave., Pasig City Pasig
Contact Number/s : 638-5373
License: 28165 Amo: Anthony B. Tanyag Org Type: Corporation Primary Classification: General Engineering

KONSTRAK INTERNATIONAL, INC.

No.2 Dagohoy St., Melitona Subd., Project 4 Quezon City
Contact Number/s : 4385110/11-12
License: 15086 Amo: Danilo M. Relucio Org Type: Corporation Primary Classification: General Engineering

□ **KORONA CONSTRUCTION**
102 Lacson St., Bacolod City Bacolod City
Contact Number/s : 495-2352
License: 10281 Amo: Ciro Y. King Org Type: Sole Proprietorship Primary Classification: General Building

□ **KRISTI CONSTRUCTION**
Km. 38 Pulong Buhangin Santa Maria Bulacan Province
Contact Number/s : 0919-5736423
License: 10233 Amo: Emmanuel C. Gener Org Type: Sole Proprietorship Primary Classification: General Engineering

□ **KV CONSTRUCTION AND SUPPLY**
Villagracia Apartment, Mercedes Rd., Daet Camarines Norte
Contact Number/s : 054-7212794
License: 17509 Amo: Efren L. Villamonte Org Type: Sole Proprietorship Primary Classification: General Building

□ **KWIKBUILT CONSTRUCTION**
2/F Rm. 240 Plaza City Mall, Plaza Mart Bldg., San Juan St., Bacolod City Negros Occidental
Contact Number/s : 034-4349249
License: 24577 Amo: Miguel M. Carriedo Org Type: Sole Proprietorship Primary Classification: General Engineering

□ **L - BETHS CONSTRUCTION**
1617 Upper Buntung Camaman-an, Cagayan de Oro City Misamis Oriental
Contact Number/s : 857-4923
License: 27165 Amo: Richard T. Bodiongan Org Type: Sole Proprietorship Primary Classification: General Engineering

□ **L W V CONSTRUCTION CORPORATION**
157 EDSA Mandaluyong CPO Mandaluyong
Contact Number/s : 725-3466
License: 29751 Amo: Miguel P. Robleza Org Type: Corporation Primary Classification: General Building

□ **L. LEGASPI CONSTRUCTION & DEVELOPMENT**
Rm.301 Executive Center, Sen Gil Puyat Makati CPO (inc. Buendia up to Edsa) Makati
Contact Number/s : 897-0927/899-6111
License: 28459 Amo: Lauro M. Legaspi Org Type: Sole Proprietorship Primary Classification: General Engineering

□ **LANSANG CONSTRUCTION**
46 Remuda St., Rancho Estate Marikina City Marikina
Contact Number/s : 9419723
License: 3430 Amo: Jovito L. Lansang Org Type: Sole Proprietorship Primary Classification: General Engineering

□ **LECO BUILDERS AND DEVELOPERS**
#1 Margarita St., cor. Carmen Ave. Bacolod City Negros Occidental
Contact Number/s : 433-0405
License: 13215 Amo: Wilfred Chan Ong Org Type: Sole Proprietorship Primary Classification: General Building

□ **LGC TRUCKING AND CONSTRUCTION**
006 PILI DRIVE, GUINGONA SUBD., BUTUAN CITY
Contact Number/s : 342-9242
License: 14464 Amo: Loreto Gaborno Chiu Org Type: Sole Proprietorship Primary Classification: General Engineering

□ **LIGAO STO. NINO CONSTRUCTION**
San Jose St., Dunao Ligao City Albay
Contact Number/s : 4808079
License: 9279 Amo: Ruben P. Quililan Org Type: Sole Proprietorship Primary Classification: General Engineering

□ **LIM GENERAL CONTRACTOR**
Pinamarbuhan, Mobo Masbate
Contact Number/s : 333-2253

License: 8482 Amo: Alejandro C. Lim, Jr. Org Type: Sole Proprietorship Primary Classification: General Engineering

 LIVING ROCK CONSTRUCTION INCORPORATED
Living Rock Compound, Telabastagan, San Fernando Pampanga
Contact Number/s : 045-9611632
License: 15087 Amo: Nelson D. Torres Org Type: Corporation Primary Classification: General Building

 LORO CONSTRUCTION
San Isidro Village, San Isidro Talisay Cebu
Contact Number/s : 273-1996
License: 11359 Amo: Romeo P. Cabading Org Type: Sole Proprietorship Primary Classification: General Engineering

 LUCKY STAR DRILLING AND CONSTRUCTION CORPORATION
21 Mapagbigay St. cor. Matiaga, V. Luna Diliman Quezon City
Contact Number/s : 9220772
License: 22258 Amo: Joseph Dexter L. Cuizon Org Type: Corporation Primary Classification: Well Drilling Work

 LVF CONSTRUCTION & DEVELOPMENT CORPORATION
243-B Rosario Bldg., Roosevelt Avenue, Quezon City Quezon City
Contact Number/s : 411-5043/40
License: 13876 Amo: Cy Lion Chuan Org Type: Corporation Primary Classification: General Building

 M & B MALIGAYA CONSTRUCTION
San Miguel Sto. Tomas Batangas
Contact Number/s : 778-35-54
License: 12185 Amo: Ma. Baylon D. Maligaya Org Type: Sole Proprietorship Primary Classification: General Engineering

 M D C L INTEGRATED CONSTRUCTION & ALLIED SERVICES CORPORATION
Rm. 209 R. Liwag Bldg. 1258 Batangas St. Makati Cit y Makati
Contact Number/s : 844-2237
License: 13327 Amo: Mario B. Libang Org Type: Corporation Primary Classification: Mechanical Work

 M. P. CALDEO CONSTRUCTION, INC.
2063 F.B. Harrison St., Pasay City Pasay
Contact Number/s : 832-3470
License: 19014 Amo: Mario P. Caldeo Org Type: Corporation Primary Classification: General Building

 M.B. GANIGAN CONSTRUCTION
21 St Claire St. Villa Lourdes Sub. Violago Hms. phll Bry. Culiat V.A Tandang Sora Quezon City
Contact Number/s : 920-8817
License: 30027 Amo: Mariberth Baitan Ganigan Org Type: Sole Proprietorship Primary Classification: General Building

 M.J. SANTOS CONSTRUCTION
No.1, Axtell Street cor. Adrian St., Fairview North Quezon City
Contact Number/s : 417-0351
License: 23058 Amo: Marcelo J. Santos Org Type: Sole Proprietorship Primary Classification: General Engineering

 M.L. PANGANIBAN CONSTRUCTION CORPORATION
29 San Agustin St., Capitol 8 Subd., Pasig City
Contact Number/s : 671-1567
License: 24824 Amo: Ma. Lenore N. Panganiban Org Type: Corporation Primary Classification: General Engineering

 M.W. HERMOGENES CONS., INC. (Formely: M.W. Hermogenes Construction)
Gulod, Pulong Buhangin, Santa Maria Bulacan Province
Contact Number/s : 0919-8372698
License: 18458 Amo: Melchor Wong Hermogenes Org Type: Corporation Primary Classification: General Engineering

☐ **M2 - VC BUILDERS AND TRADING CO.**
Villa Barrosa Phase II Dao St.,Dolores San Fernando Pampanga
License: 30014 Amo: Marvin Lising Marzan Org Type: Partnership Primary Classification: General Building

☐ **MACMAC ENTERPRISES**
20 B. Morada Avenue, Lipa City Batangas
Contact Number/s : 043-7561081
License: 24071 Amo: Paulina P. Hernandez Org Type: Sole Proprietorship Primary Classification: Electrical Work

☐ **MAMSAR ENTERPRISES AGRO-INDUSTRIAL CORPORATION**
Camague Hi-way, Tubod Iligan City
Contact Number/s : 2213345
License: 15885 Amo: Manuel C. Dasmarinas, Jr. Org Type: Corporation Primary Classification: General Building

☐ **MANPOWER CONSTRUCTION AND DEVELOPMENT CORPORATION**
Su. 205 Sunrise Condo., Ortigas Ave., San Juan CPO San Juan
Contact Number/s : 7213462
License: 8839 Amo: Rodello H. Santos Org Type: Corporation Primary Classification: General Building

☐ **MAR-DEB CONSTRUCTION & DEVELOPMENT**
Magdalena Cabatuan Isabela
Contact Number/s : 786648018
License: 6715 Amo: Mario P. Dela Fuente Org Type: Sole Proprietorship Primary Classification: General Engineering

☐ **MARIGOLD DEVELOPMENT CORPORATION**
20 Kapiligan St., Brgy Dona Imelda, Quezon City CPO Quezon City
Contact Number/s : 715-1174/75
License: 4707 Amo: Apollo Y. Chua Org Type: Corporation Primary Classification: General Building

☐ **MARK 8 PROFILE BUILDERS, INC.**
Diversion Road, Pawing, Palo, Leyte Leyte
Contact Number/s : 323-8160
License: 29429 Amo: Miguel F. Mercado Org Type: Corporation Primary Classification: General Engineering

☐ **MARK CONSTRUCTION CORPORATION**
1320 Quezon Avenue, Quezon City CPO Quezon City
Contact Number/s : 373-0740/42
License: 5859 Amo: Jaime MA Flores Org Type: Corporation Primary Classification: General Engineering

☐ **MARTIN ENGINEERING & CONSTRUCTION**
Castellano San Leonardo Nueva Ecija
Contact Number/s : 044-4684848
License: 17031 Amo: Roberto C. Martin Org Type: Sole Proprietorship Primary Classification: General Engineering

☐ **MAVIMA GROUP INCORPORATED**
Su.307 Medalla Bldg., #596 EDSA cor. Mc-Arthur Ave., Araneta Ctr., Q.C Quezon City
Contact Number/s : 9116997
License: 15056 Amo: Romeo B. Vinco Org Type: Corporation Primary Classification: General Building

☐ **MAYFLOWER CONSTRUCTION, INC.**
Km 78, Mc Arthur Highway, Brgy. Saguin, San Fernando Pampanga
Contact Number/s : 045-9634427
License: 11302 Amo: Adrian R. Briones Org Type: Corporation Primary Classification: General Engineering

☐ **MBC CONSTRUCTION**
Villa Sta. Maria Subd., Zamboanga City Zamboanga del Sur
Contact Number/s : 9917494/744-2961
License: 6682 Amo: Mario B. Capistrano Org Type: Sole Proprietorship Primary Classification: General Engineering

 MCT CONSTRUCTION AND DEVELOPMENT
Calle David, Ligtasan, Tarlac Tarlac
Contact Number/s : 9821982
License: 6596 Amo: Marcelino C. Tan Org Type: Sole Proprietorship Primary Classification: General Building

 MEDITECH TRADE & DEVELOPMENT
178 Barcelona St., San Juan
Contact Number/s : 7252634
License: 16545 Amo: John T. Tansipek Org Type: Sole Proprietorship Primary Classification: General Building

 MEGILA CONSTRUCTION DEVELOPMENT AND SUPPLY
96 A. Bonifacio St., Davao City Davao del Sur
Contact Number/s : 082-2264672
License: 19262 Amo: Gerardo G. Abrera Org Type: Sole Proprietorship Primary Classification: General Engineering

 MERCADO CONCRETE PRODUCTS
Managa, Lawaan II, Talisay Cebu
Contact Number/s : 255-6910
License: 4898 Amo: Nenito G. Mercado Org Type: Sole Proprietorship Primary Classification: General Engineering

 METRO AMPERE CONSTRUCTION INC.
74 P. Cruz St., Brgy. New Zaniga Mandaluyong CPO Mandaluyong
Contact Number/s : 418-6477
License: 23521 Amo: Manuel S. Hernandez Org Type: Corporation Primary Classification: Electrical Work

 MI-2 CONS. & DEV. CORP.
Lot 8 Blk 73 del Rosario Street, BF Resort Las Pi?as CPO Las Pi?
Contact Number/s : 083-2282335
License: 29393 Amo: Gregory J. Bautista Org Type: Corporation Primary Classification: General Engineering

 MILCRETE CORPORATION
S507 Richville Corp. Ctr. 1314 Commerce Ave. Madrigal Buss Park, Ayala Alabang P.O. Boxes Muntinlupa
Contact Number/s : 8074292
License: 26884 Amo: Emilio M. Espejo, Jr. Org Type: Corporation Primary Classification: Concrete Pre-casting and Pre-stressing Work

 MINDANAO ORIENTAL BUILDERS, INCORPORATED
59 Apollo St., Macasandig, Cagayan De Oro City Misamis Oriental
Contact Number/s : 8822727914
License: 5513 Amo: Jose B. Adriano Org Type: Corporation Primary Classification: General Engineering

 MISTER CONCRETE BUILDERS
Platinum 2000 Suite 1401, No. 7 Annapolis St., Greenhills Greenhills PO San Juan
Contact Number/s : 722-7448/722-7449
License: 27422 Amo: Emma S. Dionisio Org Type: Sole Proprietorship Primary Classification: General Engineering

 MOONDRAGON CONSTRUCTORS CORPORATION
3862 Masikap St. Bacood Sta. Mesa Manila
Contact Number/s : 642-6068
License: 21675 Amo: William C. Que Org Type: Corporation Primary Classification: General Engineering

 M-PRO INDUSTRIAL CONSTRUCTION CORPORATION
#470 (B11 L24) Romans cor. Genesis Sts., Adelina I San Pedro Laguna
Contact Number/s : 868-7124/31
License: 18994 Amo: Marcelo P. Rodelas Org Type: Corporation Primary Classification: Electrical Work

 MT. APO CONSTRUCTION
011 Labastida St., Kidapawan City Cotabato
Contact Number/s : 288-1722
License: 12183 Amo: Renato O. Rebong Org Type: Sole Proprietorship Primary Classification: General Engineering

□ **M-TRI-R CONSTRUCTION & TRADING CORPORATION**
#65 Gen. Luna st., Brgy. Banaba, San Mateo Rizal
License: 16541 Amo: Roberto T. Figueroa Org Type: Corporation Primary Classification: General Engineering

□ **MUGEN COMPANY**
19-C Germany St., Betterliving Subd., Para?aque CPO Para?aque
Contact Number/s : 821-7539
License: 28162 Amo: Nelson R. Cartagena Org Type: Partnership Primary Classification: General Engineering

□ **MYUNG SIN CONSTRUCTION PHILS., INC.**
81-Dr. A. Santos Ave., Sucat Para?aque CPO Para?aque
License: 29648 Amo: Noel Calma Sampang Org Type: Corporation Primary Classification: Electrical Work

□ **N SQUARE CONSTRUCTION**
Paligui, Apalit Pampanga
Contact Number/s : 045-3026616/931-8389
License: 8752 Amo: Emmanuel R. Nulud Org Type: Sole Proprietorship Primary Classification: General Engineering

□ **N.C. BINAG CONSTRUCTION**
Calamagui 2nd, Ilagan Isabela
Contact Number/s : 622-3211
License: 6436 Amo: Noel C. Binag Org Type: Sole Proprietorship Primary Classification: General Engineering

□ **NAIGAI PHILS., INC.**
Unit 2002-B, 20/F, Security Bank Center, 6776 Ayala Ave. Makati City Makati
Contact Number/s : 891-1162
License: 27087 Amo: Ely T. Juano Org Type: Corporation Primary Classification: General Engineering

□ **NELSON S. LEE CONSTRUCTION**
Don Anselmo, Bernad Avenue Ozamis City Ozamis City
Contact Number/s : 088-5210484
License: 6880 Amo: Nelson S. Lee Org Type: Sole Proprietorship Primary Classification: General Engineering

□ **NEW ELI DE MAYO, INC.**
Malapat, Cordon Isabela
License: 22378 Amo: Pastor S. Gamit Org Type: Corporation Primary Classification: General Engineering

□ **NINE DRAGON'S ENTERPRISES**
Jenny's Ave. cor. Francisco Legazpi St. Pasig City Manila
Contact Number/s : 643-8976
License: 29483 Amo: Felomena Deborah Y. Yam Org Type: Sole Proprietorship Primary Classification: General Building

□ **NOR-MARC BUILDERS & DEVELOPMENT CORPORATION**
Unit 206 PARC Chateau Condo. Ortigas Complex, Pasig City Pasig
Contact Number/s : 631-5785
License: 14013 Amo: Lita Marcos Roque Org Type: Corporation Primary Classification: General Engineering

□ **NORTHWELL CORPORATION**
105 Chico Street, Project 2 Quezon City
Contact Number/s : 433-8079
License: 16703 Amo: Eulogio I. Bautista, Jr. Org Type: Corporation Primary Classification: General Building

□ **O. U. A. CONSTRUCTION**
San Fermin Cauayan Isabela
Contact Number/s : 078-6345079
License: 18995 Amo: Orlando U. Agcaoili Org Type: Sole Proprietorship Primary Classification: General Engineering

□ **OBJECTS BUILDER FOR ASIA AND DEVELOPMENT CORPORATION**
2864 Finlandia St., Buendia, Makati CPO (inc. Buendia up to Edsa) Makati

Contact Number/s : 844-4368
License: 20902 Amo: Alexander E. Reyes Org Type: Corporation Primary Classification: General Engineering

□ **OCEANEERING CONTRACTORS (PHILIPPINES), INC.**
55 WASHINGTON ST., WERVILLE PARK Para?aque City Para?aque
Contact Number/s : 824-2353
License: 7643 Amo: Mariano R. Pedrigal Org Type: Corporation Primary Classification: General Engineering

□ **ONEL BUILDER RESOURCES**
1732 Pres. Quirino Ave., Ext., Pandacan, Manila Manila
Contact Number/s : 563-00-33
License: 25078 Amo: Omer S. Dela Torre Org Type: Sole Proprietorship Primary Classification: General Building

□ **ONOFRE I. BATANE CONSTRUCTION**
23 Pucay Road, Guisad Baguio City Benguet
Contact Number/s : 442-4910
License: 6300 Amo: Onofre I. Batane Org Type: Sole Proprietorship Primary Classification: General Engineering

□ **ORANI BUILDERS SUPPLY**
Arellano Avenue, Mulawin, Orani Bataan
Contact Number/s : 047-4311452
License: 5349 Amo: Antonio S. Vianzon Org Type: Sole Proprietorship Primary Classification: General Engineering

□ **ORIENT STAR CONSTRUCTION**
Roxas Mindoro Oriental
Contact Number/s : 043-2892116
License: 7183 Amo: Celia C. Manalo Org Type: Sole Proprietorship Primary Classification: General Engineering

□ **ORIENTAL SALES CENTER & CONTRACTOR**
1288 San Andres St., Cor. C. Tuazon, Malate Manila
Contact Number/s : 525-2243
License: 3816 Amo: Alberto D. Ong Org Type: Sole Proprietorship Primary Classification: General Building

□ **ORO VILLA BUILDERS MULTI-TRADING CO., INC.**
Lot 26 Blk 29, Andrew cor . Agabus Sts., Annex 35, Better Living Subd. Para?aque
License: 28911 Amo: Manuel P. Villasenor Jr. Org Type: Corporation Primary Classification: General Building

□ **P.C. BELL CORPORATION**
73 C. Tirona St., Poblacion Batangas City Batangas
Contact Number/s : 722-04-23
License: 29753 Amo: Paterno Curata Bell Org Type: Corporation Primary Classification: General Engineering

□ **P.M. MCCRANN CONSTRUCTION & TRADING**
333 Rosas St., Brgy. Margot Angeles City Pampanga
Contact Number/s : 045-3210129
License: 28126 Amo: Patrick M. Mccrann Org Type: Sole Proprietorship Primary Classification: General Building

□ **PACIFIC EAGLE CONSTRUCTION AND SUPPLY**
143 V. Sagun Ext""n., Balangasan Dist., Pagadian City Pagadian City
Contact Number/s : 214-2292
License: 23646 Amo: Damian G. Mercado Org Type: Sole Proprietorship Primary Classification: General Engineering

□ **PACIFICO AUSTRIA & SONS (ARCHITECTS/ENGINEERS/CONTRACTOR S)**
23 Scout Limbaga St., Laging Handa Quezon City CPO Quezon City
Contact Number/s : 932-5385
License: 30073 Amo: Luisito Madlangbayan Austria Org Type: Sole Proprietorship Primary Classification: General Engineering

PALAFOX CONSTRUCTION
19 Dinar St., Pasong Tamo, Quezon City CPO Quezon City
Contact Number/s : 931-7135
License: 18424 Amo: Facundo O. Palafox, Jr. Org Type: Sole Proprietorship Primary Classification: General Engineering

PAMBATO CONSTRUCTION & DEVELOPMENT CORP.
03 Calaylayan, Abucay Bataan
License: 29889 Amo: Teodoro Parrera Santiago Org Type: Corporation Primary Classification: General Building

PAP INSTRUMENTATION SUPPLIER SALES & SERVICES
Villa Mariquita Subd., Nasugbu Batangas
Contact Number/s : 9175343796
License: 27468 Amo: Pedro A. Perez Org Type: Sole Proprietorship Primary Classification: General Engineering

PARIS-MANILA TECHNOLOGY CORPORATION
Pamatec Bldg., #81 EDSA, Mandaluyong City Mandaluyong
Contact Number/s : 531-4841/44
License: 17964 Amo: Hubert D'Aboville Org Type: Corporation Primary Classification: Electrical Work

PARTAK BUILDERS
#56 Balzain Street, Tuguegarao Cagayan
Contact Number/s : 8441260
License: 17657 Amo: Ricardo H. Chua Org Type: Sole Proprietorship Primary Classification: General Engineering

PETER A. LUCIANO CONSTRUCTION
San Gabriel, Santa Maria Bulacan Province
Contact Number/s : 044-6410262
License: 7096 Amo: Peter A. Luciano Org Type: Sole Proprietorship Primary Classification: General Engineering

PHILIPPINE IRON CONSTRUCTION & MARINE WORKS, INC.
728 Pedro Gil St., Malate Manila
Contact Number/s : 5238191/95
License: 1328 Amo: Rodolfo A. Carillo Org Type: Corporation Primary Classification: General Building

PHILMARK CONSTRUCTION
53 Jacob Ext., Naga City Naga City
Contact Number/s : 473-3314
License: 8913 Amo: Romeo A. Enrile Org Type: Sole Proprietorship Primary Classification: General Engineering

PHILNUGGET CONSTRUCTION
127 Mabini Street, Tarlac, Tarlac Tarlac
Contact Number/s : 982-06-07
License: 9576 Amo: Wilfredo N. Ong Org Type: Sole Proprietorship Primary Classification: General Engineering

PHILWAYS CONST. & DEV. CORP.
121 Congressional Rd., Maderan Gen. Mariano Alvarez Cavite
Contact Number/s : 046-9720969
License: 26529 Amo: Ceferino B. Servano Org Type: Corporation Primary Classification: General Engineering

PHINTECSTAR CONSTRUCTION INCORPORATED
Su. 24 3J Heights Bldg., 35 Visayas Ave. Diliman Quezon City
Contact Number/s : 9247251/54
License: 14542 Amo: Zoilo Joaquin A. Amador Org Type: Corporation Primary Classification: General Building

PICK AND SHOVEL, INCORPORATED
296 Santolan Road San Juan CPO San Juan
Contact Number/s : 7220116
License: 1141 Amo: Dianito I. Iso Org Type: Corporation Primary Classification: General Engineering

PILES AND DEEP FOUNDATIONS EXPERTS, INC.
1116 Prince Plaza II, 101 Dela Rosa St. Legaspi Village Makati

Contact Number/s : 813-7123
License: 29526 Amo: Reynaldo A. Maliwat Org Type: Corporation Primary Classification: General Engineering

PILING & FOUNDATIONS CONTRACTORS CORP.
29 Sampaguita Street, UPS-IV, Sucat, Para?aque CPO Para?aque
Contact Number/s : 8127040
License: 23647 Amo: Dionisio S. Geron Org Type: Corporation Primary Classification: General Engineering

POWER DIMENSION, INCORPORATED
10-B Malvar St., Project 4 Quezon City
Contact Number/s : none
License: 28036 Amo: Clyde S. Nebres Org Type: Corporation Primary Classification: Electrical Work

POWERSTAR, INCORPORATED
#9, 5th Camarilla St., Murphy Cubao Quezon City
Contact Number/s : 9119343/9133470-71
License: 24937 Amo: Pedro A. Errasquin Org Type: Corporation Primary Classification: Electrical Work

PREMIUM BUILDERS CORPORATION
2/F SM OSIN Bldg., Montilla Bldg., Butuan City Agusan del Norte
Contact Number/s : 085-3417800
License: 22374 Amo: Oscar P. Lagua Org Type: Corporation Primary Classification: General Building

PRESAM CONSTRUCTION & GENERAL SERVICES, INC.
875-B, Kagitingan St., Tondo Manila
Contact Number/s : 6465518
License: 25613 Amo: Archimedes A. Cruz Org Type: Corporation Primary Classification: General Building

PRIMAVERA INT'L. CONSTRUCTION CORPORATION
195 B. Concepcion St., Buting Pasig CPO Pasig City
Contact Number/s : 6411619
License: 22110 Amo: Tito T. Cua Org Type: Corporation Primary Classification: General Engineering

PYRACRETE CONSTRUCTION
Magsaysay Ave., Singcang, Bacolod City, Negros Occ. Bacolod City
Contact Number/s : 4330845
License: 27606 Amo: Alberto C. Wong Org Type: Sole Proprietorship Primary Classification: General Engineering

QUEST-AIR TECHNOLOGY PHILS. INC.
U-402 Sycamore Bldg I Alabang-Zapote Rd. Alabang, Muntinglupa Muntinlupa
Contact Number/s : 8508007/13
License: 28609 Amo: Arturo I. Robles, Jr. Org Type: Corporation Primary Classification: Mechanical Work

R R C CONSTRUCTION
Roxas Isabela
Contact Number/s : 642-8026
License: 24369 Amo: Reynaldo R. Chua Org Type: Sole Proprietorship Primary Classification: General Engineering

R. RIGUERA CONSTRUCTION, INCORPORATED
Manuela Bldg. I, Pamplona Las Pi?as CPO Las Pi?
Contact Number/s : 872-1822 / 874-5338
License: 309 Amo: Robert H. Riguera Org Type: Corporation Primary Classification: General Building

R. ROCHA CONSTRUCTION
Panal Tabaco Albay
Contact Number/s : 052-487-4206
License: 11769 Amo: Raul R. Rocha Org Type: Sole Proprietorship Primary Classification: General Engineering

R. SEMILLA CONSTRUCTION AND MARKETING

Pioneer Drive, Bajada, Davao City Davao City
Contact Number/s : 227-2651
License: 9263 Amo: Roberto S. Semilla Org Type: Sole Proprietorship Primary Classification: General Engineering

R.A. MONTEALTO BUILDERS & TRADING
Brgy. Bugtong Lipas City Batangas
License: 29928 Amo: Raul Abrenica Montealto Org Type: Sole Proprietorship Primary Classification: General Building

R.A. PAHATI GRAVEL AND SAND
Liboton St., Naga City Camarines Sur
Contact Number/s : 472-4644
License: 22495 Amo: Rodolfo A. Pahati Org Type: Sole Proprietorship Primary Classification: General Engineering

R.C. PEKSON CONSTRUCTION
Dolores, San Fernando San Fernando Pampanga
Contact Number/s : 9616274
License: 24472 Amo: Raymundo C. Pekson Org Type: Sole Proprietorship Primary Classification: General Building

R.C. SOLEDAD CONSTRUCTION
208 Don Juan Rodriguez Sr., Davao City Davao City
Contact Number/s : 244-0056
License: 5614 Amo: Recto C. Soledad Org Type: Sole Proprietorship Primary Classification: General Engineering

R.F. DIAZ CONSTRUCTION
Katipunan Street Concepcion, Marikina City Marikina
Contact Number/s : 9414381
License: 3998 Amo: Rogelio F. Diaz Org Type: Sole Proprietorship Primary Classification: General Engineering

R.G. REYES BUILDERS & CONTRACTORS CORP.
8 Don Victorino St., Don Antonio Hts. Subd. Commonwealth Quezon City
Contact Number/s : 951-3463/65
License: 784 Amo: Reynaldo G. Reyes Org Type: Corporation Primary Classification: General Engineering

R.G. SALANATIN CONSTRUCTION
Atlantic Ave., Ecoland Phase 3, Matina Davao City Davao del Sur
Contact Number/s : 298-0135
License: 586 Amo: Remegio G. Salanatin Org Type: Sole Proprietorship Primary Classification: General Engineering

R.G. VILLANUEVA CONSTRUCTION
36 San Bernando St., San Joaquin Pasig City
Contact Number/s : 6411460
License: 22304 Amo: Renato G. Villanueva Org Type: Sole Proprietorship Primary Classification: General Engineering

R.K. MANZANO CONSTRUCTION
San Francisco, Nabua, Camarines Sur Camarines Sur
Contact Number/s : 2883624
License: 7335 Amo: Roger L. Manzano Org Type: Sole Proprietorship Primary Classification: General Engineering

R.M.L. BRAVO CONSTRUCTION
Araullo St., San Jose District, Pagadian City Zamboanga del Sur
Contact Number/s : 2151411
License: 13057 Amo: Romie M. Luy Org Type: Sole Proprietorship Primary Classification: General Engineering

R.T.C. CONSTRUCTION & CONSTRUCTION SUPPLIES
#73 Lopez Jaena Street Bacolod City Negros Occidental
Contact Number/s : 434-7679
License: 16259 Amo: Raul T. Chua Org Type: Sole Proprietorship Primary Classification: General Engineering

R-3 ENTERPRISES
No. 04 San Agustin, San Fernando, San Fernando Pampanga

Contact Number/s : 963-6913
License: 24839 Amo: Melencio S. Ramirez
Org Type: Sole Proprietorship Primary
Classification: General Engineering

RAGOJOS HERITAGE CONSTRUCTION CORPORATION
#407 Verde Oro Bldg., 535 Commonwealth Ave. Diliman Quezon City
License: 16885 Amo: Redentor D. Ragojos
Org Type: Corporation Primary Classification: General Building

RAISA CONSTRUCTION AND TRADING
San Eugenio, Aringay La Union
Contact Number/s : 072-7100502
License: 11832 Amo: Adelaida R. Juloya Org Type: Sole Proprietorship Primary Classification: General Engineering

RAM CONSTRUCTION PHILS., INC.
Km. 3, Libertad, Butuan City Agusan del Norte
Contact Number/s : 341-0002
License: 750 Amo: Joseph Y. Marasigan Org Type: Corporation Primary Classification: General Engineering

RAPOMAC CONSTRUCTION
28 St. Provident Vill. Tanong Marikina
License: 29929 Amo: Rafael Poblete Macalinao Org Type: Sole Proprietorship Primary Classification: General Engineering

RAYMUNDO H. TECSON CONSTRUCTION
Km. 8 Diversion Rd., Buhangin, Davao City Davao del Sur
Contact Number/s : 221-5233
License: 21681 Amo: Raymundo H. Tecson
Org Type: Sole Proprietorship Primary
Classification: General Engineering

RECON CONSTRUCTION
998-A A. Corea St., Tabacalera Compound Paco Manila
Contact Number/s : 522-1691
License: 3846 Amo: Ireneo S. Consumido Org Type: Sole Proprietorship Primary Classification: General Building

REGIONAL INFRASTRUCTURE DEVELOPMENT CORPORATION
Unit 17, 3/F, Legaspi Towers 300, Roxas Blvd., Manila
Contact Number/s : 5223546
License: 26373 Amo: Roberto C. Abogado
Org Type: Corporation Primary Classification: General Building

REMAJGI BUILDERS
47 San Agustin St., Pineda, Pasig Pasig
Contact Number/s : none
License: 24311 Amo: Josefina A. Antonio Org Type: Sole Proprietorship Primary Classification: General Engineering

REMJIE'S CONSTRUCTION DEVELOPMENT
9494 Gene St., Airport Village Paranaque, M.M. Para?aque
Contact Number/s : 852-06-89
License: 13768 Amo: Remedios B. Go Org Type: Sole Proprietorship Primary Classification: General Engineering

RENGAR POWER SYSTEMS, INCORPORATED
30 Meralco Ave., Ortigas Center Pasig CPO Pasig City
Contact Number/s : 6320368
License: 18428 Amo: Renato S. Garcia Org Type: Corporation Primary Classification: Electrical Work

RES ELECTRICAL SERVICES, INC.
363 Dr. J. Fernandez St., Highway Hills, Mandaluyong City Mandaluyong
Contact Number/s : 533-5198/99
License: 10001 Amo: Reynaldo B. Suarez, Jr.
Org Type: Corporation Primary Classification: Electrical Work

REYU CONSTRUCTION

Km. 3 National H-Way, Surigao City Surigao del Norte
Contact Number/s : 826-1282
License: 7416 Amo: Rogelio M. Yu Org Type: Sole Proprietorship Primary Classification: General Engineering

RFN CONSTRUCTION AND DEVELOPMENT CORPORATION
Rm. 210 Tia Maria Bldg, C.V. Star Ave., Pamplona, Las Pinas, M.M. Las Pi?
Contact Number/s : 872-4308
License: 8722 Amo: Rafael A. Ilagan Org Type: Corporation Primary Classification: General Engineering

RICHCORP SALES & DEVELOPMENT COMPANY, INC.
Mac Arthur Highway, Sampaloc, Apalit Pampanga
Contact Number/s : 743-6568
License: 25641 Amo: Soter H. Sunga Org Type: Corporation Primary Classification: General Engineering

RICOLITE, INC.
3264 Zapote St. Olympia and carmona Makati
Contact Number/s : 896-1861
License: 19404 Amo: Romeo A. Bolongaita Org Type: Corporation Primary Classification: Electrical Work

RICZEN CONSTRUCTION AND SUPPLY
#37 M.H. Del Pilar St., Bayambang Pangasinan
License: 15397 Amo: Ricardo M. Camacho Org Type: Sole Proprietorship Primary Classification: General Engineering

RIEZL LANDCARE AND CONSTRUCTION
Mamsa cor. Tulingan Stts. New Salmonan, Brgy. Wilfredo Aquino, Agdao Davao City Davao del Sur
Contact Number/s : 2275412
License: 23672 Amo: Mendrado L. Canusa Org Type: Sole Proprietorship Primary Classification: General Engineering

RIGIBILT CONTRACTORS, INC.
#33 7th Ave. cor. 8th St., Kalookan City CPO Kalookan City (South)
Contact Number/s : 3643928
License: 28732 Amo: Benedict C. Lim Org Type: Corporation Primary Classification: General Building

RJ LANDOY AND ASSOCIATES, INCORPORATED
9574 Sgt. Fabian Yabut Circle, Guadalupe Guadalupe Nuevo (inc.Palm Vill.) Makati
Contact Number/s : 882-1287
License: 10866 Amo: Romulus J. Landoy Org Type: Corporation Primary Classification: General Building

RLJ CONSTRUCTION
Rm. 305 JR Bldg., 1520 Quezon Ave., Quezon City
Contact Number/s : 373-2473
License: 8427 Amo: Lope L. Lopez Org Type: Sole Proprietorship Primary Classification: General Engineering

ROCK METAL CONSTRUCTION
Mc Arthur Highway, Dolores San Fernando Pampanga
Contact Number/s : 045-9637557
License: 21210 Amo: Librado S. Calilung Org Type: Sole Proprietorship Primary Classification: General Engineering

ROCKER BUILDER CONTRACTOR
1093 Malaspina Ilang-Ilang St., Bacolod City Negros Occidental
Contact Number/s : 4346577
License: 29882 Amo: James S. Young Org Type: Sole Proprietorship Primary Classification: General Engineering

ROMULO D. TORRES, JR. & ASSOCIATES
16 Kalinisan St., Mandaluyong CPO Mandaluyong
Contact Number/s : 5340974-84

License: 30074 Amo: Romulo De Dios Torres, Jr. Org Type: Sole Proprietorship Primary Classification: General Engineering

RONMARK CONSTRUCTION
No.118 Sta. Monica, Santa Rita Pampanga
Contact Number/s : (045) 912-703
License: 19345 Amo: Alex L. Mallari Org Type: Sole Proprietorship Primary Classification: General Engineering

ROOS INDUSTRIAL CONSTRUCTION INCORPORATED
112 Reyes Circle, 4th St. Fourth Estate, Sucat, Paranaque, M.M. Para?aque
Contact Number/s : 820-6759/60
License: 26169 Amo: Romulo R. Deiparine Org Type: Corporation Primary Classification: General Building

ROPRIM CONSTRUCTION
Lot 5, Block 5, Villa Las Palmas. Jaro Iloilo City Iloilo
Contact Number/s : 3296991
License: 8546 Amo: Ronnie P. Primaylon Org Type: Sole Proprietorship Primary Classification: General Engineering

ROY CONSTRUCTION & DEVELOPMENT CORPORATION
Unit-I, Km. 2 J.C. Aquino Ave., Butuan City Agusan del Norte
Contact Number/s : 341-9698
License: 4004 Amo: Rogelio B. Ong Yiu Org Type: Corporation Primary Classification: General Engineering

ROYAL DEVELOPMENT CORPORATION OF THE PHILS. (RDCP)
Rm. 304 Diamond Finance Bldg., 603 EDSA, Cubao Quezon City
Contact Number/s : 694-2372
License: 12236 Amo: Manuel J. Mateo Org Type: Corporation Primary Classification: General Building

ROYAL GENERAL MERCHANT AND CONTRACTOR
Calixto Zaldivar Street, San Jose Antique
Contact Number/s : 036-5408382
License: 14522 Amo: Rafael C. Haro Org Type: Sole Proprietorship Primary Classification: General Engineering

RP MALIWAT ENGINEERING
3/F Comembo Comm"l Complex J.P. Rizal Makati CPO (inc. Buendia up to Edsa) Makati
Contact Number/s : 892-8687
License: 25237 Amo: Rogelio P. De Maliwat Org Type: Sole Proprietorship Primary Classification: General Engineering

RRG ENTERPRISES, INC.
2/F P&L Bldg., 116 Legaspi St., Legaspi Vill. Makati
Contact Number/s : 8125076/8174816
License: 17743 Amo: Raul R. Gonzales Org Type: Corporation Primary Classification: General Engineering

RRMD CONSTRUCTION
123 Feliciano, Bldg., Roxas Ave., Mahayahay, Iligan City Iligan City
Contact Number/s : 063-2215182
License: 23615 Amo: Rudolf Charles Li Tamula Org Type: Sole Proprietorship Primary Classification: General Engineering

RRN, INCORPORATED
Rm. 203 Global Tower Condo. 2029 M. Reyes St., cor. Mascardo St. Bangkal Makati
Contact Number/s : 8447936-37
License: 24359 Amo: Nestor B. Cruz Org Type: Corporation Primary Classification: Electrical Work

RSL CONSTRUCTION INCORPORATED
218 Montemaria Vill., Catalunan Grande, Davao City Davao City
Contact Number/s : 297-2695
License: 5916 Amo: Roque S. Lumanlan Org Type: Corporation Primary Classification: General Engineering

RUTHLAND TRADING & CONSTRUCTION

#40 Mearle Homes, Lamuan, Sto. Nino, Marikina City Marikina
Contact Number/s : 9422171
License: 18644 Amo: Rodrigo B. Nolasco Org Type: Sole Proprietorship Primary Classification: General Engineering

RYANYX TRADING, CONSTRUCTION & GENERAL SERVICES
L-2A B-5 Green St., Stella Maris Subd., Maybunga Pasig City
Contact Number/s : 641-35-57
License: 29754 Amo: Rufino Lumacao Barinan Org Type: Sole Proprietorship Primary Classification: General Building

S & H ELECTRICAL CONSTRUCTION CORPORATION
115 D. Tuazon St., Sta. Mesa Heights Quezon City CPO Quezon City
Contact Number/s : 740-5710/15
License: 24360 Amo: Samuel Yok Yong G. Tan Org Type: Corporation Primary Classification: Electrical Work

S.C. HORTELANO CONSTRUCTION, INC.
Taft North, Mandurriao, Il Iloilo City Iloilo
Contact Number/s : 321-1054
License: 4652 Amo: Samuel C. Hortelano Org Type: Corporation Primary Classification: General Engineering

SAFETY-PLUS ERECTORS AND DEVELOPERS, INC.
30 Barcelona Cmpd., Bahay Toro Quezon City CPO Quezon City
Contact Number/s : 4556438
License: 22471 Amo: Joseph Roel D. Tiangco Org Type: Corporation Primary Classification: General Building

SALAZAR CONSTRUCTION COMPANY, INC.
211 Natalio Bacalso Avenue, Cebu City Cebu
Contact Number/s : 261-0235
License: 334 Amo: Doroteo M. Salazar Org Type: Corporation Primary Classification: General Engineering

SALEMAIRE INDUSTRIES CORPORATION
L1, B3, , Lourdes Herrera, Congressional Village 2, Quezon City CPO Quezon City
Contact Number/s : 9279344
License: 22123 Amo: Roque M. Martos Org Type: Corporation Primary Classification: Mechanical Work

SARDS CONSTRUCTION
2074 Locsin Subd., Daraga (Locsin) Albay
Contact Number/s : 4831261
License: 15408 Amo: Joevie A. Sardua Org Type: Sole Proprietorship Primary Classification: General Engineering

SEA FORM SYSTEM ASIA, INC.
Suite 208 NArra Bldg., ,2276 P. Tamo Ext Makati CPO (inc. Buendia up to Edsa) Makati
Contact Number/s : 8186721
License: 12204 Amo: Dan M. Young Org Type: Corporation Primary Classification: General Engineering

SERRA TY CONSTRUCTION
Bongtud, Tandag Surigao del Sur
Contact Number/s : 086-2112000
License: 7373 Amo: Alvin O. Ty Org Type: Sole Proprietorship Primary Classification: General Engineering

SERVICIO FILIPINO, INC.
105 West Avenue Quezon City CPO Quezon City
Contact Number/s : 371-1321
License: 24144 Amo: Luis Alberto A. Anastacio Org Type: Corporation Primary Classification: General Building

SHELYN CONSTRUCTION
1330-C MIGUELIN ST. Sampaloc Manila
Contact Number/s : none
License: 13853 Amo: Shelsahid A. Asiri Org Type: Sole Proprietorship Primary Classification: General Building

SILVER CITY GENERAL CONSTRUCTION, INC.
Rm. 3-B KKL Bldg., 1302 Masangkay St., Binondo Manila
License: 16498 Amo: Henry U. Fernandez
Org Type: Corporation Primary Classification: General Building

SITE-CON, INC.
2nd Flr. Trident Towers, 312 Sen. Gil J. Puyat Ave., Mkt. Metro Manila
Contact Number/s : 754-1500
License: 29670 Amo: Paivi Tellervo Havtajoki Org Type: Corporation Primary Classification: General Engineering

SIXTEEN ENTERPRISES-CALAPAN BRANCH
Lalud, Calapan Mindoro Oriental
Contact Number/s : 2867029
License: 18187 Amo: Marilou F. Morillo Org Type: Sole Proprietorship Primary Classification: General Engineering

SOLID ROCK CONSTRUCTION
1625-A G. Tuazon Street Sampaloc, Manila Manila
Contact Number/s : 7497671
License: 8958 Amo: Ma. Corazon S. Valenzuela Org Type: Sole Proprietorship Primary Classification: General Engineering

SOMO CONSTRUCTION
Villafrancia Street, Townsite, Limay Bataan
Contact Number/s : 244-4358
License: 10678 Amo: Isagani A. Somo Org Type: Sole Proprietorship Primary Classification: General Building

SOUTH PACIFIC BUILDERS CENTER, INC.
Corner Mabini-Delgado Sts., Iloilo City Iloilo City
Contact Number/s : 336-46-95
License: 24594 Amo: Kwong Yiu Go Org Type: Corporation Primary Classification: General Engineering

SOUTHERN FILLERS
B10, L2, Bahay Pag-ibig Heights, Catalunan Grande Davao City
Contact Number/s : 082-2962130
License: 6311 Amo: Mary Mae T. Larrabaster Org Type: Sole Proprietorship Primary Classification: General Engineering

SPATIUM, INC.
280 Tomas Morato Ave., Quezon City Quezon City
Contact Number/s : 927-3241/45
License: 12023 Amo: Manuel B. Aquino Org Type: Corporation Primary Classification: General Engineering

SPEC - MASTER, INCORPORATED
Unit 4B G&G Lumber Bldg., Ortigas Ave. Ext., Rosario, Pasig City Pasig
Contact Number/s : 641-0693
License: 22310 Amo: Manuel C. Peralta Org Type: Corporation Primary Classification: Electrical Work

SPL CONSTRUCTION & DEVELOPMENT CORPORATION
15 Gapan-Olongapo Road, Concepcion Lubao Pampanga
Contact Number/s : 045-9716522
License: 7036 Amo: Lilia G. Pineda Org Type: Corporation Primary Classification: General Engineering

ST. NICHOLAS' LUMBER AND HARDWARE
T. Fornier St. San Jose Antique
Contact Number/s : 0917-9209850
License: 11694 Amo: Soledad O. Hernaez Org Type: Sole Proprietorship Primary Classification: General Building

STA. MARIA CONSTRUCTION AND ALLIED BUSINESSES CORPORATION
103-G, Commonwealth Ave., Fairview Quezon City
Contact Number/s : 922-4447
License: 1354 Amo: Carlos A. Buenaventura Org Type: Corporation Primary Classification: General Engineering

□ **STAGES DESIGN & CONSTRUCTION**
Suite 521 Downtown Center Bldg., Quintin Paredes St., Binondo Manila
Contact Number/s : 242-4731
License: 18004 Amo: Henry Den Tee Chua Org Type: Sole Proprietorship Primary Classification: General Engineering

□ **STALL CONSTRUCTION SUPPLIES & SERVICES**
Ibabao, Cuenca Batangas
Contact Number/s : 043-342-2761
License: 29930 Amo: Nelson Aguila Larcia Org Type: Sole Proprietorship Primary Classification: General Building

□ **STARLINE CONSTRUCTION CORPORATION**
G6 GJ Apts. St. Francis Homes IV, Balibago, Sta. Rosa, Laguna Laguna
Contact Number/s : 049-8371256
License: 27850 Amo: Robert P. Resayo Org Type: Corporation Primary Classification: General Building

□ **STEEL CENTRE PHILIPPINES, INC.**
Amang Rodriguez Ave., Mangahan, Pasig CPO Pasig City
Contact Number/s : 6415690
License: 14558 Amo: Ivan Y. Ong Org Type: Corporation Primary Classification: Structural Steel Work

□ **STEELITE CONSTRUCTION CORPORATION**
#32 Uranus St., Pasig Greenland Vill., Rosario, Pasig City Pasig
Contact Number/s : 643-8009
License: 13129 Amo: Aquilino S. Dela Cruz Org Type: Corporation Primary Classification: General Engineering

□ **STRUCTURES CONTRACTORS, INCORPORATED**
Rm. M-07 Caly Building, Aurora Boulevard Quezon City
Contact Number/s : 913-8807/08
License: 4014 Amo: Edgardo S. Cabrera Org Type: Corporation Primary Classification: General Engineering

□ **SUMICON PHILIPPINES CORPORATION**
2/F Pioneer House Bldg.,108 Paseo de Roxas San Lorenzo Vill. Makati
Contact Number/s : 8404913/15
License: 20384 Amo: Mitsukazu Nakata Org Type: Corporation Primary Classification: General Building

□ **SUMISETSU PHILIPPINES, INC.**
7480 Bagtikan Cor. Dao Sts., San Antonio Vill., Makati City Makati
Contact Number/s : 897-0068/69
License: 13821 Amo: Susan B. Militar Org Type: Corporation Primary Classification: Electrical Work

□ **SYSTEM WITH RELIABILITY, INC.**
Sct. Bayoran South Triangle Quezon City CPO Quezon City
License: 29585 Amo: Crisanto C. Aquino Org Type: Corporation Primary Classification: Electrical Work

□ **SYSTEMS FACTORS COMPANY**
4/F Dona Guadalupe Bldg., 7462 Bagtikan St., San Antonio Vill.(inc. Malugay-Yakal) Makati
Contact Number/s : 8952233
License: 5019 Amo: Modesto P. Dean Org Type: Partnership Primary Classification: Electrical Work

□ **T.F. BOTONES ENGINEERING AND CONSTRUCTION**
41 Silva St., Vista Verde Exec. Vill., Antipolo Rizal
Contact Number/s : 645-8679
License: 15067 Amo: Teodolito F. Botones Org Type: Sole Proprietorship Primary Classification: General Building

□ **T.J. VELASCO CONSTRUCTION & SUPPLY**
San Vicente East, Urdaneta Pangasinan
Contact Number/s : 568-2693

License: 10560 Amo: Tolomeo J. Velasco Org Type: Sole Proprietorship Primary Classification: General Engineering

TACOLOD ENTERPRISES
Fiesta Homes Subd., Sum-ag, Bacolod City Bacolod City
Contact Number/s : 034-7034900
License: 10721 Amo: Andres G. Tacolod Org Type: Sole Proprietorship Primary Classification: General Engineering

TAPNIO AND TAN CONSTRUCTION & DEVELOPMENT CORPORATION
483 Del Monte Ave., Brgy. Manresa Quezon City CPO Quezon City
Contact Number/s : 4154900
License: 10798 Amo: Renato O. Tapnio Org Type: Corporation Primary Classification: General Building

TECHNICON ENGINEERING & DESIGN
258 Zuniga Subd., Brgy. Mangahan Rodriguez, Rizal Rizal
Contact Number/s : 942-5873
License: 21413 Amo: Julieta A. Cruz Org Type: Sole Proprietorship Primary Classification: General Engineering

TEKNOKONSTRUKT INC.
26 Helena St., Teresita Village Marikina Heights Marikina
Contact Number/s : 9416425
License: 24829 Amo: Nomel B. Lapira Org Type: Corporation Primary Classification: General Engineering

TEMPRITE ENGINEERING, INCORPORATED
Temprite Bldg. Eng'g., No. 63 Samonte St Brgy. Holy Spirit Quezon City
Contact Number/s : 951-8217
License: 8226 Amo: Virgilio F. Del Rosario Org Type: Corporation Primary Classification: Mechanical Work

THE TUSCAN STRUCTURES AND SUPPLIES
706 JP Rizal Cor. E. Aguinaldo Sts. Catarman Northern Samar
Contact Number/s : 354-1359
License: 18257 Amo: Elizer S. Unay Org Type: Sole Proprietorship Primary Classification: General Engineering

TOMSIL CONSTRUCTION AND SUPPLY
Don Francisco Village, Jaro Iloilo City Iloilo
Contact Number/s : 320-2058
License: 5244 Amo: Tomas N. Occena Org Type: Sole Proprietorship Primary Classification: General Engineering

TORQUE BUILDERS, INCORPORATED
Unit 1005 Taipan Place Emerald Ave., Ortigas Center Pasig City
Contact Number/s : 638-8868/72
License: 5023 Amo: Jaime T. Dy Org Type: Corporation Primary Classification: Electrical Work

TREVI FOUNDATIONS PHILIPPINES INC.
U5D, Country Space I Bldg., Sen. Gil Puyat Ave., Makati CPO (inc. Buendia up to Edsa) Makati
Contact Number/s : 867-3181/83
License: 22372 Amo: Delfin A. Manuel, Jr. Org Type: Corporation Primary Classification: General Engineering

TRI-AMP CORPORATION
1437 Bellevue St., Brookside Hills Cainta Rizal
Contact Number/s : 655-5222
License: 25080 Amo: Wilkie N. Mendoza Org Type: Corporation Primary Classification: Electrical Work

TRICOM SYSTEMS (PHILIPPINES), INC.
2/F, Metro House Bldg., 345 Sen. Gil Puyat Ave, Makati City Makati
Contact Number/s : 8957561
License: 29499 Amo: Edgardo B. Isleta, Jr. Org Type: Corporation Primary Classification: Communication Facilities

□ **TRI-PHASE INDUSTRIAL SERVICES AND TRADING COMPANY**
401 Aurelio Bldg. II, Rizal Avenue Extn. cor. 11th Ave., Kalookan City CPO Kalookan City (South)
Contact Number/s : 3668049-50
License: 23871 Amo: Benjamin G. Jacildo Org Type: Partnership Primary Classification: Electrical Work

□ **TRIPLE 8 CONSTRUCTION & SUPPLY**
Saog, Marilao Marilao Bulacan Province
Contact Number/s : (044)7114475
License: 10684 Amo: Wilfredo M. Natividad Org Type: Sole Proprietorship Primary Classification: General Engineering

□ **TUQUER BUILDERS**
237 Holyghost Extension Baguio City Benguet
Contact Number/s : 445-39-35
License: 13823 Amo: Theodore N. Gonzalo Org Type: Sole Proprietorship Primary Classification: General Building

□ **UNDALOC CONSTRUCTION COMPANY INC.**
Sabellano Rd., Upper Yati, Quiot Pardo, Cebu City Cebu
Contact Number/s : 272-3150
License: 26506 Amo: Cirilo A. Undaloc Org Type: Corporation Primary Classification: General Engineering

□ **UNION WELL DRILLING & STEEL WORKS**
Suite 204-206 Cecileville Bldg., 1211, Quezon Avenue Quezon City CPO Quezon City
Contact Number/s : 371-3449
License: 25125 Amo: Sofronio S. Enriquez Org Type: Sole Proprietorship Primary Classification: Well Drilling Work

□ **UNIWELL TECHNOLOGIES CORPORATION**
2F Greenfields I Bldg. 750 Shaw Blvd., Mandaluyong City Mandaluyong
Contact Number/s : 633-4841
License: 26294 Amo: Leonardo F. Valenciano Org Type: Corporation Primary Classification: Mechanical Work

□ **URACOM, INC.**
Suite Upper Penthouse, U1C 15/F Pryce Tower Bldg., , Bajada, Davao City Davao del Sur
Contact Number/s : 221-2111
License: 27743 Amo: Jimmy A. Uraya Org Type: Corporation Primary Classification: General Engineering

□ **V L CONSTRUCTION**
Dona Francisca Subd. Balanga Bataan
Contact Number/s : 237-3320/928-6242
License: 461 Amo: Celso V. Valdecanas Org Type: Sole Proprietorship Primary Classification: General Engineering

□ **V.F. LABAO CONSTRUCTION**
89 LABAO ST.LIGID,TIPAS, TAGUIG,M.M. Taguig
Contact Number/s : 641-0853
License: 630 Amo: Virgilio F. Labao Org Type: Sole Proprietorship Primary Classification: General Building

□ **V.G. GATDULA CONSTRUCTION**
#2 Kalyos cor. Malunggay Sts., Project 7, Q.C. Quezon City
Contact Number/s : 371-0004/06
License: 4878 Amo: Victor P. Gatdula Org Type: Sole Proprietorship Primary Classification: General Building

□ **V.M. ESPIRITU CONSTRUCTION**
Mabolo, Bacoor Cavite
Contact Number/s : 046-4340404
License: 706 Amo: Valeriano M. Espiritu Org Type: Sole Proprietorship Primary Classification: General Engineering

□ **VALLEY VENTURES CONSTRUCTION & DEVELOPMENT CORPORATION**
Datu Street, San Gabriel Village, Tuguegarao Cagayan
Contact Number/s : 844-3245

License: 15617 Amo: Gerry C. Alivia Org Type: Corporation Primary Classification: General Engineering

□ **VAR BUILDERS**
510 Tandang Sora Ave., Brgy. Culiat, Quezon City
Contact Number/s : 455-7427
License: 20327 Amo: Virgilio A. Reyes Org Type: Sole Proprietorship Primary Classification: General Building

□ **VELCO CONSTRUCTION**
Carolina Looc Romblon
Contact Number/s : 741-6773
License: 5308 Amo: Svell Ana F. Ang Org Type: Sole Proprietorship Primary Classification: General Building

□ **VENANCIO S. SIMBULAN JR. CONSTRUCTION & DEVELOPMENT**
265 Tinio, San Lorenzo, Gapan Nueva Ecija
Contact Number/s : 486-0336
License: 29502 Amo: Venancio S. Simbulan, Jr. Org Type: Sole Proprietorship Primary Classification: General Building

□ **VERZATEK, INCORPORATED**
6/F, Filipino Merchants Bldg., Dela Rosa Legaspi Vill, Makati City Makati
Contact Number/s : 8122194
License: 27591 Amo: Leodegario S. Domingo Org Type: Corporation Primary Classification: Electrical Work

□ **VICTOR ELECTRICAL AND CONSTRUCTION, INC.**
MacArthur Hiway Cor. T. Claudio Sts., Lourdes Sur East Angeles City Pampanga
Contact Number/s : 045-3229052
License: 20878 Amo: Edgar C. Villarosa Org Type: Corporation Primary Classification: Electrical Work

□ **VIGAN FORTUNE CONSTRUCTION**
17 Quezon Avenue, Vigan Ilocos Sur
Contact Number/s : 722-2378
License: 3887 Amo: Cirilo Lao Org Type: Sole Proprietorship Primary Classification: General Engineering

□ **VILLA VERONICA CONSTRUCTION**
#628 Diversion Rd. Brgy. 76 Fatima Vill. Tacloban City Leyte
Contact Number/s : 523-2914
License: 28079 Amo: Veronica A. Fuentebella Org Type: Sole Proprietorship Primary Classification: General Building

□ **VIRAC NRC CONSTRUCTION**
Sta. Cruz St., Virac Catanduanes
Contact Number/s : 811-1628
License: 11396 Amo: Napoleon R. Co Org Type: Sole Proprietorship Primary Classification: General Engineering

□ **VIRAY CONSTRUCTION & ASSOCIATES, INC.**
1632 Dian Street, San Isidro Makati
Contact Number/s : 843-7452
License: 957 Amo: Rozanno A. Viray Org Type: Corporation Primary Classification: General Engineering

□ **VIREN BUILDERS, INC.**
Boromeo Street Surigao City Surigao del Norte
License: 30153 Amo: Alfredo Nunez Parido Org Type: Corporation Primary Classification: General Building

□ **VIRLO CONSTRUCTION**
Guimbal, Canamucan, Compostela Cebu City Cebu
Contact Number/s : 425-8235
License: 5765 Amo: Virgilio S. Pongase Org Type: Sole Proprietorship Primary Classification: General Engineering

□ **VITES CONSTRUCTION & DEVELOPMENT CORPORATION**
868 Tayuman Street Tondo Manila
Contact Number/s : 254-3709

License: 9444 Amo: Bingson U. Tecson Org Type: Corporation Primary Classification: General Building

□ **VPM CONSTRUCTION**
#217 Bonifacio Street, San Jose City Nueva Ecija
Contact Number/s : 044-5111398
License: 2098 Amo: Vicente P. Mateo Org Type: Sole Proprietorship Primary Classification: General Building

□ **VTP CONSTRUCTION INC.**
Carrascal Surigao del Sur
Contact Number/s : none
License: 20037 Amo: Vicente T. Pimentel, Jr. Org Type: Corporation Primary Classification: General Engineering

□ **W & D RAMOS CONSTRUCTION COMPANY**
Suite 202 Erisha Condo., 1142 P. Ocampo Sr. Ave., Malate Manila
Contact Number/s : 5248630
License: 27592 Amo: Wenceslao I. Ramos Org Type: Partnership Primary Classification: General Engineering

□ **W.T.B. CONSTRUCTION AND SUPPLY**
124 Champaca St., Tahanan Vill., Paranaque City Para?aque
Contact Number/s : 809-0466
License: 9445 Amo: Wilfrido T. Bituin Org Type: Sole Proprietorship Primary Classification: General Engineering

□ **WAKOH CONSTRUCTION & DEVELOPMENT CORPORATION**
Su.302 "Ang Bahay ng Alumni" Bldg., R. Magsaysay St. UP Campus Diliman Quezon City
Contact Number/s : 4347424/25 925-4708
License: 21920 Amo: Romeo B. Santos Org Type: Corporation Primary Classification: General Building

□ **WESTERN ADVERTISING AND CONSTRUCTION INCORPORATED**
2467- E Pedro Gil St., Sta. Ana Manila
Contact Number/s : 564-7092
License: 15185 Amo: Lily Luz Chua Org Type: Corporation Primary Classification: General Engineering

□ **WESTERN PHILIPPINE CORPORATION**
5F First Life Center, 174 Salcedo St., Legaspi Village Makati CPO (inc. Buendia up to Edsa) Makati
Contact Number/s : 892-7711/892-6638
License: 12471 Amo: Alfredo C. Lim Org Type: Corporation Primary Classification: General Building

□ **WHM CONSTRUCTION**
Tiguma Pagadian City Zamboanga del Sur
License: 22644 Amo: Wilson Sy Co Org Type: Sole Proprietorship Primary Classification: General Engineering

□ **WILL DECENA & ASSOCIATES**
947 A. Maceda Street, Sampaloc East Manila
Contact Number/s : none
License: 13951 Amo: Wilfredo L. Decena Org Type: Sole Proprietorship Primary Classification: General Building

□ **Y S CONSTRUCTION**
Sagbayan, Bohol, Or Km. 3, C.P.G. North Ave., Tagbilaran City Tagbilaran City
Contact Number/s : 411-2149
License: 11928 Amo: Restituto L. Suarez Org Type: Sole Proprietorship Primary Classification: General Engineering

□ **YELLOW GOLD CONSTRUCTION**
Taglesville Subd., San Jose Balanga Bataan
Contact Number/s : 237-1428
License: 9051 Amo: Dante R. Manalaysay Org Type: Sole Proprietorship Primary Classification: General Engineering

□ **YORKS MERCHANDISING CORPORATION**
612 T. Mapua St. Sta. Cruz Manila

License: 21213 Amo: John L. Siy Org Type: Corporation Primary Classification: General Engineering

YOSHIMOTO POLE CONSTRUCTION PHILIPPINES, INCORPORATED
#21-D Congressional Ave. Ext., Project 6 Quezon City
Contact Number/s : 924-0331/08
License: 23450 Amo: Florante A. Galinato Org Type: Corporation Primary Classification: Electrical Work

YUTANI BUILDERS
144 Sunrise Subd., Bagbag Rosario Cavite
Contact Number/s : 885-1457 885-1425
License: 29597 Amo: Emilie M. Yutani Org Type: Sole Proprietorship Primary Classification: General Building

ZAMBOANGA ENGINEERS AND CONTRACTORS
G/F Zamboanga Press Club Bldg., San Jose Panigayan Street Zamboanga City Zamboanga del Sur
Contact Number/s : 991-3565/993-0426
License: 6239 Amo: Eduardo A. Catis Org Type: Sole Proprietorship Primary Classification: General Building

ZOE REALTY AND CONSTRUCTION CORPORATION
G-6 Columbia Crystal Codominium #38 Columbia St., cor. 15th ave. Cubao Quezon City
Contact Number/s : 911-79-23/421-09-71
License: 29893 Amo: Cesander Marcelino Sarenas II Org Type: Corporation Primary Classification: General Engineering

SELECTED EXPORTERS & IMPORTERS

PHILIPPINE EXPORTERS:

Berben Wood Industries Inc.	berben@mozcom.com
Basket Exports International Philippines	basket@info.com.ph
Blue Ocean Tropical	
Decorinth Trade	decorinth@skyinet.net
Diamond Star Agro Products Inc.	dsapity@skyinet.net
Filmundo Export Corp.	inquire@filmundo.com
Flower Island Art & Craft Int'l	ahrdail@skyinet.net
Gementiza Export Corp	fil@mozcom.com
Glamour Garments Inc.	kavita@skyinet.net
Goodbridge Corp	novirop@vasia.com
GPI Exports Corp	gpiexports@pesocard.com
KAMS International Inc.	kamsint@pworld.net.ph
Krexim Inc.	krexim@pworld.net.ph
Manika Inc.	manika@vasia.com
Rissant Inc.	rissant@pworld.net.ph
Santori Exports	
Statexport Asia	yves@worldtelphil.com
Tai Lin Marine Products	chisan@skyinet.net
Via Antica Export & Trading Co.	vaete@worldtelphil.com
Welltrade International Trading	welltrade@skyinet.net
Aleli International	
Asia Sampaguita Flower Perfume	
Eastern Dragon Int'l Textile	
Annas Antiques	annasmla@skyinet.net
Lavine Loungewear Mfg.	hrh@pacific.net.ph
Brittany Export	denisher@skyinet.net
Franjo Quality Exports	franjo@skyinet.net
Mighty Int'l Export	jdgrace@skyinet.net
Alcon Industries	
Anjo Export Import	

Aquarose Bijouterie	
Cardoza Handicrafts	
Cyprea International	
Dockers	
Donax International	
Edros Export International	
Island Spice Philippines	marketing@island-spice.com
Keymart Philippines	
PidroPhil Trading	pidro123@skyinet.net
Pristine International	pristine@philexport.com
Saldana & Company	trdg@saldana.com.ph
Clarson Enterprises	clarsons@philexport.com
Access Designs & Interiors	adimnl@skyinet.net
Amer Trading Company	
Baron Arts & Crafts	
Betis Crafts	bci@mozcom.com
Casa Cana Incorporated	
Cebu Fil Veneer Corp	
Cebu Rattan Comapny	ceraco@skyinet.net
F.O.B. Philippines Inc.	
Gamallosons Traders	
Govil Industries	
Kaizen Incorporated	bonok@mozcom.com
Liseco Trading	cyrene@skyinet.net
Prime Craft Incorporated	
Rattan Pacifica Inc	
Regent Rattan Furniture	
Trade Galore International	tgi@skyinet.net
Krisanta Garments	krisanta@info.com.ph
MB Garments Mfg.	
Angel whispers Gifts & Crafts	
Darsons Export	

Enriquez Handicrafts	
Fortune Baskets Philippines	
Freedom Handicrafts Incorporated	
Infini Collections	
Maniz Multicrafts	maniz@cbu.skyinet.net
Natures Craft Incorporated	
B & J Development Corp	bj@info.com.ph
The Leather Collection Inc.	sales@leather-collection.com
Craftwood Export & Mfg Corp	
Benjoy Inc	benjoy@mozcom.com
Masterpiece Garment Export Inc.	masterex@info.com.ph
Monaco Mfg. Corp	
Philippine Belt Mfg. Corp.	philbelt@webquest.com
Splash Mfg. Corp	custcare@spalsh.com.ph
TRADE ORGANIZATIONS:	
Phil. Exporters Confederation	philexport@iname.com
Community Crafts Association of the Philippines	ccapbdd@pworld.net.ph
Craft Exporters from the Philippines	
Exporter's List from the Philippines	
Confederation of Phil. Exporters Foundation	president@philexport.org
Phil. Exporters Confederation-region XI	naga.brahmas@skyinet.net
Leather Goods Exporters from the Phil.	
World Exhibitions & Conventions	wdx@amanet.net
WS Expositions Management Group	wsexpo@wsgroup.com.ph
World Trade Center Manila	wtcclub@wtcmanila.com.ph
World Trade Philippines	
GOVERNMENT AGENCIES	
Board of Investments	boiipg@mnl.sequel.net
Bonded Export Marketing Board	
Bureau of Export Trade Promotions	betp@dti.gov.ph
Bureau of Import Service	
Bureau of International Trade Relations	

Center for International Trade Expositions & Missions	citemdo@mnl.sequel.net
Department of Trade and Industry	
Philippine International Trading Corp	pitc@mnl.sequel.net
Philippine Ports Authority	gm@ppa.gov.ph
Subic Bay Metropolitan Authority	tourism@subic.com.ph

SELECTED AGRO TRADE COMPANIES

BANANA PROCESSORS

ALCEDO FRUIT INDUSTRIES	235 New Buswang, Kalibo, Aklan	(036) 262-1575			**Peter Alcedo**	Banana Brittle, Banana Chips
B-G FRUITS AND NUTS MANUFACTURING CORPORATION	Stall No. 624, Building 6, FTI Complex Taguig, Metro Manila, Philippines	(63-2) 837-0378	(63-2) 838-4563	bg@info.com.ph	**Bienvenida Badenes**	Banana chips, coconut chips, dried fruits and vegetables, nata de coco
CELEBES AGRICULTURAL CORPORATION	6th Street corner Lapu-lapu Avenue San Antonio Village, Lahug, Cebu, Philippines	(63-32) 231-2836 / 231-2837	(63-32) 231-2831 / 231-2104	sales@celebes.com	**Rory Ong Yiu**	Banana chips, dehydrated fruits, banana flour, coconut chips
EL COCO MANUFACTURING AND TRADING CORPORATION	Room 2309 Tower I, Cityland 10 6815 Ayala Avenue, Makati City, Philippines	(63-2) 815-1831	(63-2) 970-3353		**Hydie Peralta**	Banana chips, Deyhydrated fruits
GREEN AND GOLD INTERNATIONAL TRADING	Rm. 307 Solmac Building, 84 Dapitan Street corner Banaue, Quezon City	(632) 415-8714	(632) 415-8715	ggold@i-manila.com.ph	**Manuel C. Kiok**	Banana Chips
GREENVILLE AGRO CORPORATION	Matin-ao Polomolok, South Cotabato	(083) 552-6754				Banana Chips
GUARANFOOD MANUFACTURING	Everlasting Patria Village, Brgy. del Remedio, San Pablo City, Laguna	(045) 562-4968	(045) 562-4846		**Clarissa Cavero**	Banana Ketchup
ILOCOS FOOD PRODUCTS	Multinational, Paranaque City	telefax (632) 823-8702			**Bernadette Padre**	Banana Chips
JO-NA'S INTERNATIONAL	#17 Clemente Street, Brgy. San	(632) 939-3643; 936-	(632) 939-5828; 936-		**Philip C. Young**	Banana Chips

PHILIPPINES, INC.	Agustin, Novaliches, Quezon City	7239	7245		**President & CEO**	
LESLIE CORPORATION	No. 4 Dama de Noche St., United Paranaque Subd. IV, Paranaque City	(632) 823-2566/70; (632) 823-6117	(632) 823-3708			Banana Chips
MOONBAKE INCORPORATED	14 Marcos Alvarez Ave., Moonwalk Village, Talon, Las Pinas City	(632) 801-8320; 802-8301	(632) 805-9303		**Rufino R. Manrique, Jr.**	Banana Blossoms in Coconut Cream
NAMNAMA'S FOOD PRODUCTS	3 Salbans, Paoay, Ilocos Norte	(0917) 539-7793; (0917) 245-1285			**Lolita Piamonte**	Banana Chips
NEWTON FOOD PRODUCTS, INC.	#84 Ramon Dolfin Street, Marulas, Valenzuela City	(632) 291-6793/95/96; 291-6772	(632) 291-6792		**Ligaya Uy**	Banana Flower
ROYCE FOOD CORPORATION	San Antonio Village, Lahug, Cebu City	(032) 231-2836/37	(032) 528-0508		**Joey Yepes; Rory Eddie Ong Yiu**	Banana Chips
SUNBLISS INTERNATIONALE EXIMPORTS	Gensan Drive & Odi St., Koronadal, South Cotabato	(083) 228-2262	(083) 228-2028	sunbliss@marbel.webling.com	**Carlos L. Bautista**	Banana Chips
SUSAN COTTAGE INDUSTRY	03 Valeria St., Iloilo City	(033) 337-6101; 337-7941	(033) 363-3179		**Susan Tan**	Banana Chips
TENTAY FOOD SAUCES	46 Los Martirez St., San Jose Navotas, M.M.	(632) 282-1226; 281-6743	(632) 282-5169		**Velia J. Cruz**	Banana Ketchup
EXPORTER						
ALTA VISTA AGRI VENTURES INC.	Marsman Bldg., 800 Lanang, Davao del Su	(082) 234-2353	(082) 236-2209		**Irene Cabriento**	Fresh Cavendish Bananas
ALTER TRADE CORPORATION	Blk. 6-A Lily St., Bata Subd., Bacolod City, Negros Occidental	(032) 441-0051	(032) 441-0057		**Danilo Guinabo, President**	Fresh Green Bananas
AMS FARMING CORPORATION	AMS Compound, F. Torres St., Davao City	(082) 221-1415	(082) 221-1141	amsfc@skyinet.net	**Stephen Antig**	Fresh Cavendish Bananas
BFC WORLDWIDE, INC.	317 San Fernando St., Binondo, Manila	(632) 243-0553; 243-4505/06	(632) 243-0550		**Lawrence Ong**	Sweetened & Unsweetened Banana Chips in Bulk

CABADBARAN FRUITS CORPORATION	AMS Compound, F. Torres St., 8000, Davao City	telefax: (083) 221-1141			**Stephen Antig**	Fresh Giant Cavendish Bananas
CHECKERED FARMS, INC.	Malayan House, Lanang, Davao City	(082) 226-3660	(082) 226-3661		**Mr. Warlito Subayno, General Manager**	Fresh Cavendish Bananas
CINVAC TRIOUCAK FRUITS, INC	Riverview Village, Baraca 8000, Davao City	(082) 221-7580/85	(082) 226-4619		**Madeline D. Marfori**	Fresh Cavendish Bananas
DAVAO EXOTIC FRUITS CORPORATION	A & R Diamond Center, Angliongto-Ruby Sts., Lanang, Davao City	(082) 300-1033	(082) 300-1031		**Romeo J. Serra**	Fresh Lakatan Bananas
DAVAO FRUITS CORPORATION	AMS Compound, Torres St, 8000, Davao City	(082) 227-1415	(082) 221-1141	amsfc @skyinet.net	**Eduardo J. Guillergan**	Fresh Cavendish Bananas
DELTA FARMS, INC.	Maryknoll Drive, Bo. Pampanga, Lanang 8000, Davao City	(082) 226-3660; 226-4526	(082) 226-4204		**Florence C. Lupiba**	Fresh Cavendish Bananas
DIAMOND FARMS	Malayan House, Lanang, Davao City	(082) 226-3660	(082) 226-3661		**Mr. Warlito Subayno, General Manager**	Fresh Cavendish Bananas
DOLLY'S BANANA CHIPS	147 Santero Subdivision, Habay, Bacoor, Cavite, Philippines	(63-46) 434-5316	(63-46) 970-3353		**Rogelio G. Cavas**	Banana chips
EDEN CORPORATION	848 Atis st., JFM Corporate Center, Juna Subd., Matina, Davao City	(082) 299-2981/94	(082) 296-0135		**Zaldy C. Magnaye**	Fresh Cavendish/Native en Bananas
EVERGREEN FARMS, INC.	Belisario Heights, Lanang, Davo City	(082) 234-2370	(082) 226-4204		**Olivia J. Vega**	Fresh Cavendish Bananas
FS DIZON AND SONS, INC.	Riverview Village, Bacaca 8000, Davao City	(082) 221-7580/85	(082) 222-1419		**Madeline D. Marfori**	Fresh Cavendish Bananas
GREENFIELD AGRICULTURAL CORPORATION	6th St. cor. Lapu-Lapu Ave., San Antonio Vill., Lahug, Cebu City	(032) 231-3836; 231-2837	(032) 231-2831; 231-2104		**Rory Eddie Ong Yu**	Banana Chips in Bulk
GREENVILLE AGRO CORPORATION	Matin-ao, Polomolok, South Cotabato	telefax: (083) 501-0051			**Michael Rene Ong Yu**	Banana Chips in Bulk

HIGHLAND BANANA CORPORATION	505 Aguho St., Juna Subd., Matina 8000, Davao City	(082) 299-2981	(082) 299-2996		**Jose Carlos Plama Gil**	Fresh Cavendish Bananas
HIJO PLANTATION, INC. TWIN RIVERS PLANTATION, INC.	505 Aguho St., Juna Subd., Matina, Davao City	(082) 299-2981	(082) 299-2996		**Mr. Ramon M. de Vera, President and CEO**	Fresh Cavendish Bananas
INTERNATIONAL FOOD SNACKS CORPORATION	88 San Guillermo Ave., Bo. Buting, Pasig City	(632) 641-0991; 641-0995	(632) 641-0992		**Ruben See**	Banana Chips in Bulk
KOKI FOOD INTERNATIONAL	Budbud, Bunawan, Davao City	(082) 221-1528				Banana Chips
LA CONCEPCION FRUITS	A & R Diamond Center, Angliongto - Ruby Sts., Lanang 8000, Davao City	(082) 234-3329; 233-1778	(082) 235-0467		**Oliver Autor**	Fresh Lakatan Bananas
LAPANDAY FOODS CORPORATION	2263 Pasong Tamo Ext., Makati City	(632) 812-0659 to 63; 841-0971; 818-7339; 867-3004			**Luis P. Lorenzo, Jr. Chairman and CEO**	Fresh Cavendish Bananas
LAPANDAY AGRICULTURAL DEV'T. CORPORATION	Maryknoll Drive, Bo. Pampanga 8000, Lanang, Davao City	(082) 235-2551/57	(082) 234-2358		**Amanda N. Rey**	Fresh Cavendish Bananas
L. DOMETITA & SONS FOOD INDUSTRIES	15 L. Rivers St., Proj. 4, Quezon City	(632) 911-7240	(632) 911-8549	ldometita@pacific.net.ph	**Leopoldo Dometita**	Banana Chips in Bulk
MD ISALON ORGANIC BANANA AGRI-VENTURES, INC.	Bongabon, Pantukan, Compostela Valley	(632) 817-7827 c/o Marsman Drysdale	(632) 817-7836 c/o Marsman Drysdale		**Nilo Rosario, Plantation Director**	Fresh Cavendish Bananas
MALALAG VENTURES PLANTATION	Lapanday Group of Companies Compound, Maryknoll Drive, Bo. Pampanga, 8000, Davao City	(082) 235-2560; 235-2551/57	(082) 234-4488		**Jeffreynante U. Abejay**	Fresh Cavendish Bananas
MARSMAN-DRYSDALE AGRIBUSINESS GROUP	2246 Chino Roces Ave., Makati City Farm Site: Km. 7 Lanang, Davao City	(632) 817-7827	(632) 817-7836		**Roberto S. Sebastian, President & CEO**	Fresh Bananas
MARSMAN ESTATE PLANTATION, INC.	Km. 7 Lanang, 8000, Davao	(082) 235-1133/34	(082) 236-4209		**Mario B. Bongayal**	Fresh Cavendish

	City					Bananas
MICA BY THE SEA	Lana-an Hills, Roxas City, Capiz			Asingca@hotmail.com / NSingca@aol.com	**Diana Viterbo**	Processed Banana Products
NOVA VISTA MANAGEMENT AND DEV'T. CORP.	Marsman Bldg., Lanang 8000, Davao City	(082) 234-2353	(082) 236-4209		**Nilo Rosario**	Fresh Cavendish Bananas
ORIBANEX TRADING CORPORATION	2/F, Ilaico Bldg., Bgy. Ilang Tibungco, 8000, Davao City	(082) 238-0320/24	(082) 238-0328; 238-0642		**Herminio Martin, President/ Gen. Manager**	Fresh Cavendish Bananas
ORIENT MULTIFOODS MFG. CORP.	2/F, Sunshine Condominium, 9633 Kamagong St., Makati City	(632) 899-5692		alsayo@pworld.net.ph	**Antonio Ll. Sayo**	Vacuum Fried Banana Chips in Bulk
PACIFIC FRUIT PROCESSORS, INC.	# 4 Dama de Noche St., United Subd. IV, Paranaque City	(632) 823-2566 to 70	(632) 823-3708	leslie@mnl.sequel.net	**Maila Tabing**	Sweetened & Unsweetened Banana Chips
SEE'S INTERNATIONAL FOOD MANUFACRURING CORPORATION	Imperial Street, Cubao, Quezon City	(63-2) 912-2777; 438-5837	(63-2) 912-2786 / 438-4662	seesintl@skyinet.net	**Ruben See**	Banana chips, dehydrated fruits, vacuum dry fruits and snacks, mango nectar, instant noodles
SORIANO FRUITS CORPORATION	AMS Compound, F. Torres St. 8000, Davao City	(082) 221-1131/38	(082) 221-1141		**Stephen Ang**	Fresh Giant Cavendish Bananas
SOUTHERN TROPICAL FRUITS	Powerhouse Bldg., Km. 9, Bo. Pampanga, Davao City	(082) 233-1838/1843	(082) 233-1838/1843		**Cecilia D. Anuta**	Fresh Lakatan Bananas
STANFILCO, A DIVISION OF DOLE PHILS.	Stanfilco Cmpd., Belisario Heights Subd., Davao City	(082) 234-0241	(082) 233-1512; 234-1835		**Carlos Mandujano**	Fresh Bananas
STERLING GREEN INT'L. EXPORT	Rm. 512 Paramount Bldg., Quintin Paredes St., Binondo, Metro Manila	(632) 415-8714	(632) 415-8715	tianxian@info.com.ph / bogard@mailstation.net	**Manuel C. Kiok**	Banana Chips in Bulk
STOSE TRADING	52 Mt. Vernon St., Filinvest I,	(632) 95107617;	(632) 951-7489		**George P. Vallo**	Fresh Bananas

	Fairview, Quezon City	951-7489				
SOUTHERN AGRO-EXPORT CORPORATION	Samco Bldg., F. Bangoy St., 8000, Davao City	(082) 224-2287; 226-4072	(082) 221-2146		**Ferdinand Y. Maragon**	Banana Fiber
TWIN RIVERS PLANTATION, INC.	505 Aguho St. Juna Subd., Matina 8000, Davao City	(082) 299-2981/94	(082) 299-2996		**Ramon M. de Vera**	Fresh Giant Cavendish Bananas
UNIVERSAL FOOD CORPORATION	Km. 85 Center Point Bldg. Garnet Rd. cor. Julia Vargas Ave., Ortigas Ave., Pasig City	(632) 636-0279; 635-3565	(632) 633-9774	universalfood@pdx.rpnet.com	**Vincent Lopez III**	Banana Catsup
YOSHIDA FARMS & TRADING CORPORATION	185 Paseo del Carmen St., Monte Maria Village, Catalunan Grande, Davao City	(082) 297-2925; 299-3073	(082) 297-2925	yoshida@mail.dvo.info.com.ph	**Leticia Y. Ibabao**	Fresh Latundan Bananas

CALAMANSI PROCESSORS

DALISAY SWEETS INTERNATIONAL. INCORPORATED.	# 18 De Jesus Street, San Francisco Del Monte, Quezon City	(632) 373-1617/18,374-0441/ 42	(632) 373-1619	dsisales@mozcom.com	**Mr. Jim Falcatan Ms. Cristina Berroya**	Calamansi Juice, Puree
FITRITE, INC.	145 Gen. Evangelista Extension, Caloocan City	(632) 364-5920; 363-5061	(632) 361-7338; 361-4472		**Leon Solidum**	Calamansi Juice
GUIMARAS EXPORT	304 Celery Road, Bldg. 3 FTI Complex, Taguig, Metro Manila	telefax (632) 838-4752			**Regina dela Cruz**	Ready-to-Drink Calamansi, Calamansi Concentrate
HARMAN FOODS CORPORATION	46-A Bonifacio Avenue, Quezon City	(632) 740-2094/96/98; 366-5600 / 937-1651	(632) 740-2158; 937-4178		**Alfredo Yao, Grace Yao**	Calamansi Juice, Puree
KLT FRUITS, INC.	Rm. 610 Globe Telecom Plaza Bldg., Pioneer cor. Madison St., Mandaluyong City	(632) 747-9615, 747-1039	(632) 634-5823		**Michael Lao**	Calamansi Juice
R & M PRESERVES	441-B.V. Rama Ave., Guadalupe, Cebu City	(032) 825-5056 to 59	(032) 254-5777 / 254-5767; 255-3405		**Elizabeth Ong**	Dried Calamansi

ZEST-O CORPORATION	574 Edsa, Caloocan City Plant Address: 74 P. dela Cruz St., Sitio Gitna, Kaybiga, Novaliches, Quezon City	(632) 366-9192; 364-6541; 937-1651/59 (Plant)	(632) 366-5198; 937-4176 (Plant)		**Alfredo M. Yao; Francisco D. Cada**	Calamansi Soda, Dalandan Soda
EXPORTERS						
TSB ENTERPRISES	148 Pinkian St., Philang Subdivision, Bgy. Pasong Tamo, Quezon City	(632) 932-8066/67; 931-9744	(632) 932-8064	tsb@pworld.net.ph	**Thomas Emmanuel Romualdo**	Calamansi Puree
YOSHIDA FARMS & TRADING CORPORATION	185 Paseo del Carmen St., Monte Maria Village, Catalunan Grande, Davao City	(082) 297-2925; 299-3073	(082) 297-2925		**Leticia Y. Ibabao**	Calamansi Juice

COCOA / CHOCOLATE

ACTRON INDUSTRIES, INC	2662 Honduras Street, Makati City, Philippines	(63-2) 844-3041 to 44	(63-2) 815-2778	actron@info.com.ph	**Emmanuel Duenas**	Flavours, fragrances, industrial chocolates, AMF, bakery ingredients
ALASKA MILK CORPORATION	6th Floor Corinthian Plaza Building, Paseo de Roxas, Legaspi Village, 1254 Makati City, Philippines	(63-2) 840-4500	(63-2) 894-4929			Liquid milk, powdered milk, RTD-UHT milk and chocolate flavored milk
ANNIE CANDY MANUFACTURING	Kilometer 17, Aguinaldo Highway, Imus, Cavite, Philippines	(63-46) 471-0336 / 0833	(63-46) 322-2255		**John Teo Ong**	Milk chocolate candy (ube, langka, peanut)
APPLIED FOOD INGREDIENTS	Suite 2505, West Tower, Philippine Stock Exchange Center, Exchange Road, Ortigas Center, Pasig City,	(63-2) 635-7966 / 638-6515	(63-2) 635-7972 / 638-4142			Cheese powder, starches, natural and artificial flavors, natural spices, cocoa powder

	Philippines					
ASEAN COCOA CLUB	Ground Floor Eurevilla II Building, 118 Herrera Street, Legaspi Village, Makati City, Philippines	(63-2) 893-0468	(63-2) 413-4836		**Dominador S. Galvez**	Chocolate products/cocoa beans
ASIA IMPORTS AND EXPORTS CORPORATION	Room 622 Downtown Center, 516 Paredes Street, Binondo, Manila, Philippines	(63-2) 281-4114 / 282-5286	(63-2) 281-3787		**Manny Macaraig**	Noodles, condiments, fresh/frozen vegetables, dried fish, confectioneries
ASSET MARKETING CORPORATION	151 Paseo de Roxas, Makati City, Philippines	(63-2) 816-2101	(63-2) 813-3557		**Policarpio Ascalon**	
CANDY CORNER PHILIPPINES, INC.	#3 E. Rodriguez Avenue, Bagong Ilog, Pasig City, Philippines	(63-2) 671-9192 / 671-9184	(63-2) 671-9192 / 913-5374	think@info.com.ph	**Ricardo T. Andres**	Confectionary and related novelty items
UNIVERSAL ROBINA CORPORATION	43rd Floor Robinson Equitable Tower, ABB Avenue, Ortigas Center, Pasig City	(63-2) 633-9205 / 9207	(63-2) 633-9207		**James L. Go**	
COCOA SPECIALTIES, INC.	Ground Floor E. Delos Santos Avenue, Magallanes Village, Makati City, Philippines	(63-2) 804-0730 to 41	(63-2) 804-0748 / 49	cocogold@globe.com.ph / fiesta@globe.com.ph	**Armand Manawa**	
CONFECTIONERY MARKETING CORPORATION	126 Tanque Street, Paco, Manila, Philippines	(63-2) 561-6770 to 6878 / 563-9394	(63-2) 561-6775		**Patrick T. Hsu**	Chocolate coated biscuits
FCG TRADING PHILIPPINES, INC.	# 9 Guirayan Street, Araneta Subdivision, Quezon City, Philippines	(63-2) 715-1154	(63-2) 715-1165		**Ma. Corazon G. Alforja**	Frozen vegetables and fish, dried fish, tropical bottled fruit preserves, sauce and mixes, noodles, confectioneries
FILKOR INTERNATIONAL FOOD	Batuhan Palapala, Dasmarines,	(63-46) 973-0360 to 61	(63-46) 973-0359	filkor@mnl.sequel.net	**Baby Arenas**	Confectioneries, chocolate and assorted

CORPORATION	Cavite, Philippines					candies
GRAND ALPHATECH INTERNATIONAL CORPORATION	Suite 322, BPI Building, Plaza Cervantes, Binondo, Manila, Philippines	(63-2) 244-6250 / 244-6252 / 637-3386	(63-2) 244-6247 / 637-3392	jlc@webquest.com	**Josephine Go**	Biscuits and assorted cookies and confectioneries
HARMAN FOODS CORPORATION	46 A. Bonifacio Avenue, Quezon City, Philippines	(63-2_ 740-2094 / 96 / 98; 366-5600 / 03 / 04	(63-2) 740-2151 / 361-4662 / 740-2158		**Alfred Yao**	Purees, juices, chocolate
FRAFT FOODS (PHILIPPINESS) CORPORATION	8378 Dr. A. Santos Avenue, Sucat, Paranaque, Metro Manila, Philippines	(63-2) 826-5546 / 49	(63-2) 826-5546 / 49	jontangc@kraftasia.com	**Bienvenido Bautista**	Dairy products, powdered juices, chocolate and tea
MARBY FOOD VENTURES	Buenviaje Street, Plainview Subdivision, Mandaluyong City, Philippines	(63-2) 532-2348 / 2378 / 6305	(63-2) 532-0535 / 533-0460 / 532-6303		**Emelita Valderama**	Assorted biscuits and confectionery products
NESTLE PHILIPPINES, INC.	31 Plaza Drive, Rockwell Center, Makati City, Philippines	(63-2) 898-0001	(63-2) 898-0001		**Juan B. Santos**	Dairy, alpine bear brand, calcium plus, carnation, chamito, chocolait, coffeemate, fit n' fresh
NEW UNITY SWEETS MANUFACTURING CORPORATION	137 M.H. Del Pilar Street, Tugatog, Malabon, Metro Manila, Philippines	(63-2) 287-1575	(63-2) 288-7179		**John Teo Ong**	Chocolate and other candies
NOUVELLE FOODS, INC.	4th Floor, Strata Building, Emerald Avenue, Ortigas Center, Pasig City, Philippines	(63-2) 635-7961 / 65	(63-2) 632-1925		**Edwin Lim**	Crackers, biscuits, marshmallows and chocolate
NOVARTIS CONSUMER HEALTH PHILIPPINES	105 E. Rodriguez Jr. Avenue, Brgy. Ugong, Pasig City, Philippines	(63-2) 671-2840	(63-2) 671-2844		**Paulette M. Hernandez**	
ORYX INTERNAITONAL TRADERS, INC.	7351 Orchard Street, Phase 9, Marcelino Green Village, Sucat,	(63-2) 823-5332	(63-2) 823-5332		**Aida St. Garcia**	Assorted candies and chocolates

	Paranaque City, Philippines					
PHILIPPINE COCOA CORPORATION	23 M. Tuazon Street, Paranga, Marikina City, Philippines	(63-2) 942-6089 / 941-6163	(63-2) 941-5828 / 941-4489		**Conrado C. de Leon**	Cocoa products, candies, chocolates and other confectioneries
SERG'S PRODUCTS, INC.	Km. 17 Ortigas Avenue Extension, Cainta, Rizal, Philippines	(63-2) 655-0159 / 2865	(63-2) 655-0148 / 656-3195		**Gilberto P. Evaristo**	Chocolates, candies, cocoa powder, nougat
TP FOOD PROCESSING CORPORATION	34 Arthuro Drive, Bagumbayan, Taguig, Metro Manila, Philippines	(63-2) 823-8067 to 69	(63-2) 823-8838		**Edward Lim**	Cocoa butter, cocoa powder, chocolate coatings, specialty chocolates
TWIN OAKS FOODS CORPORATION	130-A, 20th Avenue, Cubao, Quezon City, Philippines	(63-2) 911-0417 / 1365 to 66	(63-2) 911-0170		**Eduardo S. Yu**	Chocolate and other confectioneries
UNIVERSAL ROBINA CORPORATION	110 E. Rodriguez Avenue, Libis, Quezon City, Philippines	(63-2) 671-8246 / 635-0751	(63-2) 671-8246 / 635-0751		**James L. Go**	Snack foods, confectionery, noodles, ice cream, biscuits, coffee, sauces, canned beans, flour and feed milling, animal help
WRIGLEY PHILIPPINES, INC.	Sitio Putting Bato, Marcos Highway, Antipolo City, Philippines	(63-2) 631-1745 / 631-1749	(63-2) 632-7645		**Melquiades Gamboa**	Chewing and bubble gum

COFFEE

COMMONWEALTH FOODS, INC.	Comfoods Building, Sen. Gil Puyat Avenue, Makati City, Philippines	(63-2) 844-5661	(63-2) 817-8845		**Archimedes Handog**	Instant and ground coffee, cocoa and chocolate and biscuit products
GENERAL MILLING CORPORATION	33rd Floor Urban Bank Plaza Building, Gil Puyat Avenue corner Pasong Tamo, Makati City, Philippines	(63-2) 887-9091	(63-2) 887-8998		**George K. Young**	Flour milling and baking, feed milling, stock food, pasta and instant noodles, cooking oil,

						coffee
NESTLE PHILIPPINES, INC.	31 Plaza Drive, Rockwell Center, Makati CIty, Philippines	(63-2) 898-0001	(63-2) 898-0001		**Juan B. Santos**	Milk, dairy, chocolate
UNIVERSAL ROBINA CORPORATION	110 E. Rodriguez Avenue, Libis, Quezon City, Philippines	(63-2) 671-8246 / 635-0751	(63-2) 671-8246 / 635-0751		**John Gokkongwei, Jr.**	Snack food, confectionary, noodles, ice cream, biscuits, coffee and sauces, canned beans, flour and feed milling

COCONUT

ATSON'S COCO, INC.	Km. 84 Maharlika Highway, San Pablo City, Laguna, Philippines	(63-49) 562-0089 / 562-3288	(63-49) 562-0088		**Sing Tiu**	Coconut milk powder, dessicated coconut
FIESTA BRANDS, INC.	1052 EDSA, Magallanes Village, Makati City, Philippines	(63-2) 851-0730 to 41	(63-2) 851-0748 to 49		**Divina Bautista**	Coconut water, coconut milk powder
MONTEREY COCONUT MILK CORPORATION	3784 Mascardo Street, Bo. Sta. Cruz, Makati City, Philippines	(63-2) 985-2166 / 896-2090	(63-2) 896-2090	monterey@philonline.com	**Rachel Arsenal**	Canned coconut milk, shredded young coconut, grated coconut meat, vegetable products, nata de coco in light syrup
ORIENT MULTIFOODS MANUFACTURING CORPORATION	32 Poseidon Street, Acropolis Greens, Bagumbayan, Quezon City, Philippines	(63-2) 910-0297	(63-2) 637-6835	alsayo@compass.com.ph	**Antonio Sayo**	Dessicated coconut, banana chips, dried fruits, coconut milk powder
SIRAWAN FOOD CORPORATION	4th Floor DACON Building, 2281 Pasong Tamo Extension, Makati City, Philippines				**Crsitina Ramos**	Dessicated coconut, coconut milk, coco chips, durian syrup

SKY BLUE IMPORT/EXPORT	17 Diamond Road, Caloocan Industrial Subdivision, Bo. Kaybiga, Caloocan City, Philippines	(63-2) 939-6096 / 927-3801	(63-2) 937-3802		**Dolly B. Cu**	Coconut chips, banana chips and other food products

CORN

ASSOCIATION OF PHILIPPINE AQUA FEEDMILLERS, INC.	2nd Floor NGC Building, 250 Ibuna Street, San Juan, Metro Manila, Philippines	(63-2) 851-3531	(63-2) 721-3599		**Engr. Napoleon Co**	
CHIEL JEDANG (CJ PHILIPPINES, INC.)	P.O. Box 1387 Ortigas Center, Pasig City, Philippines	(63-2) 851-3531	(63-2) 851-3549		**Joel Bolinao**	
CREVETTE COMPANY, INC.	23 Teodula Drive, Merlin Homes, Brgy. Sto. Nino, Marikina City	(63-2) 948-3444			**Angelo Cruz**	
CONCEPCION FARMS, INC.	Brgy. San Jose, Concepcion, Tarlac, Philippines	(63-45) 923-0623			**Alfredo G. Dy**	
EVEREST FARMS, INC.	Rm. 205 Caly Building, 986 Aurora Boulevard, Project 4, Quezon City, Philippines	(63-2) 645-1784	(63-2) 646-7450		**Alfonso Ko / Rodrigo Ko**	
FEDERAL AGRICULTURAL CORPORATION	26 Nevada Street, Northeast Greenhills, San Juan, Metro Manila, Philippines	(63-2) 724-7536 to 42 / 243-1631	(63-2) 726-1013		**Linda Typoco Chai**	
FOREMOST FARMS, INC.	448 Evangelista Street, Santolan, Pasig City, Philippines	(63-2) 645-2081 to 83	(63-2) 816-5554		**Joseph Go**	
GENERAL MILLING CORPORATION	55th Floor, Corinthian Plaza, 121 Paseo de Roxas, Makati City, Philippines	(63-2) 819-5451 to 76	(63-2) 811-3282		**Ric Pinca**	
I.O. BASIC CORPORATION	Bo. Pulang Cacutud, Angeles City,	(63-45) 602-8466 / 892-5678	(63-45) 892-0009		**Ong Ing Lee**	

	Pampanga, Philippines					
JETBEST MULTI-LINES CORPORATION	National Road, Maraouy, Lipa City, Batangas, Philippines	(63-43) 756-1076 / 756-1031			**Joselito Tapay**	
LIBERTY FLOUR MILLS, INC.	Liberty Building, Pasay Road, Makati City, Philippines	(63-2) 893-2644			**William Corpus Uy**	
MATH AGRO CORPORATION	Burol 1st, McArthur Highway, Balagtas, Bulacan, Philippines	(63-44) 693-1847 / 693-1445	(63-44) 693-2321		**Teresita Hizon**	
METRO MANILA FEEDMILLERS ASSOCIATION, INC.	1087 Northway Boulevard, Navotas, Metro Manila, Philippines	(63-2) 282-6552 / 282-6563 to 65	(63-2) 282-6556		**Andy Co**	
MONTEREY FOODS CORPORATION	PCDP Building, Sitio Sto. Nino de Bonifacio, West Bicutan, Taguig, Metro Manila, Philippines	(63-2) 810-4010 / 893-0770			**Ramon Llanos**	
NATIONAL FEDERATION OF HOG RAISERS, INC.	Penthouse Quadstar Building, #80 Ortigas Avenue, Greenhills, San Juan, Metro Manila, Philippines	(63-2) 724-8601	(63-2) 722-4473		**Nemesio Co**	
NUTRIMIX FEEDS CORPORATION	79 Dulong Bayan, San Jose del Monte, Bulacan, Philippines	(63-2) 413-4621			**Efren Bartolome**	
PHILIPPINE ASSOCIATION OF FEED MILLERS, INC.	Room 302 Maligaya Building III, 430 E. Rodriguez Sr. Boulevard, Cubao, Quezon City, Philippines	(63-2) 721-0906 / 722-2912	(63-2) 741-8532		**Soledad Agbayani**	
PHILIPPINE ASSOCIATION OF HOG RAISERS, INC.	158-C D. Tuazon Street, Sta. Mesa Heights, Quezon City,	(63-2) 453-0184	(63-2) 927-1257 / 929-8163		**Dr. Amado Baladad**	

	Philippines					
PHILIPPINE POULTRY AND LIVESTOCK COOPERATIVE	No. 62 Congressional Avenue, Quezon City, Philippines	(63-2) 453-0184	(63-2) 927-1257 / 929-8163		**Dr. Amado Baladad**	
PHILIPPINE SUPER FEED CORPORATION	1087 North Bay Boulevard, Navotas, Metro Manila, Philippines	(63-2) 724-4008	(63-2) 727-6049		**Max Bueno**	
PMI NUTRITION	Fil-Am Foods, Inc., Sto. Domingo II, Capas, Tarlac, Philippines	(63-2) 925-0505 / 925-0094	(63-2) 925-0506		**Ronald Macali**	
PULILAN AGRI. DEVELOPMENT CORPORATION	Dampol Street, Pulilan, Bulacan, Philippines	(63-2) 410-9974 to 75 / 413-4676 to 77	(63-2) 413-4621		**Buenaventura Perate**	
PUREFOODS CORPORATION	JMT Corporate Condominium, ADB Avenue, Ortigas Avenue, Ortigas Center, Pasig City, Philippines	(63-2) 634-1010	(63-2) 633-8746 to 50 / 635-2229		**Benedicto Tope**	
PURINA PHILIPPINES, INC.	14th Floor, JAKA Building, 6780 Makati City, Philippines	(63-2) 812-3489	(63-2) 812-3459		**Gary Norder**	
RIZAL POULTRY AND LIVESTOCK	Malanday, San Mateo, Rizal, Philippines	(63-2) 941-0868 / 941-1188	(63-2) 941-0868		**Joseph San Diego**	
SAN MIGUEL FOODS, INC.	PCPD Building, Nichols Interchange, Makati City, Philippines	(63-2) 819-4000 / 819-4046	(63-2) 810-4015		**Arthur Juan**	
SARIMANOK FEEDS COMPANY, INC.	86 Mayflower Street, Mandaluyong City, Philippines	(63-2) 634-8501 to 50 local 815-74	(63-2) 633-2627		**Noel Ricamata**	
UNITED SWINE PRODUCERS ASSOCIATION, INC.	3rd Floor, OR & G Tirol Building, 831 EDSA Quezon City, Philippines	(63-2) 924-2317	(63-2) 924-8884		**Jeffrey Ileto / Fransciso Gregorio**	
UNIVERSAL ROBINA CORPORATION	110 E. Rodriguez Jr. Avenue, Bagumbayan,	(63-2) 635-0751 to 85	(63-2) 635-4138 / 633-7631		**Henry Go**	

	Quezon City, Philippines					
VITARICH CORPORATION	5th Floor, Sarmiento Building III, 2316 Pasong Tamo Extension, Makati City, Philippines	(63-2) 843-3033 / 843-0237 to 47	(63-2) 711-1819 / 711-1794			

DURIAN

ANOBEI SWEETS ENTERPRISES	258 GSIS, Matina, Davao City	(082) 298-0298			**Cesar Ibañez**	Durian Sweets
70 Bigonia Circle, Ladislawa, Buhangin, Davao City	ALEJANDRO DURIAN ICE CREAM	(082) 222-3128; 224-4279			**Bernie Alejandro**	Durian Ice-Cream
KF FOODS, INC.	Kablon Farms, Tupi, South Cotabato	(083) 228-8508; 228-3050			**Ernesto Pantua, Jr.**	Durian Delicacies
LINDA'S SPECIAL DURIAN CANDY	San Antonio II, Matina, Davao City				**Erlinda Ibañez**	Durian Candy
LOLA ABON'S DURIAN CANDY	23 San Miguel Village, Matina, Davao City	(082) 297-2391; 299-2526			**Dolores Lumbab**	Durian Candy
LYNN'S DURIAN CANDY	28 San Miguel Village, Matina, Davao City	(082) 298-0998			**Aida Dayanghirang**	Durian Candy
LA ECIJANA	840 Ma. Loreto St., Juna Subd., Davao City	(082) 226-2490			**Tess Leonor**	Durian Delicacies
MINCO DURIAN	San Miguel Village, Matina, Davao City	(082) 297-2462; 298-0091			**Jose Domingo**	Durian Delicacies
ROWI'S VARIETY PRODUCTS	68-5 Fr. Selga St., Davao City	(082) 221-2793			**Romeo Guerra, Jr.**	Durian Delicacies
TATAY APO DURIAN CANDY	San Miguel Village, Matina Davao City	(082) 297-2175			**Edith Loon**	Durian Candy
PEANUTS						
PROCESSORS						
BUCAREZ FOOD PROCESSING CORPORATION	#8 New Calceta Street, Tagbilaran City, Bohol	(63-38) 411-4221	(63-38) 411-4222		**Jonathan Asunto, Felix Ibaya**	Peanut Kisses
CRYSTALLINE MARKETING	1904 Sandeja Street, Pasay City	(63-2) 521-8765	(63-2) 524-0390		**Debie Tinio Tan Kiok**	Roasted peanuts

DALISAY SWEETS, INT'L., INC.	#18 De Jesus Street, San Francisco Del Monte, Quezon City	(63-2) 373-1617/18; 374-0441/42	(63-2) 373-1619		**Cesar Falcatan**	Roasted peanuts
DOLLY'S BANANA CHIPS	147 Santero Subd., Habay I, Bacoor, Cavite	(63-46) 970-3353	(63-46) 434-5316		**Rodelio Cavas**	Roasted peanuts
FENOR FOOD PRODUCTS	26 Malboro, East Fairview, Quezon City	(63-2) 938-1621; 428-5378	(63-2) 938-1621		**Leonor Echavez**	Peanut (garlic flavor), Peanut brittle
FOOD INDUSTRIES, INC.	7582 Dela Rosa Street, Makati City	(63-2) 817-1223	(63-2) 810-0141	info@fii.ph		Cracker nuts
GORDON MARKETING, INC.	71-B DBP Avenue, FTI Complex, Taguig, Metro Manila, Philippines	(63-2) 838-4927	(63-2) 838-4598		**Zenaida Gordon**	Roasted peanuts, assorted nuts
ILOCOS FOOD PRODUCTS	Multinational, Paranaque City Factory Address: Taleb, Bantay, Ilocos Sur	(63-2) 823-8702; (077) 722-2332 c/o DOST Vigan		ilocoschichacorn@yahoo.com Website: http://ips.ph/com/ilocosfood	**Bernadette B. Padre**	Roasted peanuts
KANJI FOOD PRODUCTS	77 East Drive Marikina Heights, Marikina City, Philippines	(63-2) 942-1352	(63-2) 942-1352		**Buddy Duico**	Cracker nuts
MARISA'S FOOD	4365 L. Bernardino Street, Gen. T. De Leon Street, Valenzuela City	(63-2) 293-3736	(63-2) 323-2600		**Marisa Demin**	Peanut Butter
MARKET REACH DISTRIBUTORS, INC.	15 Scout Madrinan Street, South Triangle, Quezon City	(63-2) 371-0807	(63-2) 371-1650/51; 371-4379/93		**Mary Uy**	Roasted Peanuts
NAMNAMA'S FOOD PRODUCTS	3 Salbans, Paoay, Ilocos Norte	(0917) 539-7793; 245-1285			**Lolita Piamonte**	Roasted Peanuts
SUGARLAND MULTI-FOODS CORPORATION	102 Buendia Avenue corner Roxas Blvd., Pasay City	(63-2) 831-1889; 831-2087	(63-2) 833-3044; 551-0537		**Weena Marasigan**	Peanut butter
VICTORIA FOODS COMPANY	Soliven corner MRR Streets,	(63-2) 665-8571; 646-	(63-2) 646-3595		**Nancy D. Ordas**	Roasted Peanuts

	Manggahan, Pasig City	3595				
EXPORTERS						
DANE INT'L. COMMODITIES, INC.	Unit 53 B-I, Metrohomes, F. Benitez Street, San Juan, Metro Manila	(63-2) 722-0472; 721-0307	(63-2) 722-6472		**Aida ST. Garcia**	Roasted Peanuts and Assorted Peanuts
NEWBORN FOOD PRODUCTS, INC.	2442 Arsonvel Street, Makati City	(63-2) 844-5847; 843-5756	(63-2)) 843-1005	ftpua888@webquest.com	**Ramon Pua**	Peanut Butter
TOBI MARKETING, INC.	8526 J. De Leon Street, San Dioniso, Paranaque City, Philippines	(63-2) 825-2564 / 825-2518	(63-2) 829-3320 / 825-3710	tobi@mnl.sequel.net	**Renato Si**	Peanuts, roasted cashew nut
TROPIC RESOURCES INT'L., INC.	1977 Commonwelath Avenue, Quezon City	(63-2) 742-7720; 712-2867	(63-2) 952-6397		**Edward David**	Peanuts (Fresh)

PILI NUT PROCESSORS

MARKET REACH DISTRIBUTORS, INC.	15 Scout Madrinan Street, South Triangle, Quezon City	(63-2) 371-1650/51; 371-4379/93	(63-2) 371-0807		**Mary Uy**	Glazed Pili Nuts
NEW ALBAY CENTRAL PILI NUT CANDY	873 Rizal Street, Old Albay District, Legaspi City	(63-52) 820-3529	(63-52) 481-1161		**Rosemarie D. Battung**	Pili Nut Candies
CASHEW NUTS						
PROCESSORS						
CRYSTALLINE MARKETING	1904 Sandeja Street, Pasay City	(63-2) 524-0390	(63-2) 521-8765		**Debie Tinio Tan Kiok**	Roasted Cashew Nuts
DOLLY'S BANANA CHIPS	147 Santero Subd. Habay I, Bacoor, Cavite	(63-46) 434-5316	(63-46) 970-3353		**Rodelio Cavas**	Roasted Cashew Nuts
MARKET REACH DISTRIBUTORS, INC.	15 Scout Madrinan Street, South Triangle, Quezon City	(632) 371-1650/51	(632) 371-4379/93		**Mary Uy**	Roasted Cashew Nuts
TOBI MARKETING, INC.	8526 J. De Leon Street, San Dionisio, Paranaque City	(632) 825-2564; 825-2518; 825-3710; 825-7150	(632) 829-3320		**Renato Si**	Roasted Cashew Nuts

PAPAYA

DAVAO EXOTIC FRUITS CORPORATION (FORMERLY DAVAO EXOTIC BANANA CORPORATION)	A&R Diamond Centre, A. Angliongto Sr. corner Ruby Street, Diamond Village, Davao City, Philippines	(63-82) 235-0486 / 234-3329	(63-82) 235-0467		**Romeo J. Serra**	
DRYSDALE PRODUCTS, INC.	Philippine Far East Agro Compound, Rambutan Road, FTI Complex, Taguig, Metro Manila, Philippines	(63-2) 837-7710 to 11 / 823-6886	(63-2) 823-5321		**Esteban Pacannuayan**	
FIRST CAVITE AGRICULTURAL AND REAL ESTET DEVELOPMENT, INC.	Km. 19 Aguinaldo Highway, Bacoor, Cavite, Philippines	(63-97) 376-6129 / 378-6128	(63-96) 434-3718		**Lorena de Jesus**	
PHILIPPINE INTERNATIONAL TRADING CENTER	Apparel & Accessories Merchandising Food & Beverage Department Sen. Gil Puyat Avenue, Makati City, Philippines	(63-2) 845-4368 / 845-4376	(63-2) 845-4473 / 845-4376		**Joel Rodriguez / Janet Parreno**	Sweet potato

GINGER PROCESSORS

EM PRODUCT MIX	113 Fergusson Rd., Guisad, Baguio City Philippines	(63-32) 231-2836 / 231-2837	(63-32) 231-2831 / 231-2104		Evelyn Masaway	Ginger Candy
NARIGIN FOOD CORPORATION	602 Robert St., Bankers II Quirino Highway, Caloocan City Philippines	(63-2) 928-9510; 939-1510	(63-2) 928-9510		Julieta Navarette	Processed Ginger
EXPORTERS						
CS UMALI EXPORT	30 Sct. Borromeo St., South Triangle, Q.C. Philippines	(63-2) 372-4308; 371-1429	(63-2) 412-0487		Cezar Umali	Fresh Ginger
FRUITABLE TRADING AND DEVELOPMENT, INC.	292 Marcela St., Maypajo, Caloocan City Philippines	(63-2) 287-1536	(63-2) 288-3745	fruitable@edsamail.com.ph	Pablo B. Casimina	Fresh Ginger

SEACHAMP INTERNATIONAL EXPORT CORP.	CRW Rd., CRB Compound, FTI Complex, Taguig, M.M. Philippines	(63-2) 838-4980; 838-4467	(63-2) 838-4652		Virginia Yap Alex Malimban	Fresh Ginger
BLACK PEPPER						
PROCESSORS						
CALIFORNIA MANUFACTURING COMPANY, INC.	Km. 18 East Service Road, South Super H-way, Paranaque City	(632) 837-5086	(632) 837-5114	california@skyinet.net	Anthony N.S. Lai	Ground Pepper, Peppercorn
GANBOA HERMANOS, INC.	7431 Yakal Street, San Antonio Village, Makati City	(632) 844-8195	(632) 843-8442		Julio Ledesma IV, Executive Vice-President	Ground Pepper, Peppercorn
KAREXX INTERNATIONAL, INC.	#2 Silver Road, CIS Compound, Gen. Luis Street, Bo. Kaybiga, Caloocan City	(632) 939-6076; 939-7194; 939-9168		karexx@info.com.ph	Jesse Tanchanco, Jr.	Ground Pepper, Peppercorn
MC. CORMICK PHILS., INC.	#145 Panay Avenue, Quezon City	(632) 920-5291 to 98	(632) 920-5747	sysu@mnl.sequel.net	Lolita Cham	Ground Pepper, Peppercorn
SANDPIPER SPICES AND CONDIMENTS	131 F. Manalo Street, San Juan, Metro Manila	(632) 725-5704; 724-9435	(632) 723-5063		Kim Lapuz	Ground Pepper, Peppercorn
TENTAY FOOD SAUCES, INC.	UPY Building, No. 7 Sen. Gil Puyat Avenue, Makati City	(632) 833-4629/30; 833-4618	(632) 833-4633		Velia Cruz / Rosalie Santiago	Ground Pepper, Peppercorn

GARLIC

PROCESSORS						
BASIC FLAVORS, INC.	No. 44 3rd Street, New Manila, Quezon City	(632) 410-9256; 413-3878	(632) 700-8210	basicsauces@pacific.net.ph	Pauline Palang/ Margie Pineda	Crunchy Garlic, Garlic Chips
POTTER'S HAND PROCESSED FOODS	San Sebasatian corner Binangan McArthur H-	(63-45) 982-2041			Susana Dy	Garlic Chili Paste

	way, Tarlac City					
GIL ROY'S GARLIC ENTERPRISES	40 Rodriguez Street, Malabon, Metro Manila	Telefax: (632) 281-5881			Carmela Romero	Garlic Powder, Garlic Chips
EXPORTER / IMPORTER						
FRUITABLE TRADING & DEVELOPMENT, INC.	292 Marcela Street, maypajo, Caloocan City	(632) 287-1536	(632) 288-3745	fruitable@edsamail.com.ph	Pablo B. Casimina, President	Fresh Garlic

SUPPLEMENTS

FAQ ON CONDUCTING BUSINESS

PRIMER OF THE ESTABLISHMENT OF REGIONAL HEADQUARTERS AND REGIONAL WAREHOUSE IN THE PHILIPPINES

Question and Answers
on Regional Headquarters
The President of the Philippines on July 17, 1987 signed into law Executive Order No. 226 otherwise known as the Omnibus Investments Code of 1987 which codifies and compiles all the incentive laws of the Philippines including Presidential Decree No. 218. Book III of the Code, formerly P.D. 218, prescribes incentives to multinational companies duly established regional headquarters in the Philippines.

1. **What is a Regional Headquarters of multinational company?**

   A Regional Headquarters of a multinational company is an administrative branch which principally acts as a supervision, communications and coordination center for the subsidiaries, branches or affiliates of a multinational company in the Asia-Pacific region. All its expenses are financed by the head office or parent company.

2. **How does it differ from a branch office and a representative office?**

   A branch office of a foreign company carries out business activities of the head office and derives income from the host country. A regional office is not allowed to do business or earn income in the host county.

   A representative office, like a regional headquarters, does not derive income from the host country and is fully subsidized by its head office. However, a representative office deals directly with the clients of the parent company as it undertakes such activities as information, dissemination and promotion of the company's products as well as quality control of products for exports. The activities of a regional headquarters, on the other hand , are limited to supervisory, communications and coordinating center for its subsidiaries, affiliates and branches in the Asia-Pacific region. It is not allowed to deal directly with clients as a regular undertaking.

   A regional headquarters is granted certain incentives (tax and duty-free importation of training materials, exemption from all local licenses, fees, dues, etc.) which are not enjoyed by branches or representative offices.

3. **What is a Multinational Company?**

   A Multinational Company is a foreign firm or entity that is engaged in international trade and has affiliates, subsidiaries or branch offices in the Asia-Pacific region, which is comprised of all countries bordering the Pacific ocean on the side of Asia, including Australia and New Zealand.

4. **What are affiliates?**

Affiliates are dealers or distributors of the foreign entity granted franchises or contracts for the sale or distribution of its goods or services.

5. **How are the terms "supervision", "coordination", "communication", "management" and "investment income" defined as contemplated by the Omnibus Investments Code (Executive Order No. 226)?**

"Supervision" means superintending, overseeing and guiding the activities of affiliates, subsidiaries or branch offices in the Asia-Pacific Region to conform with approved policies and objectives, without participating directly in the executive of the work or activities necessary to implement said policies and objectives.

"Coordination" means adjusting, arranging or harmonizing the policies and workings of its various affiliates, subsidiaries or branches in the Asia-Pacific Region for their harmonious and efficient functioning.

"Communications" means transmitting, disseminating and receiving information, messages, instructions for its affiliates, subsidiaries or branches in the Asia-Pacific Region.

"Management" means direction and control of personnel in the conduct of day-to-day activities required in the operation of a business or enterprise.

"Investment income" means dividend and interest income from Philippine stocks, bonds and other securities.

6. **What incentives are given to Regional Headquarters and its executives under Executive Order No. 226?**
   a. Incentives to Regional Headquarters
      1. **Exemption From Income Tax.** Regional Headquarters shall not be subject to income tax provided they do not derive or earn income in the Philippines and they do not derive or earn income in the Philippines and they act as supervisory, communications and coordination centers for their affiliates, subsidiaries or branches in the Asia-Pacific Region.
      2. **Exemption from contractor's Tax**. The regional headquarters, including their alien executives, are exempted from the contractor's tax.
      3. **Exemption from all kinds of Local Licenses, Fees and Dues.** The regional headquarters shall be Exemption from all kinds of local licenses, fees, dues, imposts and any other local taxes or burdens.
      4. **Tax and Duty-Free Importation of Training Materials.** Regional headquarters shall also enjoy tax and duty-free importation of equipment and materials such as video equipment, slides, printed materials and visual aids exclusively appropriate and intended for use in seminars and conferences related to the functions of the regional headquarters and which are not locally available.
      5. **Importation of Motor Vehicles**. Regional headquarters shall be entitled to import motor vehicles subject to prior approval of the Board of Investments and the payment of the corresponding taxes and duties, provided that such motor vehicles shall be for the exclusive use of its expatriate executives and that the number of its expatriate shall not exceed the number of its expatriates. Such motor years from their importation.

b. Incentives to Expatriates

1. **Multiple Entry Visa**. Foreign personnel of regional headquarters of multinational companies and their respective spouses and unmarried children under twenty one years of age, if accompanying them or if following non-immigrants, shall be issued multiple entry special visas valid for a period of one year.

   Non-immigrants who have been admitted under the multiple entry special visa, as well as their respective spouses and dependents, shall be exempt from the payment of all due under the immigration and alien registration laws and obtaining immigration clearance certificates and all types of clearances required by any government department or agency.

2. **Income Tax of 15%.** While other resident foreigners working in the Philippines are required to pay on a graduated tax rate up to 35% of their income earned in the country, aliens employed by regional headquarters shall be subject to income tax equal to 15% of their gross income earned from the regional headquarters.
3. **Tax and Duty-Free Importation of Personal and Household Effects.** An alien executive of the regional headquarters shall enjoy tax and duty-free importation of personal and household effects that arrive in the Philippines within 90 days before or after the conversion of the alien executive's admission category to special non-immigrant.
4. **Travel Tax Exemption.** Personnel of multinational companies performing technical and supervisory functions in the regional headquarters and the dependents of such foreign personnel, if joining them during the period of their assignment in the Philippines shall be exempted from the payment of travel tax.

7. **What are the other advantages in establishing a regional headquarters in the Philippines?**

The Philippines has the following to offer to regional headquarters established in the Philippines:

a. **Location and Environment**- the Philippines is strategically located in the Southeast Asia. it is also a very attractive country with friendly and hospitable people.
b. **Peace and order**- the Philippines is a safe place to work and live in.
c. **Communication facilities**- existing in the Philippines involve state-of the-art technology which can service both domestic and mobile phones, which can service both domestic and international requirements. There are also exist record carriers offering both domestic and international services in terms of providing telex, telegram, data communication, packet switch, leased channels, facsimile communication and electronic mail. The satellite systems (carrier's carrier) and electronic voice/record/data circuits to service record carriers. Telephone system has shifted to digital and the use of fiber optic system. Public phones are mandatory available in all towns.
d. **Transportation Facilities**- Several major international airlines service the Philippines daily. Air, land and sea transformation facilities may be utilized for internal travel to and from all points of the islands.
e. **Banking Service**- Full banking services are available thru such international bank as Bank of America, Citibank, Hong Kong and Shanghai Bank and Standard Chartered Bank.

f. **Legal Services**- Many international law firms are representative in Manila. They provide legal advice, can assist in contract negotiations and provide taxation advice to multinationals.
g. **Office and Housing Facilities**- The Philippines has good office and housing facilities which cost very much less than comparative facilities found in other countries in Asia Pacific region, (See Appendix 6).
h. **Educational Facilities**- Educational institution of all levels and of internationally accepted standards are open to family members of alien executives.
i. **Medical and Dental Optical Facilities**- The Philippines offer the latest medical, dental and optical facilities and services.
j. **Recreational and Amusement Facilities**- A wide variety of recreational facilities and activities can be found in the Philippines such as polo-playing, scuba-diving, nightclubs, theaters, casinos, golf, and tennis.
k. **Office and Clerical Services**- Competent English-speaking office and clerical help are easy available.
l. **Household and Domestic Help**- The luxury of having household help is still available in the Philippines at reasonable costs.

8. **What are the requirements in operating a regional Headquarters under the law?**
   a. The activities of the regional headquarters should be limited to acting as supervision, communications, and coordinating center for its affiliates, subsidiaries, and branches in the Asia-Pacific region.
   b. It should not drive any income from sources within the Philippines and should not participate in any subsidiary or branch office it might leave in the Philippines.
   c. The foreign firm should remit into the Philippines the entire amount necessary to cover the operations of its regional headquarters in the Philippines but not less than US $50,000.00 annually or its equivalent in acceptable foreign currencies.
   d. The foreign executives of the regional headquarters should each receive salaries and compensation in the Philippines equivalent to at least US $1,000.00 a month.
9. **What are the procedures for establishing a Regional Headquarters?**

   The applicant may go to the nearest Philippine Embassy or Consulate and secure the prescribed application form (Please refer to Appendix 5). The application, together with the supporting documents, shall be filed with the Securities and Exchange Commission (SEC) through the Board of Investments (BOI). Upon the favorable recommendation of the BOI, the SEC may issue to the applicant a certificate of Registration and license to establish and operate a regional headquarters in the Philippines.

   If the applicant - firm is in the Philippines, it can go directly in One- Stop Action Center of the BOI for the filling of its application.

10. **What documents are needed from the Philippine Commercial Attaché or Philippine Consul?**
    a. A certification from the Philippine Foreign Trade Senior Officer or, in his absence, the Philippine Consul in the foreign firm is an entity engaged in international trade with affiliates, subsidiaries of branch offices in the Asia- Pacific Region.
    b. Certificates from the Philippine Commercial Attaches of Consuls in at least two countries in Asia-Pacific region verifying the existence of an affiliate, subsidiary or branch office in each country.
11. **Where and how does the alien executive secure the multiple entry special visa to enter the Philippines?**

The alien executive, his spouse and unmarried children under 21 years of age accompanying or joining him after his admission into the Philippines, shall be issued multiple entry special visa(s) by the Philippine Consulate in the country whence he is departing for entry into the Philippines. The multiple entry special visa will be issued upon submission of an affidavit from a responsible officer of the applicant company to the effect that:

a. The person who seeks entry into the Philippines is an executive of an applicant company and will work exclusively for the applicant's regional headquarters which is duly licensed to operate in the Philippines.
b. He will receive a salary to be paid by the headquarters in the Philippines in an amount equivalent to at least US$12,000 per annum.
c. A copy of the regional headquarters' certificate of registration and license should be attached to the certificate.

12. **If the alien executive and his family have already entered the Philippines with visas other than those provided under Executive Order No. 226, can he apply for a change of visa category without having to leave the Philippines? If so how?**

Yes, the alien executive can apply for himself, his wife and unmarried children under twenty one (21) years of age, for a change of category of admission with the Bureau of Immigration. The change will be effected upon submission of the documents specified in no. "11" and three (3) copies of his and his dependent s' passports indicating the portion with their Passport Numbers and the immigration stamp showing the date of arrival in the Philippines.

13. **How does a Regional Office executive apply for visa renewal?**

The executive applying for visa renewal must submit the following:

1. Affidavit confirming his status as a Regional Office executive.
2. Copy of the SEC Registration Certificate
3. Three (3) copies of his and his dependents' passports showing their Passport Numbers and most recent date of arrival in the Philippines.
4. Last year's letter from the Bureau of immigration approving his visa renewal/conversion.

The documents shall be submitted to the Alien Registration Section of the Bureau of immigration. Upon receipt of notice of visa approval, the applicant shall present he passport for stamping.

14. **What is the procedure for information of training materials or equipment?**

Prior to importation, the approval of the Board of Investments should be obtained. To do this, the applicant should submit a letter of request to the BOI, particularly describing the materials or equipment, and their intended use. A sample of the training materials may be submitted to expedite evaluation of request.

If the request is approved, the BOI shall indorse the same to the Department of Finance which, after approval, shall likewise indorse the request to the Bureau of Customs for the release of the materials.

15. **What is the procedure of the importation of motor vehicles?**

Prior to importation, the approval of the BOI should be obtained. To do this, the applicant should submit to the BOI a letter-request indicating the brand, model, engine displacement and kerbweight of the vehicle. Under the energy Conservation Law, gasoline-powered passenger cars must have an engine displacement not exceeding 2800 cubic centimeters or kerbweight not exceeding 1500 kilograms, inclusive of accessories.

Upon approval, the request shall be indorsed to the Bureau of Import Services, Department of Trade and Industry for issuance of authorization to release, subject to payment of the corresponding duties and taxes.

16. **May the Regional Office transfer the ownership of the vehicle to another person?**

The Regional office may resell or otherwise dispose of the vehicle after three(3) years from the date of original registration provided that the Board of Investments is notified prior to the disposition.

17. **On what income of the alien executive does the 15% income tax apply?**

The tax of 15% applies only on the gross income the alien executive receives in the Philippines from the regional headquarters.

18. **What is the procedure for filing income tax returns?**

All foreign executives should secure a tax Account Number (TAN) with the BIR. A 15% income tax should be deducted by the Regional Office from the salary of the executive and remitted monthly within the first 10 days of the following month to the BIR. Regional Headquarters executives are also required to file income Tax Returns on or before April 15 of every year.

19. **Is the alien executive liable to tax on any income earned or derived outside the Philippines?**

No. Under Section 22 of National International Revenue Code, the alien executive of a regional headquarters is considered a non resident alien, and as such, he is not liable to tax on any income earned outside the Philippines.

20. **What expenses can be paid out of the required minimum annual remittance of US$50,000?**

The peso proceeds of the US$50,000 can be used for the ordinary and necessary expenses of the regional headquarters, including the tickets for travel abroad of its executives or to pay the peso equivalent of the US$1,000 minimum monthly salary of the alien executives.

. **Can a multinational company with dividend income from its subsidiary in the Philippines use said income to cover all or part of the US$50,000 minimum annual budget if its regional headquarters?**

Yes. Said dividend income may be used to cover the operating expenses of the regional headquarters provided that:

Said income is eligible for remittance under Central Bank rules and the transfer of such fund to the regional headquarters is made with the approval of the Central Bank;

The taxes on said income are duly paid;

The multinational company remits to the Philippines any part of the said US$50,000 minimum which is not covered by its peso income;

An appropriate report by the regional headquarters concerned in each case shall be submitted to the Securities and Exchange Commission, Central Bank (Foreign Exchange Regulations Department) and the Board of Investments.

21. **Can a multinational company buy or own private lands in the Philippines?**

    No. A multinational company being foreign - owned cannot buy or own private lands in the Philippines.

22. **Can a multinational company own condominium units?**

    Yes. The multinational company may own condominium units subject to the condition that its membership or stockholding in the condominium corporation owning the common areas including the land shall not exceed 40% of its entire capital stock

23. **What steps should be taken in applying for withdrawal/closure of regional headquarters or suspension of its operations?**

    The headquarters shall submit an application for closure, withdrawal or suspension of operations to the Securities and Exchange Commission, accompanied by a duly authenticated Board resolution of the parent office. The application should be submitted at least fifteen (15) days before such decision is effected.

On Regional Warehouse

1. **Who may establish a regional warehouse in the Philippines?**

   Multinational companies organized and existing under a foreign law which is engaged in international trade, and supplies spare parts or manufactured components and raw materials to its distributors and markets in the Asia-Pacific Region and other foreign areas, and which has established or will simultaneously establish a regional headquarters in the Philippines, may establish a regional warehouse in the Philippines.

2. **Are there tax incentives for imported articles destined for re-exportation?**

   Yes, imported spare parts or manufactured components, raw materials and other items as may be allowed by the Board of Investments for use exclusively on the goods stored, if brought and stored into the regional warehouse and re-exported directly therefrom shall not be subject to customs duty, internal revenue tax, export tax nor to local taxes. These tax exemptions also apply to goods transferred from the regional warehouse to a bonded manufacturing warehouse in the Philippines and eventually re-exported.

3. **Are the goods stored in the regional warehouse subject to the maximum storage period under the staff and customs code?**

   No. Articles duly entered for warehousing may remain in the warehouse for a period of two (2) years from the time of their transfer to the regional warehouse, which period may be extended with the approval of the Board of Investments for an additional period of one (1) year upon payment of the corresponding storage fee.

4. **What are the requirements to be submitted in applying for a regional warehousing license?**

   The requirements are:

   a. A certificate from the foreign Trade Officer or, in his absence, from the Philippine Consul in the firm's home country that said foreign firm is engaged in international trade, and supplies or will supply spare parts or manufactured components and raw materials to its distributors or markets in the Asia-Pacific Region.
   b. A certification from a principal officer of the foreign entry to the effect that said foreign entity has been authorized by its Board of Directors to establish its regional warehouse in the Philippines.
   c. The multinational company shall pay the Board of Investments and the appropriate Regional Collector of Customs the corresponding license fees and storage fees to be determined by said offices.
   d. A written application for the establishment of a regional warehouse to be submitted to the Board of Investments upon recommendation of the Bureau of Customs. The application shall describe the premises, the location and capacity of the regional warehouse and the purpose for which the building is to be used.

5. **What are the conditions to be observed in operating a regional warehouse?**
   a. The activities of the regional warehouse shall be limited to serving as a supply depot for the storage, deposit, safekeeping of its spare parts or manufactured components and raw materials including the packing, covering, putting up, marking, labeling and cutting altering to customer's specification, mounting and/or packaging into kits or marketable lots thereof, to fill up transactions and sales made by its head offices or parent companies and to serving as a storage or warehouse of goods purchased locally by the home office of the multinational company for export abroad.
   b. The regional warehouse shall not directly engage in trade nor directly solicit business, promote any sale, nor enter into any contract for the sale or disposition of goods in the Philippines.
   c. The regional warehouse will not derive any income from sources within the Philippines and its personnel will not participate in any manner in the management of any subsidiary, affiliate or branch office it might have in the Philippines.
   d. The entry or importation, storage or re-export of the goods destined for or to be stored in the regional warehouse will not involve any dollar outlay from Philippine sources.
   e. A separate accounting system shall be installed for the operation of the regional headquarters and regional warehouse.
   f. The personnel of the regional headquarters shall be responsible for the operation of the regional warehouse unless the exigencies of the service requires a separate set of the personnel to handle the operation of the regional warehouse.

g. Only articles authorized by the Board to be imported shall be transferred and stored at the regional warehouse.

6. **With what agency may the application for the establishment of a regional warehouse be filed?**

   The application may be filled with the Board of Investments.

7. **What is the procedure for the processing of the application?**

   The Board of Investment shall endorse the application to the Bureau of Customs. Upon receipt of the recommendation of the Bureau of customs, the Board shall evaluate the application and order the examination of the premises to be made with reference particularly to its location, construction and means by provided for the safekeeping of its articles in accordance with Customs rules and regulation.

   If the documents submitted for the application are found to be satisfactory, the Board shall issue in favor of the applicant a due Course Letter, specifying the terms and conditions for compliance.

   Upon acceptance of the terms and conditions, and compliance with the pre-registration requirements, the Board shall issue in favor of the applicant company a certificate of Registration and License authorizing it to establish a regional warehouse upon payment to the Board of a license fee of P5,000.00

8. **What government official is in charge of the supervision of regional warehousing operations?**

   Supervision of warehousing operations shall be under the jurisdiction of the District Collector of Customs concerned and shall be undertaken in accordance with the applicable Customs rules, regulations and Memorandum Orders.

9. **What are limitations on withdrawals for domestic use?**

   Withdrawal of articles for domestic use may be allowed to fill up orders or contracts of sale, distributors or indentors and the head office or parent company of the regional warehouse. Such withdrawal shall, in no case, exceed thirty (30%) per cent of the value of the goods it has brought into the Philippines in any given year. spare parts or manufactured components which are sold to and used by international carriers in connection with the rendering of services abroad or in the international routes are exempted from the 30% limitation, subject to the payment of taxes, duties and other changes due thereon.

10. **May the regional warehouse also be used for the storage of locally purchased goods?**

    Yes, the regional warehouse may be used as a storage or warehouse of goods purchased locally by the parent company or home office for export provided that such purchases shall be stored in the regional warehouse only after they have been cleared for export in accordance with the laws and regulations including those of the Central Bank, and stored separately from the imported items.

EXECUTIVE ORDER NO. 226
THE OMNIBUS INVESTMENTS CODE OF 1987
BOOK III

INCENTIVES TO MULTINATIONAL COMPANIES ESTABLISHING REGIONAL OR AREA HEADQUARTERS IN THE PHILIPPINES

CHAPTER I - LICENSING OF THE MULTINATIONAL COMPANY

ART. 58. **Qualifications of multinational company** - any foreign business entity formed, organized and existing under any law other than those of the Philippines whose purpose, as expressed in its organizational documents or by resolution of its Board of Directors or its equivalent, is it supervise, superintend, inspect or coordinate its own affiliates, subsidiaries, or branches in the Asia-Pacific Region may establish a regional or area headquarters in the Philippines, after securing a license therefor from the Securities and Exchange Commission, upon the favorable recommendation of the Board of Investments.
The Securities and Exchange Commission shall, within thirty (30) days from the effectively of this Code, Issue the Implementing rules and regulations. The following minimum requirements shall, however, be complied with by the said foreign entity.

a. A certification from the Philippines Foreign Trade Senior Officer or in the absence of such an official, a Philippine Consul in the foreign firm's home country that said foreign firm is an entity engaged in international trade with affiliates, subsidiaries or branch offices in the Asia-Pacific Region.
b. A certification from a principal officer of the foreign entity to the effect that the said foreign entity has been authorized by its Board of Directors or governing body to establish its regional headquarters in the Philippines, specifying that:
    1. The activities of the regional headquarters shall be limited to acting as a supervisory,
    2. communications and coordinating center for its subsidiaries, affiliates and branches in the region;
    3. The headquarters will not derive any income from sources within the Philippines and will not derive any income from sources within the Philippines.
    4. The headquarters shall notify the Board of Investments and the Securities and Exchange Commission of any decision to close down or suspend operations of its headquarters or terminate the services of any expatriate at least fifteen (15) days before the same is effected.
c. An undertaking that the multinational company will remit into the country such amount as may be necessary to cover its operations in the Philippines but which amount will not be less than fifty thousand United States dollars or its equivalent in other foreign currencies annually. Within thirty (30) days from receipt of Certificate of Registration from company will submit to the Securities and Exchange Commission a Certificate of inward remittance from a local bank showing that it has remitted to the Philippines the amount of at least thirty thousand United States dollars or its equivalent in other foreign currencies and converted the same to Philippine currency. Annually, within (30) days from the anniversary date of the multinational company's registration as a regional or area headquarters with the Securities & Exchange Commission, it will submit proof to the Securities & Exchange Commission of inward remittance amounting to at least fifty thousand United States dollars or its equivalent to other foreign currencies during the past year.
d. Any willful violation by the regional or area headquarters of a multinational company of any of the provisions of this Code, or its implementing rules and regulations, or other

terms and conditions of its registration, or any provision of existing laws, shall constitute a sufficient cause for the cancellation of its license or registration.

CHAPTER II - INCENTIVES TO EXPATRIATES

ART. 59. **Multiple entry visa** - Foreign personnel or area headquarters of multinational companies, their respective spouses and unmarried children twenty-one years of age, if accompanying them or if following to join them after their admission into the Philippines as non-immigrant shall be issued a multiple entry special visa, valid for a period of one year, to enter the Philippines ; Provided, that a responsible officer of the applicant company submits a certificate to the effect that the person who seeks entry into the Philippines is an executive of the applicant company and will work exclusively for applicant's regional or area headquarters which is duly licensed to operate in the Philippines, and that he will receive a salary and will be paid by the headquarters in the Philippines an amount equivalent to at least twelve thousand United States Dollars, or the equivalent in other foreign currencies per annum.

The admission and stay shall be co-terminus with the validity of multiple entry special visa. The stay, however, is extendible yearly upon submission on immigration and Deportation of a sworn certification by a responsible officer of the regional area headquarters: that its license to operate remains valid and subsisting; that he has been paid the Philippines from the date of original admission, the equivalent of at least one thousand United States dollars per month. or its equivalent in other foreign currencies; and that the regional or area headquarters has with held the tax due on said compensation and the same has been paid to the Bureau of Internal Revenue.

Non-immigrants who have been admitted under the multiple entry special visa, as well as their respective spouses and dependents, shall be exempt from: the payment of all fees due under the immigration and alien registration laws; securing alien certificates of registration; and obtaining immigration, clearance certificates, and all types of clearances required by any government, department or agency, except that upon final departure from the Philippines the employer of the said non-immigrants shall so advise in writing the commission on Immigration and Deportation at least five (5) working days prior to the non-immigrant's departure, and the finally departing non-immigrant employee shall be required to submit to the said office a tax clearance from the Bureau of Internal Revenue.

ART.60. **Withholding Tax of 15%** - Aliens employed by regional or area headquarters of multinational corporations shall be subject for each taxable year upon their gross income received from the regional or area headquarters established in the Philippines by multinational companies as salaries, wages, annuities, compensations, remuneration's and emoluments to a tax equal to fifteen percentum of such gross income.

ART.61. **Tax and Duty Free Importation** - An alien executive of the regional or area headquarters of a multinational company shall enjoy tax and duty free importation of personal and household effects as provided for under Section 105 (h) of the tariff and Customs Code, as amended, and Section 169 (b) (4) of the Internal Revenue Code, as amended.

ART.62. **Travel Tax Exemption** - Personnel of multinational companies performing technical and supervisory functions with regional headquarters at, but not engaged in business in the Philippines and the dependents, of such foreign personnel if joining them during the period of their assignment in the Philippines, as certified to by the Board of Investments, shall be excepted from the payment of travel tax imposed under Section 1 of Presidential Decree No. 1183 by securing a travel Tax Certificate from the Philippine Tourism Authority.

CHAPTER III - INCENTIVES TO THE REGIONAL HEADQUARTERS

ART.63. **Exemption from Income Tax.** - Regional or area headquarters established in the Philippines by multinational Corporation and which headquarters do not earn or derive income from the Philippines and which act as supervisory communication and coordinating center for their affiliates, subsidiaries, or branches in the Asia-Pacific Region shall not be subject to income tax.

ART.64. **Exemption from Contractor's Tax.** - The regional or area headquarters established in the Philippines by multinational corporations, including their alien executives, are exempted from the contractor's tax.

ART.65. **Exemption from all Kids of Local Licenses, Fees, Dues**.- The regional or area headquarters of multinational companies shall be exempt from all kids of local licenses, fees, dues, impost or any other local taxes or burdens.

ART.66. **Tax and Duty Free Importation of Training Materials, Importation of Motor Vehicles.** - Regional or area headquarters shall also enjoy tax and duty free importation of equipment and materials for training, conferences which are needed for the functions of the regional or area headquarters and which are not locally available subject to the prior approval of the Board of Investments. Regional or area headquarters shall be entitled to the importation of motor vehicles subject to the prior approval of the Board and the payment of the corresponding taxes and duties: Provided, That such motor vehicles shall be for the exclusive use of its expatriate executives and that such motor vehicle may be replace every three (3) years from their importation.

ART. 67. **Exemption from Registration Requirements.** - The regional or area headquarters of multinational companies shall be exempt from the provisions from the provisions of Book II of this Code.

RULES AND REGULATION TO IMPLEMENT EXECUTIVE ORDER NO.226 OTHERWISE KNOWN AS THE OMNIBUS INVESTMENTS CODE OF 1987

PART IV - INCENTIVES TO MULTINATIONAL COMPANIES ESTABLISHING REGIONAL OR AREA HEADQUARTERS IN THE PHILIPPINES

RULE XVII. APPLICATION FOR REGISTRATION

SECTION 1. **Filling of Application.** - Any multinational company may file, upon payment of filling fee, an application with the Securities and Exchange Commission through the One Stop Action Center (OSAC), Board of Investment for the establishment of its regional or area headquarters in the Philippines, in accordance with the form prescribed for the purpose, accompanied by the following documents:

1. A Certification from the Philippines Foreign Trade Senior Officer or, in his absence, The Philippine Consul in the foreign firm's country that said foreign firm is an entity engaged in international trade with affiliates, subsidiaries or branch offices in the Asia-Pacific Region.
2. A Certification from the principal officer of the foreign entity to the effect that the said foreign entity has been authorized by its board of directors or governing body to establish its regional headquarters in the Philippines, specify that:
    a. The activities of the regional headquarters shall be limited to acting as a supervisory, communications and coordinating center for its affiliates, subsidiaries or branches in the region.
    b. The headquarters will not derive any income from sources within the Philippines and will not participate in any manner in the management of any subsidiary or branch office the parent company might have in the Philippines.
    c. The headquarters shall notify the Board of Investments and the Securities and Exchange Commission of any decisions to close down or suspend operations of its headquarters or terminate the services of any expatriate at least fifteen (15) days before the same is effected.
3. An undertaking that the multinational company will remit into the country such amount as may be necessary to cover its operations in the Philippines but which amount will not be less than fifty thousand United States dollars ($50,000) or its equivalent in other foreign currency annually. Within thirty (30) days from receipt of the certificate of registration from the Securities and Exchange Commission, the multinational company will submit to the SEC and the BOI a certificate of inward remittance from a local bank showing that it has

remitted to the Philippines the amount of at least thirty thousand United States dollars (30,000) or its equivalent in other foreign currency.

SEC.2. **Issuance of Certificate of Registration and License.** Upon submission of all the required documents and the application having been favorably endorsed by the Board of Investments, The SEC shall issue to the applicant company a Certificate of Registration and License authorizing it to establish a regional or area headquarters in the Philippines.
SEC.3. **Reporting requirement**. - Every registered area headquarters of a multinational company shall submit to the Board of Investment and the Securities and Exchange Commission the following reports:

1. A general information sheet in the prescribed from showing, among other, the names, positions, titles and salaries of all the officers and personnel of the regional or area headquarters in the Philippines, within thirty (30) days after the issuance of the Certificate of Registration and License.

   Any change in the composition of its personnel shall likewise be reported within ten (10) days after such change occurs.

2. A certificate of inward remittance from a local bank showing that it has remitted to the Philippines the amount of at least 30,000 U.S. dollars or its equivalent in other foreign currency and converted the same to Philippines currency, within thirty (30) days from receipt of the certificate shall be submitted within ten (10) days from receipt of every additional inward remittance for the maintenance of the regional or area headquarters in the Philippines.
3. An annual report showing its operations in the Philippines, including proofs of inward remittance amounting to at least 50,000.00 U.S. dollars or its equivalent in other foreign currencies converted into Philippine Pesos, and its expenditures in the Philippines during the past year. All funds of the Regional Headquarters shall be utilized for salaries and other emoluments, including fringe benefits of personnel, rental of offices, transportation expenses, communication fees and similar costs for the maintenance of the regional or area headquarters in the Philippines

SEC.4. **Travel Tax Exemption.** - Travel tax exemptions may be granted only to personnel of multinational companies performing technical and supervisory functions and the dependents of such foreign personnel if joining them during the period of their assignment in the Philippines as certified by the Board of Investments.
SEC.5. **Tax and Duty-Free Importation of Personnel and Household Effects.** - This privilege may be enjoyed by an alien executive of the regional or area headquarters provided that the personal and household effects arrive in the Philippines within ninety (90) days before and after the conversion of the alien executive's admission category to special non-immigrant.
SEC.6. **Importation of Training Materials.** - Training materials qualified for tax and duty-free importation under Article 66 of the Code shall refer to equipment exclusively appropriate and shall be used in holding seminars and conference, such as video equipment, slides, printed materials and other visual aids.
SEC.7. **Importation of Motor Vehicles**. - Importation of motor vehicles intended as replacements for those already imported as provided under Article 66 of the Code, shall be with prior Board approval and subject to existing laws, rules and regulations.
SEC.8. **Personnel of Regional Headquarters.** - Foreign personnel of regional headquarters of multinational companies in the Philippines and their respective spouses and unmarried children under twenty-one (21) years of age shall be entitled to a multiple entry visa and all the benefits under Art. 59 of the Code subject to the conditions provide therein.

SEC.9. **Suspension of Availment of Incentives**.- No availment of incentives by regional headquarters shall be allowed if found delinquent in compliance, with any of terms and conditions for registration including such report and statistical data which may be required by the SEC or the Board.

SEC.10. **Visitorial Powers.** - In the public interest and /or for the enforcement of any applicable law, rules or regulation, the Board of Investment, SEC or any government office having jurisdiction on the matter may, through any of its duly authorized representatives, conduct necessary examination of records in the Philippines, make pertinent inquiries from its officials and take such action as may be necessary for the proper exercise of its authority.

SEC.11. **Withdrawal/Closure of Regional Headquarters.** - Applications/ petitions for withdrawal or closure of regional headquarters shall be filed with the Securities and Exchange Commission for appropriate consideration: Provided, That any final action thereon shall be made only after consultation with the Board of Investments.

SEC.12. **Penalties.** - Any willful violation by the regional or area headquarters in the Philippines of any of the provisions of Book III of the Omnibus Investment Code of 1987 or these rules and regulations, or other terms and conditions of its registration, or any existing applicable laws shall constitute a sufficient cause for the cancellation of its Certificate of Registration and License.

EXECUTIVE ORDER NO. 226
THE OMNIBUS INVESTMENTS CODE OF 1987
BOOK IV
INCENTIVES TO MULTINATIONAL COMAPANIES ESTABLISHING REGIONAL WAREHOUSES TO SUPPLY SPARE PARTS OR MANUFACTURED COMPONENTS AND RAW MATERIALS TO THE ASIA-PACIFIC REGION AND OTHER FOREIGN MARKETS

ART.68. **Qualification.** - A multinational company organized and existing under any law other than those of the Philippines which is engaged in International trade and supplies, spare parts or manufactured components and raw materials to its distributors or market in the Asia-Pacific Area and other foreign areas and which has established or will simultaneously establish a regional or area headquarters in the Philippines in accordance with the provisions of Book III of this Code and the rules and regulations implementing the same may also establish regional warehouse or warehouses in the Philippines, after securing a license therefor from the Board of Investments. The following minimum requirements shall be submitted or complied with by the said foreign entity in accordance with the rules and regulations to be issued by the Board of Investments as provided for in Article 7 (2) of this Code.

a. A certification from the Foreign Trade Officer or in the absence of such an official, a Philippine Consul in the foreign firm's home country that said foreign firm is engaged in international trade and supplies or will supply spare parts or manufactured components and raw materials to its distributors or markets in the Asia-Pacific Region.
b. A certification from a principal officer of the foreign entity to the effect that said foreign entity has been authorized by its Board of Directors or governing warehouse in the Philippines, specifying that:
    1. The activities of the regional warehouse shall be limited to serving as a supply depot for the storage, deposits, safekeeping of its spare parts of manufactured components and raw materials including the packing, covering, putting up, marking, labeling and cutting or altering to customer's specification, mounting and /or packaging into kits or marketable lots thereof, to fill up transactions and sales made by its head offices or parent companies and to serving as a storage or warehouse of goods purchased locally by the home office of the multinational for export abroad: Provide. that said locally purchased for export may be stored in the regional warehouse only after they have been cleared for export in accordance with the laws and regulations including those of the regional Central Bank and simplified procedures governing exports. The regional warehouse shall

not directly engage in trade nor directly solicit business, promote any sale nor enter into any contract for the sale or disposition of goods in the Philippines.
2. The regional warehouse will not derive any income from the source within the Philippines and its personnel will not participate in any manner in the management of any subsidiary, affiliate or branch office it might in the Philippines.
3. The personnel of the regional headquarters shall be responsible for the operation of the regional warehouse subject to the provision of this Code.

c. The Multinational company shall pay the Board of Investments and the appropriate Regional Collector of Customs the corresponding license fees and storage fees to be determined by said officers.
d. An Application for the establishment of a regional warehouse shall be made in writing to the Board of Investments upon recommendation of the Bureau of Customs. The application shall describe the premises, the location and capacity of the regional warehouse and the purpose for which the building is to be used.

The jurisdiction and responsibility of supervising the regional warehouses shall be vested on the Bureau of Customs.

The Board of Investments, in consultation with the Regional Director of Customs of the district where the warehouse will be situated shall cause an examination of the premises to be made with reference particularly to the location, construction and means provided for the safekeeping of its articles and if found satisfactory, it may authorize its establishment without complying with the requirements of any other government body and aimed at providing speedy procedure for its establishment, subject to the following conditions;

1. That articles to stored in the warehouse are spare parts of manufactured components and/or raw materials of the multinational company operator of distribution and supply to its Asia-Pacific markets including packaging, covering brands, labels and warehouse equipment as provided in Art.69 (a) hereof;
2. That the entry or importation, storage or re-export of the goods destined for or to be stored in the regional warehouse will not involve any dollar outlay from Philippines sources;
3. That they are of such character as to be readily identifiable for re-export ; and in case of local distribution they shall be subject to Article 69 paragraph (b) and the guidelines implementing Book IV of this Code;
4. That they shall be allowed provisional entry expeditiously by means of a pro forma invoice of the parent company identified, examined and appraised by the Regional Collector of Custom and they shall be directly delivered to and kept in the regional warehouses and released therefrom only in accordance with Article 69 paragraphs.(a) and (b) and the guidelines implementing Book IV of this Code:

   In the absence of a Regional Collector of Custom where the volume of the establishment of regional warehouse does not yet warrant the creation of said offices, and duties of the Regional Collector of Customs shall be performed by the Collector of Customs of the district where the regional warehouse will be located.

5. Each shipment of goods which will be stored in the regional warehouse shall be covered by an affidavit of the multinational company operator setting forth that said articles shall be exclusively used as supply for its Asia-Pacific markets and stating C & F price thereof;
6. That it shall file an ordinary warehousing bond in an amount equal to ONE HUNDRED PER CENT (100%) of the ascertained customs duties on the articles imported without

prejudice to its filling a general warehousing bond in lieu of the ordinary warehousing bond.

7. The percentage of annual allowable withdrawal for domestic use shall be subject to the approval of the Board of Investment: Provided, however, That in no case shall such withdrawals exceed thirty per cent (30%) of the value of goods it has brought in for any given year and the payment of the corresponding taxes and duties.

ART. 69. **Tax Treatment of Imported Articles in the Regional Warehouse.-**

a. **Tax Incentives for Qualified Goods Destined for Re-exportation to the Asia-Pacific and other Foreign Markets**.- Except as other wise provided in this Code, imported spare parts or manufactured components, raw materials and other items including any packages, coverings, brands and labels and warehouse equipment as may be allowed by the Board of Investments for use exclusively on the good stored, except those prohibited by law, brought into regional warehouse from abroad to be kept, stored/or deposit or used therein and re-exported directly therefrom under supervision of the Regional Collection of Customs for distribution to its Asia-Pacific and other foreign markets in accordance with the guidelines implementing Book IV of this Code including to a bonded manufacturing warehouse in the Philippines and eventually re-exported shall not be subject to customs duty, internal revenue tax, export tax nor to local taxes, the provisions of law to the contrary notwithstanding.
b. **Payment of Applicable Duties and Taxes on Qualifies Goods subject to Law and Regulations Covering Importation Merchandise if destined for the Local Market.-** Any spare parts, manufactured components, raw materials and other items sent, delivered or taken from the regional warehouse to the local market in accordance with the guidelines implementing Book IV of this Code shall be subject to the payment of customs duties, taxes and other charges and for which purpose, the proper commercial invoice of the head offices of parent companies shall be submitted to the Regional Collector of Customs; and shall be subject to laws and regulation governing imported merchandise, Provided, that in case any of the foregoing items are sold, bartered, hired or used for purpose other than they were intended for without prior compliance with the guidelines implementing Book IV of the Code and without prior payment of the duties, tax or other charge which would have been due and payable at the time of entry if the articles had been entered without the benefit of this decree, shall be subject to forfeiture and the importation shall constitute a fraudulent practice against customs revenue punishable under section 3602, as amended, of the tariff and Customs Code of the Philippines; Provided, further, that a sale pursuant to a judicial order shall not be subject to the preceding provision without prejudice to the payment of duties, taxes and other charges.

ART.70. **Exemption from the Maximum Storage Period under the Tariff and Custom Code: Period Storage in the Regional Warehouse.-** The Provision of the law in section 1908 of the Tariff and Customs Code of the Philippines, as amended, to the contrary notwithstanding, articles duly entered for warehousing may remain in the regional warehouses for a period of two (2) years from the time of their transfer to the regional warehouse, which period may be extended with the approval of the Board of Investments for an additional period of one (1) year upon payment of the corresponding storage fee on the unexported articles, as provided for under Article 69 paragraph (c) for each extension until they are re-exported in accordance with the guidelines implementing Book IV of this Code. Any articles withdrawn, released or removed contrary to the provisions of Article 69. paragraph (b) hereof.

ART.71. **Rules and Regulation on the Jurisdiction, Operation and Control over Qualified Goods Stored in the Regional Warehouse.** - The Board of Investment and the Bureau of Customs shall jointly issue special rules and regulations on the receiving, handling, custody, entry, examination, classifications, delivery, storage, warehousing, manipulation and packaging,

release for re-exportation and for the safekeeping, recording, inventory and liquidation of said qualified goods, any existing law notwithstanding. Such rules and regulations shall be formulated in consultation with the applicants/ operators of regional warehouse in order to be responsive to the objective of providing a procedure for the speedy inflow and outflow of the qualified goods which are destined for the Asia-Pacific and other foreign markets and keeping a proper balance between promoting the Philippines as a center for multinational regional warehouse and safeguarding the revenue laws of the country.
The Commissioner of the Customs is directed to expedite the immediate re-exportation or transshipment of the foregoing goods destined for regional warehousing to their Asia-Pacific and other foreign markets, including the emergency withdrawal for re-exportation by air and ship and the partial liquidation of bonds adopting simplified export procedures therefor.
ART.72. **Penalties**. - Any willful violation by the regional or area headquarters of a multinational company which has established regional warehouse or warehouses of the provisions of existing laws and implementing guidelines of Book IV of this Code shall constitute a sufficient cause for the cancellation the cancellation of its license or registration in addition to the penalties here in above provided in article 69. paragraph (b) hereof.
ART.73. The regional or area headquarters of multinational companies establishing regional warehouses shall exempt from the provisions of Book II of this Code.

RULES AND REGULATIONS TO IMPLEMENT EXECUTIVE ORDER NO. 226 OTHERWISE KNOWN AS THE OMNIBUS INVESTMENTS CODE OF 1987

RULE XVIII. MULTINATIONAL COMPANIES ESTABLISHING REGIONAL WAREHOUSES

SECTION 1. **Application for the Establishment of a Regional Warehouse.** - Multinational companies who have established regional headquarters under Book III hereof shall file as application for the establishment of regional warehouse(s) with the Board of Investment in a form prescribed for the purpose, accompanied by the following documents:

a. A certification from the foreign trade officer or, in his absence, the Philippines consul in the foreign firm's home country that said foreign firm is engage in international trade and supplies or will supply spare parts or manufactured components and raw material to its distributors or markets in the Asia-Pacific Region.
b. A certification from a principal officer of the foreign entity to the effect that the said foreign entity has been authorized by its Board of Directors or governing body to establish its regional warehouse in the Philippines, specifying that:

1. The activities of the regional warehouse shall be limited to serving as a supply depot for the storage, deposit, safekeeping of its spare parts or manufactured components and raw materials including the packing, covering, putting up, marking, labeling and cutting or altering to customer's specification, mounting and/or packaging into kits or marketable lots thereof, to fill up transactions and sales made by its head offices or parent companies and to serving as a storage or warehouse of goods purchased locally by the home office of the multinational for export abroad; Provided, That, said locally purchase goods for export may be stored in the regional warehouse only after they have been cleared for exports in accordance with the laws and regulations including those of the Central Bank and simplified procedures governing exports. The regional warehouse shall not directly solicit business, promote any sale, nor enter into any contract for the sale or disposition of goods in the Philippines.
2. The regional warehouse will not derive any income from sources within the Philippines and its personnel will not participate in any manner in the management of any subsidiary, affiliate, or branch office its parent company might have in the Philippines.

3. The personnel of the regional headquarters shall be responsible for operation of the regional warehouse subject to the provisions of Book IV of this Code unless the exigencies of the service requires a separate set of personnel to handle the operation of the regional warehouse.
4. A separate accounting system shall be installed for the operation of the regional headquarters and the regional warehouse.

1. Propose list contract (or ownership papers) covering the proposed warehouse.
2. Plant location showing area of access to the property.
3. Plant layout showing and describing the size and contraction of the proposed warehouse together with the intended use for each room, section or compartment as well as the surrounding premises.
4. List of proposed machineries and equipment for packing, covering, branding, labeling, mounting and cutting or altering of articles to customer's specification.
5. List propose spare parts, manufactured components or raw materials to be stored in the regional warehouse.

   The Board shall endorse the application to the Bureau of Customs for determining compliance of the provision of Section 3 hereof.

SEC.2. **Multinational companies without Regional headquarters.** - Multinational companies who have not established regional headquarters in the Philippines under Book III hereof shall be allowed to file simultaneously an application to establish regional headquarters under Book III and an application to establish a regional warehouse(s) under Book IV of the Code in a form prescribed for the purpose accompanied by the documents mentioned in the preceding sections and under Section 1, Rule XVII of these Implementing Rules and Regulations.
The application for the establishment of the regional warehouse filed by the applicant with the Board of Investments shall be processed upon receipt thereof. The Board shall endorse to the Bureau of Customs the multinational company's application for regional warehouse(s). Action thereon shall, however, be held in abeyance until the issuance of the certification and License by the Securities and Exchange Commission to establish regional headquarters under Book III of the Code and receipt of the recommendation of the Bureau of Customs. The Board shall then evaluate the multinational company's application for regional warehouse in accordance with these rules and regulations.
SEC.3. **Examination of Proposed Regional Warehouse Premises.** - The BOI or its duly authorized representative, in consultation with the Regional Collector of Customs or his duly authorized representative of the district where the warehouse will be situated, shall cause an examination of the premises to be made wit reference particularly to its location and means provided for the safekeeping of its articles in accordance with Customs rules and regulations.
SEC.4. **Due Course Letters.** - The Board of Investment, upon submission by the application of all the documents required in Section 2 hereof and said documents having been found satisfactory, shall issue in favor of the applicant a Due Course Letter, specifying the terms and conditions for compliance.
SEC.5. **Certificate of Registration and License.** - Upon acceptance of the terms and conditions and compliance with the pre-registration requirements, the Board shall issue in favor of the applicant company a Certificate of Registration and License authorizing it to establish regional warehouse (s) upon payment to the Board of a license fee of P5,000.00. Subsequent annual payment of the license fee in the amount of P5,000.00 shall be made within the first twenty (20) days of January of each year.
SEC.6. **List of Articles to be Imported.** - Only articles authorized by the Board to be imported shall be transferred and stored at the regional warehouse. For this purpose, the Board shall furnish the District Collector of Customs a list of importable articles as well as amendatory or supplemental lists.

SEC.7. **Period of Storage of Imported Articles.** - The provisions of Section 1908 of the Tariff and Customs Code notwithstanding, articles duly entered for warehousing in the regional warehouse may remain therein for a period of two (2) years from the time of their transfer to the warehouse, which period may be extended, with the approval of the Board for an additional period of one (1) year upon payment of the corresponding storage fee as penalty on the un-exported articles for each extension until they are finally exported.
SEC.8. **Supervision of Warehousing Operations**. - Supervision of warehousing operations shall be under the jurisdiction of the District Collector of Customs concerned and shall be undertaken in accordance with applicable Customs rules, regulations, and Memorandum Orders.
SEC.9. **Manipulation of Articles in the Warehouse.** - All work on articles shall be done inside the warehouse. The Articles being prepared for re-export or for local consumption may be repacked, packaged, covered, put up, marked, labeled, cut or otherwise altered but in no case shall processing be undertaken unless authorized by the Board.
SEC.10. **Limitation on Withdrawals for Domestic use.** - Withdrawal of articles for domestic use may be allowed to fill up orders or contracts of sale, distributors or indentors and the head office or parent company of the regional warehouse to the extent as may be authorized by the Board. Such withdrawal shall, in no case, exceed thirty (30%) per cent of the value of the goods it has brought into the Philippines in any given year except spare parts or manufactured components which are sold to and used by international carries in connection with the rendering of services abroad or in the international routes (e.g. shipping airlines companies) subject, however, to the payment of taxes, duties and other charges due thereon.
SEC.11. **Storage of Locally Purchased Goods for Export.** - The regional Warehouse may also serve as a storage or warehouse of goods purchased locally by the parent company or home office for export provided that such purchases shall be stored separately from importations.
SEC.12. **Assignment of Customs Personnel to the Regional Warehouses.** - The District Collector of Customs shall assign such customs personnel as may be necessary to supervise the operations of the regional warehouse. the operator shall provide customs personnel with suitable working space complete with office supplies and equipment.
SEC.13. **Books and Records.** - Books of Account and other records as may be prescribed by the Bureau of Customs shall be maintained by the operator and kept at all times in their place of business subject to immediate inspection on demand by the authorized customs officials and/or Board representatives.
SEC.14. **Visitorial Power.** - In the public interest and/or for the effective implementation of Book IV of this Code, the Board of Investment and the Bureau of Customs may, through any of its duly authorized representative, exercise the following function:

a. Conduct such investigations as it deems necessary to determine whether or not a multinational company which has registered its regional warehouse in the Philippines is complying with the provisions of Book IV of this Code or of any applicable laws, rules and regulations, including but not limited to:
    1. Conducting necessary examination of the book and records of accounts of the regional 2. warehouse;
    2. Determing all the facts and circumstances concerning the manner to be investigated, including making pertinent inquiries from its personnel; and
    3. Taking such action as may be necessary for the proper exercise of its authority.
b. Request such other reports, financial or otherwise, as may be necessary in the public interest or for the proper compliance of this code: Provided, That such requirement shall be applicable to all those similarly situated;
c. Take such proper proceeding to revoke or cancel the license or registration of the regional headquarters of the multinational company which has established a regional warehouse in the Philippines in case the same is found to have willfully violated any provision of this Code and these implementing rules and regulations.

SEC.15. **Penaties and/or Cancellation of License of Registration.** -

1. Any spare parts, manufactured components, raw materials and other items used on the said parts, components or materials for packing, covering, putting up, marking, labeling, cutting or altering to customer's specification, mounting and/or packaging into kits and marketable lots, which are withdrawn, released, removed, sold, bartered, into or used for any purpose contrary to the provisions of Article 69 (b) of this Code and for purpose other than what they were intended for without prior payment of the duty, tax or other charges which would have been due and payable at the time of entry if the article had been entered without the benefits of the Code, shall be subject to forfeiture and the importation shall constitute a fraudulent practice against Customs revenue punishable under Section 3602, as amended, of the Tariff and Customs Code of the Philippines. A sale pursuant to a judicial order not be subject to this provision without prejudice to the payment of duties, taxes and other charges.
2. Any willful violation by the regional headquarters or a multinational company which has established regional warehouse or warehouses of any provision of this Code or its implementing rules and regulations, or any provision of existing laws shall constitute a sufficient cause for cancellation of its license or registration, in addition to the penalties provided for Article 69 (b) of the Code.

APPLICATION FORMS

Republika ng Pilipinas Kagawaran ng Kalakal **KOMISYON SA MGA PANAGOT AT PALITAN** (Securities and Exchange Commission) Maynila

The ____________________hereby applies with the Securities and Exchange Commission under the 1987 Omnibus Investment Code (Executive Order No.226) Book III for registration and license to establish a regional or area headquarters in the Philippines, and submits the following statements, undertaking and accompanying documents:

1. The ____________________is a foreign company organized and existing under the laws of __________________engaged in international trade with affiliates, subsidiaries, or branch offices in the Asia-Pacific Region.
2. The location of its principal or home office is at
____
3. That it has affiliates, subsidiaries or branch offices in the following places:
____
4. Bank references (Foreign and Local) Address
____
5. That the activities of the regional or area headquarters to be established in the Philippines shall be limited to acting as supervision, communications and coordination center for its affiliates, subsidiaries or branches of the region;
6. That the regional headquarters will not derive any income from source within the Philippines and will not participate in any manner in the management of any subsidiary or branch office the foreign entity might have in the Philippines;
7. That The MULTINATIONAL COMPANY will remit into the country the entire amount necessary to cover the operations of its regional headquarters in the Philippines which will not be less than FIFTY THOUSAND ($50,000) U.S. DOLLARS or its equivalent in other acceptable foreign currencies annually;

   That within thirty (30) days from receipt or license from the Securities and Exchange Commission, the MULTINATIONAL COMPANY will submit a certification of inward remittance from a local bank showing that it has remitted to the Philippines the amount of at least THIRTY THOUSAND (30,000) U.S. DOLLARS or its equivalent in other foreign currencies and converted the same to Philippines currency.

That the headquarters shall notify the Board of Investments and the Securities and Exchange Commission of any decision to close down or suspend operations of its headquarters or terminate the services of any expatriate at least fifteen (15) days before the same is effected.

8. ____________________________ residence or office address at _____________ __________________________ is its local agent in the Philippines empowered to accept service of summons and processes in all legal proceedings against the company and of all notices affecting the same.
9. Attached hereto are:
   a. Certification from the Philippines Commercial Attaché or Philippines Consul in the home country of this firm to the effect that it is engaged in international trade with affiliates, subsidiaries or branch offices in the Asia-Pacific Region;
   b. Sworn certification from a principal officer of the firm that it has been authorized by its board of directors of governing body
   c. Verification issued by the Commercial Attaché of the Philippine Consul to the effect that in his country of assignment there exists an affiliate, subsidiary or branch office of the form.

WITNESS the signature of _________________________hereunto duly authorized to sign for and in behalf of the applicant at____________________on the _____________ _____________day of ________,19___.

____
(Name of Company)

By:

____
(Authorized Representative)

SUBSCRIBED AND SWORN to before me this _____________day of _______________19_____at__________________ Affiant exhibited to me his/her Passport NO.________________issued at ______________________on ________________,19____.

____
Notary Public
Until December 31, 19____

Doc. No. ________
Page No. ________
Book No. ________
Series No.________
(If executed abroad the signature of the Notary Public must be duly authenticated by the Philippine Consul in the Place of execution).

CERTIFICATION

This is to certify that ____________________, is a company duly organized and existing under the laws of ________________ with principal office or General Headquarters in ____________________ and engaged in international trade having affiliates, subsidiaries or branch offices in the Asia Pacific Region particularly in ____________according to the pertinent documents presented to and verified by this office and may, therefore, be qualified to establish Regional or Area Headquarters in the Philippines, pursuant to the provisions of Headquarters in the Philippines, pursuant to the provisions of Executive Order No. 226.

This certification is issues upon the request of

__________________.

Name of person

requesting ______________________ capacity or position of

____

Person requesting in the corporation

______________________ ______________________
(Place) (Date)

COMMERCIAL ATTACHE
or
PHILIPPINE CONSUL

STATEMENT OF MONETARY INWARD REMITTANCES
FOR THE REGIONAL OR AREA HEADQUARTERS OF
____

Received on ______________________

1. Name of Recipient: ______________________
2. Address of Recipient: ______________________
3. Amount Received: ______________________
4. Equivalent in Philippine Peso After Conversion: ______________________
5. Form of Remittance (Demand Draft, Cash, Traveler's, Cheque, Bills of Exchange, Letter of credit, etc.) ______________________
6. Name and Address of Bank: ______________________
7. Purpose of Remittance: ______________________

Attached hereto is the back certificate of inward remittance.

____
Head of Regional or Area Headquarters

(To be Submitted in triplicate within ten (10) days after receipt of inward remittance).

BASIC PUBLICATIONS ON PHILIPPINES

TITLE	ISBN
Philippines A Spy" Guide"	1438738684
Philippines Agricultural Sector Business Opportunities Handbook	1438738692
Philippines Air Force Handbook	1438738706
Philippines Army Handbook	1438738714
Philippines Army, National Security and Defense Policy Handbook	1438738722
Philippines Banking & Financial Market Handbook	1438738730
Philippines Business and Investment Opportunities Yearbook	1438738749

Philippines Business Intelligence Report - Practical Information, Opportunities, Contcts	1438738757
Philippines Business Law Handbook - Strategic Information and Basic Laws	1438738765
Philippines Clothing & Textile Industry Handbook	1438738773
Philippines Country Study Guide - Strategic Information and Developments	1438738781
Philippines Customs, Trade Regulations and Procedures Handbook	143873879X
Philippines Diplomatic Handbook - Strategic Information and Developments	1438738803
Philippines Ecology & Nature Protection Handbook	1438738811
Philippines Economic & Development Strategy Handbook	143873882X
Philippines Energy Policy, Laws and Regulations Handbook	1438738838
Philippines Export-Import Trade and Business Directory	1438738846
Philippines Financial Market Business Opportunities Handbook	1438738854
Philippines Foreign Policy and Government Guide	1438738862
Philippines Government and Business Contacts Handbook	1438738870
Philippines Industrial and Business Directory	1438738889
Philippines Internet and E-Commerce Investment and Business Guide - Strategic and Practical Information: Regulations and Opportunities	1438738897
Philippines Investment and Business Guide - Strategic and Practical Information	1438738900
Philippines Justice System and National Police Handbook	1438738919
Philippines Medical & Pharmaceutical Industry Handbook	1438738927
Philippines Mineral & Mining Sector Investment and Business Guide - Strategic and Practical Information	1438738935
Philippines National Police Force Handbook	1438738943
Philippines Navy Handbook	1438738951
Philippines Oil & Gas Sector Business & Investment Opportunities Yearbook	143873896X
Philippines President Handbook	1438738978
Philippines Privatization Programs and Regulations Handbook	1438738986
Philippines Science and Technology Policy Handbook	1438738994
Philippines Telecommunication Industry Business Opportunities Handbook	1438739001
Philippines Trade Policy Handbook	143873901X
Philippines Transportation and Communication Policy Handbook	1438739028

BASIC LAWS AND REGULATIONS AFFECTING BUSINESS[2]

COUTRY	LAW TITLE
Philippines	Act no 9255 Act allowing illegitimate children to use the surname of their father
Philippines	Act No. 4003 - The Fisheries Act
Philippines	Agriculture and Fisheries Modernization Act of 1997
Philippines	Amendment to RA 7170 - Organ Donation Act of 1991
Philippines	An act amending Republic Act No. 9160, otherwise known as the "Anti-Money Laundering Act of 2001"

[2] For ordering tests of specific laws in English or French, Please contact Global Investment Center USA at ibpusa3@gmail.com

Philippines	An Act Establishing a Provident Personal Savings Plan, known as the Personal Equity and Retirement Account (PERA) R.A. 9505
Philippines	Anti-Money Laundering Act of 2001
Philippines	Biofuels Act of 2006
Philippines	Citizenship Retention and RE-acquisition Act of 2003
Philippines	Civil Code
Philippines	Community Intellectual Rights Protection Act - CIRPA (2001, draft)
Philippines	Comprehensive and Integrated Shelter Financing Act of 1994
Philippines	Constitution of the Republic of the Philippines
Philippines	Cotton Industry Development Law of 1998
Philippines	Department of Energy Act of 1992
Philippines	Ecological Solid Waste Management Act of 2000
Philippines	Electric Power Industry Reform Act of 2001
Philippines	Family Code
Philippines	Health Law
Philippines	Implementing Rules and Regulations of R.A. 9505
Philippines	Implementing Rules and Regulations of The Securitization Act of 2004 (Republic Act No. 9267)
Philippines	Implementing Rules and Regulations of the Seed Industry Development Act of 1992
Philippines	Indigenous Peoples Rights Act (1997)
Philippines	Intellectual property Code
Philippines	Juvenile Justice and Welfare Act 2006
Philippines	Labor Code
Philippines	New Central Bank Act (Republic Act No. 7653)
Philippines	Philippine Accountancy Act 2004
Philippines	Presidential Decree No. 1067 - The Water Code of the Philippines
Philippines	Presidential Decree No. 1152 - Philippine Environment Code
Philippines	Presidential Decree No. 1433 - Plant Quarantine Law of 1978
Philippines	Presidential Decree No. 1899 - Small-Scale Mining Law
Philippines	Presidential Decree No. 601 - Revised Coast Guard Law
Philippines	Presidential Decree No. 705 - Revised Forestry Code of the Philippines
Philippines	Presidential Decree No. 856 - Code on Sanitation of the Philippines
Philippines	Presidential Decree No. 979 - Marine Pollution Decree of 1976
Philippines	Renewable Energy Act of 2008
Philippines	Repbulic Act No. 9184 - Government Procurement Reform Act
Philippines	Republic Act N0. 1364 - Sanitary Engineering Law
Philippines	Republic Act No 9194 - Amendment to the Anti-Money Laundering Act
Philippines	Republic Act No. 3019 - Anti-Graft and Corrupt Practices Act
Philippines	Republic Act No. 4226 - Hospital Licensure Act
Philippines	Republic Act No. 4566 - Contractors License Law
Philippines	Republic Act No. 544 - Civil Engineering Act
Philippines	Republic Act No. 5921- Pharmacy Act
Philippines	Republic Act No. 6425 - Dangerous Drugs Act of 1972
Philippines	Republic Act No. 6552 - Realty Installment Buyer Protection Act
Philippines	Republic Act No. 6657 - Comprehensive Agrarian Reform Law of 1988

Philippines	Republic Act No. 6675 - Generics Act of 1988
Philippines	Republic Act No. 6713 - "Code of Conduct and Ethical Standards for Public Officials and Employees
Philippines	Republic Act No. 6727 - Wage Rationalization Act
Philippines	Republic Act No. 6728 - Government Assistance to Students and Teachers in Private Education Act
Philippines	Republic Act No. 6770 - Ombudsman Act of 1989
Philippines	Republic Act No. 6969 - Toxic Substances and Hazardous and Nuclear Wastes Control Act of 1990
Philippines	Republic Act No. 6975 - Department of the Interior and Local Government Act of 1990
Philippines	Republic Act No. 6981 - Witness Protection, Security and Benefit Act
Philippines	Republic Act No. 7042 - Foreign Investments Act
Philippines	Republic Act No. 7076 - People's Small-Scale Mining Act of 1991
Philippines	Republic Act No. 7080 - Act Defining and Penalizing the Crime of Plunder
Philippines	Republic Act No. 7156, "An Act Granting Incentives to Mini-Hydro-Electric Power Developers and for Other Purposes
Philippines	Republic Act No. 7160 - The Local Government Code of 1991
Philippines	Republic Act No. 7192 - Women in Development and Nation Building Act
Philippines	Republic Act No. 7279 - Urban Development and Housing Act of 1992.
Philippines	Republic Act No. 7305 - The Magna Carta of Public health Workers
Philippines	Republic Act No. 7308 - Seed Industry Development Act of 1992
Philippines	Republic Act No. 7394 - Consumer Act of the Philippines
Philippines	Republic Act No. 7581 - Price Act 1992
Philippines	Republic Act No. 7600 - Rooming-in- and Breastfeeding Act of 1992
Philippines	Republic Act No. 7641 - Retirement Pay Law
Philippines	Republic Act No. 7648 - Electric Power Crisis Act of 1993
Philippines	Republic Act No. 7658 - Prohibiting the Employment of children Below Fifteen (15) Years of Age in Public and Private Undertakings
Philippines	Republic Act No. 7718 - BOT Law
Philippines	Republic Act No. 7719 - National Blood Services Act of 1994
Philippines	Republic Act No. 7727 - Magna Carta for Disabled Persons
Philippines	Republic Act No. 7832 - Anti-electricity and Electric Transmission Lines/Materials Pilferage Act of 1994
Philippines	Republic Act No. 7844 - Export Development Act of 1994
Philippines	Republic Act No. 7875 - National Health Insurance Act of 1995
Philippines	Republic Act No. 7877 - Anti Sexual Harassment Act of 1995
Philippines	Republic Act No. 7880 - Fair and Equitable Access to Education Act
Philippines	Republic Act No. 7883 - Barangay Health Workers' Benefits and Incentives Act of 1995
Philippines	Republic Act No. 7916 - The Special Economic Zone Act of 1995
Philippines	Republic Act No. 7942 - Philippine Mining Act of 1995
Philippines	Republic Act No. 8042 - Migrant Workers and Overseas Filipinos Act of 1995
Philippines	Republic Act No. 8043 - Inter-Country Adoption Act of 1995
Philippines	Republic Act No. 8048 - Coconut Preservation Act of 1995
Philippines	Republic Act No. 8187 - Paternity Leave Act of 1996
Philippines	Republic Act No. 8188 - Law Increasing Penalty for Violation of Wage Laws

Philippines	Republic Act No. 8282 - Social Security Act of 1997
Philippines	Republic Act No. 8293 - Intellectual Property Code of the Philippines
Philippines	Republic Act No. 8353 - The Anti-Rape Law of 1997
Philippines	Republic Act No. 8369 - Family Courts Act 1997
Philippines	Republic Act No. 8370 - Children's Television Act of 1997
Philippines	Republic Act No. 8423 - Traditional and Alternative Medicine Act (TAMA of 1997)
Philippines	Republic Act No. 8424 - National Internal Revenue Code of 1997
Philippines	Republic Act No. 8425 - Social Reform and Poverty Alleviation Act
Philippines	Republic Act No. 8479, "Downstream Oil Industry Deregulation Act of 1998"
Philippines	Republic Act No. 8485 - Animal Welfare Act of 1998
Philippines	Republic Act No. 8491 - Flag and Heraldic Code of the Philippines
Philippines	Republic Act No. 8493 - Speedy Trial Act of 1998
Philippines	Republic Act No. 8495 - Mechanical Engineering Act of 1998
Philippines	Republic Act No. 8504 - HIV Prevention and Control of 1988
Philippines	Republic Act No. 8505 - The Rape Victims Assistance and Protection Act of 1998
Philippines	Republic Act No. 8550 - Fisheries Code of 1998
Philippines	Republic Act No. 8749 - Clean Air Act of 1999
Philippines	Republic Act No. 8750 - Seat Belts Use Act of 1999
Philippines	Republic Act No. 8751 - Countervailing Act of 1999
Philippines	Republic Act No. 8752 - The Anti-Dumping Act of 1999
Philippines	Republic Act No. 8762 - Retail Trade Liberalization Act of 2000
Philippines	Republic Act No. 8792 - E-Commerce Law
Philippines	Republic Act No. 8800 - Safeguards Measures Act
Philippines	Republic Act No. 8972 - The Solo Parents' Welfare Act of 2000
Philippines	Republic Act No. 8976 - Philippine Food Fortification Act of 2000
Philippines	Republic Act No. 9003 - Ecological Solid Waste Management Act of 2000
Philippines	Republic Act No. 9135 - Transaction Value Act.
Philippines	Republic Act No. 9147 - Wildlife Resources Conservation and Protection Act
Philippines	Republic Act No. 9155 - Governance of Basic Education Act of 2001
Philippines	Republic Act No. 9165 - Dangerous Drugs Act of 2002
Philippines	Republic Act No. 9168 - Philippine Plant Variety Protection Act of 2002
Philippines	Republic Act No. 9175 - Chain Saw Act of 2002
Philippines	Republic Act No. 9208 - Anti-trafficking in Persons Act
Philippines	Republic Act No. 9211 - Tobacco Regulation Act
Philippines	Republic Act No. 9225 - Citizenship Retention and RE-acquisition Act of 2003
Philippines	Republic Act No. 9231 - The Special Protection of Children against Child Abuse, Exploitation and Discrimination Act
Philippines	Republic Act No. 9239 - Optical Media Act of 2003
Philippines	Republic Act No. 9239 - Optical Media Act of 2003
Philippines	Republic Act No. 9255 - Family Code of the Philippines
Philippines	Republic Act No. 9257 - Expanded Senior Citizens Act of 2003
Philippines	Republic Act No. 9262 - Anti-Violence Against Women and Their Children Act of 2004
Philippines	Republic Act No. 9275 - Clean Water Act
Philippines	Republic Act No. 9285 - Alternative Dispute Resolution Act of 2004
Philippines	Republic Act No. 9288 - Newborn Screening

Philippines	Republic Act No. 9341 - Rental Law
Philippines	Republic Act No. 9344 - Juvenile Justice System
Philippines	Republic Act No. 9346 - Act Prohibiting the Imposition of Death Penalty in the Philippines
Philippines	Republic Act No. 9422 - Amendment to the Migrant Workers and Overseas Filipinos Act of 1995
Philippines	Republic Act No. 9482 - An Act Providing for the Control and Elimination of Human and Animal Rabies, Prescribing Penalties for Violation Thereof and Appropriating Funds Therefore
Philippines	Republic Act No. 9482 - An Act Providing for the Control and Elimination of Human and Animal Rabies, Prescribing Penalties for Violation Thereof and Appropriating Funds Therefore
Philippines	Republic Act No. 9497 - Act Creating the Civil Aviation Authority of the Philippines
Philippines	Republic Act No. 9502 - An act providing for cheaper and quality medicines
Philippines	Republic Act No. 9504 - Amendment to the National Internal Revenue Code
Philippines	Republic Act No. 9510 - Act Establishing the Credit Information System
Philippines	Republic Act No. 9512 - Environmental Awareness Act
Philippines	Republic Act No. 9514 - Revised Fire Code of the Philippines of 2008
Philippines	Republic Act No. 9653 - Rent Control Act
Philippines	Republic Act No.9136 - Electric Power Industry Reform Act of 2001
Philippines	Revised Non-Stock Savings and Loan Association Act of 1997
Philippines	Revised Penal Code
Philippines	Seed Industry Development Act of 1992
Philippines	Social Reform and Poverty Alleviation Act
Philippines	Tax Reform Act of 1997
Philippines	The Labor Code of the Philippines
Philippines	The Philippine Fisheries Code of 1998
Philippines	The Securitization Act of 2004
Philippines	Traditional and Alternative Medicine Act (1997)
Philippines	Wildlife Resources Convservation and Protection Act (RA 9147) (2001)

WORLD INVESTMENT AND BUSINESS GUIDE LIBRARY

Ultimate guides for business and investment operations in the country.

Price: $99 each

1.	**Afghanistan Investment and Business Guide**
2.	**Aland Investment and Business Guide**
3.	**Albania Investment and Business Guide**
4.	**Algeria Investment and Business Guide**
5.	**Andorra Investment and Business Guide**
6.	**Angola Investment and Business Guide**
7.	**Anguilla Investment and Business Guide**
8.	**Antigua and Barbuda Investment and Business Guide**
9.	**Antilles (Netherlands) Investment and Business Guide**
10.	**Argentina Investment and Business Guide**
11.	**Armenia Investment and Business Guide**
12.	**Aruba Investment and Business Guide**
13.	**Australia Investment and Business Guide**
14.	**Austria Investment and Business Guide**
15.	**Azerbaijan Investment and Business Guide**
16.	**Bahamas Investment and Business Guide**
17.	**Bahrain Investment and Business Guide**
18.	**Bangladesh Investment and Business Guide**
19.	**Barbados Investment and Business Guide**
20.	**Belarus Investment and Business Guide**
21.	**Belgium Investment and Business Guide**
22.	**Belize Investment and Business Guide**
23.	**Benin Investment and Business Guide**
24.	**Bermuda Investment and Business Guide**
25.	**Bhutan Investment and Business Guide**
26.	**Bolivia Investment and Business Guide**
27.	**Bosnia and Herzegovina Investment and Business Guide**
28.	**Botswana Investment and Business Guide**
29.	**Brazil Investment and Business Guide**
30.	**Brunei Investment and Business Guide**
31.	**Bulgaria Investment and Business Guide**
32.	**Burkina Faso Investment and Business Guide**
33.	**Burundi Investment and Business Guide**
34.	**Cambodia Investment and Business Guide**
35.	**Cameroon Investment and Business Guide**
36.	**Canada Investment and Business Guide**
37.	**Cape Verde Investment and Business Guide**

38.	Cayman Islands Investment and Business Guide
39.	Central African Republic Investment and Business Guide
40.	Chad Investment and Business Guide
41.	Chile Investment and Business Guide
42.	China Investment and Business Guide
43.	Colombia Investment and Business Guide
44.	Comoros Investment and Business Guide
45.	Congo Investment and Business Guide
46.	Congo, Democratic Republic Investment and Business Guide
47.	Cook Islands Investment and Business Guide
48.	Costa Rica Investment and Business Guide
49.	Cote d'Ivoire Investment and Business Guide
50.	Croatia Investment and Business Guide
51.	Cuba Investment and Business Guide
52.	Cyprus Investment and Business Guide
53.	Czech Republic Investment and Business Guide
54.	Denmark Investment and Business Guide
55.	Djibouti Investment and Business Guide
56.	Dominica Investment and Business Guide
57.	Dominican Republic Investment and Business Guide
58.	Ecuador Investment and Business Guide
59.	Egypt Investment and Business Guide
60.	El Salvador Investment and Business Guide
61.	Equatorial Guinea Investment and Business Guide
62.	Eritrea Investment and Business Guide
63.	Estonia Investment and Business Guide
64.	Ethiopia Investment and Business Guide
65.	Falkland Islands Investment and Business Guide
66.	Faroes Islands Investment and Business Guide
67.	Fiji Investment and Business Guide
68.	Finland Investment and Business Guide
69.	France Investment and Business Guide
70.	Gabon Investment and Business Guide
71.	Gambia Investment and Business Guide
72.	Georgia Investment and Business Guide
73.	Germany Investment and Business Guide
74.	Ghana Investment and Business Guide
75.	Gibraltar Investment and Business Guide
76.	Greece Investment and Business Guide
77.	Greenland Investment and Business Guide
78.	Grenada Investment and Business Guide
79.	Guam Investment and Business Guide
80.	Guatemala Investment and Business Guide
81.	Guernsey Investment and Business Guide
82.	Guinea Investment and Business Guide
83.	Guinea-Bissau Investment and Business Guide
84.	Guyana Investment and Business Guide
85.	Haiti Investment and Business Guide
86.	Honduras Investment and Business Guide
87.	Hungary Investment and Business Guide
88.	Iceland Investment and Business Guide

89. India Investment and Business Guide
90. Indonesia Investment and Business Guide
91. Iran Investment and Business Guide
92. Iraq Investment and Business Guide
93. Ireland Investment and Business Guide
94. Israel Investment and Business Guide
95. Italy Investment and Business Guide
96. Jamaica Investment and Business Guide
97. Japan Investment and Business Guide
98. Jersey Investment and Business Guide
99. Jordan Investment and Business Guide
100. Kazakhstan Investment and Business Guide
101. Kenya Investment and Business Guide
102. Kiribati Investment and Business Guide
103. Korea, North Investment and Business Guide
104. Korea, South Investment and Business Guide
105. Kosovo Investment and Business Guide
106. Kurdistan Investment and Business Guide
107. Kuwait Investment and Business Guide
108. Kyrgyzstan Investment and Business Guide
109. Laos Investment and Business Guide
110. Latvia Investment and Business Guide
111. Lebanon Investment and Business Guide
112. Lesotho Investment and Business Guide
113. Liberia Investment and Business Guide
114. Libya Investment and Business Guide
115. Liechtenstein Investment and Business Guide
116. Lithuania Investment and Business Guide
117. Luxembourg Investment and Business Guide
118. Macao Investment and Business Guide
119. Macedonia Investment and Business Guide
120. Madagascar Investment and Business Guide
121. Madeira Investment and Business Guide
122. Malawi Investment and Business Guide
123. Malaysia Investment and Business Guide
124. Maldives Investment and Business Guide
125. Mali Investment and Business Guide
126. Malta Investment and Business Guide
127. Man Investment and Business Guide
128. Marshall Islands Investment and Business Guide
129. Mauritania Investment and Business Guide
130. Mauritius Investment and Business Guide
131. Mayotte Investment and Business Guide
132. Mexico Investment and Business Guide
133. Micronesia Investment and Business Guide
134. Moldova Investment and Business Guide
135. Monaco Investment and Business Guide
136. Mongolia Investment and Business Guide
137. Monserrat Investment and Business Guide
138. Morocco Investment and Business Guide
139. Mozambique Investment and Business Guide

140. Myanmar Investment and Business Guide
141. Namibia Investment and Business Guide
142. Nauru Investment and Business Guide
143. Nepal Investment and Business Guide
144. Netherlands Investment and Business Guide
145. New Caledonia Investment and Business Guide
146. New Zealand Investment and Business Guide
147. Nicaragua Investment and Business Guide
148. Niger Investment and Business Guide
149. Nigeria Investment and Business Guide
150. Niue Investment and Business Guide
151. Northern Mariana Islands Investment and Business Guide
152. Norway Investment and Business Guide
153. Oman Investment and Business Guide
154. Pakistan Investment and Business Guide
155. Palau Investment and Business Guide
156. Palestine (West Bank & Gaza) Investment and Business Guide
157. Panama Investment and Business Guide
158. Papua New Guinea Investment and Business Guide
159. Paraguay Investment and Business Guide
160. Peru Investment and Business Guide
161. Philippines Investment and Business Guide
162. Pitcairn Islands Investment and Business Guide
163. Poland Investment and Business Guide
164. Polynesia French Investment and Business Guide
165. Portugal Investment and Business Guide
166. Qatar Investment and Business Guide
167. Romania Investment and Business Guide
168. Russia Investment and Business Guide
169. Rwanda Investment and Business Guide
170. Saint Kitts and Nevis Investment and Business Guide
171. Saint Lucia Investment and Business Guide
172. Saint Vincent and The Grenadines Investment and Business Guide
173. Samoa (American) A Investment and Business Guide
174. Samoa (Western) Investment and Business Guide
175. San Marino Investment and Business Guide
176. Sao Tome and Principe Investment and Business Guide
177. Saudi Arabia Investment and Business Guide
178. Scotland Investment and Business Guide
179. Senegal Investment and Business Guide
180. Serbia Investment and Business Guide
181. Seychelles Investment and Business Guide
182. Sierra Leone Investment and Business Guide
183. Singapore Investment and Business Guide
184. Slovakia Investment and Business Guide
185. Slovenia Investment and Business Guide
186. Solomon Islands Investment and Business Guide
187. Somalia Investment and Business Guide
188. South Africa Investment and Business Guide
189. Spain Investment and Business Guide
190. Sri Lanka Investment and Business Guide

191. St. Helena Investment and Business Guide
192. St. Pierre & Miquelon Investment and Business Guide
193. Sudan Investment and Business Guide
194. Sudan South Investment and Business Guide
195. Suriname Investment and Business Guide
196. Swaziland Investment and Business Guide
197. Sweden Investment and Business Guide
198. Switzerland Investment and Business Guide
199. Syria Investment and Business Guide
200. Taiwan Investment and Business Guide
201. Tajikistan Investment and Business Guide
202. Tanzania Investment and Business Guide
203. Thailand Investment and Business Guide
204. Togo Investment and Business Guide
205. Tonga Investment and Business Guide
206. Trinidad and Tobago Investment and Business Guide
207. Tunisia Investment and Business Guide
208. Turkey Investment and Business Guide
209. Turkmenistan Investment and Business Guide
210. Turks & Caicos Investment and Business Guide
211. Tuvalu Investment and Business Guide
212. Uganda Investment and Business Guide
213. Ukraine Investment and Business Guide
214. United Arab Emirates Investment and Business Guide
215. United Kingdom Investment and Business Guide
216. United States Investment and Business Guide
217. Uruguay Investment and Business Guide
218. Uzbekistan Investment and Business Guide
219. Vanuatu Investment and Business Guide
220. Vatican City Investment and Business Guide
221. Venezuela Investment and Business Guide
222. Vietnam Investment and Business Guide
223. Virgin Islands, British Investment and Business Guide
224. Wake Atoll Investment and Business Guide
225. Wallis & Futuna Investment and Business Guide
226. Western Sahara Investment and Business Guide
227. Yemen Investment and Business Guide
228. Zambia Investment and Business Guide
229. Zimbabwe Investment and Business Guide

Made in the USA
Monee, IL
14 September 2026

63198324R00157